THE DEVIANT
MYSTIQUE

THE DEVIANT MYSTIQUE

Involvements, Realities, and Regulation

Robert Prus and Scott Grills

Westport, Connecticut
London

Library of Congress Cataloging-in-Publication Data

Prus, Robert C.
    The deviant mystique : involvements, realities, and regulation / Robert Prus and
Scott Grills.
        p. cm.
    Includes bibliographical references and index.
    ISBN 0–275–97822–2 (alk. paper)
        1. Deviant behavior.   2. Symbolic interactionism.   3. Subculture.   4. Social
control.   I. Grills, Scott.   II. Title.
    HM811.P78   2003
    302.5′42—dc21   2002030333

British Library Cataloguing in Publication Data is available.

Library of Congress Catalog Card Number: 2002030333
ISBN: 0–275–979822–2

First published in 2003

Praeger Publishers, 88 Post Road West, Westport, CT 06881
An imprint of Greenwood Publishing Group, Inc.
www.praeger.com

Printed in the United States of America

The paper used in this book complies with the
Permanent Paper Standard issued by the National
Information Standards Organization (Z39.48–1984).

10   9   8   7   6   5   4   3   2   1

This volume is dedicated to everyone who has experienced the deviant mystique and especially those who have attempted to move beyond the deviant mystique in pursuing the study of human group life.

Contents

Preface

As used herein, *the deviant mystique* refers to the allures and fascinations, the anxieties and fears, and the disaffections and repulsions that people associate with wrongdoing and morality. This statement is not intended to encourage or intensify the deviant mystique, but instead acknowledges these human viewpoints and the ways that people engage the deviance phenomenon. Accordingly, this material is intended to address any and all instances of anyone (person or group) doing anything that any audience (person or group) might consider "deviant" in some manner.

While the study of deviance extends much beyond the auras or intrigues that people develop with respect to certain realms of activity, it is important to consider the ways in which the deviant mystique enters into people's theaters of operation so that we might more adequately move through and beyond the various intrigues that people may experience en route to a more complete examination of the deviance-making process.

In developing this volume, we have not only endeavored to generate more comprehensive interlinkages of social theory and enacted realities as these pertain to the study of deviance as something in the making, but also have attempted to produce a statement that would put newcomers to the field in closer contact with those who are actively involved in examining deviance as a socially constructed phenomenon.

Our objective, thus, is to generate a sustained focus on the ways in which people define, experience, and act toward deviance within the many arenas of activity that constitute the human community. There is no interest in controlling or rehabilitating those considered deviants from one or other standpoints. Likewise, there is no attempt to condemn, liberate, or change any forms or fields of activity. Instead, the emphasis is on examining the ways in which people engage the various life-worlds in which they find themselves and suggesting ways in which the study of deviance, as reflected in instances of humanly engaged activity, might be pursued in more direct, participant-informed terms.

Our approach to the study of deviance is a relativist one, in the sense that deviance is seen as a matter of variable audience definitions. At the same time, however, deviance is not simply a matter of definition (or disembodied text). That is, although people may develop different notions of what constitutes deviance and how they might deal with these matters, deviance definitions become important whenever (but only to the extent that) people take these into account in formulating their own behaviors and attending to the situations of others.

Focusing on the humanly known and enacted world, this volume has been organized around a series of generic social processes. Thus, while recognizing that human life takes place in enacted, situated instances and is to be studied in manners that are mindful of the ways in which people actually do things, we also have sought to develop concepts that encourage an explicit comparative or transcontextual analysis of those instances along processual dimensions.

Addressing the ways in which deviance-making ventures take shape within the broader community, these social processes enable scholars to make comparisons and contrasts across and between any two or more realms of human activity. Starting with some basic social processes, the objective is to learn more about the humanly engaged world by examining the ways in which these matters are articulated in the course of ongoing community life.

In writing this volume, we have built on the existing interactionist literature, particularly the work on deviance that is more ethnographic in quality. Still, this volume also is intended as a research agenda for the study of deviance. Accordingly, the statements presented here are envisioned as tentative or working formulations, as conceptual approximations whose eventual value and extensions are contingent on subsequent examinations of instances of deviance in the making.

In contrast to many texts on deviance, the material developed here does not attempt to synthesize an assortment of approaches to the study of deviance. Indeed, few approaches in the social sciences actually deal with the experiences of living, breathing, acting, and interacting human beings. Concentrating on humanly known and enacted realities, we have taken a distinctively *symbolic interactionist* approach to the study of deviance.[1]

Although rooted in a broader European scholarly tradition that can be traced back to the early Greeks (Prus, 2003), symbolic interaction more directly represents a sociological extension of American pragmatist philosophy. While pragmatist philosophy is concerned with the ways that people make sense of and act toward the humanly known world, symbolic interaction has been formulated more centrally by George Herbert Mead (1934) and Herbert Blumer (1969). Interactionism also has been informed by several decades of Chicago-style ethnographic research.

Emphasizing the interlinkages of theory, methods, and research, symbolic interactionism (a) contends that people engage the world (and one another) in

ways that are symbolically or linguistically meaningful; (b) encourages researchers to examine the world as known to the various participants in the
human community through direct interchange with the people whose life-
world situations one studies; and (c) fosters the development of process-
oriented concepts that transcend particular situations and, thus, allow
researchers and analysts to develop fuller understandings of human enacted
realities. These three concerns identify the theoretical and methodological emphases that undergird this statement.

When approached in this manner, the study of deviance becomes a study of
community life in the making. Instead of developing a special theory for the
study of "deviance" (or "deviants"), the objective is to generate an approach
to the study of community life that encompasses people's participation in all
of the arenas in which matters of deviance and morality become envisioned as
problematic.

In keeping with the interactionist tradition, we have relied primarily on
ethnographic materials to provide the baseline instances necessary for the study
of matters pertaining to human knowing and acting within the context of
human group life. Relatedly, we have given comparatively little attention to
materials that fail to acknowledge the centrality of human lived experience
(i.e., that disregard human knowing and acting).

Adopting the viewpoint that nothing is inherently deviant (i.e., that deviance
reflects audience moralities and definitions), we have incorporated a considerable amount of ethnographic material that one would not encounter in more
conventional or topical discussions of deviance. This is advantageous for three
reasons. First, once one approaches the study of human lived experience in
more generic terms, it becomes apparent that some very powerful, comparative
analytic insights into people's involvements in aspects of deviance can be obtained by examining people's activities in other (seemingly more respectable)
arenas of human group life and attending to the conceptual parallels therein.
Second, many things that people may take for granted from one or other moral
viewpoints appear disreputable when approached from another notion of propriety. Third, it should be emphasized that deviance and respectability are not
two separate issues but, instead, are part of the same basic set of community
processes.

As well, despite a heavy emphasis on ethnographic materials as the primary
reference points for the study of community life in the present text, it should
be observed that ethnographic accounts are far from even in quality, scope,
emphasis, detail, and clarity. Quite directly, some ethnographies are much more
informative in substantive, conceptual, and analytical terms than are others.
Some also cover their subject matters in more encompassing manners and/or
provide much more detail about the situations at hand than do others. Further,
ethnographies vary notably in the extent to which they are attentive to participant viewpoints.

Although certain recent ethnographies offer a great deal of insight into people's perspectives, identities, relationships, and so forth, it would be folly to
assume that recent work is necessarily of higher quality than earlier statements.
Thus, ethnographies that are developed more fully around people's activities
and attend more directly to participant viewpoints not only have an enduring
relevance to the study of human group life, but also offer analysts invaluable
transcontextual and transhistorical comparison points (and resources).

We do not claim to have represented all of the ethnographic materials that
are pertinent to the study of deviance and no doubt will have missed some
very valuable studies. However, in developing this text, we also have observed
that a comparatively small number of ethnographies have provided a great deal
of highly insightful material across the broader parameters of the deviance-
making process and have cited these works more frequently as a result. Given
the overall theoretical emphasis of this text, we have not been able to represent
any of the ethnographies referenced as fully as they merit. Still, it is our hope
that readers will examine these studies on their own and find that these materials, along with the conceptual frame developed in this volume, represent
sources of inspiration for engaging the study of the human condition in much
more sustained ethnographic terms. In this way, by locating themselves and
their works within a broader community of scholars who focus on the matters
of human knowing and acting, readers will be in a much better position to
benefit from these earlier materials and to contribute more directly and effectively to future analyses of deviance as well as achieve a more viable, activity-
based understanding of ongoing community life.

Shifting the focus somewhat, we would like to briefly acknowledge the contributions that a wide array of people have made to this project. First, and in
the most basic, enabling, and essential of respects, this volume is very much a
tribute to the community of symbolic interactionists and kindred academics.
Working with a vision of how the materials produced by these scholars might
be organized, presented, and shared with others, we hope that we can be of like
service to others who are interested in the study of human knowing and acting.

Because this book has been some years in the making, we undoubtedly will
miss the opportunity to thank many people to whom we are indebted. We hope
that they will be understanding of our more implicit gratitude. Minimally,
however, we would particularly like to acknowledge Peter and Patti Adler,
Cheryl and Dan Albas, Julia Arndt, Michael Atkinson, Hans Bakker, Michael
and Elizabeth Berger, Joel Best, Kieran Bonner, Scott Brandon, Robert Broad-
head, Dick Brymer, Matthew Burk, Fatima Camara, Kathy Charmaz, Carl
Couch, Donna Darden, Mary Lou Dietz, Helen Rose Ebaugh, Timothy Epp,
Bob Farmer, Scott Harris, Lori Holyfield, Ruth Horowitz, Styllianoss Irini, John
Johnson, Bruce Kanters, David Karp, Russell Kelly, Steve Kleinknecht, John
Lofland, Stan Lyman, Charlene Miall, Richard Mitchell, Jr., Tom Morrione, Gil
Musolf, Adie Nelson, Dorothy Pawluch, Tony Puddephatt, Larry Reynolds,
Carrie Sanders, Clint Sanders, Marvin Scott, Bill Shaffir, C.R.D. Sharper, Bob

Stebbins, Angus Vail, Beert Verstraete, Steve Worden, and Bill Yoels. We very much appreciate the interest that these people have taken in our work.

Still, Lorraine Prus and Sheilagh Grills deserve special consideration for their support and encouragement throughout this project. We would very much like to thank them for their continued interest in our studies and the many contributions they have made to *The Deviant Mystique*.

In addition, we would like to thank Suzanne Staszak-Silva (Acquisitions Editor) for her interest in this volume and for her highly congenial and thoughtful guidance throughout this venture, as well as Wendy Schlosberg (Copy Editor) and the staff at Praeger Press for their assistance in making this book available to the readership. Thanks also to Angela Williams Urquhart and Thistle Hill Publishing Services. We also are grateful to the anonymous reviewers for their helpful suggestions on an earlier draft of this manuscript.

Finally, we would like to express our appreciation to the readers for their interests in learning about the human condition in all of its manifestations. We very much hope that they will permeate the deviant mystique in their own scholarship and extend the study of human knowing and acting across the parameters of community life.

NOTE

1. Readers more familiar with the field will recognize many affinities of symbolic interaction with the phenomenological sociology of Alfred Schutz (1962, 1964) and its intellectual offshoots ethnomethodology (Garfinkel, 1967) and social constructionism (Berger and Luckmann, 1966). This volume has benefited considerably from the insights generated by Schutz and others working within this tradition. This project also has been informed by the hermeneutic social theory of Wilhelm Dilthey (Ermarth, 1978) and Georg Simmel's (1950) emphasis on social process.

Part I

The Conceptual Frame

1

Encountering the Deviant Mystique
Fascination, Indignation, and the Dramatization of Evil

[T]hey say that if a group of people should collect from all the nations of the world their disgraceful customs and then should call everyone together and tell each man to select what he thinks is seemly, everything would be taken away as belonging to the seemly things. (Dissoi Logi or Dialexeis [circa 400 B.C.E.]; Sprague, 1972:284)

For our purposes, the term deviance refers to any activity, actor, idea, or humanly produced situation that an audience defines as threatening, disturbing, offensive, immoral, evil, disreputable, or negative in some way. At the very heart of this standpoint is the notion that nothing is inherently good or bad, appropriate or inappropriate. Rather, deviance is *social* in its very definition, or conversely, deviance is brought into existence only when something is so defined by an audience.

Envisioning deviance as a negative quality attributed to some activity (or actor) by an audience, this volume deals with deviance as a phenomenon that is fully the product of human activity. The emphasis throughout is on the "social construction of deviance" and people's involvements in all aspects of the deviance-making process.

Much more is involved in the study of deviance than acknowledging that deviance is a matter of definition or that deviance signifies both realms of moral disapproval and arenas of intrigue for those in the human community. By explicitly recognizing the negativities associated with deviance, we may begin to appreciate just how very fundamentally and extensively deviance is a socially constituted essence. We may begin to acknowledge how central the activities and interactions of an assortment of people in the community are for what eventually becomes known and acted toward as "instances of deviance."

The objective is to develop a theoretical statement on deviance that is informed by research that deals with people's experiences and practices as they engage one another in the various life-worlds that constitute the human community. It is intended that the material presented here will enable people to embark on research that more directly examines people's experiences with deviance in the community and, thus, serve to further (re)inform scholarly notions of deviance. Consequently, rather than providing "facts, figures, and trends" regarding various forms of deviance, this volume lays out the parameters of an approach that deals with deviance as a socially constructed phenomenon.

Likewise, although we will be referencing many firsthand or ethnographic studies of "deviance in the making," this volume clearly is not intended to replace field studies of people's activities. Quite directly, there is no substitute for the in-depth familiarity with one's human subject matter that is attainable through sustained field research. Not only does ethnographic research on deviance represent essential background information for comprehending the materials highlighted herein, but these direct examinations of instances of deviance also connote the primary criteria for assessing the viability of materials developed in this volume or any other statement in the social sciences.

FRAMING THE ANALYSIS

Viewing deviance as a relativist but inevitable component of community life, this volume examines the processes by which people: (1) establish definitions of phenomena as "deviant;" (2) become identified as "deviants;" (3) become involved in deviance-implicated activities and networks; (4) sustain involvements in (and/or become disinvolved from) those practices and life-worlds; and (5) attempt to regulate deviance both informally and through control agencies.

Focusing on the humanly known and enacted world, the emphasis is on the ways in which people engage one another in community contexts and how notions of deviance (and morality) are constituted in the course of their activities and interchanges. Thus, although people with applied orientations may find this volume useful in understanding the deviance phenomena, this statement is not directed toward the control, elimination, acceptance, or promotion of deviance or (alternatively) the restructuring of society.

Speaking more generally, the approach taken here is notably distinct from the standpoints adopted by (a) the moralists, (b) the idealists, and (c) the structuralists. Those assuming moralist approaches to deviance focus on the matters of judging, directing, and controlling people's situations, behaviors, and experiences. Denying the authenticity of human knowing and acting, the idealists often attempt to talk deviance out of existence by reducing everything to the realm of words, concepts, or ideas, wherein anything can be anything (i.e., totalizing linguistic relativism). Envisioning themselves as a great deal more grounded or empirical than the moralists and idealists, the structuralists (also positivists) attempt to explain deviance by virtue of an interplay of (internal and external) factors thought to cause people to act in certain manners.[1]

By contrast, the interactionist approach (Mead 1934; Blumer 1969; Strauss 1993; Prus 1996b) adopted in this volume has a distinctively pragmatist emphasis and envisions deviance as a social essence that is produced by minded, acting, and interacting people who engage one another in the full range of community contexts.

Thus, although acknowledging the centrality of moral viewpoints for defining deviance, the interactionist position is distinct from the moralists. In contrast to the moralists who promote or invoke particular evaluative standpoints by which deviance may be defined, deviants may be identified, and control efforts may be implemented, the interactionists study the processes by which human group life, in all of its moralities and other manifestations, takes place.

Likewise, while appreciating the diversity or relativism of moral standpoints, the interactionists differ from the idealists in (a) recognizing the authenticity of people's knowledge, moralities, interpretations, and judgments as meaningful (versus arbitrary or capricious) foci of study, and (b) emphasizing the centrality of activity (and humanly engaged objects) for comprehending the human condition.

Recognizing that people engage "the world out there" in sensory-enabled terms, the interactionists also share some common concerns with the structuralists. However, instead of asking "why" or "what makes" people do things in more typical structuralist terms, the interactionists ask "how" people make sense of the situations in which they find themselves and act toward the things of their awareness. Likewise, while acknowledging that people operate in a world of objects, the interactionists contend that it is people who give things meanings or bring objects into existence (as meaningful essences) by the ways in which they attend to things. The emphasis, accordingly, is on the things that people consider meaningful in symbolic or linguistic terms. The interactionists do not deny notions of causality but instead ask when and how people infer causality (or draw linkages between things) and how people enter into (and endeavor to shape) the causal process as knowing, anticipating, deliberating, interacting, assessing, and adjustive agents.[2] Because humans have abilities to define and engage the things of their awareness in linguistically informed, reflective, and adjustive manners, it may be expected that any adequate theory of deviance would not only attend to matters of human agency and association in very direct, detailed, and sustained terms, but also would examine these matters from the points of view of the participants in the settings under consideration.

Thus, while acknowledging the viability of structuralist (positivist, quantitative) approaches for studying nonhuman essences or the biophysical features of humans, the interactionists insist on a social science that attends to the unique, socially achieved or constructed nature of all meaningful human endeavor. Quite directly, a different theoretical and methodological emphasis is required when one studies the ways in which *people* (as linguistically and experientially enabled agents) knowingly do things within the context of the human community. In this respect, the interactionists are neither subjectivists nor objectivists, but instead adopt an intersubjectivist stance, focusing on the symbolically enabled and actively constituted nature of the human community.[3]

Seven premises form the theoretical base of this volume.[4] While discussed in greater detail in chapter 2, it may be useful to introduce these assumptions to help frame the interactionist approach at the outset. These premises are: (1) the human world is linguistically understood, constructed, and experienced; (2) the "world" can have multiple meanings to people; (3) people develop capacities for taking themselves into account in developing lines of action; (4) human group life is organized around the doing or accomplishing of activity; (5) people are able to influence (and resist) others; (6) people develop and attend to particularistic bonds or associations with others; and (7) group life has an emergent quality. Thus, we view group life as *intersubjective, (multi)perspectival, reflective, action-oriented, negotiable, relational,* and *processual.*

Concerned with analyzing group life from the viewpoints of the people involved in instances of deviance, the emphasis in this volume is on the ways in which people define, interpret, and engage situations in conjunction with others. Because nothing is seen as inherently deviant or disrespectable, the imputations of negativity that undergird definitions of deviance reflect consequential realms of human enterprise and human moralities, as do all of the activities that revolve around the production of "those things" that are viewed, somehow, as offensive, threatening, disturbing, bothersome, and the like. Envisioning deviance as a realm of human lived experience, our fundamental concern is one of *connecting social theory and human activity* within the "here and now" of ongoing community life.

Whereas the people who constitute particular communities may adopt a variety of moralities and pursue rather different interests in the process of engaging others in various realms of community life, deviance achieves its essence within the context of humanly enacted theaters of operation. Attending to the *deviant mystique* or the auras that people generate in the process of defining something in negative or disreputable terms, this statement not only identifies a number of roles that people in the community may invoke vis-à-vis the deviance phenomenon, but also shows how thoroughly notions of deviance may be embedded as enacted realities within human communities.

Thus, beyond acknowledging the ways that those adopting roles as "deviants" and "control agents" engage their situations (and one another) in more central and direct terms, consideration is given to the people who become involved in (and sustain concerns with) the deviance phenomenon in other ways. Paralleling the activities of those involved in theatrical productions as members of the supporting cast, stagehands, directors, entrepreneurs, audiences, and so forth, these other people may be less obvious than those assuming roles as perpetrators and control agents, but they, too, may play consequential roles in the production and maintenance of the deviance phenomenon.

By considering this broader base of community involvement and focusing on the ways that people actually do things, we become increasingly aware of the practical limitations of attempting to explain deviance by commonly referenced structural factors such as class, gender, age, and race on the one hand and matters of intelligence, personalities, and attitudes on the other.[5]

Likewise, in contrast to the postmodernists or other idealists who might contend that they can talk or redefine deviance out of existence, the material developed here acknowledges the fundamentally engaged (enacted and inter-active) nature of community life. The totalizing (and debilitating) relativism associated with pure idealism (and postmodernist cynicism) might attain via-bility in a world in which no one ever did anything, but *the human world is a world of activity*.[6] In order to do things, from dealing with the human strug-gle of existence at the most fundamental levels to the pursuit of any other interest or objective, people rather inevitably *engage* objects (including other humans and themselves) within the context of symbolically mediated realities. Thus, deviance is not rendered a mythical phenomenon in the community because analysts observe that deviance has a relativist or linguistic quality. While recognizing the linguistically mediated nature of all human knowing and meaningful activity, the interactionists insist on the necessity of attending to humanly engaged realities.

As an enacted essence, deviance exists because and when people invoke def-initions of negativity in dealing with one another. And, people may generate and attend to definitions (or assessments) of these sorts whenever they deem these appropriate. Deviance has a multiperspectival or relativist quality, but *deviance achieves its essence* as a substantive phenomenon when specific no-tions of negativity are invoked (envisioned, articulated, implemented, shared, projected, resisted, adjusted to, reassessed, and so forth) in this and that in-stance as people engage ongoing group life. Because instances of deviance are developed in the *activities* entailed in the accomplishment of community life, all matters pertaining to deviance are most adequately understood within the context of group life "in the making."

ACKNOWLEDGING THE DEVIANT MYSTIQUE

> Twofold arguments concerning the good and the bad are put forward in Greece by those who philosophise. Some say the good is one thing and the bad another, but others say that they are the same and that a thing might be good for some persons but bad for others, or at one time good and at another time bad for the same person. (Dissoi Logi or Dialexeis [circa 400 B.C.E.]; Sprague, 1972:279)

While some sociologists have focused on the processes by which people de-fine, identify, manage, and promote deviance (i.e., the social construction of deviance),[7] a great many sociologists and other social scientists have been re-miss in not attending more fully to the ways in which and extent to which people experience deviance as a form of fascination or intrigue within the com-munity. We are referring here to what may be termed *the deviant mystique*—the auras, fascinations, repulsions, interests, curiosities, and related images that people develop with respect to deviance. This theme has been very much neglected in the social sciences, but it has great importance for understanding deviance as a community phenomenon.

Like other activities that may be viewed in a plurality of manners on a simultaneous or sequential basis (e.g., something may be considered interesting, but also difficult, costly, and dangerous), activities designated as "deviant" may be viewed in positive and more neutral terms by both different and the very same people. That is, although things defined as deviant may be shrouded in disrespectability, it should *not* be assumed that they are necessarily unattractive to people in other respects. Something may be considered forbidden or disreputable, but viewed simultaneously as interesting, fun, adventurous, or exciting.

Indeed, certain activities or situations may appear even more alluring to some people because they are forbidden or people may find themselves (curiously) attending more intensively to certain things because of the public notoriety those activities receive. Notably, the very act of defining something as deviant in a community often fosters a sense of drama and intrigue as these things are made to stand apart from the routines of everyday life.

While everyday routines may be punctuated by the exceptional acts of "heroes," "villains," and "fools" (Klapp, 1962), the essence of deviance is found in the attribution of some *negative* quality. Deviance is not simply an exception or noteworthy difference of some sort, it also implies a sense of disrespectability; that some notion of morality or propriety has been threatened, denigrated, offended, or defiled. These negative attributions hold the potential to offer a variety of intrigues as people (a) consider offender motivations, activities, and possible apprehension; (b) experience a range of emotions around acts, actors, and outcomes; (c) become involved in issues of guilt and innocence; and (d) reflect upon the appropriateness of various sanctions as well as matters of reintegration of offenders into the community and broader notions of deterrence.

In addition to focusing people's attention on "exceptional" activities, the implied constraints associated with regulating deviance also tend to direct people's attention to those actors engaged in disreputable activities. Although images of evil, danger, foolishness, stupidity, and the like are often imputed to those participating in deviance, people also may associate auras of pleasure or hedonism, freedom and independence, intrigue and adventure, daring and courage with these same performers. Some of those taking this latter position subsequently might become willing participants in endeavors of these sorts, but others sharing these intrigues may have little opportunity to embrace those lifestyles or find themselves unable to reconcile the risks (e.g., physical dangers, moral reactions, financial costs, or community sanctions) that they associate with the activity.

Although presumably at odds with the moral ideals of the broader community, the more or less simultaneous definitions of instances of deviance

involvements as interesting, alluring, and excitingly dangerous seem somewhat commonplace and appear to form the base of people's interest in deviance
and the foundations for "the deviance mystique" in the community at large.[8]

PERMEATING THE DEVIANT MYSTIQUE

Given the fears, indignations, intrigues, and other dramatizations associated
with deviance in the community, it is often difficult for social scientists to
approach the study of deviance with the same care and dedication that they
might use to examine other subject matters. Nevertheless, the study of deviance
very much requires the same sort of conscientious and open-minded conceptual
and methodological rigor that one would employ in other realms of inquiry.

In order to achieve this analytical plane, it is necessary to first overcome or
permeate the deviant mystique—to look past or through the condemnations,
repulsions, fascinations, and other auras that surround deviance and to concentrate, explicitly and intensively, on the ways in which the people involved
in all aspects of the deviance process work out their activities in conjunction
with others in the community. This requires a scholarly attentiveness to all
aspects of human enterprise, including notions of interpretation and definition,
activity and adjustment, influence and resistance, intimacy and distancing, control and tolerance, as well as related matters such as cooperation, conflict, compromise, negotiation, and renegotiation.

This is not to deny the importance of "the deviant mystique" as a phenomenon of study, but rather to emphasize the importance of researchers and analysts *not* becoming personally caught up or entrapped in moralistic or
sensationalistic aspects of the sociological puzzle. Comprehending the mystique
that surrounds deviance is an essential aspect of the sociological venture, but
an appreciation of this aura is best achieved through a detailed understanding
of the community enterprise entailed in the production of deviance.

Approaching deviance as an enacted feature of ongoing community life, we
attend to the experiences (viewpoints and activities) of a wide assortment of
players or participants. This includes those who (a) define deviance,[9] (b) become
involved in deviance, (c) experience deviance because of others, and (d) attempt
to control deviance, as well as those who use deviance as (e) venues of entertainment or (f) sources of political or theological advantage, and those who
(g) try to explain deviance for others.

Minimally, too, it is necessary that social scientists approach the study of
deviance in ways that are unencumbered by any moralisms, idealisms, and
structuralisms that might distance or otherwise obstruct students of human
behavior from attending to the careful, thorough study of human activity and
the ways in which people work out their lines of action with other people.

This focus on the meaningful, ongoing production of human activity represents *the primary anchorage point* for an interactionist approach to deviance.
This standpoint not only allows for a fuller appreciation of the mystiques that

people associate with the activities under consideration, but also enables scholars to attend to the humanly known and enacted life-worlds in which all instances of deviance take place.

LOOKING AHEAD

Addressing the matter of human knowing and acting in more sustained
theoretical terms, chapter 2 provides the central conceptual frame for this volume. Thus, following a brief overview of the roots of interactionist thought,
chapter 2 attends to the premises that undergird the interactionist approach
and briefly considers the ethnographic methodology that informs interactionist
analysis.

Focusing more specifically on deviance, chapter 3 considers the great many
theaters in which members of the community operate and the ways in which
they engage aspects of the deviance-making process. Acknowledging a variety
of roles that people develop as they experience deviance, manage trouble, and
participate in public forums, deviance is envisioned in more comprehensive,
panoramic, and humanly enacted terms.

Chapters 4 and 5 attend more directly to the matters of people designating
deviance. Chapter 4 deals with the preliminary matter of people defining things
as deviant, evil, troublesome, and the like. While appreciating the relativism
signified by people's notions of deviance and the moralities that are foundational to these notions of negativity, it is in the definition of things that deviance is brought into play as a meaningful human essence. Thus, chapter 4
draws particular attention to the (often considerable) human enterprise entailed
in articulating, identifying, engaging, promoting, stabilizing, experiencing, and
resisting definitions of deviance within the human community.

Reflecting people's notions of moralities and deviance, chapter 5 considers
the ways in which particular people are implicated in the deviance-making
process and the ways in which these targets manage the imputations, identities,
and reactions they encounter from others. Although subsequent chapters cast
further insight into the processes by which certain activities and specific people
are defined as troublesome or disreputable in some way, an appreciation of the
labeling process is fundamental for comprehending people's participation in,
and regulation of, all manners of deviance.

Whereas chapters 4 and 5 centrally reflect the initiatives, practices, and adjustments of the people involved in defining realms of deviance and the participants within, chapters 6 through 9 focus more directly on those who become
caught up in or otherwise engage in the activities and life-worlds that others
define in negative or disreputable terms. Although it is always particular people
who do things, closer examinations of deviance reveals just how much specific
people's activities are interfused with those of other people. As a result, a direct
and sustained consideration of the group or subculture, as an interacting unit,
is essential to an adequate appreciation of an exceptionally wide range of human

involvements. Indeed, because so much human lived experience takes place within subcultural arenas, these interacting units merit extended attention on the part of social scientists.

Examining the ways in which people become involved in, continue, disengage from, and become reinvolved in particular realms of deviance, chapter 6 considers people's histories or careers of participation in the various life-worlds or subcultures in which they work out aspects of their lives in conjunction with others. Whereas chapter 6 more specifically details the ways in which people become initially involved in disreputable situations, chapters 7 and 8 follow people's experiences in subcultures in more extended terms.

Focusing on people's experiences as participants in ongoing subcultural arenas, chapter 7 attends to the ways in which people engage these life-worlds with respect to matters such as acquiring perspectives, achieving identities, developing relationships, doing activities, experiencing emotionality, and participating in collective events. Addressing subcultural involvements from a third, but related vantage point, chapter 8 examines the grouping process or the ways in which people go about forming and coordinating associations. In addition to considering the more preliminary ways in which people develop associations with others, attention also is directed to the ways in which people attempt to intensify and sustain particular associations as well as the manners in which insiders and those outside the group envision and act toward one another.

Chapter 9 deals primarily with solitary deviance. While more pointedly acknowledging people's capacities for developing more isolated or idiosyncratic ventures, this chapter also considers the ways in which people experience deviance and disrespectability on their own. Still, even when people appear to "strike out on their own," their activities and experiences are generally much more interconnected with those of other people than first seems. Representing a series of contradictions for those inclined to reduce solitary deviance to individual properties or isolated activities, the viewpoints and practices of those involved in solitary deviance cannot be adequately understood apart from their relations and interchanges with others.

Shifting the emphasis somewhat, from those participating in problematic realms of activity to matters of control and disinvolvement, chapters 10 through 13 revisit and extend some regulatory themes introduced in chapters 4 and 5. Chapter 10 considers the commonplace, but comparatively neglected matter of handling deviance informally. Although much of the literature on deviance focuses on the formal regulation of deviance by control agents, most instances of trouble are identified and dealt with by people in the community at large. Attending to regulatory matters more generically, attention is given to the ways in which people define instances of trouble, respond to those whom they define as troublesome, and consider tactical exchanges with targets.

Even though there is no assurance that instances of deviance will be handled more effectively or viably by "formal control agencies" than by citizens acting on their own, control agencies often assume central roles in the deviant-making process. Thus, chapter 11 focuses on control agencies or those persons and groups in the community who have undertaken the task of regulating deviance on a more official, systematic, and sustained basis. Particular attention is given to agency concerns with achieving support for the control agency, accessing cases to be processed, classifying the cases encountered, emphasizing treatment, restoring justice, and pursuing internal order.

Chapter 12 more specifically considers the ways that people assume and implement roles as regulatory agents within agency settings. The emphasis, here, is on the ways that these officeholders attend to organizational objectives, adjust to existing organizational practices, maintain order within the agency, engage (and treat) the targets with whom they work, and strive for personal viability within somewhat precarious organizational contexts.

Attending to the experiences of people targeted for control and the related problematics of people becoming disinvolved from deviance more generally, chapter 13 provides another, highly consequential set of viewpoints on control efforts. As with chapters 10 through 12, the emphasis is on the ways in which the participants define their situations and deal with others on a day-to-day basis. Thus, particular attention is given to the ways in which those targeted for regulatory endeavors encounter, interpret, engage, experience, assess, resist, and adjust to the situations in which they find themselves.

Overviewing the volume in certain respects, chapter 14 addresses some of the more enduring features of deviance as an enacted community essence. Thus, consideration is given to the matters of developing, assessing, and refining concepts that correspond with the humanly enacted realities that constitute community life and to the importance of ethnographically examining the instances of humanly engaged sets of activities that take place in people's theaters of operation. Rather than envision deviance as something that is at odds with community life (as many theorists have done), we ask how social scientists may better understand community life through the careful, sustained examination of deviance as an enacted feature of everyday life.

NOTES

1. While acknowledging a series of divides between the moralists, idealists, structuralists, and interactionists, we have no intention of providing a more sustained overview of the various competing popular, theoretical, and methodological debates characterizing the field of deviance in this volume. This is not to deny the importance of attending to these matters (and the great many variants one finds within) in more direct, comparative terms. However, this not only would be a massive undertaking on its own but it also would represent a significant diversion from the central (and substantial) task of this immediate volume. Still, conceptual matters pertaining to an array of theoretical (as in functionalist, Marxist, postmodernist, constructionist, and interactionist) and methodological (quantitative and ethnographic) positions in the social sciences are addressed in rather direct terms in Prus (1996b, 1997, 1999).

Readers seeking a more sustained overview of the various theoretical perspectives in the sociology of crime and deviance are directed to the text developed by Downes and Rock (1998) as well as the edited volumes of Farrell and Swigert (1988), Rubington and Weinberg (1995), and Traub and Little (1999). For collections of materials that have a more distinctive interactionist focus, see Herman (1995), Kelly (1996), Adler and Adler (2000), and Rubington and Weinberg (2002).

2. As Blumer (1928, 1969) observes, the interactionist (and pragmatist) opposition to structuralism does not reflect people's attempts to engage the world in practical (means-ends) terms or scholarly attempts to be scientific (as in being thorough, systematic, and concept-oriented, or insisting on the primacy of information gathered through sustained inquiry into the instances of things). Clearly, as well, the interactionists do not deny humans the relevance of physiologically enabled thought processes (as in human capacities for making distinctions, developing categories, attending to sequences, inferring effects, behaviorally engaging things, and making adjustments). The opposition to structuralist thought and research, instead, reflects the comparative disregard of linguistically achieved human knowing and acting.

3. For more extended statements on people's notions of "obdurate reality," see Blumer (1969) and Prus and Dawson (1996).

4. While reflecting a considerably broader pragmatist-intersubjectivist theoretical base (Prus, 1996b), readers may appreciate that the premises outlined here very much represent variants or reconfigurations of materials developed by Mead (1934), Blumer (1969), and Strauss (1993).

5. As materials from the past several decades of publication in flagship journals such as the *American Journal of Sociology*, the *American Sociological Review*, the *American Journal of Psychology*, and the *Journal of Personality and Social Psychology* indicate, the predominant emphasis in the sociological and psychological literature has been on discerning quantitative relationships between factors of these sorts and particular sets of outcomes. Surprisingly little consideration has been given to the ways in which people actually do things as reflective, deliberative, acting, and interacting beings.

6. Fuller considerations of the centrality of activity for the study of human group life and other differences between interactionist and idealist (more specifically postmodernist) approaches to the human condition are available in Dawson and Prus (1993a, 1993b, 1995) and Prus (1996b).

7. For other texts that feature an interactionist approach to the study of deviance, see Becker (1963), Lofland (1969), Hawkins and Tiedman (1975), Goode (1978), Pfuhl (1980), Best and Luckenbill (1982), Dotter and Roebuck (1988), and Pfuhl and Henry (1993). We also acknowledge Rubington and Weinberg's (1968) interactionist approach to the study of deviance. Like many others, we benefited from their explicit organizational emphasis on social process. At a more fundamental level, Blumer (1969), Lofland (1976), Strauss (1993), and Prus (1996b, 1997, 1999) address the theoretical and methodological dimensions of symbolic interaction and ethnographic research.

8. These mixtures of disapproval, intrigue, and risk represent instructive dimensions for the study of deviance. Beyond (a) the inadvertent predicaments in which people find themselves in some instances and (b) certain pragmatic or instrumental advantages that may be associated with deviance involvements in other cases, it also might be noted that (c) the disrespectability associated with deviance sometimes represents part of its appeal.

9. Here and elsewhere, we stress the fundamentally relativistic aspect of people's definitions of deviance. This is not to imply that definitions of deviance are completely capricious or arbitrary, for notions of deviance inevitably reflect the concerns and viewpoints with which particular audiences work in engaging or dealing with the world about them. At a very basic conceptual level, though, it is necessary to acknowledge the highly diverse sets of concerns and viewpoints that people may invoke in defining deviance both over time and across contexts.

Intersubjective Accomplishment
Human Knowing and Acting

In setting up studies of human group life and social action there is need to take social interaction seriously. It is necessary to view the given sphere of life under study as a moving process in which the participants are defining and interpreting each other's acts. It is important to see how this process of designation and interpretation is sustaining, undercutting, redirecting, and transforming the ways in which the participants are fitting together their lines of action. Such a necessary type of study cannot be done if it operates with the premise that group life is but the result of determining factors working through the interaction of people. Further, approaches organized on this latter premise are not equipped to study the process of social interaction. A different perspective, a different set of categories, and a different procedure of inquiry are necessary. (Blumer, 1969:53)

Addressing the central features of symbolic interaction, this statement establishes the theoretical and methodological frame for the considerations of deviance in the chapters following. Focusing on the study of human knowing and acting, symbolic interaction is associated most directly with the works of George Herbert Mead (1934) and Herbert Blumer (1969). Still, the roots of symbolic interaction go much deeper. Conventionally, the origins of interactionism are located in American pragmatist philosophy and the ethnographic research tradition associated with the University of Chicago. However, symbolic interaction also is indebted to European scholarship (Wilhelm Dilthey and Georg Simmel) and can be traced even further back to the classical Greek era.[1]

ATTENDING TO HUMAN LIVED EXPERIENCE

Although Herbert Blumer introduced the term "symbolic interaction" in 1937, the scholarly tradition that would become known as symbolic interaction took shape somewhat simultaneously with the emergence of the Department of Sociology at the University of Chicago in 1895. The first four department members, Albion Small (as the chair and principal facilitator), Charles Henderson, George Vincent, and W.I. Thomas, clearly could not anticipate that

Chicago would be the site in which interactionist thought would develop. However, by building on the sociology of Georg Simmel, attending to the emergent ethnographic tradition in anthropology,[2] and encouraging their students to view the city as their own laboratory in which to explore community life, these early sociologists were not only laying the foundations for an ethnographic methodology but also for what would become a more sustained interactionist tradition. Other Chicago sociologists, including Robert Park, Ernest Burgess, Ellsworth Faris, Everett Hughes, and Herbert Blumer, in turn would foster these interests in city life and people's involvements therein.

These early developments in Chicago sociology took place somewhat concurrently with the emergence of American pragmatist philosophy. Given their intellectual overlaps, the traditions of anthropology and pragmatist philosophy would become intertwined in Chicago sociology. Whereas anthropological inquiry was at a rudimentary state of development and was quickly eclipsed by methodological developments in sociology (see Palmer's [1928] account of fieldwork in sociology), American pragmatism provided a highly consequential conceptual frame for what would become known as symbolic interaction.

American pragmatism developed mainly around the works of Charles Peirce, William James, John Dewey, F.C.S. Schiller (a British scholar), Charles Horton Cooley, and George Herbert Mead. Disenchanted with what they envisioned as the general irrelevance of philosophy for the everyday lived situations in which people find themselves,[3] the American pragmatists generally were opposed to both "idealist" or "absolutist" standpoints on the one hand and "structuralist" or "determinist" (i.e., positivist/structuralist) philosophies on the other.

Although their emphases were somewhat diverse (e.g., as in education, child development, and art) and their approaches were interdisciplinary in many respects, the pragmatists focused on the ways (*actualities* and *practices*) that people do things. The emphasis is on the ways that people make sense of and actively engage in problem-solving activities in the "here and now."

While not dispensing with notions of truth, scientific endeavor, or logic, the pragmatists consider the ways in which people in all realms of life might define and deal with [reality]. Thus, the pragmatists work with multiplistic, situated, emergent notions of reality and rationality, wherein things acquire meaning by virtue of the ways in which people *act* toward them.

The pragmatists varied in the extent to which they explicitly asked about the social processes by which community life took its shape, but there was a more general emphasis (especially via Peirce, Dewey, and Mead) on attending to people as community-based, language-using, reflective beings who possess capacities to act mindfully of their own situations and in conjunction with others. Far removed from notions of activity as an inherent response to some stimulus or even a learned adaptation to some socially defined situation, activity was envisioned in process terms, as something in the making. Thus, activity was seen not only as a humanly generated product but also as a deliberative, developmental, adjustive process that could be modified (relative to people's experiences with the past, assessments of the present, and anticipations of the future) even as it was being developed.

Working within this evolving philosophy of human knowing and acting, George Herbert Mead provided what would become the central theoretical frame for symbolic interaction.[4] Still, it was Herbert Blumer who most directly synthesized Mead's pragmatist philosophy with the ethnographic research tradition that was developing at Chicago. While observing that the social sciences would be unable to match the rigor and precision of the physical sciences, Blumer (1928, 1969) argued for the necessity of a methodology that examines the ways in which people make sense of and actively engage the world about them.[5]

Although many "social theorists" disregard the ethnographic components of symbolic interaction and, consequently, miss the relevance of the study of human lived experience for the sociological enterprise, field research is an integral feature of symbolic interactionism. As an empirically informed approach to human knowing and acting, interactionist theory exists as a developmental process in which the instances of human group life examined in ethnographic research are used to inform, adjust, and extend earlier conceptions of human group life. Because interactionist theory is so extensively interfused with field research, symbolic interactionism cannot be adequately understood apart from this methodological emphasis and the database that this approach has generated. Further, whereas the subject matter of deviance is but one theme explored by early Chicago sociologists, some of the most consequential material on deviance has its foundations in early Chicago ethnography.

Somewhat ironically, as well, because the Chicago faculty were primarily involved in teaching, administration, and writing manuscripts in the style of the day, it was largely their students who generated the actual field research that was to become the methodological mainstay of symbolic interaction. Thus, contemporary students of deviance might appreciate that the methodological practices of symbolic interaction were importantly facilitated by the inputs of a hobo turned sociologist named Nels Anderson (1923) who wrote *The Hobo*; a "street kid" who worked with Clifford Shaw (1930) in *The Jack-Roller*; some "taxi-dance hall" girls and their associates who helped Paul Cressey (1932) develop *The Taxi-Dance Hall*; and a professional thief who enabled Edwin Sutherland (1937) to produce *The Professional Thief*.

Although the University of Chicago would remain a prominent center of symbolic interaction until the 1960s (prior to Herbert Blumer's departure for the University of California, Berkeley and Everett Hughes's move to McGill University),[6] Chicago sociology was a mix of different approaches. These included a quantitatively oriented ecological sociology; functionalism and social disorganization; pluralist (value) conflict theory; cultural transmission; and differential association.[7] Even in the midst of considerable diversity, though, Chicago sociologists generally maintained focus on the processual or the emergent nature of community life. In contrast to European sociologists, who generally were content to discuss social life in more abstract terms, the early Chicago sociologists also were much more intent on examining things on a firsthand basis.

Thus, while sociologically more diverse than the term symbolic interaction implies, Chicago viewpoints were notably at variance from those promoted by the social pathologists of the same era (late 1800s onward). Reflecting a variety of reform backgrounds (as in medicine, corrections, social work, religion, and feminism), the social pathologists saw deviance as the product of biological or character flaws of individuals, often combined with or generated by disreputable living conditions (Platt, 1969a, 1969b). Still, because definitions of deviance, crime, and the like always reflect moral standpoints and are typically accompanied by the quest for solutions, people adopting moralist stances on deviance are likely to find that theories of these sorts (and related remedies) have great appeal. Thus, notions of crime and deviance as pathologies, sicknesses, character flaws, or products of undesirable living conditions are expressed in a great many forums and have seeped into various academic agendas and explanations. By contrast, the Chicago sociologists approached deviance as a natural product and process of human group life.

Although Chicago sociologists often focused on things considered troublesome or deviant in the community at large (as in homelessness, crime, control agencies, and policy), they also resisted the tendency to explain deviance in psychological, psychoanalytic (Freudian), or medical terms. Attending to pragmatist thought more generally, the broader emphasis was on the ways that people engage one another amidst the various associations, interactional contexts, and transitions that constitute group life in the making.

The task of maintaining a position that is distant from the moralists (and others caught up in the deviant mystique) has been only part of the intellectual struggle facing the interactionists. The interactionists also are highly attentive to both the idealist-pragmatist and the structuralist-intersubjectivist divides. Thus, while adopting a relativist stance on the meanings of things and attending to the mediating quality of language, the pragmatists differ from the idealists (who reduce everything to arbitrary text or language) by virtue of the pragmatist emphasis on (a) people engaging in activity within a world of objects and (b) focusing on the production of action in sustained analytical and methodological (interactionist) terms.

In contrast to the structuralists who insist on studying the things that affect human behavior, the pragmatists not only attend to (a) a linguistically enabled reality, but also (b) focus on the ways in which people, as agents, enter into the causal process (or engage the world of objects as meaningful, deliberative, agents). The interactionists do not deny the value of science or logic for human endeavor, but insist that a science of the human condition respect the human subject matter that is at the very core of the social science enterprise. From an interactionist standpoint, science and logic also represent human constructions and are to be approached in the same way that researchers might study any other instances of human group life in the making. For these reasons, the interactionists have not only been critical of what passes for social science in a set of disciplines dominated by structuralist viewpoints, but also are concerned about articulating the premises of a social science that is genuinely attentive to human lived experience.

SYMBOLIC INTERACTIONISM

Developed most explicitly by George Herbert Mead (1934) and Herbert George Blumer (1969), symbolic interaction may be envisioned as the study of the ways in which people make sense of their life-situations and accomplish their activities, in conjunction with others, on a day-to-day basis. It is an approach that insists on rigorously grounding its notions of the ways in which people do things within the context of community life.

Central to the interactionist approach is the notion that human life is group life; that *human life is thoroughly intersubjective in its essence*. At base is the recognition that humans (and human behavior) cannot be understood apart from the community context in which people live. People derive their (social) essences from the communities in which they are located, and human communities are contingent on the development of shared (or intersubjectively acknowledged) sets of symbols or languages. This means that there can be no self without the (community) other.

It is in the course of developing familiarity with the language of a community that people are able to approximate rudimentary understandings of, or perspectives on, human life-worlds. Only once people develop some fundamental conceptualizations of the *socially known* world may they begin to exhibit some sort of reflectivity and meaningful human agency. Only with the acquisition of a language-based set of understandings or perspectives are people able to take themselves into account in developing and pursuing particular lines of action. As Mead (1934) observes, it is the attainment of language that makes the possession of a "self" possible.

Accessing or sharing a language does not presuppose that people will automatically act in cooperative ways or in manners that others might deem rational. However, language provides the basis on which people establish common (community) understandings and it is through ongoing (symbolic) interaction with the other that people may achieve more precise levels of intersubjectivity or more comprehensive understandings of the viewpoints of the other as well as more intricate senses of self.

Because people are born into preexisting groups or communities (each with its own prevailing stocks of knowledge), the individuals within do not bring the objects of their awareness into existence on their own, at least not on a meaningful, foundational level. Thus, while recognizing people's capacities for creativity (and extensions of current object images and applications), the social world of (delineated, meaningful) objects precedes (and "objectifies") one's existence and experience as a knowing, reflective essence.

As interacting, self-reflective beings, people not only develop ways of viewing and acting toward other objects (including other people and themselves), but they also can direct, monitor, assess, and adjust their own behaviors over time. The recognition that people do not merely act toward objects, but also can make self-indications (i.e., attend to, consider, and alter their own behaviors) in the very process of developing particular lines of action toward things, has profound implications for the study of human behavior.

The human capacity for achieving intersubjectivity (mutuality of mindedness or a sharedness of meanings), as indicated by language and cultural development, meaningful interaction, self-reflectivity, and minded behavior, introduces complexities that require an entirely different theoretical and methodological approach than those that may be appropriate for studying other objects.[8] Likewise, it is not enough to ask about people's attitudes or backgrounds and then correlate these with people's behaviors (or the products of their behaviors). As Blumer (1969) so cogently argues, it is a fundamental error to view people as mediums through which various structures may find expression. As entities that are able to think, anticipate, act, interact, assess, and adjust to situations, people knowingly enter into the causal process as agents. However, they do so only by invoking intersubjectively achieved and sustained symbolic realities.

This emphasis on intersubjectivity is to be appreciated within the context of human activity. People are not perpetually or uniformly active, but human group life is characterized by *activity*. As reflective entities, people may pursue activities on their own on a meaningful basis, but also are commonly faced with the tasks of coordinating (cooperation, competition, conflict) their activities with those of others.

Human activity does not simply involve someone invoking behavior of some sort, but more accurately entails several subprocesses. Some instances of human activity are developed much more extensively than others, but a fuller sense of human activity centrally includes such things as: people defining the situation at hand, considering and anticipating both particular lines of action and potential outcomes, implementing behavior, monitoring themselves along the way, assessing situations both in process and in retrospect, and adjusting or modifying their own behavior both during immediate events and following earlier episodes. This way, people may align their activities to more adequately fit with their intentions, shifting interests, and any other matters that they take into consideration in their more immediate situations.

Human activity, thus, *cannot* be reduced to sets of preexisting individual properties or learned dispositions. As meaningful ventures, human behavior takes shape as people make indications to themselves and others in the process of working their way through specific situations. Human behavior is fundamentally informed by, and emerges within, the ongoing interchanges that humans have with one another.

Basic Assumptions

Recognizing the centrality of the standpoint adopted here for the comprehension and study of deviance, it may be instructive to specify a set of assumptions that people working within an interactionist tradition normally make (sometimes explicitly, sometimes implicitly) as they approach the study of human lived experience:[9]

1. *Human group life is intersubjective.* Human group life reflects a shared linguistic or symbolic reality that takes its shape as people interact with one another. Human group life is community life and human behavior cannot be reduced to individual properties. All meaningful essences, including the more solitary experiences of (linguistic-enabled) members of human groups, derive from or are built on comprehensions of "the reality of the other."

2. *Human group life is (multi)perspectival.* Rather than posit the existence of a singular or objective reality that people would experience in some uniform manner, people distinguish and develop meanings for [objects] as they interact with one another and develop styles of relating to those objects. Both the identification of phenomena as "objects" and the meanings attached to objects are problematic in their existence and directions. However, when groups of people establish consensus among themselves on the existence and meanings of particular objects, they tend to envision their definitions of situations as "real" or "objective."[10] Although the adoption of certain worldviews may enable a group of people to do things that others may not be able to accomplish, these viewpoints represent the paramount realities for understanding people's participation in the situations at hand. Thus, people are seen to operate in versions of (multiple) realities that they share, albeit imperfectly, with others at an "intersubjective" level.

3. *Human group life is reflective.* Through interaction with others, and by taking the viewpoint of the other with respect to oneself, people develop capacities to become objects of their own awareness. By attending to the viewpoint of "the other" (what Mead [1934] terms, "role-taking"), people are able to attribute meanings to their own "essences" and to develop lines of action that take themselves (and other objects) into account. Enabling people to see themselves from the standpoint of the other and to "converse with themselves about themselves," the acquisition of self-reflectivity fosters meaningful initiative (i.e., human agency, deliberation, intentionality) as people develop their activities in manners that take themselves into account. As reflective entities, people may pursue activities on their own as well as resist unwanted inputs from others.

4. *Human group life is activity-based.* Whereas human behavior is meaningful only within intersubjectively constructed, conveyed, and mediated contexts, and implies an ongoing interpretive process with respect to behaviors invoked in both solitary and collective instances, human group life is organized around the doing, constructing, creating, building, forging, coordinating, and

adjusting of behavior. There is no requirement that the activity in question need be successful as intended, nor need it be viewed as wise or rational by others or even by the actors themselves. Activity draws attention to the centrality of human enterprise; to the constituent notions of people defining, anticipating, invoking, encountering resistance, accomplishing, experiencing failure, reassessing and adjusting to things, on both interactive and more solitary realms of involvement.[11]

5. *Human group life is negotiable.* Acknowledging the abilities of people to influence and resist the influences of others, this premise makes the interactive dimension of human reflectivity especially explicit. Thus, the diverse range of interests and activities implied in cooperation, competition, conflict, and compromise are recognized as central to human interaction. Although people's exchanges with others may be quite uneven, some element of mutuality, sharedness, or intersubjectivity is evident whenever people attend to others, endeavor to shape the behaviors of others, and attempt to "get their own way" in dealing with others.[12]

6. *Human group life is relational.* People do not associate with one another in random or undifferentiated manners but tend to associate somewhat selectively (as in relevancies and affectations and disaffections) with others as they develop affiliations with other members of the communities in which they find themselves. This premise not only acknowledges the differing identities (i.e., self and other definitions) that people attach to one another, but it is also mindful of the interconnections, dependencies, instrumentalities, intrigues, loyalties, disenchantments, oppositions, and other interactional motifs that develop between people in the course of human interaction.

Thus, in addition to the perspectives characterizing the community at large, many of the activities in which people engage are made particularly meaningful and shaped in certain manners because of people's attentiveness to specific others in the setting. People's definitions of reality (including language) and ensuing negotiations, thus, depend centrally on people's involvements and embeddedness in particular groups within the broader community of others.

7. *Human group life is processual.* Human lived experiences are viewed as emergent or ongoing social constructions or productions. The emphasis is on the ways in which human group life is shaped or constructed by particular people as they go about their activities at specific points in time. While notions of intersubjectivity, particularized worldviews, reflectivity, activity, negotiated interchange, and relationships are all central to the ways in which the interactionists approach the study of human lived experience, so is the matter of process.

Reflecting the emergent or ongoing nature of group life, process is integral to an understanding of these other themes. Intersubjectivity (and the sharing of symbolic realities) is an ongoing process. Perspectives also are best approached in process terms, as the meanings that people attach to objects are developed, acted upon, and changed over time. Likewise, reflectivity is not only a product of ongoing association, but assumes its significance as "human agency" when people go about their activities. Reflectivity is processually experienced and expressed as people engage in instances of definition, interpretation, intentionality, assessment, and minded adjustments over time. While acknowledging the perspectives that people acquire through association with others and contingent upon people's invoked notions of (reflective) self-agency, activity is also fundamentally tied to process.

Denoting (experiential and behavior) sequences of definitions, anticipations, implementations, assessments, and adjustments, which build up over time (techniques, practices, skills, stocks of knowledge, and manners of engaging objects), activity provides a very powerful sense of emergence, transition, or process. Instances of negotiation or persuasive interchange also assume a processual dimension as people define situations (and selves), work out tentative lines of action, make indications to others, interpret the indications of others, and make ensuing adjustments to others in the form of subsequent definitions, plans, and indications. Relationships, as well, are best understood in developmental terms (or as having natural histories) with respect to their emergence, intensification, dissipation, and possible reconstitution, as people attend to specific others and attempt to develop their life-worlds in conjunction with those with whom they associate over time.

The primary conceptual and methodological implication of this processual emphasis is this: Because all aspects of group life take place in process terms or develop over time, it is essential that the human condition be conceptualized and studied in manners that are acutely mindful of the emergent nature of human lived experience.

ETHNOGRAPHIC RESEARCH: QUESTING FOR INTIMATE FAMILIARITY

In contrast to the physical scientists who study nonminded or noninterpreting objects, the interactionists contend that those in the social sciences require a methodology that is sensitive both to the intersubjective nature of the human condition and to human activity as a formulative process. To ignore any of the earlier discussed features of group life (intersubjectivity, perspectives, reflectivity, activity, negotiability, relationships, and processes) is to violate central qualities of the human subject matter.

The research implications of these assumptions are highly consequential. It means that people studying people should attend to: (1) the intersubjective nature of human behavior; (2) the viewpoints of those whose worlds they purport to examine; (3) the interpretations or meanings that people attach to themselves, other people, and other objects of their experiences; (4) the ways in which people do things on both a solitary and interactive basis; (5) the attempts that people make to influence (as well as accommodate and resist the inputs and behaviors of) others; (6) the bonds that people develop with others over time and the ways in which they attend to these relationships; and (7) the processes, natural histories or sequences of activities, exchanges, and events that people develop and experience over time.[13]

Although each inquiry into the life-worlds of the other will assume a somewhat different emphasis from the next, ethnographers generally rely primarily on three sources of data (observation, participant-observation, and interviews) in their attempts to achieve intimate familiarity (Blumer, 1969) with the life-worlds of those they study.

Observation encompasses not only those things that one witnesses through one's visual and audio senses, but also includes any documents, diaries, records, frequency counts, maps, and the like that one may be able to obtain in particular settings. While these materials can be valuable, it is imperative to recognize that the worth of any observation (or artifact) is contingent on researchers' abilities to achieve clear and accurate definitions of how that phenomenon or aspect of the situation was experienced and constructed by those participating in the situations under consideration.

Even when richly detailed, observational material is too limited on its own (i.e., is much too inferential; intersubjectively inadequate) to serve as a basis on which to build an ethnographic study. However, observational materials (particularly those that are more detailed, more descriptive in essence) can be very valuable in helping researchers formulate questions to be pursued in interviews as well as in providing a means of assessing and contextualizing the information one obtains through interviews and participant observation.

Participant-observation adds an entirely different and vital dimension to the notion of observation. Although the practice of describing and analyzing one's own experiences has often been dismissed as "biased" or "subjective" by those who think that researchers should distance themselves from their subject matters, the participant-observer role allows the researcher to get much closer to the lived experiences of the participants than does straight observation. While beset by problems of representation (as in concerns with typicality, authenticity, depth, and scope), researcher experiences as participants may provide scholars with invaluable vantage points for appreciating certain aspects of particular life-worlds.

As well, these role-involvements generally enable researchers to access (through conversation) the experiences of others in these settings in much more meaningful fashions than can be accomplished through questionnaires or experiments. Still, researcher participants in the field should strive for as much balance in representation as possible in attending to the experiences of those who constitute the setting under consideration. In particular, it is critical that researchers develop a thorough appreciation of where and in what ways researchers' own experiences may approximate and differ from those of others in the setting.

Like those doing straight observation, researchers engaged in participant-observation normally try to remain fairly unobtrusive or nondisruptive in the setting being studied. However, participant-observation entails a more active (and interactive) and ambiguous role as researchers attempt to fit into the dynamic settings at hand. Insofar as more sustained participant-observation typically allows researchers to experience many aspects of the life-worlds of the other on a firsthand basis, it offers a rather unique and instructive form of data to those able and willing to assume the role of the other in a more comprehensive sense.

Additionally, since participant-observation typically puts researchers in close, sustained contact with others, this methodology generates further opportunities for researchers to gain insight into the viewpoints and practices of others through ongoing commentary and other interactions. Insofar as researchers use these related opportunities to discuss other participants' experiences in more detail, they may achieve a doubly privileged form of contact with their human subject matter.

Interviews or extended, open-ended inquiries into the experiences (circumstances, viewpoints, dilemmas, activities, adjustments) of others represent the third, and generally the single most important, method of gathering ethnographic data. Because interviews enable researchers to achieve enhanced levels of intersubjectivity with the other better than any other method of research, these more sustained inquiries constitute the primary source of data for field researchers.

By inquiring extensively into the experiences of others, interviewers may learn a great deal more about the life-worlds of the other than is possible in either observation or participant observation. However, the viability of interview material is contingent on researchers maintaining good working relations with those in the field as well as researchers' attentiveness to detail and concerns about making careful records of the information communicated to them. Interview material is much more valuable, too, when researchers concentrate on developing a fuller, more open sense of the world as is experienced by (and in the terms of) the other. Relatedly, the most valuable interviews are apt to be obtained by researchers who listen more carefully, exercise greater interest in learning about the other, and display genuine receptivity to all manners of activity in which the participants in the field engage.

Thus, the emphasis is on a sustained examination of the *what* and *how* of the life-world of the other; to comprehend the substance and process of the other's experiences, particularly as this can be achieved by examining instances of people's activities in the making. Rather simultaneously, too, this implies that researchers open themselves to participant viewpoints and practices and avoid imposing their own concepts and moralities on the other.

When researchers are able to establish high levels of trust and openness with people who are willing to share their experiences and teach them about their life-worlds, extended, open-ended interviews can be extremely valuable. Even here, however, it is most instructive to supplement interviews with extended observation and, wherever possible, more extensive instances of participant-observation, being particularly mindful in all instances that the objective of ethnographic research is to *represent the other* as fully, accurately, and carefully as possible.

Thus, even the very best interview materials are apt to be enhanced by sustained observation and participant-observation. When people are unable to assume participatory roles that directly parallel those whom they are studying, researchers still may be able to achieve a greater sense of participant viewpoints and activities by adopting other roles in the setting or spending more time in related field settings. On some occasions, more marginal roles may advantage researchers in the field, as these roles reduce threats that researchers may represent (as competitors or agents of control) to more central participants in the setting.

One more methodological caveat may be in order. This pertains to the necessity of researchers suspending their own notions of deviance (and morality) while in the field. It is essential that researchers attend to the things that people do from the viewpoints of the participants rather than the moralities of researchers or others. For those engaged in the study of deviance (as with any other realm of human endeavor), the approach developed by Mead and Blumer addresses a general theory of human behavior. The interactionists do not require one theory for the "deviants" and another for the "normals." The interactionists approach the study of deviance as but one of many manifestations of the human condition that people may develop in dealing with one another in the course of community life.

Whereas these and other matters pertaining to the study of deviance will be addressed further in subsequent chapters, we now turn to a more direct consideration of the various theaters of operation in which people engage deviance in one or other ways. As with chapter 2, chapter 3 frames the ensuing analysis of deviance as a community process.

NOTES

1. In another project, Prus (2003) has been examining the development of pragmatist social thought from the early Greeks (c700–300 B.C.E.) to the present time. In the absence of a more distinctive social science over the intervening centuries, it has been most instructive to examine scholarship in the areas of rhetoric, poetics, theology, history, and philosophy as the intellectual bridges spanning the centuries.

In the briefest of terms, the early Greeks explicitly addressed a number of themes that we would presently identify as more distinctively pragmatist or interactionist in essence. Thus, some Greek philosophers (notably, Heraclitus, Protagoras, Plato, and Aristotle) explicitly discussed matters of process, community, language, activity, relativism, and influence work, as well as people's deliberative capacities, and interpersonal and intergroup relationships. However, these analytical themes were developed amidst wide arrays of theological, moralist, and philosophical standpoints.

Although aspects of pragmatist thought would persevere in a wide variety of humanly engaged European theaters (as in law, politics, education, religion, and entertainment) over the millennia, these emphases would largely assume applied dimensions, with more explicit scholarly considerations of pragmatist thought receding into the background, amidst various political, military, and religious ventures, diverse intellectual intrigues, and assortments of natural and humanly precipitated disasters.

Following the rediscovery of various Greek texts, Thomas Aquinas (1225–1274), Francis Bacon (1561–1626), Thomas Hobbes (1588–1679), and John Locke (1632–1704) would explicitly engage notions of pragmatist social theory. However, these emphases would be obscured as subsequent European philosophers emphasized matters pertaining to theology, idealism, moralism, structuralism, and socialist utopias as opposed to concerns with studying the humanly known and enacted world. Thus, it is not until the last century, with the efforts of some German interpretivists (especially Wilhelm Dilthey, 1833–1911) and the American pragmatists that we begin to see a more sustained emphasis on the study of human knowing and acting.

2. Far from being a recent innovation, the ethnographic research tradition is more appropriately rooted in the works of Greek ethnohistorians Herodotus (c484–425 B.C.E., *The Histories*); Thucydides (c460–400 B.C.E., *The History of the Peloponnesian War*); and Xenophon (c430–340 B.C.E., *Hellenica and Anabasis*). However, social scientists typically envision ethnography as a much more recent development. For overview statements on the development of nineteenth- and twentieth-century ethnography in anthropology and sociology, see Wax (1971) and Prus (1996b).

3. Morris (1970) provides one of the best accounts of the American pragmatist movement, but readers also may wish to consult Rucker (1969) who also provides some valuable material on the Sociology Department at Chicago, Mills (1969) who oddly omitted Mead from his discussion, and Scheffler (1974). Konvitz and Kennedy (1960) provide a collection of statements extracted from ten scholars they identify as American Pragmatists. For summary statements on the American Pragmatists, including Charles Peirce, William James, John Dewey, Charles H. Cooley, and George Herbert Mead, with respect to the development of symbolic interactionism, see Meltzer et al. (1975), Shalin (1986), Hammersley (1989), Reynolds (1993), and Prus (1996b).

4. For a valuable account of Mead's career as a scholar, see Joas (1985). Mead never completed his doctoral studies with Wilhelm Dilthey in Germany. However, when Mead returned to the United States, he pursued a line of scholarship regarding human knowing and acting that conceptually paralleled the position taken by Dilthey (Prus, 1996b).

Drawing philosophical inspiration from the hermeneutic or interpretivist tradition associated with religious studies (and especially the scholarship of Friedrich Schleiermacher), Wilhelm Dilthey (1833–1911) introduced the concept of *Verstehen* (interpretive understanding) to the study of the human condition about a century ago. Not only does Dilthey (Ermarth, 1978) address *Verstehen* earlier and in much more comprehensive terms than does Max Weber (with whom sociologists typically credit this concept), but Dilthey also explicitly and centrally argues for the development of a human science that entails a different set of premises than that associated with the physical sciences. Like Mead, Dilthey does not argue against the concept of science (as the careful, sustained study of some phenomenon), but rather insists that people are very different from other objects of study. Because people differ from other things by virtue of a community-based language and (relatedly) their linguistically mediated senses of reality, social scientists require a theory and a methodology that respects these unique features of human lived (i.e., linguistically defined and knowingly enacted) experiences.

5. Although Charles Horton Cooley spent his career at the University of Michigan rather than at Chicago, Cooley (1909, 1922, 1926, 1928) contributed notably to the development of what would later become known as symbolic interaction. A student of John Dewey, Cooley provides some highly consequential justifications for ethnographic research (what Cooley termed "sympathetic introspection"). Cooley also indicates the relevance of this methodology for studying more molar aspects of social life as well as smaller associational units. Blumer (1928) is acutely attentive to Cooley's work and is highly instrumental in synthesizing the conceptual dimensions of American pragmatism with the methodology of ethnographic research.

6. Even with these groundbreaking studies, Chicago sociologists did not consistently sustain a substantial ethnographic thrust. Thus, after a comparative hiatus, one finds a renewed emphasis on ethnographic research at Chicago in the early 1950s and 1960s. Especially noteworthy in this latter period are the works of scholars such as Howard Becker, Donald Roy, Anselm Strauss, Erving Goffman, and Fred Davis.

7. Building on insights from his earlier ethnographic study of professional thieves, Edwin Sutherland (1939) subsequently developed his theory of "differential association." Focusing primarily on criminal involvements, Sutherland outlines a set of processes that would very much parallel notions of deviance within the interactionist tradition. Thus, Sutherland (1955:77–80) contends that criminal behavior (1) is learned behavior; (2) this learning takes place through interaction with other people; and (3) this learning occurs primarily and most effectively within small intimate groups. He also states that (4) the learning of criminal behavior includes both attitudes (rationale, justifications) and techniques and (5) people concurrently learn attitudes that are both favorable and unfavorable toward criminal and conventional behavior. Sutherland further contends that people (6) are more likely to engage in criminal behavior when they have an excess of definitions favorable to law violation over those unfavorable to law violations. As Sutherland describes his theory, people's associations (7) vary in terms of: frequency (how often persons associate with particular others; duration (how long particular associations have been in effect); priority (how early in people's lives particular relationships develop); and intensity (how significant particular relationships are to the people involved). Relatedly, people may learn criminal and conventional behavior patterns through association with both criminal and noncriminal persons. As well, Sutherland stresses, criminal behavior (8) is an expression of the same interests that persons would have in engaging in other (law-abiding) behavior.

Because it fits so well with people's experiences in subcultural settings, differential association is a compelling theory for understanding people's involvements in deviance. However, Sutherland's theory of differential association was not conceptually developed as fully or inclusively as George Herbert Mead's (1934) social behaviorism or Herbert Blumer's (1969) formulation of symbolic interaction. Notably, too, Sutherland fails to address the enacted features of crime (i.e., as activity in the making). Still, readers may appreciate that the present text addresses in some detail a number of ideas that Sutherland introduced in his formulation of differential association.

8. For a most instructive ethnographic account of the relationship of language to knowing and communication, readers are referred to Evans and Falk (1986) and Evans (1994) who examine the processes by which nonhearing, pre-linguistic children "learn to be deaf."

9. We are particularly indebted to Mead (1934) and Blumer (1969) in developing this list of assumptions.

10. See Schutz (1962, 1964), Berger and Luckmann (1966), Blumer (1969), Strauss (1993) and Prus (1996b, 1997) for elaborations of the "objectification" (and typification) process as this pertains to people's sense of reality and their "stocks of knowledge."

11. Developing a pragmatist research agenda for the social sciences, Prus (1997) addresses activity across a wide range of substantive fields (and human-object relations).

12. For more sustained analysis of influence work (and resistance) over a wide range of interactional contexts, see Prus (1999).

13. For some other materials that deal with the practice of ethnographic research, see Becker (1970), Wax (1971), Bogdan and Taylor (1975), Lofland and Lofland (1984, 1995), Jorgensen (1989), Shaffir and Stebbins (1991), Lofland (1995), Prus (1996b, 1997), and Grills (1998).

3

Theaters of Operation
Deviance as Community Enterprise

If one is to permeate the deviant mystique in a more adequate sense, it will be necessary to consider the ways in which the many people involved in the production of deviance at a community level engage their activities at hand.

In what follows, we identify the major sets of players in the various theaters of operation that constitute "deviance in the making."[1] Clearly, only some people (and perhaps only one) may be involved in any "instance of deviance," but an attentiveness to this broader set of interactive arenas is essential for comprehending (and studying) deviance as a consequential and generic feature of community life.

Because it draws attention to the fuller set of roles that people may engage with respect to deviance as a community phenomenon, this statement on people's *theaters of operation* serves to set the stage for the chapters that follow. For purposes of presentation, the "players" are located within three major arenas of involvement: (1) *experiencing deviance*; (2) *managing trouble*; and (3) *participating in public forums*. These distinctions are *not* mutually exclusive and we should expect some overlap of people's involvements across these realms of endeavor. Although people often engage single roles in specific instances of deviance, it should be recognized that some people may assume multiple roles in single settings and frequently become involved in a variety of theaters of operation as they move from one context to another.

EXPERIENCING DEVIANCE

When discussing people's involvements in what are allegedly deviant enterprises within the community, it may be instructive to delineate five forms of participation. We refer here to those who may be envisioned as *practitioners, supporting casts, implicated parties, vicarious participants,* and *targets*. Thus, in addition to those who directly engage in activities designated as deviant, however tentatively or intensively they may pursue these roles, we should also recognize those who opportunistically develop roles that support particular deviants or forms of deviance; those who become implicated through intimate association with particular deviants; those who experience deviance vicariously; and those who assume a variety of target roles. Clearly, this does not exhaust the set of participants in the deviance-making scenarios that unfold in the community at large, but it provides an instructive starting point for appreciating and permeating some of the complexities surrounding the deviant mystique.

Being Practitioners

A review of the career contingencies (i.e., involvement processes—see Becker, 1963; Prus, 1987, 1996b, 1997) literature on deviance indicates that people may become involved in this or that form of deviance through multiple routings (seekership, recruitment, and closure) and that they may do so with a variety of definitions (and reservations) pertaining to the situations at hand.

Sometimes, people actively pursue situations in which they have developed earlier fascinations, but at other times they find that other people are highly concerned about encouraging (i.e., facilitating, recruiting, promoting) their participation in specific situations. On still other occasions, people may become involved in deviance on a most reluctant level as they experience closure or envision themselves to have no viable alternatives.

Whereas some people may become involved in and sustain participation in various forms of deviance without developing any particular fascinations or experiencing any exciting sensations regarding those activities, others may define their anticipations and participation in the same activities as fascinating, thrilling, exciting, intriguing, and the like. These latter participants may be seen to be enthralled, encapsulated, or engrossed in what they define as appealing aspects of the deviant mystique.[2]

As reflective entities or "objects unto themselves" (Mead, 1934), people seem able to develop intensities and excitements on their own, but these interests assume collective dimensions whenever other people become involved in these fascinations as co-participants (more casually or in focused associations) or provide other opportunities for individuals and groups to pursue their practices in these areas.

People may actively participate in particular forms of deviance with wide variations in the scope and intensity of involvements. Given the range of people's perspectives, their uneven commitments to particular activities, their varying senses of self, and their diverse relationships with others, we should not expect this to be otherwise.[3]

Thus, in contrast to outsiders who only know deviance from a distance, those who participate more actively in particular forms of deviant activity are not only apt to experience a much fuller sense of what "deviance involvements are all about," but often have to move far beyond notions of the deviant mystique in order to be effective participants in those settings.[4]

As well, while people sometimes pursue these interests in more solitary fashions (see chapter 9), those involved in "group endeavors" (chapters 6 through 8) are apt to find that other people enter into one another's involvements (and experiences) in a great many ways.

In addition to those more centrally involved as participants in deviance, it is important to consider those who become involved in deviance in more marginal manners. These other people may assume roles that parallel supporting casts and stagehands in certain respects, but they tend to be much more consequential for understanding the actual production of deviance than first seems.[5]

Assuming Supporting Roles

Although they may make contact with particular deviants or realms of deviance in any number of ways (including their own prior or concurrent involvements in particular forms of deviance), some people may begin to envision various personal and economic advantages to catering to particular deviants (as individuals or groups).

Those involved in these supplementary activities may experience some disrespectability, but members of supporting casts may play integral roles in facilitating and accommodating deviance. These people may have little personal interest in becoming "practitioners" in more direct senses, but may become extensively involved in providing places for disreputable people to meet and do things as well as offering more specialized goods and services to these people.

Providing Forums

Much like sociologists who initially may have difficulty identifying and accessing those participating in particular realms of deviance, those pursuing particular modes of deviant involvements may face parallel challenges in forming relations with like-minded others (i.e., a failure to gain access to others may limit or preclude participation altogether). People operating various businesses may envision the services entailed in providing "meeting places" to be financially lucrative.

As Whyte (1934) points out, one of the characteristics of relatively stable slum communities is the existence of legitimate business interests surviving alongside various less respectable trades. Establishments such as hotels, bars, and restaurants sometimes organize their activities in such a way as to facilitate the patronage of people involved in a wide variety of deviant activities. Anderson's (1923) study of hobos effectively illustrates the linkages of homeless people with slum businesses, while Cressey (1932), Roebuck and Frese (1976), and Prus and Irini (1980) note the importance of sex trade for financial survival of some bars. In like manner, Wolf (1991) observes that biker patronage may be highly consequential to the financial well-being of some bars. Similarly, Steffensmeier's (1986) portrayal of "fencing" depicts another variation of a meeting place for people involved in the exchanges of stolen goods. In such cases, people running businesses expect to benefit from the support of those associated with deviance.

Those involved with deviance more directly (as practitioners and prospective practitioners) also benefit from these arrangements. Having access to settings in which they may be both seen and unseen, accessible but not too openly so, enables practitioners to make desired contacts with others and sustain particular forms of activities. Further, as establishments come to be recognized as "hooker bars," "biker bars," "meeting places," or other viable settings, they facilitate the initial and continuing involvements of others with deviance. The print (e.g., newspapers, magazines) and electronic media also may serve as contact forums, for exchanges of ideas and subsequent face-to-face interaction between people with similar or interdependent interests. As noted in Bartell's (1971) research on mate-swapping, Correll's (1995) consideration of lesbian "cyberspace," and Ekins's (1997) study of transgendering, arenas of these sorts may be particularly appealing for those attempting to manage the stigma of "coming out."

Providing Specialized Goods and Services

Many deviance involvements also require continuing access to certain goods and services. As Becker (1963) points out, continued access to marijuana is essential to sustaining one's involvement as a drug user. His point is logically obvious but sociologically complex. He asks us to recognize the interpersonal and relational (i.e., organizational) quality of deviance that allows participants to access illegal, restricted, or otherwise disrespectable goods.

Although the distinction between illegal goods and legal goods hinges on matters of morality and definition, considerably more is involved. To be successful, those who provide illegal goods and services in the support of deviance must, in some way, organize their activities around the "social fact" of this illegality. This adds additional elements of risk to the business at hand and, if practitioners are to survive in these arenas, added precautions will likely be advantageous. Though the concept of organized crime brings with it the burden of mass-media images, the organization of crime normally focuses on those goods and services (e.g., drugs, sex, and gambling) for which there are continuing demands and interests. This is not to deny some of the rougher elements that may be associated with businesses involving deviant and/or criminal interchange. However, those embarking on trade that involves "illicit goods" or a "deviant clientele" are apt to find it most productive to organize and manage their operations in manners that parallel the ways in which people might run any other viable business venture.[6]

In addition to those businesses that are more explicitly organized around illegal endeavors, a wide range of other businesses engage in legal (if at times disreputable) activities that may be more or less oriented to participants in deviant enterprises. Some publishers and filmmakers, for instance, may heavily target their work for people involved in particular forms of deviance. In the process, they may provide a series of moral claims or justifications for those lifestyles as well as distribute practical information (of the "how-to" variety) to facilitate participation. Some deviant involvements may also be "paraphernalia intensive" or involve certain kinds of commercial products.

Whereas some retailers may make concerted efforts to appeal to those involved in certain deviant endeavors, other merchants may quite unexpectedly find that a significant portion of their routine business effectively brings them in frequent contact with those pursuing particular forms of deviance.

Becoming Implicated

A third category of people involved in deviance includes those who live with or have other close associations with those they know to be "deviants." Typically, these people find themselves learning about particular forms of deviance not by choice, but because one or more of their associates is involved in some particular realm of deviance.

As family members, friends, or neighbors of those more directly engaged in deviance, these *implicated parties* find themselves privy to the (generally not so pleasurable) back regions (Goffman, 1959) that they witness in living with and attempting to deal with those assuming roles as deviants. Although their definitions of the deviance at hand often reflect general community sentiments of disgust, embarrassment, and frustration, these people also may become caught up in various themes of the deviant mystique (curiosities, explanations, indignations, control efforts, vicarious fascinations, and active participation) by virtue of the impact of the deviant other on their personal lives.[7]

Relatedly, it might be appreciated that these people often have "privileged" access to these roles should they be so inclined. Not only are they more apt to occupy positions of trust relative to their deviant associates, but as "intimates" of sorts, these people also are likely to learn viewpoints and techniques that foster entry into particular realms of deviance.

Living Vicariously

Role-taking (or the ability to share, or evoke in oneself, a meaning possessed or experienced by the other), as Mead (1934) observes, is an essential feature of human group life. Foundational to all symbolic communication and a requirement of all human language, the ability to adopt the standpoint of the other enables people to make indications to themselves, as well as to communicate with, adjust their behaviors to, and coordinate their activities with others.

Still, in addition to more open sharing of meanings with the other, people also may attempt to adopt (and experience) the viewpoints of the other as a more personal and private form of activity. As internal, personally containable experiences, people's reflections about the situations of others (and often related, personal anticipations and daydreams) on matters of these sorts offer people a degree of autonomy, privacy or safety.

To live vicariously requires that one experience aspects of the situation of the other in one's mind or attend to an imagined sense of what the other is experiencing in some situation. The "mindedness" of role-taking allows one to *play at* deviance—to invoke images of identity, activity and risk—without totally or completely embracing these notions in practice. Those living vicariously may openly share in the experiences of others, but they also may "sin from a distance" by more covertly (unobtrusively, discreetly, and safely) pursuing activities that are publicly devalued.

However, like children who play at adult activities only to find that imagination fails at the limits of their own experience, those pursuing deviance as an imagined pleasure must rely on their acquired knowledge to carry them from imagined act to imagined act.

Although those engaged in deviance (as practitioners) also may be interested in hearing about accounts of their life-worlds (and many practitioners also may live somewhat vicariously, working with dreams of much greater success and daring in these settings than they actually expect to achieve), those experiencing deviance more exclusively at a vicarious level are apt to be among the heavier *consumers* of materials pertaining to deviance in this or that setting. Some of these people eventually may become insider (actual) participants in the very situations that they presently experience only at a vicarious level. In the interim, however, they are apt to be highly receptive to accounts (both interpersonal and media-generated) of the experiences of those whose lifestyles they find so alluring.[8]

As with those experiencing other success in their daydreams (e.g., envisioning themselves as stars or celebrities), the people experiencing deviance vicariously have another advantage over their insider counterparts. As objects of their own reflection, those living vicariously can more readily selectively focus their fascinations. Because these people are experiencing deviance via self-generated accounts, they have greater abilities to control the directions that their fascinations and fantasies assume than can most insiders who (as actual participants) are highly dependent on those they encounter for their experiences of the world.

Thus, in addition to embellishing aspects of deviant roles that they find particularly alluring, those living vicariously also can diminish or minimize the more negative or potentially abrasive aspects of particular roles. Hence, those vicariously entering deviant worlds can do so in idealized settings, free from the hazards that mark the lived experience of full participants. People living vicariously may be quite aware of, as well as frustrated by, the limits and artificiality of their experiences. Nevertheless, they may deeply appreciate the entertaining features of experiencing deviance, even from a distance.

In addition to those who find certain forms of deviance more intriguing in more direct participatory or vicarious respects, it also may be observed (somewhat ironically) that some people involved in condemning or regulating particular forms of behavior also may develop (more covert, sometimes intense) fascinations with the very things they seek to suppress or the treatments (and ensuing target reactions) that they or others administer to the "deviants" in question.

Experiencing Target Roles

Without denying, in any way, people's senses of injury, loss, or righteous indignation, it is essential that social scientists, as analysts, be extremely cautious about mystifying, emphasizing, or dramatizing the experiences of those who identify themselves as the recipients of (presumably) unwanted features of the behaviors of others.

Thus, in addition to (a) the ways that people sometimes experience (define and deal with) direct injury and loss as a consequence of the actions of others, it is important that students of human behavior also be acutely attentive to such things as (b) the diverse moral frames and differential sensitivities that people may invoke in defining themselves as victims or injured parties; (c) the activities in which these people themselves have engaged that contribute to the joint or ensuing production of the circumstances in which they define as troublesome or threatening;[9] and (d) the ways in which people sometimes claim victim roles or injuries as rhetorical devices intended to advantage themselves (and any missions they may pursue) or punish those of whom they disapprove.[10]

Our objective is not to justify deviance or encourage greater tolerance of deviants as perpetrators. However, it would be no more desirable for analysts to assume roles as dramatists, moralists, or advocates with respect to those assuming target roles. Although it may be tempting for researchers to identify with one or other sets of parties in the setting or to pursue analysts' own notions of justice in the setting, this viewpoint is apt to result in a skewed representation (and mystification) of the experiential and enacted foundations of the situation under consideration.

Rather than deny the integrity of the target role or, more accurately, target roles (since any and all parties may envision themselves as targets at various points) in the situations under consideration, what is required is a rigorous attentiveness to the viewpoints of *all* parties involved and an extended consideration of the ways in which the various participants define and act toward themselves and others over time as they engage the situation at hand. This means acknowledging such things as people's interests, affiliations, obligations, reservations, and senses of vulnerability and accountability. This also requires an appreciation of the various tactician roles that people defining themselves as targets may assume during their involvements in particular situations.

This attentiveness to people's multiple roles *and* interchangeable positions as targets and tacticians (see Prus, 1999) enables social scientists to move beyond highly simplistic, singularistic, or reductionist notions of villains and victims. It also allows researchers to compare and contrast cases in which targets may be subject to more unilateral treatments from tacticians with those in which those considered to be targets engage tacticians in more interactive and sustained manners. Distinctions of these sorts are fundamental if analysts are to move past the deviant mystique.

Albeit also highly compacted, the following consideration of people "managing trouble" draws attention to the *reactive behaviors* that serve to isolate and objectify (Berger and Luckmann, 1966; Prus, 1997) particular forms of deviance and an assortment of roles within.

MANAGING TROUBLE

Drawing particular inspiration from Becker's (1963) portrayal of "moral entrepreneurs," Blumer's (1971) depiction of "social problems as collective behavior," and Gusfield's (1989) discussion of "troubled person" professionals, we turn to the roles that those concerned with conventional morality play in fostering deviance and the deviant mystique within the community.

Following Becker (1963), we use the term moral entrepreneur to refer to those who define trouble in the setting at hand and attempt to regulate people's behaviors therein. It is these people who assume responsibility for defining and enforcing the rules whose violations constitute deviance. These definitions and regulatory efforts vary greatly in explicitness, formality, consensus, and the like, but the enterprise involved in the production of morality (and deviance) represents an important departure point for subsequent analysis.

Mindful of this emphasis, we distinguish five roles that people involved in the control of deviance may engage: *spotting trouble; raising consciousness; identifying deviants; regulating deviance;* and *providing secondary aid*. Though people (e.g., parents dealing with their offspring, teachers in a classroom, pedestrians on a street) may embark on more than one of these pursuits in given settings, a closer examination of each of these activities significantly contributes to notions of deviance in a here-and-now sense. Further, even when people are more directly involved in "rooting out" or otherwise dealing with trouble, it should be recognized that these same people may occasionally develop sympathies, curiosities, or fascinations with the deviance they are endeavoring to manage. Likewise, those regulating deviance may develop and sustain a wide range of relationships with those targeted for control.

Spotting Trouble

Consistent with the interactionist approach more generally, we take the viewpoint that deviance or trouble does not exist as an objective or inherent state but rather reflects some audience's (person or group) definition of that situation. Like all definitions of objects, people's notions of "trouble" entail interpretations of instances within conceptual frames.

Spotting or identifying instances of trouble refers to the matter of someone first defining particular things (e.g., activities, appearances, episodes, outcomes) as disruptive, threatening, bothersome, and the like. These definitions may be vaguely experienced or pointedly explicit in thrust. The matter in question may be something encountered for the first time or it may be a more recurrent phenomenon and may involve the same or different people. The point is, though, that someone has defined something as troublesome, threatening, disconcerting, and so forth. Whereas people's definitions of deviance may be seen to reflect their broader notions of morality or propriety, these preliminary definitions are not automatic and they do not determine people's ensuing reactions to the episodes in question.

Indeed, even when people explicitly define something as troublesome or deviant and envision others to concur with their definitions of the situation, they may still invoke rather different (one to another) lines of action in engaging the deviance at hand. Even clearly defined and consensually validated instances of deviance may mean rather different things to the people in a particular community. As well, although particular people may assume specific tactics in one instance, it should not be assumed that they would do the same things in subsequent, seemingly identical instances. If we are to permeate the deviant mystique, it will be necessary to attend to the ways that the people in the setting make sense of and actually approach the instances of deviance that they see themselves as encountering.

Raising Consciousness

As referenced herein, "consciousness-raising" denotes people's attempts to (a) promote particular moral codes within the community under consideration; (b) alert others to some pressing problem at hand; and (c) seek solutions to that problem. While instances of consciousness-raising may subsequently form a basis on which trouble later may be defined, these ventures normally begin with someone proffering definitions of a situation or type of situation as both problematic and undesirable.

Given the great many things that people may define as troublesome or deviant on a day-to-day basis, broad-scale consciousness-raising, especially of a more sustained sort, seems apt to occur in a minority of cases. Still, because these moral frames may become focal points for highly intensive realms of enterprise, this aspect of deviance merits considerable attention on the part of analysts (especially see chapter 4).

People embarking on these activities typically presume a moral or ethical position and attempt to generate an awareness of disparities between community ideals and the activities of particular individuals or groups within the

community. While the targets of moral crusades can be exceedingly wide ranging (e.g., vagrants, drinkers, television viewers, and sinners), the advocates typically assert that the behaviors or situations in question seriously jeopardize
some important aspect of community life.[11] Notably, as well, while highlighting
certain practices as problematic and in need of attention, these crusades also
tend to thrust the consciousness-raisers into the spotlight.

Stepping out of their (often banal) community routines to take action of
more exceptional proportions, moral entrepreneurs (Becker, 1963) or crusaders
(Klapp, 1969) may both pursue and be pursued by the media,[12] as well as
become the focal points of public interest more generally. Thus, the quests for,
and benefits of, celebrity status associated with moral campaigns should not be
overlooked by analysts.

Likewise, inspired by a sense of moral indignation, and envisioning themselves as "championing" noble causes, moral entrepreneurs may take exceptional liberties and aggressively embark on highly confrontational and
emotionally charged pursuits as they challenge villainy, complacency, and other
human obstacles in the pursuit of morality (Grills, 1989).

In drawing attention to their causes, consciousness-raisers and those they
encounter in these missions become sources of intrigue and entertainment in
the broader community. Also, by virtue of their experiences in "combating the
forces of evil," these people may be envisioned by their supporters and others
as authorities or experts in dealing with particular kinds of problems in the
community.

Interestingly, those individuals or groups who oppose the definitions of the
situation promoted by consciousness-raisers may become the targets of greater
contempt and hostility on the part of the consciousness-raisers than those engaging in activities that represent the topic of initial affront.[13] Whereas those
defined as "the deviants" may be excused on various grounds (e.g., as sick,
victims, or inadequately socialized), people who oppose the agendas being promoted may be viewed as intentionally disrespectful, obstructive, or as threatening the basic moralities of the community.

Identifying Deviants

As with people identifying instances of trouble or attempting to define morality for the community more generally, we also may consider those who
"label" or more openly designate particular targets as deviants of this and that
sort. These focused identifications of disreputable persons may lack some of
the fervor characterizing broader instances of consciousness-raising, but these
definitions may also be interrelated with the former, as when particular cases
(targets) are seen to epitomize particular causes or crusades.

As well, whereas some designations may be quickly dropped or even re-
tracted, and others may proceed rather quietly, some accusations and claims
often become sites of dramatic encounters or character contests (see Garfinkel,

1956; Klapp, 1964; Prus, 1975a, 1975b) and may add elements of considerable intrigue and excitement to ongoing community life.[14] Insofar as definitions of deviance more sharply thrust individuals (the accused and accusers) into public theaters, these people become singled out as objects of attention, reflection, and conversation, as may all of those participating more directly in the ensuing episodes.

Regulating Deviance

When people define particular others as troublesome, they may ignore these "targets" or engage them in more direct manners. Although people encountering troublesome behaviors (and actors) may (a) "do nothing" for a variety of reasons, those bothered by these occurrences also may (b) alter their own behaviors, (c) attempt to change the perpetrators in some way, and (d) refer troublesome cases to third parties for disposition.

Troubled parties also may (e) develop alignments with other concerned parties in order to embark on activities designed to deal with troublesome cases on a collective basis. These latter sorts of endeavors may assume relatively enduring and highly formalized dimensions in some instances, accompanied by the development of a variety of offices and service specialists. On many occasions, though, these collective ventures may be relatively short-lived and may dissipate before handling even a single case.

To the extent that their activities denote selective treatments applied to those considered to be deviants, those involved in attempting to regulate or control deviance further objectify the deviant mystique. This seems especially true when these activities are accompanied by heightened senses of moral indignation and trust violation. Although people in the community generally seem to anticipate some discrepancy between target activity and eventual treatments (reflecting detection, apprehension, justifications, judgements and the like), people often take interest in the dramas of human interchange that take place in specific instances of deviance regulation. To this end, people may attend to treatment decisions, the implementation of treatments, and reactions from targets and others, and longer term implications of treatments for the targets and others in the community more generally.

Though much trouble-spotting, consciousness-raising, identification of deviants, and regulatory activity is conducted at a more informal or casual level, the development of more formal or more sustained roles of rule enforcers (and control agencies) carries the deviance-making process much further along the lines of "professionalism" and industry. Here, people may specialize in the production, identification, and regulation of deviance on a full-time basis.

Insofar as the primary clientele with whom full-time regulators work consists of discreditable if not discredited people, much of this work may be seen to have a "dirty work, dirty hands" quality to it. Relatedly, many outsiders seem entirely happy to distance themselves from these activities as a consequence. However, these same settings do afford images of contact with, and control over the lives of, disreputable others that some outsiders may find intriguing.

Some people may be attracted to this type of work as a consequence of the opportunities offered to make "legitimated contact" with particular kinds of deviants, but others (vicariously) also may want to know what it is like to work with the more sinful, troublesome, "incorrigible," or "bizarre" elements of society. Thus, the control agents dealing with troublesome cases on a more intimate or long-term basis may be accorded a certain aura.

Providing Secondary Aid

In addition to those working more directly as control agents, there are other people whose work roles bring them into contact with deviants as "troubled persons." One may think, here, of lawyers, counselors, therapists, social workers, and the clergy, as well as a host of other social service personnel, who work with people participating in deviance or those who have become implicated in other ways.

As with those involved more explicitly in rule enforcement directed at particular deviants, these secondary aid professionals tend to develop industries around deviance and help to sustain a focus on particular forms of deviant activity. Although they generally are thought to have less confrontational forms of contact with practitioners (or their associates), some mystique may also be associated with their involvements with deviants (as in criminal lawyers, psychiatric social workers, and so forth).

PARTICIPATING IN PUBLIC FORUMS

Because all of those who talk about deviance in some capacity also may contribute to one another's stocks of knowledge about community life, even those who discuss aspects of deviance more casually with others may be seen as cultural entrepreneurs of sorts.

It is not implied that people who talk about deviance possess or provide accurate information on the subject matters. However, in whatever ways talk about deviance is generated and presented to others, this information contributes to people's general images and understandings of deviance.

In the process, as well, we begin to see some other roles (even if somewhat more distant) that people in the broader community may assume with respect to both particular instances of deviance and the deviant mystique more generally. Thus, we may delineate five important sources of talk about deviance: *interpersonal exchange; educators and scientists; politicians and political advocacy; religious and ethical moralists;* and the *mass media*. As will become evident, too, those informing us about deviance in one or other ways assume a variety of motives and motifs, but one of the more central themes is that of being compelling in the process. Indeed, being relevant, entertaining, or, otherwise able to sustain audience interest may significantly overshadow many people's concerns with accuracy and authenticity.

Interpersonal Exchange

Despite a tendency on the part of some people to focus on the mass media almost to the exclusion of interpersonal networks, casual talk about or conversation regarding (respectable and disrespectable) others remains one of the, if not the single, most central means of conveying information about specific people within communities.[15] Many of these discussions may be of little interest to people outside of particular settings, but talk (accurate or otherwise) can affect people's life-chances in very important ways within those smaller communities (as well as in larger communities where someone has achieved broader attention).

Talk about others seems a regular aspect of community life and particular rumors may be started by anyone. Still, it should be noted that not all talk about other people is equally interesting even when the alleged behaviors are the same and not everyone is equally adept at generating, spreading, and sustaining rumors. Not only may certain people be seen as more interesting topics of conversation because of their existing situations or earlier reputations in the community, but particular members of the community may routinely make more effective use of gossip as a resource for attempting to shape community sentiments than do others in the setting.

As people become more adept at using talk about others as a resource, and establish links with others who tend to do so as well, then we may speak of the development of rumor mills. Further, gossip, rumor, and rumor mills are not only the precursors to the mass media, they also may be quite intertwined in some instances. Not only may some community members find themselves in positions to feed material to the mass media (with agents tapping into these sources whenever they think it will serve their purposes), but those involved in gossip also may feed off the media (using information gleaned from the media to embellish, contemporize, objectify, or otherwise dramatize talk about particular targets).

Because deviance implies notions of exceptionality as well as negativity, talk about deviance, however well founded or fabricated, adds an element of interest to many people's daily routines. Importantly, too, it also thrusts the messengers into somewhat privileged positions as a consequence of the informative and entertainment potential they represent.

As Simmel (1950) notes, people's abilities to share secrets with others represent a form of interpersonal advantage with respect to both targets and audiences. In addition to being in a position to wrest concessions or favors from (and blackmail) targets in some instances, those with interesting information to disclose may be able to use these materials to gain special considerations from other audiences. As long as they can sustain interest in particular episodes, these messengers also may be imbued with a celebrity status of sorts.

Educators and Scientists

When people in the community desire more careful, reliable or thorough information about deviance they sometimes turn to educators and scientists. Although there is no guarantee that this information will be any better than that available "on the street," and may be confounded by the roles that some educators and scientists maintain as moral entrepreneurs, this group of people tend to be viewed as experts because of their claims to particularized realms of knowledge.

In general, as well, members of the academic community are more apt to be discouraged from unduly sensationalizing deviance. Still, some academics do become heavily involved in the dramatization or sensationalization of evil. This seems more likely when they attempt to promote particular political ideologies (i.e., become moral entrepreneurs under the guise of being academics); pursue (the sometimes large) research grants available for studying particular aspects of deviance; attempt to become celebrities (and experts) as authors, speakers, and consultants; or attempt to use deviance as a focal point for entertaining or evoking greater levels of emotionalism from readers and the other audiences.

Albeit less wittingly, academics may also contribute to the deviance mystique when they attempt to explain deviance as if the behaviors involved were somehow "inherently deviant" or "require the development of theories unique to deviants or deviance" (i.e., theories at variance from those used to explain other instances of human activity and interchange). Such conclusions may be far from their respective intents, but scholars working in avenues of these sorts suggest that deviance represents a separate, specialized form of the human condition.

Like those involved in deviance and those working with deviance (as regulators, secondary aid professionals), academics doing research on, or merely talking about, particular forms of deviance may find that the deviant mystique also extends to them. As Henslin (1972), who studied cab drivers, drug users, abortion, and suicide, pointedly observes, researchers may find themselves recipients of inferences of both intrigue and disrespectability in the eyes of outsiders (academics and laypeople alike). Hence, simply alleging to know about or speaking with people who engage in particular forms of deviance may be enough to alter the reputations of scholars.

Politicians and Community Arenas

Those engaged in activities associated with the political forums (e.g., pursuing support, promoting party membership, seeking election, and constructing, implementing, and defending legislation) also may play significant roles in shaping people's understanding of deviance. Because spokespeople in political forms often lay claim to community interests in addressing the formal regulation of troublesome behavior, political activities can be highly instrumental in drawing attention to or amplifying troublesome behaviors. As Gusfield (1963) notes, political attentiveness to deviance may take on the qualities of a "symbolic crusade" with groups attempting to preserve their interests through the regulation, restriction, or criminalization of the behavior of others.

Because governments purport to act in the interests of the community, political responses to deviance often objectify the deviant qualities attributed to acts and influence people's understandings more generally regarding dangers to person and community (Blumer, 1971). As Becker (1963) posits, political activity plays a part in creating crime by passing laws whose violation constitutes criminal activity and promoting "deviance agendas" that designate some forms of offense as more urgently problematic than others.

The central participants also may actively pursue and cultivate identities as "deviance experts" or champions of morality, law and order, and the like, by promoting definitions of self as someone who is "tough on crime" or who can "clean up" problems not successfully attended to by others. Such strategies may attempt to place deviance at the forefront of political agendas.

Those using deviance as "political footballs," however, are reliant upon the continuance of the deviance that they purport to regulate. To be effective over the longer term, political crusades constructed around the regulation of morality require the continued threat of offense. Thus, partisan actors may selectively attend to deviance as a means of nurturing solidarity by providing others with a common target for derision and fostering a public sense of fear (Altheide, 1996), often independently of the representations that social scientists might develop of the same realms of trouble.

In permeating the deviant mystique, it is important that analysts attend to political processes in a more comprehensive sense and, yet, simultaneously avoid the trap of undue cynicism. Thus, although politicians may (a) use deviance (and criminality, law and order) themes as rhetorical emphases with which to garner support (e.g., position, votes, funding) and (b) promote particular political positions in order to pursue personal agendas or those encouraged by special interest groups, politicians may also (c) implement, alter, or nullify rules or legislation pertaining to certain realms of deviance in response to perceptions of more widespread sentiments among the constituency as well as more pervasive concerns about the well-being of the community.

Consequently, it is essential that analysts be attentive not only to the full range of options that those invoking political decisions may entertain, but also to the processual, reflective, interactive nature of those situations. Unfortunately, social scientists have developed very little ethnographic research on officeholders and the decisions associated with those offices. Only by achieving intimate familiarity with this realm of endeavor will we be able to further demystify this aspect of the deviance-making process.

Religious and Secular Moralists

Although the practices of those assuming roles as spokespeople for religious and secular moralities parallel those of politicians in certain respects and often directly overlap with political advocacy, it is important to recognize (Klapp, 1969) that politicians are generally more reluctant to "go out on a limb" or more independently assume roles as crusaders because of the greater risks of sustaining public support amidst the more extreme positions that theologians and moralists sometimes represent. Likewise, it is appropriate to recognize that these parties not only may attempt to influence one another but also commonly strive for greater acceptance of their own viewpoints relative to the populace at large.

Recognizing the substantive diversity reflected in human religious expression, we follow Geertz's (1973) lead in understanding religion minimally as a system of meaning. Still, because each claims to deal with ultimate reality or truth, specific versions of religion are often privileged as the interpretive frame from which the intersubjective reality of everyday life is understood, analyzed, and evaluated. The experience of the Holy (Otto, 1970) is sometimes so pervasive that the totality of a person's life-world is understood in reference to particular religious frameworks.[16] Religious meanings may be considerably less salient for some members of the community and possibly reflect little more than fantasy worlds for others. However, denouncements on the part of skeptics do not render religious standpoints inconsequential for understanding deviance within the broader community.

Assuming roles as spokespeople for the community at large, religious leaders may find themselves holding positions of relative authority and attributed expertise on aspects of deviance. Thus, while perhaps unanticipated and undesired in some cases, these people may find themselves immersed in community debates concerning such issues as homosexual rights, contraception and abortion, poverty and the distribution of wealth, and sexual assault. Such debate and discussion may prove divisive and may alter the relationship between adherents within groups but, by joining in the activities that accompany the designation of deviance, religious leaders typically also assume opportunities to proclaim the relevancy of religious perspectives for the world at large. By so doing, these religious voices may effectively contribute to the mystique associated with deviance by locating and vilifying particular acts and actors within the context of struggles over "good and evil" or the "sacred and profane."

Albeit often disidentified with particular religious communities, more secular moralities such as concerns with "state consciousness," "ethical behavior" and "political correctness" are often invoked in similar manners. These stances may not only be employed to denounce or condemn behaviors and actors deemed offensive from certain viewpoints, but also may be used to proclaim or express moral positions intended to direct (and justify) the activities of the community at large. Although some of these endeavors may be imbued or interfused with preexisting religious moralities, others fostering these moralities may intend that these will become the "new religion" of a secularized society.

Media Materials

As a concept, "the media" or "mass media" is both a useful notion and a source of immense confusion. Because the term, "media" (a) encompasses so many forms of print and electronic communication, (b) covers such a wide range of communication formats and messages, and (c) is so interlinked with people's interpersonal communications, most discussions of the media are much more ambiguous and vacuous than they might first seem.

Rumor mills and other interpersonal exchanges not only represent note-worthy precursors to the print and electronic media, as also do public and quasi-public assemblies and theatrical productions,[17] but they also connote contemporary alternatives to, and introduce interactive effects (as in the enhancement, neutralization, or denigration) of, media messages. Still, in addition to other ways that one might learn about deviance, we should be attentive to the ways that people in the contemporary scene collectively shape, promote, and derive images of deviance through the use of, and encounters with, the mass media. While our immediate emphasis is on deviance, readers may appreciate that the matters of *generating* and *engaging* the media represent two different, but interrelated aspects of the broader community theater.

Generating the Media

Regardless of whether one is discussing books, movies, television, radio, newspapers, magazines, direct mailing, signs, or other print and electronic media, a great many images of deviance abound in the mass media. Likewise, numerous industries have developed around the mass media and many people are actively employed in producing material for consumption in the community. Only some of this material deals with deviance, but much media attention still is given to the definition, regulation, and participation of people in activities that are considered deviant in the community.

Further, while some mass-media producers (agents) profess to "just report" matters pertaining to deviance, considerable profile may be given to matters encompassed by the deviant mystique (e.g., as in television or newspaper versions of the news). Uses of the media range from allegedly factual descriptions to extended fabrications that are clearly intended to have extensive entertainment value. Arguing that "deviance sells," those working with the media may claim that they only give their audiences what they desire.

Attending to aspects of deviance, media personnel (writers, producers, actors, television hosts) also may establish themselves as celebrities and experts on deviance. Thus, various people involved in the media may benefit from the "dramatization of evil" and may cater to, where they do not extensively embellish, the deviant mystique.

Whether they engage the media as moral entrepreneurs, educators, entertainers, or advocates, people may use the media to pursue vastly different agendas along these lines. In actual practice, by conveying, reaffirming, and creating particular images of deviance (and morality), those involved in the media may contribute somewhat to all of these things, depending on how their productions are interpreted by their audiences.

Interestingly, as well, despite a great deal of talk in academic circles and among the general public about the media and the impact of the media on people in contemporary society (i.e., the media mystique), social scientists know surprisingly little about the ways in which people attempt to use the media to promote definitions of reality (including that material that reflects aspects of deviance). Likewise, little is known about the ways in which people (as consumers) attend to, make sense of, and incorporate into their lives and practices any messages they might encounter through the media.[18]

Encountering the Media

Given the diverse and uneven range of media messages to which people may be exposed, it is an overwhelming task to even try to consider (a) all the images of deviance that people might obtain from the media. This complexity is heightened when one acknowledges the various ways in which people (b) attend to, (c) interpret, and (d) synthesize these notions with respect to their existing definitions of the world around them, as well as (e) actually incorporate these images into their day-to-day activities. The matter is further complicated in that (f) people commonly receive many images of deviance and morality from sources other than the media, and (g) any media messages are only comprehensible within people's existing notions of reality (and deviance). Likewise, people may (h) reconsider earlier interpretations of media messages when they encounter definitions of these messages and other aspects of deviance from other sources. Consequently, the use of frequency (and averaging) counts or "content analysis" (denoting some third party viewpoint) to discern the affects of media messages is most inadequate, if not highly misleading (despite scientistic appearances),[19] for comprehending the ways in which people actually experience and deal with media messages.

If researchers want to understand how people deal with images of deviance from the media or any other sources, it will be necessary to spend time examining (achieving intersubjectivity through ongoing observation, participation, and extended dialogue) the ways that people experience their life-worlds and work out their lines of action with respect to particular realms of involvements (deviant and otherwise) on a here-and-now basis.

This means attending to people's (i.e., as consumers, actors) *images* of deviance (and morality), how these notions have been formed, and how people deal with the particular situations they encounter. It also means learning, through sustained, interactive contact with the other: when and how people find themselves attending to messages pertaining to particular aspects of deviance; how they make sense of these materials over time; and in what ways, if any, they notice that their viewpoints or their activities in particular realms of endeavor may have changed over time, relative to various messages or other experiences that they may have with respect to any particular realms of deviance.[20]

Since people often discuss media messages with others and interpret and reinterpret media messages in these contexts, it is necessary to consider the *interactive* aspects of media exposure. Because media messages are interpreted, synthesized, and implemented in experiential, situated, and interactive contexts, any attempts on the part of social scientists to discuss the "impact of the media" without centrally acknowledging these basic dimensions of the human condition will be futile.

Although it would be a mistake of vast proportion to view consumers as mere recipients of the media, people still may be more exposed to a much greater cross-section of deviance through the media and other communications than they may desire. That is, even though people may selectively pursue and avoid exposure to certain media materials or talk about deviance, they are apt to be exposed to various expressions of deviance as a consequence of the activities of others. Some exposures may represent incidental or inopportune disclosures or revelations from others, but other exposures may be deliberately imposed on targets by practitioners, moral entrepreneurs, or others who attempt to use these contact occasions to foster their own interests or agendas.

Until we have materials that examine, in sustained ethnographic detail, the ways in which people experience interpersonal talk and media messages about deviance and incorporate these into their behaviors on a day-to-day basis, we can only make some very elementary observations about those consuming more frequent and varied messages about deviance.

First, people in contemporary society have opportunities to learn about a great many forms and assessments of deviance (these exposures may very well exceed their interests). These materials commonly are generated by (a) people who wish to share their experiences with others; (b) those who intend to eliminate or regulate particular activities; (c) by those who wish to promote particular activities as normal and desirable; (d) academics who intend to elaborate upon aspects of deviance; (e) those who seek to promote the involvements of others in political, religious, or other moral crusades; and (f) those who use deviance as a means of entertaining audiences or enhancing their own positions with or without regard to the ensuing images of deviance that they foster on the part of others. As well, however, (g) people with highly diverse interests may intentionally seek exposure to generalized or specific aspects of deviance by pursuing particular others and mediums.

Second, as people encounter these diversely initiated materials, they may find that their existing viewpoints are reaffirmed, challenged, or disregarded. As well, people also may find themselves feeling fascinated with or disgusted by particular images of deviance as well as experiencing sensations of disinterest, boredom, and banality with respect to the images they encounter.

Third, regardless of the authenticity, specificity, and comprehensiveness of any representations of deviance (and deviants) that they encounter, people's images of aspects of deviance are apt to be moderated or contextualized within their existing stocks of knowledge. The ensuing images, thus, are apt to reflect the condemnations, fears, and fascinations pertaining to people's notions of human behavior more generally.

Fourth, even when not so intended, exposure to aspects of deviance seems likely to increase the likelihood of people's participation in particular forms of deviance.[21] While part of learning about deviance may include expressions of perspectives or rationales conducive to particular forms of deviance, audiences also may find aspects of the deviant life-worlds appealing in other ways (including their shocking or forbidden qualities).

In addition to learning about the existence of particular practices and practitioners, people also may learn where and how to make contact with particular groups of deviants, as well as some techniques for engaging in certain disreputable practices through these various sources. Further, people may develop identifications with particular characters who participate in this or that form of deviant activity and may view these people as heroes of sorts (including those deliberately portrayed as villains).

Fifth, regardless of the origins or intentions of the messages, these materials also may provide opportunities for people to experience deviance vicariously. Although specific communications may denote disgust, disenchantment, and indignation to some audiences, they may represent sources of adventure, excitement, and fantasy to the same or different audiences. Further, some of these intrigues with deviance can be pursued under the guise of getting entertainment, getting an education, or being a moral entrepreneur. Thus, irrespective of the articulated interest of the participants, all encounters with deviance enable people to engage aspects of the deviant mystique.

In the chapters that follow, we address a series of processes through which people enact roles of the sorts outlined in the present chapter. It is impossible to discuss all of the activities entailed in these various theaters at once, but by drawing attention to the many different ways in which people engage aspects of the deviance-making process, we may be better able to concentrate on the human enterprise that constitutes community life. Focusing on the ways in which people define what constitutes deviance and implicate particular sets of others in their notions of disrespectability, chapters 4 and 5 not only establish "the reality" of deviance as a community essence but also centrally frame the ensuing analysis by introducing sets of meaningful concerns and reference points for subsequent action.

NOTES

1. For a fuller sociological appreciation of the dramaturgical essence of everyday life, see Goffman (1959), Klapp (1962, 1964), and Lyman and Scott (1975, 1989).

2. Some of these notions are evident in Katz's (1988) *Seductions of Crime* in which he argues for the necessity of attending much more closely to the experiential nature of crime. Although his data is selectively focused, Katz draws our attention to the intensities of human experience that sometimes characterize deviance involvements. What Katz has in mind are the sights, sounds, and other physical sensations to which people may attend in anticipating, participating in, and assessing their (deviant) activities and how they define and interpret these features of deviance as well as the actions (and reactions) of others toward them.

In addition to positively esteemed fascinations or attractions, Katz also considers the more acute sensations of moral revulsion or righteous indignation that people may experience as they approach various situations and develop lines of action toward objects (including other people) in those settings. Whereas matters of fascination and indignation can be quite encapsulating in particular instances at the levels of both individual and group participation, it is important to note that even in these instances people may view other aspects of their involvements in deviance as quite unexceptional or mundane. Thus, while recognizing people's "seduction to the deviant mystique" with respect to some instances of initial involvements and continuities in deviance, it seems instructive to attend to a fuller range of definitions that people might assign to their activities.

3. At the same time, it should be recognized that even the most enthusiastic of participants may find aspects of their situations to be onerous, boring, unsettling, or offensive, while others may be more decidedly negative about their experiences in this or that realm of deviance.

4. Although certain fascinations or intrigues may significantly contribute to some people's initial involvements in things such as juvenile delinquency (Shaw, 1930, 1931), theft (Sutherland, 1937; Maurer, 1955, 1964; Prus and Sharper, 1977), systematic check forgery (Lemert, 1967:109–134), marijuana use (Becker, 1963), the jazz community (Becker, 1963), gambling (Lesieur, 1977), bar and hotel life (Roebuck and Frese, 1976; Prus and Irini, 1980), drug dealing (Adler, 1985; Jacobs, 1999), and the outlaw biker community (Wolf, 1991), a fuller examination of these same materials also reveals both a diverse set of orientations toward initial involvements and the necessity of moving past the deviant mystique in order to understand the ways in which people accomplish and sustain their activities in these settings.

5. Albeit informed by dramaturgical analysis as developed by Goffman (1959, 1963), Klapp (1964), and Lyman and Scott (1989), the emphasis in the present text is more directly on "the ongoing accomplishment of human group life" (i.e., a more sustained emphasis on "activity" or the "doing," "enterprising," or "engaging" of all aspects of community life). This includes those matters envisioned and acted toward as "deviant" by various audiences within particular settings.

6. Readers may find it instructive to compare accounts of drug dealers (Adler, 1985), fences (Steffensmeier, 1986) and those doing business in disreputable bar settings (Roebuck and Frese, 1976; Prus and Irini, 1980) with more conventional marketing and sales activities (Prus, 1989a, 1989b; Prus and Frisby, 1990).

7. See, for instance, family encounters with "mental illness" (Yarrow et al., 1955), prison sentences (Fishman, 1990), and drinking problems (Jackson, 1954; Wiseman,

1991; Asher, 1992). Goffman (1963) is also quite attentive to the tendency for stigma to spread and implicate people other than those more centrally participating in disreputable activities. As well, family members and friends (as convenient and trusted others) often encounter additional opportunities to participate in the activities of their disreputable associates. See, for instance, Shaw's (1930) discussion of delinquency, Becker's (1963) consideration of jazz musicians and marijuana users, Prus and Irini's (1980) study of the hotel community, and Wolf's (1991) study of outlaw bikers.

8. Part of the fascination with computer-simulated "virtual reality" is that it allows people to participate in aspects (i.e., experience certain sensations) of life in fuller manners than they might otherwise achieve. Still, although they may offer some sensual enhancements, computer-generated simulations are not unique as enabling devices. Thus, people may use any feature of a situation (e.g., visual aids, aromas, sounds) to intensify vicarious closeness (approximations) with the particular kinds of sensations they wish to experience.

9. In addition to those who may inadvertently become involved in escalating situations involving others, it should also be recognized that people sometimes seek out contact with (and influence from) others whose activities they have defined as more interesting, exciting, or beneficial than more conventional practices. These people need not define themselves as victims in any sense, whatsoever, but on occasion may claim victim status to avoid imputations of culpability when confronted by third parties who seem intent on punishing them for these involvements.

10. Holstein and Miller (1990) provide a very insightful analysis of victimization as a socially constructed identity.

11. Readers may refer to Cressey (1932), Becker (1963), Klapp (1969), Blumer (1971), Mauss (1975), Best (1989, 1995a), and Grills (1989, 1994) for materials that deal with moral entrepreneurs, crusaders, and consciousness-raising regarding "social problems." Also see chapter 4.

12. Relatedly, because of their existing community profiles, celebrities may be sought out to endorse particular viewpoints. However, celebrities whose fame is on the decline may be eager to regain some of their former public auras by assuming figurehead roles in these other arenas.

13. Those opposing any particular moral entrepreneurs also may assume similar roles. Thus, they too may promote moral viewpoints, recruit members for crusades, and engage other moral entrepreneurs in political ventures. Consequently, it is often difficult to distinguish the tactics of one set of moral entrepreneurs from those of oppositionary groups.

14. Although representing comparatively recent matters of the intellectual focus within the social sciences, concerns with identity work can be readily traced back to the early Greeks (especially, see Aristotle's [c384–322 B.C.E.] Rhetoric).

15. Readers interested in rumors more generally may refer to Shibutani (1966) and Rosnow and Fine (1976). Unfortunately, neither of these works attends to deviance or deviants in any significant manner. Goffman's (1963) Stigma and Klapp's (1964) Symbolic Leaders, thus, remain among the most insightful materials in the area.

16. For religious believers, the relationship between theological standpoints and deviance (as in sin) may be particularly well developed. This could include proscriptions, earthly sanctions, and modes of redemption as well as explanations of human conduct and extrapolations to other life-world experiences associated with the perpetrators of particular activities and others in the community. Somewhat relatedly, the identity of

the sinner may signify a spiritually tainted "master status" (Becker, 1963) with respect to those who are "fallen," "evil," "damned," or "possessed."

17. One also might appreciate the roles of poets, chroniclers, and other bearers of news who travel about reporting developments taking place in other settings. These people still represent alternatives to the print and electronic media, as also do those who memorize and recite materials for others (i.e., perpetuating oral traditions).

18. Once one moves past general discourse, "models of communication," and quantitative research on consumption, one finds only few ethnographic studies in the social (and communication) sciences that examine the ways in which people either use the media as influence devices (Prus, 1989b; Prus and Fleras, 1996) or experience the media as consumers (Blumer, 1933; Blumer and Hauser, 1933; Prus, 1993; Harrington and Bielby, 1995).

19. People conducting studies of these sorts not only presume to know the parameters of situations that are more or less continuously in flux, but that they also can, somehow, accurately access, sort out, and indicate the significance of these notions for people's behavior in practice. Still, these limitations likely will not stop some academic entrepreneurs from pursuing these ventures and presenting the results as "facts" about deviance to interested audiences. On a more relativistic note, it might be observed that reports of this sort are probably no more distorted than most others one might obtain from the mass media.

20. Although largely neglected by scholars in both communication and sociology, Blumer (1933) and Blumer and Hauser (1933) provide two very insightful studies of the ways in which young people experience the movies. While some may be tempted to view these studies as dated, to do so would be to miss the very insightful depiction of the ways in which adolescents attend to the mass media and the manners in which they incorporate images (gleaned inadvertently as well as selectively pursued) of human behavior from the mass media into their daily routines. What we require is much more ethnographic research, not just with respect to people's experiences with the movies, television, magazines, Internet communications, and other media-generated messages, but also with regard to the ways that people learn about deviance through talk (with interpersonal others) more generally.

21. Although some "dramatization of evil" may serve, as Durkheim (1895) suggests, to reaffirm community morality, it may also be the case that with the increased attention given to deviance in the media and in community talk at large, more conventional lifestyles may come to be viewed as increasingly irrelevant and banal, as unworthy of the efforts required to sustain them.

Part II

Designating Deviance

4

Defining Deviance
Perspectives and Practices

A social problem is always a focal point for the operation of divergent and conflicting interests, intentions, and objectives. It is an interplay of these interests and objectives that constitutes the way in which a society deals with any one of its social problems. . . . (T)he career and the fate of social problems in a process of collective definition calls for an analysis of the course of this process. (Blumer 1971:301)

One of the major tasks facing students of deviance revolves around the question of how people develop definitions of things as "deviant" (also troublesome, illegal, taboo, evil, and the like). Recognizing great variations in what is and is not considered deviant across communities and over time within the same communities, we may begin by considering definitions of conduct (rules, norms, deviance, crime, and the like) as problematic, emergent, and negotiable aspects of group life. From this viewpoint, the emphases are on uncovering the processes by which definitions of acceptable and unacceptable conduct come about and attending to the implications of these definitions of morality and deviance for ongoing group life.

Referring to our earlier definition, deviance denotes any situation (activity, actor, ideas, or state of affairs) that an audience defines as threatening, disturbing, offensive, immoral, disreputable, or negative in some way.[1]

Working from this definition, it becomes apparent that any quality may be considered deviant, acceptable, or desirable when approached from two or more viewpoints. Although variations of this sort are often associated with different audiences, a single audience (person or group) could simultaneously judge an activity as deviant and also exciting, fun, worthwhile, or desirable.[2] To envision things in more exclusive (either good or bad) terms is to fall into a philosophical trap (that things can not be assigned multiple properties at the same time).[3]

From an interactionist perspective, all members of the community may be seen as *definers* (interpreters) of deviance; *promoters* of particular notions of reality insofar as they make their definitions known to others or otherwise attempt to shape the viewpoints and behaviors of others; potential *supporters* of the definitions and other initiatives taken by others; and *resistors* of the viewpoints and enterprises of others. The extent to which other people are exposed to, and accept, any particular definitions of deviance that someone suggests is problematic, as are the processes by which these interchanges occur.

However, it is when those promoting specific notions of deviance are successful in having their definitions accepted by others that these definitions become objectified (Berger and Luckmann, 1966). When definitions of deviance are thought to achieve "intersubjective consensus" within some community (i.e., made explicit, visibly accepted, shared, promoted, sanctioned), these notions attain a sense of realism that individuals and subgroups within those settings may find difficult to resist even were they so inclined.

In what follows, consideration is given to the processes by which people invoke, promote, support, and contest what Peter Berger and Thomas Luckmann term "the social construction of reality."[4] Focusing more particularly on the notions of deviance (and morality) that people develop in community contexts, attention is directed toward *moral entrepreneurs, moral crusades, social problems as collective behavior, cultures of social problems, toys and other fictionalizations*, and the matters of people *striving for success* and *resisting moral impositions*.

The focus, thus, is very much on the enacted features of morality; on the enterprise (speech, action, and interaction) involved in conceptualizing, invoking, and contesting morality (and deviance) in humanly engaged theaters of operation.

Moral Entrepreneurs

Like other aspects of meaningful endeavor, definitions of deviance (and their regulation) entail human initiative and ongoing enterprise. Howard Becker (1963) uses the term moral entrepreneurs to refer to those who assume (or are assigned) the tasks of defining ("rule creators") and regulating ("rule enforcers") particular realms of deviance. Although these notions may seem most readily applied to formal control agents, such as those involved in the judicial system or religious orders, it is apparent that people attempting to promote or eliminate particular lifestyles can be found in all levels and areas of society.

Thus, for instance, parents and teachers would be included herein, as well as any others who attempt to supervise, direct, or oversee people's activities in any realm of endeavor. Although less commonly envisioned in these terms, it might also be acknowledged that many others, in capacities such as roommates, spouses, and friends, also may embark on similar (directive or remedial) practices, as might people who envision themselves in subordinate roles. Consider, for example, children who attempt to educate their parents or otherwise shape parental behaviors with respect to matters of being "cool," extending curfews, increasing allowances, and shopping wisely (as with teen-tastes in mind).[5] Most research on this topic has focused on larger-scale definitions of deviance, but it might be observed that similar processes seem operative in smaller groupings as well.[6]

While Becker's (1963) work on moral entrepreneurs provides testimony to the importance of people engaging deviance in collective, group-based manners, we may develop a further appreciation of moral entrepreneurs in action in the following considerations of moral crusades and social problems as collective behavior.

Moral Crusades

Denoting group-based programs of social change or reform, crusades represent attempts on the parts of certain sectors of the community to pursue particular ideals or moral standpoints in collectively focused and enabled manners. Although some crusades are comparatively fleeting and only haphazardly developed, others are much more sustained and may last for centuries, albeit with varying levels of intensity, activity, and points of confrontation.

When characterizing crusades and crusaders, Klapp (1969: 257–311) references (a) a vigorous, militant sense of mission; (b) a determinism to persist in the venture in spite of considerable, potentially intense opposition; (c) a sense of urgency for action, particularly of a direct, interventionist sort; (d) a willingness to commit oneself and others to the cause in a more totalizing manner; (e) a pervasive emphasis on the moral righteousness of the mission being undertaken; (f) a heightened sense of evil (and moral hatred) associated with certain targets; and (g) an unwillingness to compromise the moral principles of the venture.

Although the people involved in particular crusades may only approximate these notions in varying degrees over the duration of these ventures, those who join together with others often are more effective in pursuing their objectives as a collectivity than they might be on their own. Thus, while not all crusades are effective in achieving even the more minor of their objectives, people (as moral entrepreneurs) who engage situations in collective manners, even if these are not thoughtfully, carefully, or extensively coordinated, may be able to affect some other sectors of community life.

Because of the complexity of collective behavior more generally, one finds few carefully developed examinations of moral crusades in the social sciences. Although not explicitly interactionist in emphasis, Anthony Platt (1969a, 1969b) provides a valuable illustration of the roles of moral entrepreneurs in the rise of the child-saving movement in North America in the late 1800s.

Reflecting medical notions of pathology, infection, and treatment, combined with concerns pertaining to crime control, social welfare, and the protection of the young, the child-savers were not only instrumental in creating (a) a new category of deviants (delinquents), but also were responsible for generating (b) a new legal administrative process (juvenile court) and (c) a new correctional system (juvenile reformatories).

Contending that children were born with defects that could foster a life of crime and/or could be corrupted by undesirable living conditions, the intention was to use medical expertise combined with an emphasis on social welfare and religious and moral direction to reform youthful offenders and to protect other young people from undesired influences.

As the movement took shape, a wide variety of people became involved, including physicians, clergy, court personnel, welfare workers, and educators. Still, Platt describes the child-saving movement predominantly as a feminist movement. He also indicates that antifeminists, as well as feminists, were inclined to see the matters pertaining to child rearing as an essentially female domain.

Acknowledging the heavily prohibitionist stance that the feminists and others in the child-saving movement adopted on youthful activities, Platt observes that the desire to help children in difficult circumstances soon became engulfed within a broader agenda of moral absolutism. Thus, young people were to be kept from alcohol, cigarettes, unsavory literature, the movies, or anything else that the reformers thought might detract from people's virtue.

As well, many matters pertaining to young people that formerly had been handled informally now became matters of the court. Instructed to act in the best interests of the child, juvenile court judges assumed the rights of parents in all matters pertaining to the welfare of those that had been referred to them. In attempts to destigmatize and otherwise protect the young, children were no longer accused of crimes per se, but were to be given whatever assistance, instruction, or regulation the court deemed appropriate. Civil rights and procedural formalities were considered irrelevant because judges were expected to deal with the cases falling in their charge in manners paralleling the practices of physicians, therapists, and parents.

Recognizing that some children might require more extensive correctional treatment, a reformatory system was emphasized as an alternative to more conventional penal programs. Further, in the case of youthful offenders, the emphasis was on making these facilities more homelike with cottages and farm schools seen to provide viable alternatives to undesirable urban lifestyles. The hope was that in providing young people with higher levels of individual attention and the opportunities to express themselves in more benign settings, they would have greater opportunities to become responsible, law-abiding citizens. Platt observes that there is little justification for optimism in programs of these sorts, but a great many people continue to insist that with skilled workers, proper facilities, and humanitarian emphases, successful treatment will be achieved.

In another account of moral entrepreneurs at work, Louis Zurcher and his associates (1971) examined the natural histories of two anti-pornography campaigns. Like Platt's, the Zurcher study also provides scholars with an indication of the intensity and devotion with which people may pursue instances of morality in their community. However, this account more directly indicates the sorts of resistances that moral entrepreneurs may encounter even when they appear to have strong, associational, and multifaceted bases of support within those settings.

Thus, whereas the child-savers (invoking policy on youthful targets) were able to avoid direct confrontation with people able to resist their agendas, the targets of the two anti-pornography campaigns that Zurcher describes were not so compliant. In Midville, the bookstore that was the primary focus of extended attack on the part of the Interdenominational Citizens Council for Decency (ICCD) emerged as a formidable opponent. Thus, the moral onslaught was terminated after the bookstore launched a major lawsuit against the ICCD (invoking rights to the freedom of expression under the U.S. Constitution). The Southtown crusade, the Uprising for Decency (UFD), was much more constrained and legalistic in its approach. Still, though successful in passing two pieces of legislation at the state level, these were very limited in scope. In both Midville and Southtown, the predominantly adult consumers (with greater rights of freedom than juveniles) continued to patronize bookstores and theaters appealing to their interests. In both cases, the results might best be described as minimal and Zurcher notes an increase in the number of outlets featuring erotic material in both Midville and Southtown.

Somewhat similar limitations are evident in Joseph Gusfield's (1963, 1996) depictions of people's attempts to reduce or eliminate the consumption of alcohol and related social problems (such as violence, poverty, and drinking and driving). Despite massive levels of support (governmental, religious, industrial, public, and extended financial investments), it is not an understatement to say that control programs in this area have been rather ineffectual.

Part of the problem is that the people pursuing these and other remedial programs do not attend to the complex set of social processes that policy programs of all sorts entail. Neither do they give adequate attention to people's capacities to define and pursue interests at variance with those intended by the moral entrepreneurs. To better understand the issues involved, we turn to Herbert Blumer's work on social problems.

Social Problems as Collective Behavior

Considering the ways in which situations become publicly defined and treated as "social problems," Herbert Blumer (1976) emphasizes that, rather than signifying "objective conditions" of some sort, social problems are most fundamentally *matters of community definition*. As Blumer observes as well, there is no guarantee that any attempts that people make to define situations as "social problems" will be acknowledged or acted upon within the community.

Although arenas of community concern may include many things other than "deviance," Blumer identifies five processes as central to the matter of publicly defining situations or practices as "social problems." These processes include: *emergence* (initial awareness and publicity); *legitimation* (public and official acknowledgement); *mobilization for action* (assess information, suggestions, and probabilities); *formation of an official plan*; and *implementation of the official plan* (and the problematics of successfully doing so).

At each point, Blumer suggests, the process is problematic, adjustive, and negotiable. Social problems, thus, represent sites of collective enterprise and generally involve multiple viewpoints and contested bodies of knowledge and beliefs. Accordingly, most social problems are characterized by political ma-neuverings of various sorts as persons and groups endeavor to promote their interests relative to the issues at hand and resist those taking action that appears to be at variance with their objectives.[7]

When discussing *emergence* (i.e., creating awareness) of a problematic situation,[8] Blumer attends to practices such as (a) defining situations as more troublesome, threatening, and enduring; (b) dramatizing conditions;[9] (c) spreading information within the community; (d) striving for audience at-tention amidst other concerns (distractions); and (e) using (and enlisting) the media.

The matter of *legitimating definitions* of the situation encompasses such things as (a) justifying the positions taken; (b) pursuing endorsements and support of influential community members; (c) providing evidence; (d) refer-encing experts; and (e) credentialing people who speak on behalf of the cause.

The third process that Blumer delineates, *mobilizing for action*, includes subprocesses such as (a) emphasizing the necessity of immediate, effective ac-tion; (b) coordinating activities with supportive others; (c) neutralizing contro-versy and alternative viewpoints; (d) developing alliances; and (e) confronting opponents.

If people's interests in certain situations are sustained, they may become involved in *formulating an official plan*. The more central matters entailed here include (a) defining and promoting preliminary agendas; (b) encountering obstacles, resistances, and blockages; and (c) negotiating and redefining the agendas with insiders and outsiders.

Should developments reach the next stage, that of *implementing the official plan*, the focus turns to such things as (a) announcing policies and programs; (b) assigning responsibility and culpability; (c) establishing rule enforcers; (d) encountering resistance from targets, rule enforcers, and other third parties; (e) assessing the effectiveness of the official plan; and (f) enforcing and adjust-ing the official plan in attempts to make it more readily implementable.

While Blumer presents these processes as "stages" of sorts, he also is highly attentive to several features of association within each of these stages. Thus, although some variation is inevitable from one instance of a social problem to the next, and within each of the five stages that Blumer delineates, within, we may expect to find that the people involved commonly (a) invoke assort-ments of perspectives or viewpoints at each stage; (b) engage in focused enter-prise; (c) pursue cooperation from others; (d) embark on influence work;

(e) encounter resistance; and (f) make adjustments that are mindful of the developmental contexts in which they operate.

Although among the earliest of the Chicago school ethnographies, Paul Cressey's (1932) The *Taxi-Dance Hall* remains one of the very best illustrations of social problems as collective behavior. Focusing on a variant of commercialized sexuality, Cressey traces the development of taxi-dance halls (wherein men would buy tickets [10¢] to dance with the young woman of their choice) in Chicago in the 1920s and 1930s.

Developing a natural history of people's experiences with taxi-dance halls, Cressey considers the ways in which the owners of public dance halls attempted to come to terms with shifting public interests and lifestyles and how they dealt with competition, public images, social control, and an assortment of patron and dancer interests and practices. In related terms, Cressey also endeavors to provide readers with the sense of the viewpoints and practices of the other participants in the setting.

In the process, Cressey shows how an extended assortment of people engage one another in a collectively developing set of interchanges. Attending to the considerable diversity of interests that one encounters in this theater of operations, Cressey acknowledges the pursuits of (a) taxi-dance hall operators (who might support and cooperate with one another at times but also engage one another in openly antagonistic terms); (b) patrons with varying concerns and intrigues; (c) dancers invoking an assortment of work and related side interests; and (d) control agents adopting an array of standpoints and adjustive strategies. Thus, one begins to understand the notions of ambiguity and frustration that permeate the taxi-dance hall setting more generally. This also helps explain the uneven tactical-adjustive efforts on the part of different participants and the ensuing interchanges that take place as people attempt to pursue and sustain their interests amidst the diverse, often oppositionary viewpoints and agendas of others in the setting.

Accordingly, although developed some forty years prior to Blumer's (1971) statement on social problems as collective behavior, Cressey's statement provides multiple illustrations of the processes (i.e., emergence, legitimation, mobilization, formation of an official plan, and the problematics of implementation) that Blumer delineates.

Jacqueline Wiseman's (1970) research on agencies dealing with skid row alcoholics also effectively depicts the dilemmas and obstacles entailed in "the people work" pertaining to implementing official plans. Much like those involved in the child-saving movement, those campaigning against drunkenness and homelessness have been successful in establishing a wide range of programs designed to care for and help rehabilitate skid row alcoholics. However, as Wiseman's rich ethnographic research reveals, the implementation and eventual success of these programs (as with so many others) is notably removed from the hopes of those promoting and funding these campaigns.

On a broader, more scholarly level, thus, Blumer's statement represents a highly enabling foundational statement for examining social problems as instances of community life in the making. This is because of the way Blumer focuses attention on the actualities of human interchange (especially multiple viewpoints, persuasive endeavor, and motivated resistance).

Cultures of Social Problems

In addition to the processes underlying the production of social problems that Blumer delineates, it is important that we be attentive to the ways in which people organize their lives around these events along the way. As Joseph Gusfield (1989) notes, we appear to be experiencing a rapid proliferation of social problems in our society, as well as an increase in "the troubled persons professions" and the industries that people develop around these arenas of activity.

In Gusfield's terms, we have become caught up in a *culture of public problems*. Relatedly, Gusfield also notes that (a) there is an inflationary trend to expand the areas described as "social problems;" (b) the identification and naming of situations as social problems implies the creation and perpetuation of particular "structures" to deal with these situations; (c) each problem expands the potential for professions (and experts) to emerge around that new arena; and (d) proportionately more community "industries" are defining social problems as their primary, public directive.

Although it is not apparent just how far this trend will continue, the implication is that we may increasingly become legally and financially bogged down in the production and implementation of social problems. Accordingly, we may expect the broader social problems process to become increasingly politicized as groups (defining particular situations as social problems in need of remedy) campaign more intensively amidst other associations (including oppositionary, functionally parallel, and unrelated groups) for attention, legitimacy, and funding.

Indeed, despite various noble motives and alleged concerns with people's rights and potentials, a great deal of agency activity is focused on sources of public and private funding. While the arguments for funding are typically pitched in terms of the general support of the cause at issue, much of this (generally financial) support is normally targeted for the maintenance and growth of the agency promoting the cause. Relatedly, this funding has considerable implications for the careers (e.g., continuity, finances, prestige, and empire building) of the professionals involved more specifically.

Toys and Other Fictionalizations

Although the objects of children's play and other fictional representations or imitations may seem innocent on the surface, virtually nothing is exempt from deviance definitions (and control efforts) in the human community.

Mindful of the relativist nature of deviance definitions, Joel Best (1998) provides a particularly thoughtful consideration of the ways that some moral entrepreneurs have defined toys as social problems.

This is done by *imbuing* specific objects that children may engage in playful manners with a variety of negative meanings (e.g., hazardous, violent, sexist, racist, occultist). Thus, despite the absence of careful research that relates children's use of toys to these negativized claims or even a significant body of literature that examines how children *actually play* with toys and *assign meanings* to objects,[10] we find some highly concerted realms of censorship and reform that revolve around the manufacture and use of toys.[11]

Condemnation and censorship of the sort that have developed around children's playthings are not limited to children's activities, nor are they somehow unique to the present generation or contemporary society.

Thus, for instance, in setting up guidelines for the development of a socialist state, Plato (420–328 B.C.E.; see *Republic, Laws, Ion*) not only envisions poetic (any fictionalized) representations of things as inferior and wasteful human endeavors, but also argues that fictional endeavors of all sorts are things that should be censored (not only with respect to content, but also with regard to words, references, styles, and tempos) to ensure that they do not lead children or other persons astray.

If there is to be poetry (and Plato recognizes the humanly alluring potential of fictional representations), Plato's proposal is that only those materials that are developed by state authorized poets would be acceptable.[12]

Striving for Success

While it is most unlikely that people will or could be successful in having all of the definitions of deviance and the remedies that they propose accepted (even at more rudimentary levels), we may still ask when they are apt to fare better in these regards. Notably, too, as with marketing ventures more generally (see Prus, 1989a, 1989b), people's successes as moral entrepreneurs are contingent on other people accepting these notions as viable and making commitments in those directions.

Attending to the works of Cressey (1932), Sutherland (1950), Garfinkel (1956), Becker (1963), Klapp (1969), Blumer (1971), Gusfield (1981, 1989), the Best (1989, 1995a) collections, and others, it appears that parties promoting definitions of deviance are more likely to be successful in having their definitions of (and remedies for) deviance accepted when they (are seen to) provide more extensive indications that: (1) the activity is morally and/or theologically undesirable; (2) the activity represents an immediate, powerful, and active threat to both the public good and widespread individual well-being; (3) the definitions proffered have the support of prominent, respected, and knowledgeable figures (and groups) in the community; (4) any opposition is defined as ill-informed, irresponsible, self-serving, or otherwise suspect of motive; and

(5) the proposed definitions (and other control efforts) could be implemented with a minimum of disruption (money, inconvenience, suffering) to community members.

As well, given the centrality of public recognition of particular problems for achieving sympathy and financial support, it might be observed that these definitional ventures are apt to fare better when promoters are able to: (6) generate, dramatize, and sustain public attention regarding the situation at hand; (7) develop coalitions with other groups and agencies that are also willing to express their moral indignation about the situation in question; (8) establish and maintain social movements around these themes by creating agencies (that not only represent the potential for full-time employment and career development, but that also serve as central reference points for claims-making activities, internally benign sources of "expertise," and the ardent pursuits of financial support); and (9) make politicians and other publicly accountable figures appear responsible for the "deplorable" circumstances being discussed.

When successful in establishing their versions of deviance, the same "entrepreneurs" may not only (a) articulate the dominant working definitions of deviance in the community and (b) determine the ways in which deviants are categorized and explained, but also (c) generate and shape the agencies, personnel, practices, and treatments involved in regulating deviance.

However, before we presume or overemphasize the success of specific moral ventures on either larger or smaller scales, it is instructive to acknowledge people's capacities for diversity of interest and resisting those things that they may find disenchanting. Thus, the matter of defining what constitutes deviance may be seen as an ongoing, intermittent struggle in both smaller and larger sectors of community life.

Accordingly, despite the high levels of enterprise, the intensity of emotional involvement, and the comparative prominence and profile that various crusades or morals campaigns achieve, the overall effects are generally less evident, enduring, and extensive than advocates and supporters anticipate. In addition to (a) the more visible sources of resistance that crusades encounter in the form of counter-crusades, those embarking on various agendas also face (b) the prospects of managing dissension within the association and (c) the difficulties of effectively implementing programs even should they reach this point. It is mindful of these limited notions of success that Joseph Gusfield (1989, 1996) suggests that a major outcome of many crusades is that of publicly reaffirming participant viewpoints among people already committed to the cause; that is, to indicate that their convictions have been expressed in a broader public arena.

Resisting Moral Impositions

Somewhat simultaneously with people's attempts to define deviance and control (and censor) others, we often find (as Becker [1963] and Blumer [1971] observe) attempts on the part of others to oppose or contest these endeavors.

In the case of toys (Best, 1998), for instance, children and others may maintain interest in playthings that others define as objectionable. Likewise, one finds (following Plato's condemnation of poetics) that hundreds of people over the millennia have written statements "in defense of poetics" (also theater and acting).[13]

On some occasions, definitions of deviance are resisted by people on a more individualized basis as particular people become caught up in the control efforts of others. Here, however, many individualized resistances revolve around efforts to avoid stigmatizations of self (and related sanctions) rather than to contest more abstract definitions of morality.

Further, once implicated through accusation, targets are generally disadvantaged in contesting viewpoints that previously had been taken to represent the best interests of the larger community. That a number of people may be implicated through accusation also seems inadequate in itself to alter prevailing community definitions of morality,[14] although things may be changed when increasingly larger numbers of people are implicated as a consequence of the reactions of sympathetic associates and/or the practical problems of managing an increasingly larger proportion of the population.

More typically, while seemingly only partially successful in most cases, it is through instances of collectivized resistance that prevailing definitions of deviance are more likely to be altered. Before leaving this chapter then, some consideration is given to this aspect of the deviance-making process.

The notion of collectivized resistance draws attention to an interactive, coordinated focusing of effort on the part of two or more people to challenge (also obstruct, contest, change) prevailing notions of morality. These efforts need not be highly sustained or thoroughly coordinated, and all of the participants need not have direct knowledge of or contact with one another. Nevertheless, collectivized resistance implies some interlinkages of supporters and some generally shared sense of targets and objectives.

As well, while many or all of those involved in collective resistance may be implicated (or potentially implicatable) in the deviance at issue, particular instances of collective resistance may involve a variety of people who have no direct involvements in the deviant categorizations at hand. These other supporters (and possibly initiators, coordinators) may include family members and friends of involved parties, sympathizers to particular and related causes, and people (e.g., lawyers, journalists and publicists, certain business owners, and some politicians) who anticipate benefiting by supporting particular causes or specific disreputable people.

Regardless of the bases of their involvements, these outsiders bring a wide assortment of material, associational, and tactical resources into contested arenas. As well, as outsiders, these supporters may claim to represent the interests of the broader community in ways that those who have become more directly "tainted by deviance" may be unable to accomplish on their own.

Those resisting prevailing notions of morality may seem some distance re-moved from those championing earlier (and possibly now contested) definitions of morality as these people may be seen to contradict one another with respect to moral viewpoints and agendas. However, when viewed more directly in pro-cess-terms (i.e., with respect to activities, coalitions, tactics), oppositionary par-ties frequently approximate mirrored images of one another as they adopt somewhat parallel roles as targets and tacticians on a sequential, if not also a more simultaneous, basis.

Mindful of people's tendencies to invoke and contest moralities across the entire range of human experience, a great deal of careful, sustained research is warranted with respect to the deviance-defining process. For our more imme-diate purposes, though, this chapter establishes a conceptual frame within which we may more fully appreciate situationally enacted notions of morality and deviance, relative to both the broader interfaces of community life and people's more specific, localized theaters of operation within.

We now turn to a consideration of the ways in which notions of morality may be applied more directly to specific individuals and groups who become the targets of disaffection under one or other definitions of morality.

NOTES

1. Definitions of deviance may be seen to vary with respect to the degree of con-demnation associated with the particular act or quality being considered; the degree of consensus across and within audiences; the explicitness and formality of any codes designating deviance; the degree of specificity with which qualities are defined as de-viant; the targets to whom such definitions may be applied; and the duration of the existence (and application) of these definitions.

2. This position is in basic agreement with Sutherland (1939) who in discussing the theory of "differential association," states that persons may simultaneously hold defi-nitions favorable and unfavorable to criminal activity. The tendency to "average out attitudes" represents a fundamental conceptual error in some people's attempts to un-derstand human behavior.

People may also assign differing meanings to activities and their consequences. Even though an activity may be defined as desirable, for instance, some consequences asso-ciated with it may be viewed negatively, and vice-versa.

3. Some may appreciate a related observation that Plato makes in one of his dia-logues:

> *Visitor:* Let's give an account of how we call the very same thing, whatever it may be, by several names.
>
> *Theaetetus:* What, for instance? Give me an example.
>
> *Visitor:* Surely we're speaking of a man even when we name him several things, that is, when we apply colors to him and shapes, sizes, defects, and virtues. In these cases and a million others we say that he's not only a man but also is good and indefinitely many different things. And similarly on the same account we take a thing to be one, and at the same time we speak of it as many by using many names for it. (Plato, *Sophist* 251a–b [Trans. by N.P. White; Cooper, 1997])

4. Those familiar with the broader tradition in which Peter Berger and Thomas Luckmann (1966) and Harold Garfinkel (1967) work will recognize their extended indebtedness to Alfred Schutz (1962, 1964).

5. This viewpoint recognizes the capacities for all interactants to assume roles as targets and tacticians on a sequential or simultaneous basis (Prus, 1999).

6. For an instructive statement on "the micro-politics of trouble," see Emerson and Messinger (1977). These and related matters are discussed further in chapter 10 (informal regulation of deviance), chapter 12 (control agents at work), and chapter 13 (target encounters with treatment).

7. Working in similar veins, Wiseman (1979) and Estes and Edmunds (1981) make concerted pleas for a "theory of policy analysis and implementation" (vs. interventionist sociology).

8. The descriptive listings of Blumer's five processes are adapted from Prus (1997: 139–140). For some "natural history" accounts of the emergence of legislation that address matters that Blumer highlights in his analysis of social problems, see Cressey, 1932; Sutherland, 1950; Gusfield, 1955, 1963; Lindesmith, 1959; Sinclair, 1962; Becker, 1963; Chambliss, 1964; Zurcher et al., 1971; Platt, 1969a, 1969b; and Connor, 1972. Also relevant are the materials developed by Mauss (1975), Spector and Kitsuse (1977), Gusfield (1981, 1989), and Best's (1989, 1995a) edited volumes. Organized around the social construction of social problems, Best's collections include materials on child abuse, missing children, elderly abuse, AIDS, learning disabilities, drug use, smoking, drunk driving, music, and immigration. Whereas knowledge and science are not commonly viewed as social problems, further awareness of the ways in which communities deal with troublesome situations may be gained by examining paradigm conflicts in the physical and social sciences (Kuhn, 1970; Prus, 1992b).

9. Although crusades represent only one aspect of the construction of community morality, these collective ventures can be particularly noteworthy with respect to dramatizing "troublesome" situations. Crusades seem especially consequential in settings in which the proponents of particular positions find themselves in competition with other groups or agendas in the quest for control of community practices.

Klapp (1969: 257–311) contends that the mounting of moral crusades typically reflects concerns of the following sort: achieving a vigorous sense of mission; emphasizing urgency of remedial action; expressing righteousness and moral indignation; indicating and countering evils; and maintaining an unwillingness to compromise. The most intense clashes seem apt to occur when the participants of two or more "righteous" crusades find themselves in opposition to one another. Grills (1989, 1994) provides an account of a political party's (Christian Heritage Party) attempt to organize around a particularized version of morality.

10. It is to be appreciated that objects do not have inherent meanings to people. Thus, even what is viewed as a "toy" requires some definitional activity on the part of an audience. To assume that others (e.g., children or others) view things in the same fashions as do some sets of adults who have adopted certain moral viewpoints is quite unwarranted, sociologically, but this practice seems rather commonplace among those operating as moral entrepreneurs (Becker, 1963) in this setting.

11. Readers familiar with Platt's (1969a, 1969b) analysis of the emergence of the juvenile justice system may envision concerns with children's toys as an extension of the "child-saving" movement.

12. Readers who are unfamiliar with the early Greek literature may be surprised to see how extensively contemporary Western censorship (as with religious, secular, Marxist, and "postmodernist" emphases) parallels (where these efforts do not build more directly on) the notions that Plato articulates in *Republic* and *Laws*.

13. Classical Greek notions of poetics not only encompass the sorts of rhyme and versification that many people associate with "poetry," but also would include all manner of fictionalized representation (as in theater and prose). It is worth noting that Aristotle (*Poetics*) assumes a much more sustained analytical and scholarly position than does Plato. Thus, Aristotle represents a central counterpoint to Plato in many debates and analyses of poetics.

14. Connor's (1972) depiction of the Soviet Purge is instructive here, as also is Erikson's (1966) account of the Salem witch trials.

5

Labeling Deviants
Disrespectable Persons

One of the most crucial steps in the process of building a stable pattern of deviant behavior is likely to be the experience of being caught and publicly labeled as a deviant. . . . (B)eing caught and branded as a deviant has important consequences for one's further social participation and self image. The most important consequence is a drastic change in the individual's public identity. (Becker, 1963:32)

For the purpose of this volume, labeling refers to (a) the processes by which people acquire identities and reputations as certain kinds of people within the community and (b) the ways in which people take these designations of others and self into account in formulating their activities within the settings at hand.[1] As with other objects, humans are not inherently meaningful entities, but take on specific meanings by virtue of the ways that people define and act toward these phenomena.

Like other objects of their awareness, people identify or categorize one another, associate certain qualities or attributes with those identity marks, and act toward others in terms of the meanings that they associate with those targets. The primary differences between the labeling of people and other objects revolve around the capacities of human targets to enter meaningfully into the labeling process. As "objects of their own awareness," people not only can (a) assign meanings to themselves and others, but they also can (b) attempt to shape the images that others have of them, and (c) contest or otherwise resist designations that they think have been undesirably or inappropriately applied to themselves or others.[2]

While the labeling processes entailed in identifying and acting toward "particular kinds of people" seems comparatively parallel for both "deviants" and "others," the term "labeling theory" has largely been developed with respect to deviance. Thus, whereas labeling theory often is envisioned as that body of literature that focuses on the role that verbal designations play in the definition, emergence, regulation, and stabilization of deviance, those in the interactionist community are apt to view the labeling of people as deviants as but one variant of a broader naming process.

Although most labeling theory has been developed in reference to the identities and reputations of individuals, labeling theorists would generally posit that similar processes would come into play in categorizing, attributing qualities to, and acting toward groups or categories of people as well. Further, because people are able to take the role of the other (Mead, 1934), they not only can assign identities and attributes to themselves, but also can objectify themselves or act toward themselves in manners that they deem appropriate for persons of that sort.

As most people know from personal experience, one's present and future encounters with others can be affected, sometimes very dramatically, by the ways in which people define one another since these identities often suggest ways that people may act toward oneself or others.

While these notions have been incorporated in the study of deviance by sociologists primarily since the 1960s (Becker, 1963; Lemert, 1967), it may be observed that scholarly concerns with people's images and reputations can be traced back throughout recorded history, perhaps most notably in the development of rhetoric as a realm of practice and study in early Greek and Roman society.

Addressing a number of different themes pertaining to speakers, speeches, and judges, Aristotle's (384–322 B.C.E.) classic statement, *Rhetoric*, is directly concerned with the matters of assigning and challenging people's identities across a range of occasions and an assortment of judges. While identity work was only one aspect of the persuasive process that Aristotle and others associated with rhetoric (which is concerned with the influence process and decision-making more generally), identity work was given prominent emphases in the areas of political, ceremonial, and forensic rhetoric.

As indicated in the subsequent works of Cicero (106–43 B.C.E.) and Quintilian (35–100 C.E.), the matter of achieving desired and contested identities through the practice of rhetoric also was a central theme in early Roman life. However, with the passage of time, those involved in rhetoric programs seemed more concerned about the form and style of language than enacted human interchange and the implications of group relations for people's social identities, careers, and life-world experiences.

Interestingly, and despite the centrality of linguistic interchange for all realms of human endeavor, few social scientists have given concerted attention to rhetoric as a social process. Instead, working with the positivist emphases on causes and factors intended to explain human behavior, most social scientists (following Auguste Comte, John Stuart Mill, Emile Durkheim, and Wilhelm Wundt) have overlooked both the ways in which people acquire identities and the implications of these identities for people's activities and associations. Thus, it is not until the mid-twentieth century that we find some social scientists explicitly attending to this aspect of the socially constructed (and definitionally shaped) world of human experience. It is to the development of this tradition we now turn our attention.

LABELING THEORY

While labeling theory is sometimes traced back to Frank Tannenbaum (1938),[3] it is Edwin Lemert (1951, 1967) and Howard Becker (1963) who seem to have been most instrumental in popularizing the concept of labeling in sociology. Labeling theory has led to important understandings in many substantive areas of deviance, but at the same time, there has been relatively little synthesis of the research and insight that this tradition has generated. Thus, for people beginning the study of criminality and deviance, as well as for those actively working in these areas, the literature on labeling theory can be rather perplexing. Rather centrally, then, one faces the tasks of (1) sorting out some very different perspectives on labeling, and (2) addressing some of the more noteworthy issues and research foci that have fallen under its umbrella.

To contextualize labeling theory somewhat more broadly within the sociological literature, four variants or approaches to the identification of deviants may be delineated: societal reactions, functionalism, Marxism, and symbolic interactionism. There is some overlap among these approaches, but each is characterized by notably different assumptions and concerns. Thus, after briefly acknowledging these different approaches to this aspect of the deviance-making process, we will return more directly to the interactionist approach.

The *societal reactions* approach (Lemert, 1951, 1967) has considerable affinity with symbolic interaction and will be synthesized into the present analysis. Still, the societal reactions viewpoint emphasizes the role that control agents play in the perpetuation of deviance and gives comparatively little attention to people's involvements and activities more generally. The *functionalists* are most concerned with the interplay of system requirements, demands, and capacities for the tolerance and production of deviant behavior.[4] Operating from an assortment of moralist agendas, those in the *marxist nexus* insist that criminalization (and deviance-making more generally) is used by those in power to oppress or exploit the weak and disadvantaged.[5] In contrast to the functionalists and those adopting Marxist standpoints, the interactionists subscribe neither to the notion that organizational structures determine human behavior nor that people's positions with respect to domination and conflict represent the key features of community life. Likewise, instead of prescribing morality for others (as do those in the marxist nexus), the interactionists attend to the differing ways that people define deviance in their respective communities and (acting in terms of their viewpoints) identify and deal with particular individuals and groups as deviants. Thus, the interactionist emphasis is on the ways in which people as minded agents make sense of the world and develop lines of action toward all objects of their awareness, including people who in one or other ways are linked to the notions of deviance that particular sets of people develop within the context of ongoing community life.

Over the past several decades, labeling theory has received most attention (research and theoretical specification) from the symbolic interactionists. Although labeling theory is not synonymous with interactionism, the amount of interchange between those working in labeling theory and interactionism has been so great that the two have become largely synonymous in many discussions of deviance. While Erving Goffman (1959, 1963), Orrin Klapp (1962, 1964, 1971), and John Lofland (1969) contributed notably to this tradition,[6] it is important to unravel some aspects of the labeling process so that these might be used to better comprehend the deviance phenomenon. Thus, consideration is given to the matters of *constructing social identities, stabilizing identities and involvements*, and *dealing with disrespectability*.

CONSTRUCTING SOCIAL IDENTITIES

As a social essence, a major aspect of the deviance-making process pertains to the identification of particular people (individuals or groups) as deviants. Although a basic theme in labeling theory (Tannenbaum, 1938; Lemert, 1951, 1967; Becker, 1963) is that people act toward others (targets) in terms of the meanings they attach to them and thus tend to stabilize target identities and involvements, this notion is premised on an antecedent *naming process*. Thus, before turning to a consideration of the implications of people's (public) identities for their involvements in deviance, attention is given to the ways in which people affix names or labels, particularly of a negative sort, to particular targets (individuals and groups) in the community. Accordingly, more immediate attention is given to (a) the naming process and (b) degradation ceremonies.

The Naming Process

Building on discussions of "social identities," "type-casting," and "impression management" by Goffman (1959, 1963), Klapp (1962, 1964, 1971), Becker (1963), and Lofland (1969), all of whom draw attention to the socially constituted and processual essence of identities and reputations, Prus (1975a, 1975b; 1982) delineates four processes operative in the naming process or the formation of social identities: typing; designating; assessing; and resisting. Although implied in these earlier depictions of labeling, the fifth process also should be made explicit, that of people readjusting their images or definitions of targets following their interchanges with others.

Typing refers to the process by which one person (agent) arrives at a private definition of another (target).[7] Not all typings are made known to the target and/or others, and although agents may occasionally blurt out their private typings, they are seen to make decisions as to whether or not to make these typings known to others.

Designating occurs when agents make indications (verbal and/or behavioral) about targets to others, thus more publicly defining targets as particular types of people.[8] As others (including the target) learn of these designations, they tend to *assess* these for their appropriateness or "goodness of fit" relative to their knowledge and views of the target.[9] Where target references are seen as inappropriate (too soft, too harsh, inaccurate), interested persons then decide whether to *resist* target designations,[10] and in what ways to do so.[11] Relatedly, even if labels are contested at one or more points in time, those invoking the initial designation or others need not accept these challenges as viable. They may *readjust* their notions of the targets, but they need not do so. Likewise, the other parties (targets included) involved in any instance of labeling also may reconsider their earlier target definitions, possibly reassessing and shifting their views of the targets a number of times, either on their own or through further interchange with others. Indeed, some instances of contested labels may be extended indefinitely.

It should be recognized that not all instances of labeling will reflect this fuller sequence. For instance, people may never make their private typings of targets known to others; targets or others learning of target designations need not resist publicly imputed identities; and so forth.

As well, because people (as individuals and groups) may define situations in different ways, we should be attentive to *the multiple target identities* that may be assigned to particular individuals and groups across various sectors of the community. Thus, as Klapp (1962) suggests, people may more or less simultaneously be viewed as "heroes," "villains," and "fools" within various segments of the same community or across different communities.

Relatedly, it is important to attend to the ways in which people acknowledge target definitions, both more immediately and in the longer term, mindfully as well of the fuller range of interactional settings in which people may be referenced as deviants. While the prominence of earlier designations often fade with time and are apt to be of varying relevance to different audiences, these identifications nevertheless denote interpretative frames in which any subsequent activities may be conceptualized. Consequently, much of the effect of targets attempting to adjust or reform their own behavior may not only be nullified by the ways that others define and treat them, but (once identified) targets also become much more vulnerable to designations of a related nature (and consequently more subject to manipulation by other persons).

As Simmons (1969) notes, one important residual effect of negative labels is to reduce the ability of discredited persons to be competitive on other levels. Not only are these persons more apt to be subject to disproportionate surveillance, but their participation in even "innocent activities" also may become readily suspect or recast in manners that may be used to discredit them.

As well, one might also observe that as people's reputations become more widespread or entrenched within a community, targets are apt to find it increasingly difficult to resist or otherwise alter those definitions. Not only may target identities become more firmly fixed or objectified in the process, but particular people in the community also may find it advantageous to perpetuate these target definitions even in the face of contrary evidence. Thus, other than trying to distance themselves from disrespectability by relocating in another community, people wishing to resist unwanted imputations are faced with the prospects of living with those imputations until such time as members of the community become diverted by other concerns and other troublesome cases (and even these diversions may be more sporadic than enduring).

Degradation Ceremonies

Attending to the social construction of identity work, particularly as this pertains to the instances of moral indignation revolving around some allegedly disrespectable target, Harold Garfinkel (1956) sheds valuable light on the "ritual destruction" of respectability or, conversely, the "objectification of deviance."

Viewing public hearings in which persons' identities are called into question as moral battles, Garfinkel posits that degradation ceremonies are most likely to be successful when (1) the alleged "activity" is considered more unusual, is presumed intended by the perpetrator, and is at variance with fundamental group values; (2) the "denouncer" is perceived to act in the interest of the group, has the authority to speak on behalf of the group, and is himself considered an honorable member of the group; (3) "witnesses" to the activity in question are void of personal interests relative to the target; and (4) the "perpetrators" are considered disrespectable in other ways.

Approaching degradation ceremonies in a more generic sense, it should be noted that (a) the targets (of disreputable allegations) may be individuals or groups; (b) the agents of denunciation may operate in all manners of organizational or group contexts; (c) the agents may adopt a variety of viewpoints and pursue a diverse set of interests in making their allegations; and (d) the targets may or may not be present, and if present they may speak on their own behalf or have others to speak for them. In developing his analysis, Garfinkel assumes that the agents and targets will endeavor to appeal to particular sets of adjudicators, suggesting (e) that those invoking judgements may operate with wide ranges of concerns and receptivities.

Locating instances of target degradation, disrespectability, discreditation, or stigmatization within the drama of community interchange, Garfinkel's work not only testifies to the problematic (fragile) nature of people's identities within social settings, but also portrays several important contingencies affecting their outcomes.

STABILIZING IDENTITIES AND INVOLVEMENTS

Having considered the processes by which people acquire identities as deviants, we now turn to the related theme of asking about the implications of deviant identities for people's subsequent involvements in activities (and lifestyles) within the community. Especially pertinent in this respect are notions of *the dramatization of evil* (Tannenbaum, 1938); *societal reactions* (Lemert,

1951, 1967); and *career contingencies* (Becker, 1963). Although these statements were developed earlier than the preceding discussion of the naming process, these materials assume that the naming process has been invoked.

The Dramatization of Evil

In what is otherwise a rather vague depiction of "crime and the community," Frank Tannenbaum (1938) provides a highly compelling set of insights on the definition, dramatization, and objectification of delinquency. In a few brief pages (16–22), Tannenbaum eloquently outlines some of the central features of the labeling process. Extracts from Tannenbaum's material are presented here:

In the conflict between the young delinquent and the community there develop two opposing definitions of the situation. In the beginning the definition of the situation by the young delinquent may be in the form of play, adventure, excitement, interest, mischief, fun. Breaking windows, annoying people, running around porches, climbing over roofs, stealing from pushcarts, playing truant—all are items of play, adventure, excitement. To the community, however, these activities may and often do take on the form of a nuisance, evil, delinquency, with the demand for control, admonition, chastisement, punishment, police court, truant school. This conflict over the situation gradually becomes redefined. The attitude of the community hardens definitely into a demand for suppression. There is a gradual shift from the definition of the specific acts as evil to a definition of the individual as evil, so that all his acts come to be looked upon with suspicion. (17)

Only some of the children are caught though all may be equally guilty. There is a great deal more delinquency practiced and committed by the young groups than comes to the attention of the police. The boy arrested, therefore, is singled out in specialized treatment. This boy, no more guilty than the other members of his group, discovers a world of which he knew little. His arrest suddenly precipitates a series of institutions, attitudes, and experiences which the other children do not share. (19)

The process of making the criminal, therefore, is a process of tagging, defining, identifying, segregating, describing, emphasizing, making conscious and self-conscious; it becomes a way of stimulating, suggesting, emphasizing the very traits that are complained of. (19–20)

The point of view here developed rejects all assumptions that would impute crime to the individual in the sense that a personal shortcoming of the offender is the cause of the unsocial behavior. The assumption that crime is caused by any sort of inferiority, physiological or psychological, is here completely and unequivocally repudiated. (Tannenbaum, 1938:22)

Societal Reactions

Focusing centrally on themes paralleling those outlined by Tannenbaum, Edwin Lemert (1951, 1967) is primarily concerned with the impact of community responses to deviance for the perpetrator's subsequent involvements in deviance.

Drawing upon notions of community definitions, target identities, and community sanctions, Lemert posits that the responses of concerned citizens and formal control agents to (assumed) deviants in the community serve to (a) stabilize community and self-definitions of these people (targets) as deviants, and (b) restructure targets' options so as to make deviant behavior comparatively more appealing than was formerly (or would have otherwise been) the case.[12]

Although somewhat problematic conceptually, Lemert's distinction between "primary" and "secondary" deviation is pivotal to his analysis. Lemert observes that many instances of "deviance" go undetected or might be responded to only in more fleeting manners, whereby perpetrators maintain essentially acceptable identities in the community (i.e., retain the definition of "normal" despite involvements in deviance). Lemert uses the term, primary deviation to refer to these unknown, overlooked, or audience-tolerated instances of (problematic or potentially deviant) behavior and largely eschews interest in accounting for the existence or emergence of these activities.

While acknowledging instances of primary deviation, Lemert's emphasis is on explaining secondary deviation or those behaviors that develop as a consequence of community attempts to control instances of behavior that they define as troublesome and in need of regulation, modification, or sanction (ergo, the term, societal reactions). Lemert, thus, envisions people as more likely to continue their involvements in deviance when they are subject to more extensive and persistent identification (and reaction, including exclusion) as deviants in the community.

Lemert clearly does not see targets' subsequent involvement in deviance as inevitable, but contends that continuity is more likely to occur when others in the community more extensively act toward (identify, isolate, sanction) particular targets as if they were deviants (and no longer entitled to the full range of opportunities that would be accessible to people in otherwise similar positions).

By sharpening and emphasizing definitions of the alleged perpetrators as deviants and recasting their options, control agents or other "upstanding citizens" may promote the stabilization or intensification of the very behaviors that they had defined as troublesome:[13]

Secondary deviation refers to a special class of socially defined responses which people make to problems created by the societal reaction to their deviance. (Lemert, 1967:40)

When a person begins to employ his deviant behavior or a role based upon it as a means of defense, attack, or adjustment to the overt and covert problems created by the consequent societal reaction to him, his deviation is secondary. (Lemert, 1951:76)

Crystallizing people's self-identities and reputations within the community, these deviant designations may serve to foster the very involvements that were deemed troublesome (i.e., self-fulfilling prophecies [Thomas, 1928] may be brought into play). Intentionally or otherwise, both the targets and other members of the community may act in ways that serve to reaffirm targets' (deviant) identities in the community.

Not only may targets find more conventional options limited, but as a result of their ensuing disrespectable community images, targets may also decide that they have less interest in pursuing available conventional routines (thereby making them more receptive to deviant pursuits). Should these other (deviant) options become rewarding in particular respects, they may be pursued more intensively.

Relatedly, to the extent that people more fully organize their lives around these activities, they are apt to find it increasingly difficult to "go straight" even when they might so desire. Further while one incident (actual or imputed) may be sufficient to start this process in some instances, Lemert indicates that more extensive labeling (definitions and reactions) often follows a series of unsuccessful attempts on the part of the community to curb the troublesome behavior.[14]

In discussing imputations of deviance, Lemert recognizes that people may be differentially disposed to identify particular targets as deviants and that some targets may be more susceptible to imputations of deviance than others, but he elaborates little on the naming process. Lemert also devotes minimal attention to the ways in which societal reactions are interpreted by the targets at hand, as these might be qualified by people's prior experiences, existing options, contacts, or other resources to which targets might have uneven access. Further, although Lemert indicates that outcomes are always problematic (deviance imputations need not result in secondary deviation), his theory largely emphasizes exclusionary effects.[15]

Exclusionary reactions may be effective in perpetuating deviance, but it seems instructive to sort out the (often considerable) varieties of community responses to which the same people might be subjected and the ways in which these are defined and experienced by the targets.[16] The matter of deviance stabilization becomes further complicated by Lemert's tendency to minimize the role that others (e.g., peers, family) may play in recruiting or otherwise encouraging or facilitating targets' involvements in deviant activities. While Lemert suggests that those identified as deviants are likely to be rejecting of their condemners and more receptive to deviant behavior as a result of exclusion from more conventional situations, he provides limited commentary on either the conditions affecting people's successes as deviants or the conditions under which people may resume more conventional routines.

The concept of societal reactions seems vital for understanding the stabilization of deviance in a great many cases, but it is important to obtain a clearer understanding of when and how those labeled (named and treated) as deviants may resist (minimize, overcome, or exit from) these imputations and tendencies of exclusion.

Synthesizing Garfinkel's (1956) and Lemert's (1951; 1967) statements on labeling, it may be suggested that further involvement in deviance is more likely when "discrediting sources" (formal or informal) (1) define targets as more villainous (ill-intentioned), persistent, and powerful threats; (2) are more highly esteemed in the community; (3) provide more widespread publicity regarding the targets and their "improprieties;" (4) are more exclusionary in their reactions relative to conventional options; and (5) have greater control over community activities (can more effectively neutralize conventional avenues of target support).

It is suggested, however, that persons interested in the impact of control efforts on systematic deviance not neglect (6) targets' prior experiences and interpretations of the situation at hand, or (7) the affiliational networks (deviant and conventional) to which the target has access (and the target's receptivity therein). When persons have been more intensively engaged in deviance prior to official processing and/or are better connected with networks of deviants, the effects of control agent responses may be very different from those experienced by targets who are largely conventional in orientation and whose contacts with "the underlife" are exceedingly limited.

Career Contingencies

Although accepting Lemert's contention that community responses to deviance (via labeling and exclusion of deviants) can effectively promote intensified involvements in deviance, Howard Becker (1963) views deviance even more fundamentally as social activity.[17] Working much more squarely within the interactionist tradition, Becker views deviance as a product of human association; as reflecting the interchanges that take place between any implicated persons and all of those with whom (conventional and otherwise) they interact.

Using *career contingencies* as his organizing concept, Becker posits that deviance is best examined in process terms, by an attentiveness to the conditions affecting people's participation in activities over time.[18] Thus, Becker posits that just as someone might have a career as a doctor, ballerina, movie-goer, or student, so might one have a career as a burglar, gambler, exotic dancer, or drug dealer.

In this way, Becker not only helps to demystify the study of deviance, but also suggests that we might profitably approach the study of deviance in much the same way that one might approach the study of any other line of people's involvements in community life (see Becker, 1986). The difference revolves not around the activities that people do or do not do, but around the meanings that people attribute to their activities and associates. Viewed in this way, one may draw all sorts of conceptual parallels across people's deviant and other involvements, while still recognizing that imputations of deviance and the ensuing disrespectability may serve to further complicate the lives of those engaged in practices that are defined as deviant in the community.

From Becker's work, the following issues emerge as having central significance for the study of deviance: (a) how definitions of deviance emerge and are
enforced; (b) how (as opposed to why) people become involved in deviant activities and groups; (c) how people overcome the disrespectability associated
with deviant activities; (d) how people avoid getting drawn more exclusively
into conventional routines; (e) how those who denunciate particular forms of
deviance deal with those they define as deviants; and (f) how deviants individually and collectively (e.g., subcultural rationales, motives, ideologies, identities, opportunities, and techniques) go about their activities as well as deal with
the attempts on the part of others to regulate and control their behaviors.

Relatedly, Becker's concept of career contingencies avoids many of the difficulties characterizing Lemert's notion of secondary deviation. It allows researchers to trace particular instances and realms of people's activities from A
to Z and to examine these involvements mindfully of (a) all of the actors'
preceding experiences; (b) the full range of interactional contexts in which
people pursue their activities; and (c) participants' emergent definitions of the
situations in which they find themselves. Likewise, Becker's (1963) ethnographic considerations of jazz musicians and marijuana users are particularly
instructive for illustrating the processes of initial involvements, continuities,
and disinvolvements of people from activities deemed disrespectable by the
larger community.

DEALING WITH DISRESPECTABILITY

While people's sense of disrespectability or stigmatization is centrally interlinked with attributions of deviance, this theme allows us to focus a little more
directly on the ways that deviance is experienced by those singled out as targets
in negative terms. Following a more direct consideration of Erving Goffman's
Stigma, attention is given to some related matters of identity work.

Experiencing Stigma

Attending to the discrediting qualities that people may attribute to others
(and oneself), Erving Goffman's (1963) statement on stigma can be readily
located within the interactionist tradition. Like Howard Becker, Goffman is
highly attentive to "naming" as a socially constituted process.

Adopting an interactionist viewpoint, Goffman views *stigma* as a negative
quality or evaluation attributed to some person or group rather than an inherent or objective quality of some target. Attending to variants within, Goffman distinguishes three types or realms of stigma: tribal (or group association);
body (or physiological qualities); and character (traits, habits, mannerisms) imputations.

Although it does not focus directly on the ways in which people become
involved in deviance (as activity), Goffman's *Stigma* represents a powerful

testimony to the potentially deeply discrediting and socially debilitating aspects of (negative) labeling ventures on the part of others. However, this volume also depicts the reflective, resourceful, and resistant capacities of human targets and their associates. Thus, while he acknowledges the fragility of human identities (and people's vulnerabilities within the community of the other), Goffman also addresses the problematic, resilient, and constructed nature of human association. Building on his analysis of impression management in The Presentation of Self in Everyday Life (1959), Goffman's Stigma considers the dilemmas and difficulties that people whose identities are problematic encounter in their attempts to maintain respectability among their associates.

The material following is organized around Goffman's distinction between *being discreditable* and *being discredited*, but it should be emphasized that his work adds a very consequential element of "target agency" to the labeling process. Not only may people assume active roles in attempts to minimize the unwanted negativity (and the implications thereof) associated with imputations of deviance, but they also may attempt to project images of self that encourage others to define them (as targets) in more desired (respectable) manners. Thus, Goffman's work draws particular attention to the roles that potential and actual targets of deviant designations may play in the social construction of their own identities.

On Being Discreditable

When people anticipate that others might condemn their activities were they to learn of them, they approximate an important subset of Goffman's "discreditables." Like those inadvertently involved in situations that others might disparage, those knowingly participating in deviance as secretive or clandestine actors could quickly become stigmatized should information of their practices become more public.[19] The differences between discreditable and discredited statuses, thus, reflect (a) people's abilities (and willingness) to conceal aspects of their situations; (b) the astuteness of their audiences; (c) inopportune discoveries; and (d) self-disclosures.

The concept of passing is particularly noteworthy to the distinction between being discredited and discreditable. In passing, one allows oneself to be viewed as normal, respectable, unblemished, and the like (despite possessing some quality that others would consider discrediting). In addition to those who pass inadvertently, people may deliberately resort to a variety of tactics designed to keep others from learning about these attributes.[20] Goffman uses the term *natural cycle of passing* to refer to situations in which people (a) pass inadvertently, (b) come to see advantages of avoiding discreditation, and (c) embark on practices explicitly intended to enable them to avoid being discredited by others.

Thus, actors may conceal particular interests, activities, appearances, or associations from others lest they become discredited as a result. Likewise, people may engage in fabrications (and "misdirections") intended to shift audience's attention to other aspects of the situation (away from potentially discrediting pieces of information), as well as minimize contact with others so that these audiences would have less opportunity to learn about any disreputable features of their situations.

As Goffman observes, people's abilities to pass are contingent not only on their abilities to manage the impressions they give off to others (and control the information that others might acquire about them more generally), but also on the attentiveness of particular audiences to certain pieces of information as indications of people's circumstances more generally. Thus, in addition to those who might have vested interests in uncovering things that they might use to discredit targets, people who are "wise" in Goffman's terms (by virtue of involvement in similar practices or knowledgeable through intimate awareness of other practitioners) may develop suspicions about discreditable attributes that would go unnoticed by other audiences.

In some instances, people become aware of someone's discreditable attributes, through inopportune discoveries. These may reflect carelessness on the part of practitioners or unfortunate occurrences (from the practitioner's viewpoint). On some other occasions, others may become suspicious or make shrewd deductions about someone's situation. Whether they represent direct discoveries or suspicions of various sorts, these inferences of deviance may dramatically alter the situations in which the formerly discreditable now find themselves. Audience reactions are often compounded, as Goffman (1963) notes, not only (a) as a consequence of any condemnation of the stigmatized quality now associated with the actor(s) at hand, but also because of (b) the sense of moral indignation that may accompany related inferences of target deception (trust violations).

Despite the advantages of remaining undetected (being treated as a "normal" or respectable person), people sometimes knowingly reveal their disrespectable qualities to others. This may reflect people's (a) interests in facilitating their activities or situations more generally; (b) concerns with doubts, dilemmas, guilt, anxiety, and the like; and (c) desires to educate, crusade, shock, or arouse sympathy from others. In general (Grupp and Schmidt, 1980; Prus, 1982), disclosures seem more likely when audiences are defined as (a) necessary others (e.g., suppliers, assistants, targets), (b) sympathetic to the discloser, (c) disinterested (anonymous, nonjudgmental), and (d) trustworthy (keep confidences).

To the extent that those engaging in self-disclosure are able to determine the times and modes of revelation (e.g., "testing the ice," softening designations, selecting audiences), they may not only be able to lessen the impact of these revelations, but also to avoid the indignation that frequently emerges when people (audiences) envision themselves to have been deceived. Regardless of whether the "disreputables" disclose their disreputable qualities to others or these others learn of these in other ways, these people now join the ranks of the "identified" deviants and typically face new sets of audience reactions.

On Being Discredited

Once identified as disreputable, people often experience a sense of isolation or distancing from those seen to judge (and reject) them. This seems especially likely for people lacking subcultural supports. In contrast to those more caught up in subcultural deviance (with fuller, shared senses of perspectives, identities, relationships, and the like), discredited solitary targets "stand alone." As a consequence, these people seem considerably more susceptible to the definitions and suggestions of judgmental others than do those participating in subcultural deviance.[21]

Still, even when they are identified as deviants, people may be able to nullify some of the impact of deviant attributions. To this end, they may attempt to (a) reduce the visibility of their discreditable qualities by "covering" (Goffman, 1963) their stigma or making themselves less obtrusive in certain regards; (b) distance themselves from others;[22] (c) discount the relevance of stigmatizing qualities by acting as if these were nonproblematic; (d) joke about things that might be taken too seriously (i.e., disrupt interaction with) by others; and (e) embark on diversionary practices in attempts to refocus people's attention away from discrediting qualities.[23] Those whose identities have been impugned may also try to neutralize the stigma to which they may be subjected by (f) accounting for (justifying, providing excuses for, explaining) their predicaments (Scott and Lyman, 1968), as well as (g) challenging deviant imputations (Hewitt and Stokes, 1975; Prus, 1975b).

Sometimes, too, discredited persons may be able to (h) enlist the activities of supporters who may help them completely pass in front of some audiences or minimally attain greater respectability in the situation at hand (Edgerton, 1967). In all cases, the success of these endeavors is contingent on the ways in which audiences interpret and respond to these efforts.

Further, although some audiences may be very critical of those deemed disrespectable, others may (i) attempt to support those so identified.[24] Thus, some people with whom discredited individuals associate may normalize the situation by overlooking even highly visible stigma (see Davis, 1961; Goffman, 1963) or acknowledging the stigmatized person's efforts to retain (or regain) "normalcy." However, the success of discredited persons achieving acceptance in interactional contexts is contingent on the receptivity (sympathies, other interests) of their audiences to their circumstances and the particular relationships that targets invoke with these others.

For discredited people, a central interactional problem revolves around what Goffman terms *ambivalence of identity*. They do not know when (or to what extent) they will be accepted as normals or treated as deviants by their associates. Even when others seem accepting of them on a fairly consistent basis, people who earlier have been identified as deviants may be quickly reminded of their discreditable circumstances.

Mindful of ambivalences and shifts of these sorts, Goffman (1963) uses the term *moral career* to refer to people's sense of self-worth over time. Although people's moral careers may be seen to encompass notions of self over time (past, present, and future), these valuings of self also reflect the ways that others define and act toward them (as the targets in question) on a more situated basis. Thus, there is a continuity of self in certain respects, but this is to be appreciated within the context of ongoing sets of situated encounters wherein the same people may be treated (and envision themselves) as normal, respectable, or esteemed on the one hand and deviant, discredited, or stigmatized on the other. Everyone, in this sense, is apt to experience some ambivalence or contradiction of identity both over time and across interactional contexts.

Acknowledging the concept of "minstrelization," Goffman also observes that those who envision themselves as subject to deviant statuses also may openly dramatize, flaunt, or otherwise emphasize these identities or other aspects of their roles, thus drawing attention to this problematic sense of self.

Other Aspects of Identity Work

In what follows, attention is given to three somewhat related aspects of identity work. These notions build on Goffman's work in some respects but focus more directly on *self-identified deviants; displaying disrespectability;* and *defining victim-status.*

Self-Identified Deviants

While people may very much wish to avoid imputations of deviance by others and may experience considerable losses of self when others define them as disrespectable in some manner, people also apply definitions of deviance to themselves in the absence of other audiences. Because (a) people achieve notions of morality by "taking the role" (i.e., adopting the viewpoint of the other; Mead, 1934) and (b) have access to specific realms of information about themselves (as in activities, thoughts, or relations with others), they may apply definitions of deviance and disrespectability to themselves without any particular prompting from other people. Defining themselves as disreputable, people may experience senses of disappointment, shame, or embarrassment even when on their own.

Relatedly, the human capacity for reflectivity that enables people to view their own activities as deviant also allows them to impose penalties of varying severity on themselves. Likewise, should people come to see themselves as no longer "worthy" or "fit" for particular relationships (e.g., employment, marriage, friendship), they may withdraw from others as a part of the extended context of privately defined deviance.

As well, because people can take the role of the generalized other (Mead, 1934) or anticipate how others might judge them were they to act in certain ways, this capacity for negative self definitions fosters social control at a community level even when people are on their own. Indeed, as Mead (1934) would observe, much deviance may be avoided because people have capacities to anticipate others, experience guilt, and sanction themselves as "objects of their own awareness."

Displaying Disrespectability

While Goffman uses the concept of "minstrelization" in *Stigma* to refer to people who flaunt disreputable identities, the matter of expressing or displaying disrespectability appears to warrant yet more attention. By considering those occasions when people intentionally convey aspects of disreputability to others, we may achieve a fuller understanding of the deviance-making process from the viewpoints of both "deviant insiders" and "outsider judges."

Although people acting on a more solitary basis may knowingly express themselves disrespectfully in dealing with others, subcultural or groups-related displays appear especially consequential for comprehending people's concerns about conveying "integrity" and "coolness" with respect to self and others. Clearly, not all of those involved in (deviant) subcultures wish to be known as deviants and many, as Goffman (1959, 1963) suggests, may go to great lengths (both as individuals and in more collective fashions) to conceal or otherwise minimize the obtrusiveness of any activities, appearances, or associations that might be viewed as disrespectable. At the same time, however, other people may knowingly display deviance, either as individuals or within group-related contexts.

The nonconformist, rebel, or "hip" images that Howard Becker (1963) describes in his portrayal of jazz musicians is illustrative here, as are depictions of bravado, outlaw, and intimidation orientations on the part of street and biker gangs (Thrasher, 1927; Keiser, 1969; Wolf, 1991). Tattoos (Sanders, 1989; Vail, 1999) and other fashion items (Klapp, 1969) also may be used as expressions of freedom, defiance, intimidation, and the like.

As with people's involvements more generally, those invoking stances as disreputables may assume a variety of viewpoints, possibly mixed on occasion. Thus, while people may display disrespectability with the intention of (a) indicating personal disaffection with self or others, (b) claiming independence from others, and (c) pursuing stylistic individuality or particularistic genres, people may also express disrespectability as a means of (d) proving themselves to others, (e) questing for prestige among others, (f) pursuing cooperation from others, or (g) seeking entertainment derived from other people's reactions to these displays. As well, some expressions of disrespectability may also be the natural consequence of (h) knowingly pursuing particular in-group agendas that are at variance from out-group standpoints.

Like other realms of involvement, it appears that people may not only approach any given expression of disrespectability from multiple, often mixed, viewpoints but also may shift viewpoints over time (even where they maintain what may appear as consistent expressions of disreputability or mere variants of a theme to outsiders). Relatedly, one may find that members of particular groups may disagree on the practice of displaying deviance, even when expressing collectively developed viewpoints. Thus, some may intend that the group be more intense or overt in expressing group consciousness (and/or contempt for outsiders), while other members may encourage the adoption of more neutral or more subdued displays.

Whereas citizens at large may invoke any variety of standpoints in making sense of the instances of disrespectability that they encounter, the problem for analysts is much more complex. Given the diverse meanings that various participants and audiences may attach to particular displays, it is essential that analysts are mindful of just whose behaviors they are trying to explain and that they attend carefully to the viewpoints that those people invoke. Clearly, the matter of displaying disrespectability is *not* a single thing and attempts to explain these instances as if they were one thing are fraught with error.

Similarly, it should *not* be assumed that those who knowingly engage in deviant bravado or "flaunt their deviance" are unconcerned about being identified or treated as deviants. Thus, although people sometimes seem quite willing to display disrespectability, they may still resent and resist efforts to be designated as deviants by those who are prepared to hold them accountable for their activities.

Like others who become implicated in deviance, those involved in disreputable displays later may try to avoid culpability. To this end, they may attempt to disclaim responsibility for their activities, cast themselves as helpless victims of circumstance, or project more acceptable roles as repentant sinners. When no longer in situations in which they may be held accountable, they may resume their former bravado (expressive) stances.

Defining Victim-status

In addition to people's self- and other-initiated definitions of themselves as deviants, we may also consider the processes by which people come to be known as victims or parties thought to experience injury or loss and some of the implications of people claiming victim-status.

In an instructive commentary on the "victimology" literature, James Holstein and Gale Miller (1990) address victim-status as a *socially constructed* phenomenon. Observing that the literature dealing with victims (a) concentrates on contexts, correlates, and consequences of victimization; (b) assumes a static as opposed to a dynamic or processual viewpoint; and (c) presumes the objectivity of victim claims, Holstein and Miller reconceptualize the victim phenomenon as an interactively constituted identity-status.[25]

As Holstein and Miller note, the "victimization" process fundamentally is a categorization device. Like other labels, victim-related identities (suggesting ways that people may act toward particular people in the setting) are highly problematic in their emergence, application, acceptance, duration, and so forth.

When considering victims, people often assume that (a) those to whom the victim-status is applied are not fully responsible or accountable for their present circumstances and failings; (b) others have intervened in the victims' situations in undesirable, causal fashions; and (c) certain remedies and redresses may be appropriate.

Those claiming victim-status are often accepted at their word, but when issues of victim integrity arise, audiences may ask about (a) general victim competencies, (b) particular victim follies or mistakes, and (c) contributory victim-initiatives, encouragements, or cooperative activities. Audiences also may become concerned about people invoking victim-status in order to (d) avoid normal responsibilities, (e) evade culpability for their own misdeeds, (f) realize personal gains, and (g) injure others with whom they have become disenchanted.

Where victim-status implies losses, liabilities, and punishments for others, claims to victim-status may assume a negotiated or contested quality. Thus, although those claiming victim-status may engage in a variety of designation practices (of self and other) intended to "objectify" their claims (Berger and Luckmann, 1966), these contentions may be challenged as other parties contest or resist victim-related definitions of the situation at hand. Relatedly, a variety of third parties may become involved in the process as judges, witnesses, representatives, and curious onlookers.

As well, although victims are often seen as helpless participants, they may assume tactician roles wherein they seek certain advantages relative to others. Thus, they may pursue compensations for losses, increased privileges and freedoms, resources, and publicly acknowledged justifications for any current shortcomings. On the other hand, even when successful in gaining victim-status, this too may come with a loss. Thus, "victims" may be envisioned by some members of the community as less competent, less trustworthy, less congenial, and more political in their styles of relating to others more generally.

In some instances, too, the cases at hand may assume more abstract dimensions, wherein the specific players become cast into broader theaters as the representatives of "good" and "evil." Accordingly, those involved may benefit (as well as lose) from the potentially diverse public and personal sentiments and agendas that judges of all sorts may bring into play in deciding on the characters (and claims) of the participants in any identity contest.

As with stigma (Goffman, 1963) more broadly, an important implication of Holstein and Miller's analysis is a recognition of the enacted nature of influence work; that everyone (central actors and third parties) involved in a setting may assume roles as targets and tacticians on an interchangeable (and sequential if not also more or less simultaneous) basis as they define "what is deviant" and "what is not" within the many contexts or theaters of interchange that constitute the human community.

LOOKING AHEAD

Because people live, act, and experience self within a community (if only a small subgroup within) of others, being discredited often has implications for people's involvements in deviance that extend far beyond any sense of shame or personal embarrassment that they may experience. Although clearly not subscribing to the idea that labels will automatically "stick" and thereby ensure people's continued involvements in particular realms of deviance, the labeling theorists (Tannenbaum, 1938; Lemert, 1951, 1967; Goffman, 1959, 1963; Becker, 1963) have drawn attention to the tendencies of people (as audiences / associates) to act in ways that confirm or objectify the deviance implied in deviant designations. Where imputations of deviance are more widely acknowledged (and more consistently acted upon) within community contexts, it may be difficult for identified deviants to pursue other options even should they intend to disengage or distance themselves from these practices.

Whereas those involved in subcultural deviance are apt to have others to whom they more directly may turn when encountering imputations of deviance, those experiencing deviance definitions on a more isolated (solitary) basis seem likely to find the experience more disconcerting overall. Although the fragility of one's former identities is particularly evident when one's normality is questioned on a more intense basis, those who encounter instances of discreditation, distancing, and distrust while on their own seem particularly susceptible to self-doubts and denigrations.

When envisioned along the lines just discussed, an appreciation of the discreditation process enables researchers to consider the ways in which audiences identify and act toward those they consider deviants. It also allows scholars to consider the ways that these definitions and treatments are experienced by those encountering demarcations as deviants of sorts. Although chapters 6 through 9 examine people's involvements in realms of activity (and life-worlds) considered deviant by others in the community and chapters 10 through 13 focus more specifically on regulatory efforts and the disinvolvement process, these statements very much build on the definitional processes addressed in chapters 4 and 5.

NOTES

1. Readers may appreciate some of the parallels of labeling individuals (and groups) as deviant with chapter 4, wherein the emphasis is on defining situations as problems.

2. As self-reflective entities, people also may anticipate the attribution process on the part of others. Thus, they may selectively present (as in revealing and concealing information about) themselves to others in attempts to obtain and sustain more favorable definitions of self on the part of others (see Goffman, 1959; 1963).

3. Although they are seldom referenced as labeling theorists, many of the ideas associated with labeling theory (particularly as an interactionist approach to the study of deviance) can be traced back to Thrasher (1927) and Shaw (1930), whose books, *The*

Gang and *The Jack-Roller*, respectively, provide compelling insights into the intersubjective nature of subcultural deviance and people's careers as delinquents. Indeed, Tannenbaum's (1938) overall work pales in comparison to Thrasher's *The Gang*, a source on which Tannenbaum partially builds.

4. Some functionalist variations of labeling theory can be seen in the works of Erikson (1962; 1966), Connor (1972), Cohen (1974), and Lauderdale (1976). In general terms, these authors derive inspiration from an oft-neglected statement by Emile Durkheim. Durkheim (1895) posits that deviance is an inevitable aspect of group life, and definitions of deviance are profoundly social, reflecting community reference points. Functionalist scholars typically focus on issues such as the "elasticity," "inevitability," and "functionality" of deviance, as well as the conditions affecting labeling endeavors on a general societal level. Working on a larger and often historical level, they endeavor to indicate the ways in which community responses to deviance are shaped by the forces affecting the social system at large. Parsons (1951), Merton (1957), and Cohen (1959) provide more general statements on functionalist notions of order and deviance.

5. Those in the marxist nexus (as in Marxism, cultural studies, critical theory, marxist-feminism, political economy, critical criminology, left realism, and postmodernism) generally do not define themselves as labeling theorists, but instead have entered into the process as vociferous critics both of other sociological positions regarding deviance and of people who do not share their moral viewpoints. Contending that those in power use criminalization and the other imputations of deviance as tools with which to oppress (and exploit) those who are disadvantaged, these authors allege that they alone are morally equipped not only to define the true essence of deviance and to determine who the real deviants are, but also to determine the appropriate remedies for society's ills.

While emphasizing a number of different themes (such as property ownership, class, gender, sexual orientation, race, age, and knowledge) as the basis for invoking instances of the oppression thesis, this literature stresses the centrality of generating new moral orders (informed by one or other perspectives within the marxist nexus) rather than examining the what and how of human group life in more empirical (either quantitative or ethnographic) terms. As a result, this literature tends to be heavily rhetorical rather than scientific in quality.

Most of these authors have moved away from fundamentalist Marxist images of "worker revolutions" and some explicitly claim to be dubious of "utopian Marxist states." Nevertheless, virtually all of these spokespeople continue to perpetuate highly moralistic and politicized approaches to understanding crime and deviance. This is no less true for the "left realists" whose positions, on the surface, might seem highly consistent with a more conventionalist, if not also a more conservative, citizenry-oriented vision of crime.

Similarly, although the progenitors of postmodernism express disenchantment with the grand ideologies of fundamentalist Marxism, these same spokespeople retain much of the imagery associated with the marxist oppressionist/conspiracy thesis but now locate polarization and oppression within smaller domains or fields of community life. Like other moral entrepreneurs (Becker, 1963) who claim privileged standards for judging the substance of deviance, the standpoints adopted by those in the marxist nexus are subject to various contradictions. However, postmodernist (a) criticisms of existing (modernist) moral orders and (b) their own claims to provide enlightened guidance for future moral orders (where pertinent power differentials, oppression, and deviance presumably would be eliminated) are particularly paradoxical because the postmodernists also (c) explicitly deny the authenticity of any claims that anyone (or any group of people) can know anything about anything.

More sustained overviews of socialist (also communist, Marxist, and related) agendas, are available in Cole (1959) and Kolakowski (1978). While Taylor et al., (1973), Quinney (1974), and Young (1986) typify marxist nexus positions in many respects, Downes and Rock (1998) provide a more extended review of the marxist literature pertaining to crime and deviance. Readers interested in issues in feminist (and marxist-feminist) epistemology (i.e., interlinkages of theory and research) are apt to find Stanley and Wise (1993) a particularly instructive source. Given the relative obscurity of the postmodernist (and poststructuralist) literature, readers may find Rosenau's (1992) overview of some assistance in sorting through this literature. For some material that addresses the flaws of postmodernist approaches to the social sciences, see Dawson and Prus (1993a, 1993b, 1995), Best (1995b), Charmaz (1995), Sanders (1995), Maines (1996), and Prus (1996b). A more sustained interactionist critique of cultural studies, postmodernism, and other variants of the marxist nexus with respect to power as a humanly engaged phenomenon can be found in Prus (1999).

6. Others who have contributed to an interactionist conceptualization of labeling theory include Garfinkel (1956), Sykes and Matza (1957), Rubington and Weinberg (1968), Scott and Lyman (1968), Thorsell and Klemke (1972), Schervish (1973), Rogers and Buffalo (1974), Hewitt and Stokes (1975), Levitan (1975), Prus (1975a, 1975b, 1982), Cullen and Cullen (1978), and Grupp and Schmidt (1980). This does not include the many instructive ethnographic accounts of identity work (see chapters 6–9) that also deal with the labeling process.

7. In arriving at private definitions of targets (Prus, 1975a), people may utilize information that they themselves encounter directly as well as that disclosed to them by others. On a firsthand basis, people commonly develop impressions of targets reflecting (1) "appearances" (the settings in which the targets are observed; nonaction personal effects such as dress, grooming, and physique); (2) "activities" in which targets were observed (or assumed) participating; (3) "consequences" (of activities) observed directly or attributed to the target; (4) the levels of "responsibility" attributed to targets for appearances, activities, or consequences; and (5) "values" (interests, motives) thought to characterize the targets. Where agents have prior knowledge of the targets under consideration, incoming information is subjected to this context. Existing typings may provide powerful interpretative frames, particularly when people believe they know the target in more complete senses or when incoming information is more ambiguous or incomplete. However, when incoming information is seen to be more extensive, or more central to the agent's interests, it may form a frame in which earlier information is recast.

8. When making target typings known to others (Prus, 1982), agents may affect not only the social lives of the targets about whom these disclosures are made, but also that of any others with whom these targets have contact (including the designators). Given the potential ramifications of disclosures, agents may be selective in making target references. Typically, as agents define the disclosure of target typings as (1) more significant (more newsworthy) to others, (2) situationally more relevant, (3) reflecting their duties, or (4) promoting their interests, they seem more desirous of making their typings known to others. However, persons' actual disclosures tend to be moderated by their perceptions of external accountability. In general, as agents envision themselves

as (a) more knowledgeable, (b) more esteemed, (c) more influential, and (d) more independent (i.e., autonomous), they seem more likely to make target disclosures in line with their current interests.

Should agents wish to make target disclosures, but experience little designating autonomy, they may (a) disclose their typings more selectively, picking and choosing their audiences; (b) soften disclosures, while maintaining much of the essence of their typings (e.g., referring to the target as a "little slow," rather than "dumb"); and (c) obscure accountability for disclosures by presenting these in the context of double talk, humor, and sarcasm. Other disclosures may come about (d) inadvertently; (e) in conjunction with moral indignation (wherein the agent, sensing injustice, feels less constrained); or (f) as a consequence of consulting a third party regarding difficulties involving the target. Not all disclosures are truthful, and agents (in an attempt to better their position relative to a target) may misrepresent (miscontextualize, distort, or falsify) information concerning a target.

9. Regardless of the authenticity of a disclosure, once a target typing is made known to others, these others (including the target) face the prospect of assimilating this incoming information with their other knowledge of the target. Typically, recipients of information seem most comfortable with material that confirms their present images of the target. When inconsistencies appear, the direction of their resolution seems contingent on the amount, centrality, and internal consistency of prior target information in contrast to the amount, centrality, and internal consistency of the incoming information; and the credibility of the source(s). Even though more recent information may be seen as more relevant, recipients of information seem to attribute greater credibility to sources they envision to (1) have higher community prestige; (2) assume perspectives more similar to those of the recipient's in reference to the target; (3) provide more verifiable cues in making the disclosure; (4) act with greater conviction in their designations; (5) be free of "personal motives;" and (6) possess casts of supporting others (multiple others, particularly those seemingly independent of one another, appear more convincing).

10. Should proposed labels be judged inappropriate, undesired, and such, persons (and groups) may challenge or attempt to neutralize these designations in a variety of manners (Prus, 1975b). It should not be assumed, however, that all undesired or inaccurate labels are resisted by the targets or other interested parties. Designations seem more likely to go uncontested as potential resisters anticipate that (1) designations will be less permanent; (2) designations will be less consequential; (3) the costs or risks of resisting the designations will be more extensive; and (4) their challenges are less likely to be successful. As well, undesired labels may go uncontested because (5) targets may simply not be aware that they are being so defined or (6) targets are uncertain about the ways in which they might challenge these unwanted imputations.

11. When interested parties (targets and/or others) decide to resist target definitions they may (1) contest the validity of the typing as applied to the target (indicate inconsistencies between the typing and the "target as is," deny and/or provide alternative explanations for the "evidence," or contend that the target should not be held responsible for the evidence); (2) challenge the agent (often on the basis of vested interests or incompetence); (3) suggest a compromise typing (whereby the agent retracts some, but not all elements of the earlier designation); or (4) ask the agent to retract the designation (by acknowledging the agent's good will and/or indicating the regret of the target, a "repentant sinner"). Should these options (individually or in any combination) be

thought or found insufficient, targets may endeavor to resist undesired labels by (5) seeking out others with whom to associate. This latter option seems more effective when the interactive distance between the two sets of audiences is maximized. Targets may also attempt to resist designations by (6) invoking new appearances or behavioral alignments, thus providing demonstrations of inconsistencies between suggested typings and their personas or routines.

12. Ed Lemert (personal communication) traced his attentiveness to "secondary deviation" back to his interest in stuttering (as a socially developed pattern of activity) and credits L. Guy Brown as a source of intellectual inspiration. Brown (1931), in turn, links his work to that of G. H. Mead.

13. Although Lemert (1962) does not use the term "secondary deviation" in his analysis of "paranoia and the dynamics of exclusion," this remains one of the very best illustrations of both labeling theory and the dynamics of human interchange.

14. While formal intervention may be seen to crystallize people's deviant involvements in some instances, particular modes of individual behavior also may become highly systematic prior to official consultation or intervention. See research on families (Jackson, 1954; Yarrow et al., 1955; Lemert, 1962; Blum, 1991; Wiseman, 1991; Asher, 1992), drug usage and drinking (Becker, 1963; Prus, 1983), gambling (Lesieur, 1977), theft (Sutherland, 1937; Ditton, 1977; Prus and Sharper, 1977; Prus and Irini, 1980), homosexuality (Reiss, 1961; Warren, 1974; Humphreys, 1975; Ponse, 1978; Newton, 1979; McNamara, 1994; Correll, 1995), depression (Karp, 1996), and transgendering (Ekins, 1997).

15. Noting that negative labels may also promote conventional behavior on the part of some targets, Thorsell and Klemke (1972) suggest that (1) societal reactions may have different effects on targets depending on when these occur (e.g. early/ late) during their careers; (2) confidential reactions are less likely to promote subsequent involvements in deviance than are those of a more public nature; (3) targets accepting of the agent's perspectives are more likely to respond in conventional ways; (4) easily removed labels are more likely to promote conventional behavior; and (5) targets receiving greater social support (as opposed to exclusion) from conventional sources, are more likely to conform to community standards.

16. It should also be recognized that reactions intended as benign, helpful, and the like, may be interpreted quite differently by targets and may (effectively) have exclusionary results.

17. While Edwin Lemert views himself primarily as a "deviance theorist" and has only marginally aligned himself with symbolic interaction, the Chicago-trained Howard Becker much more centrally assumes an interactionist viewpoint. Both scholars (see Lemert, 1951:23–24) encourage a more generic appreciation of the implications of the identification process for people's participation in deviance and other settings.

18. The concept of deviant involvements as "careers" may be traced to Frederick Thrasher's (1927) *The Gang*, Clifford Shaw's (1930) *The Jack-Roller*, Paul Cressey's (1932) *The Taxi-Dance Hall*, and Edwin Sutherland's (1937) *The Professional Thief*. All of these works very much envision deviance in enacted, process terms. The occupational metaphor is particularly direct in the Cressey and Sutherland statements, wherein deviance involvements are seen as denoting financial alternatives to more conventional occupational endeavors.

19. Ball (1970), Denzin (1970), Douglas (1970), and Lyman and Scott (1989) provide valuable conceptual accounts on the more general phenomenon of disrespectability.

Although virtually all ethnographic research on deviance addresses the matter of disrespectability, the following works are instructive in this regard: Edgerton's (1967) study
of mentally retarded people; Prus and Irini's (1980) examination of the hotel community; Schneider and Conrad's (1983) account of epilepsy; March's (1994) study of adopt-
ees; Karp's (1996) research on depression; and Ekins' (1997) depiction of transgendering
practices. As well, because of the contrasts this material provides, readers may find it
instructive to examine people's experiences with disrespectability in an assortment of
homosexual life-worlds (Reiss, 1961; Warren, 1974; Humphreys, 1975; Ponse, 1978;
Newton, 1979; Broadhead and Fox, 1990; Sandstrom, 1990; Correll, 1995).

20. For some ethnographic examinations of "passing" endeavors (and related dilemmas), see Edgerton's (1967) study of the mentally retarded, Kando's (1973) and Ekins'
(1997) considerations of transgendering, Prus and Sharper's (1977) depiction of card
and dice hustlers, Higgins (1980) statement on people's experiences with deafness,
Schneider and Conrad's (1983) study of epilepsy, Haas and Shaffir's (1987) portrayal of
medical students, and Arluke's (1991) consideration of those engaged in experimental
research with animals.

21. Somewhat similar experiences are evident among members of subcultures who
are more abruptly isolated from their associates.

22. Distancing may be invoked on a more situated or occasioned basis within ongoing
interactional contexts or may represent people's attempts to achieve more comprehensive or total identity breaks by seeking out new life-worlds and leaving former associates
far behind.

23. It is in reference to these sorts of "preventive" information-control strategies that
the works of Davis (1961), Goffman (1963), Edgerton (1967), Himmelfarb and Evans
(1974), Petrunik (1974), Higgins (1980), Petrunik and Shearing (1983), Arluke (1991),
and Albas and Albas (1993) are especially relevant.

24. In addition to one's more situated associates and help specialists of various sorts,
one of the attractions of (deviant) subcultures is that people have opportunities to interact with others who seem likely to support them and their activities. These and many
other aspects of subcultural life are addressed in chapters 6 through 8.

25. For some other insightful analyses of victim-status and the interrelated roles of
heroes and villains, see Klapp (1962, 1964, 1971).

Part III

Experiencing Deviance

6

Becoming Involved
Subcultural Mosaics and Careers of Participation

Although so much of the gang boy's life is fanciful, it often has the utmost reality for
him, and many times he does not distinguish between what is real and what is not.
He interprets his own situations in his terms and with the utmost seriousness.

To understand the gang boy one must enter into his world with a comprehension,
on the one hand, of this seriousness behind his mask of bravado, and on the other,
of the role of the romantic, in his activities and in his interpretations of the larger
world of reality. (Thrasher [1927] 1963:96)

Although often used with specific reference to the life-worlds of those involved
in group-related deviance of some sort, the term subculture may be quite appropriately (generically) applied to any group or association that exists within
some larger community context. Referring to any group of people who associate with one another around some common theme or realm of activity, the
notion of subculture draws attention to the collectively achieved nature of
much human activity; that people generally do things mindfully of, or in conjunction with, others.

Chapter 6 is the first of three chapters that deal with subcultures in a more
sustained manner. Whereas chapter 7 examines the multifaceted nature of subcultural life and chapter 8 attends to the ways in which people develop and
maintain subcultural associations, chapter 6 establishes the groundwork for a
subcultural approach to deviance.

In what follows, consideration is given to (1) subculture as an analytic concept; (2) the importance of envisioning community life as a subcultural mosaic;
and (3) people's careers of participation in particular subcultural settings. While
addressing people's involvements in deviance more specifically, the material
presented here has a much more generic quality and is relevant to any realm
of meaningful human activity. Thus, although the concepts introduced herein
have been explicitly cast in deviance terms at times, these notions are not
bounded by any particular standpoints on morality (or definitions of deviance)
that one or other groups of people might endorse.

SUBCULTURE AS AN ANALYTIC CONCEPT

In contrast to those who envision society as embodying a single overarching culture, the interactionists (following Simmel and Mead) have long viewed society as composed of a great many realms of association, with the people involved in each of these interactional arenas, life-worlds, or subcultures representing a reality (ergo, multiple realities) somewhat unto itself.

Following Prus (1997: 41), the term *subculture* is used to refer to a set of interactionally linked people characterized by some sense of distinctiveness (outsider and insider definitions) within the broader community. The people involved in particular subcultures may range from two-person groups to much larger associations in which all of those participating need not be directly aware of one another's involvements in the grouping at hand. Likewise, whereas the members of many subcultures will be in one another's presence for extended periods of time, others may meet in person only occasionally, if at all (as in people who communicate or share associational involvements through other people or through the use of mediums such as written text, telephone, and computerized technology).

In very direct terms, subcultures are constituted as people do things and work out the strands of their lives in conjunction with others in the grouping. Although the term subculture is often used in reference to gangs, cults, drug use, and the like, this concept also is highly relevant to other life-worlds, such as police departments, parole offices, and therapy groups. One may speak, as well, of subcultures seemingly quite removed from popular notions of deviance and control, as in the case of families, friendship groups, work groups, or recreational associations.

In some cases, people readily seek out subcultural involvements. Consider for instance, those who participate in shopping activity, sports, gambling, or hobby groups. In other instances, people may find themselves in subcultural settings only reluctantly, as frequently holds for hospitalization, prison sentences, or (compulsory) education and many work roles. Thus, while people (as minded beings) often do things on their own, a great deal of deviance achieves its essence only through people's involvements in one or other subcultural contexts.

Subcultures develop around particular realms of activity, but people may become involved in particular subcultures in a variety of manners and capacities. As well, people may engage particular subcultural ventures in varying levels of intensity over the duration of their careers as participants. Similarly, though subcultures often appear highly cohesive and unified in thrust, it is important to appreciate the ambiguities, contradictions, tensions, fragmentations, and confrontations that are apt to characterize human associations (including those that seem highly organized, formalized, or bureaucratic in nature).

Not all interactionist ethnography employs the term subculture, but almost all ethnographic research on deviance has been developed around one or more subcultural contexts. Consider, for example, early work on hobos (Anderson, 1923), delinquency (Thrasher, 1927; Shaw, 1930), divorce (Waller, 1930), taxi-dance halls (Cressey, 1932), and professional thieves (Sutherland, 1937). These and other interactionist ethnographies not only indicate the necessity of ex-amining human group life (and deviance) in the making, but also attest to the importance of developing better conceptual understandings of subcultures as community phenomena.

Building on the existing ethnographic literature, the material following pro-vides a conceptual frame that could be used as an analytical reference point (for drawing comparisons and assessing, as well as extending, prevailing conceptual notions) in developing research on people's participation in *any* subcultural setting.

Whereas the remainder of this volume deals with many other aspects of subcultures, this chapter focuses more specifically on (a) subcultures as these exist within a broader subcultural mosaic and (b) people's involvements within subcultural life-worlds. In this regard, we very much heed the advice of George Herbert Mead (1934) and Herbert Blumer (1969) who insist on the importance of explaining the behavior of individuals from the standpoint of the groups in which they are embedded. Indeed, it is only within the realities of human group life that people may be seen to act in deliberative, meaningful terms.

SUBCULTURES AND SUBCULTURAL MOSAICS

Rather than envisioning society as somehow consisting of one central or unitary essence, the approach taken here views society as something that is not only more or less continuously in the making, but also is constituted through the activities of a variety of groups within.[1] Society, thus, is generated by and achieves its essence through the activities of the groups subsumed within this convenient, more encompassing term of reference. Accordingly, though a community may be defined by notions of location, duration, and interaction, communities achieve existence whenever two or more people come together to do something in conjunction with one another.[2]

The notion of a *subcultural mosaic* draws attention to the idea that far from representing singular or global entities, human societies or communities are constituted and sustained only as people pursue specific realms of activity in conjunction with others. Even when the broader membership of the groups involved is constant, each realm of activity represents the focal point for an-other set of interactions, identities, relationships, viewpoints, and priorities on the part of those assembled therein.[3] Relatedly, although one often finds great variations from life-world to life-world within a community, subcultural in-volvements reflect variants of sorts from a (hypothetical) dominant or central culture with respect to people's perspectives, identities, activities, relationships, expressions of emotionality, and communicative styles.

Each subculture may be seen as a forum in which several basic facets of people's lives may take shape. While subcultures are fundamentally enabled by the more encompassing *intersubjectivities* (most especially through common language) of the larger community, each subculture affords participants opportunities to experience another paramount or operational reality.

Viewed thusly, subcultures represent *interactional contexts* in which various aspects of people's earlier or outside lifestyles may be disregarded or challenged as particular alternatives are introduced, developed, sustained, and dropped within those associational contexts. Relatedly, any variety of interests and practices may be entertained and managed in any way that those involved in the situations at hand deem appropriate. Subcultural participants may deliberately strive to be different from others (outsiders) on a sustained or sporadic basis, but in many other cases, the differences emerge rather incidentally with respect to outsiders as the people involved attend to this or that pursuit or subtheme within particular associational contexts.

Despite some surface appearances, it should not be supposed that the participants in any subculture consistently are of one mind on matters pertaining to their particular associations. As with the broader community in which particular subcultures are embedded, one may expect sporadic if not more enduring occurrences of confusion, cooperation, competition, conflict, and compromise within each subculture.

Likewise, whereas dyadic relations may be uneven in their development and operations, subcultures involving three or more participants (as Simmel [1950] observes) offer yet more varied associational dimensions (as in alliances, suspicion, competition, and factions). Shifting membership and individual disengagement also may be expected as matters of routine, as may reconciliations, realignments, and reinvolvements.

Subcultures may endure for extended periods of time, but they may also be highly fleeting in essence. Likewise, associations may fold abruptly; have a precarious, disjointed existence; or wither away over time as factions develop, people's interests change, or members depart or become dispersed in various ways. On occasion too, subcultures may be reconstituted after extended periods of time where there is some memory and renewed collective vision of their value to the people in this setting.

Because specific subcultures exist within larger subcultural mosaics, and individual participants are typically involved in several associations, the matter of "identifiable differences" (on any basis that people may make distinctions) becomes important for appreciating people's ongoing associations or more enduring subcultural affiliations. While participants sometimes intend that their associations will be viewed as unique, people need not embark on any elaborate or intensive identity work to achieve recognition as a unit (consider two people who are seen together on an intermittent but somewhat sustained basis).

Still, both insiders and outsiders are more likely to view associations in more concrete or objectified (Berger and Luckmann, 1966) terms when they associate some noteworthy qualities (e.g., focused activity, celebration, trouble, threat) with this or that associational nexus. It does not matter, in this respect, whether the subculture is viewed in friendship, recreational, task, honorable, or disreputable terms, or whether people involved actually wish to be there. A sense of distinctiveness draws attention to specific associational forums as settings in which certain kinds of things are done by particular groups of people.

Although *attributions of deviance* further differentiate some subcultures from others, and may complicate the lives of the participants of those associations so designated, it is important to appreciate that the interchanges characterizing deviant subcultures very much parallel those of any other human group.[4] Relatedly, the sociological task revolves around the matter of attending to the ways in which the people both inside and outside of any groups defined as deviant deal with this aspect of their situation, while not becoming so overwhelmed or enraptured by the deviant mystique that scholars fail to comprehend (and examine) the more fundamental aspects of association experienced by participants in those settings. Mindful of this broader quest for a sociological understanding of subcultural life, the present chapter focuses on the ways that people become involved and sustain participation in specific subcultural settings.

CAREERS OF PARTICIPATION

Albeit pitched at a more generic level, the present discussion attends to the ways that people first become involved in particular associations or subcultures and follows their involvements (as in continuities, disinvolvements, and reinvolvements) within those settings.

The emphasis, thus, is on examining instances of the historical flows or careers of people's participation in specific subcultures with the eventual goal of learning more about the ways that people become involved in situations more generally. The objective is to arrive at a better understanding of the career contingencies or things that people take into account as they participate adjustively in particular subcultural arenas.

As a way of considering people's participation in subcultural settings, the concept of "career" was popularized by Becker (1963). However, it can be traced back to early Chicago-school ethnographies, including Thrasher (1927), Shaw (1930) and Cressey (1932). The implication is that people involved in theft, drinking, drug use, or other realms of deviance may be seen to have careers in those fields of activity, just as people might have careers as doctors, accountants, or homemakers. By invoking the occupational metaphor, these early sociologists were able to permeate the deviant mystique and began to focus more precisely on the nature of people's involvements within discredited realms of activity.

Relatedly, while we may follow the history of individual careers of participation over time, the notion of career contingencies (Becker, 1963) encourages analysts to ask about things to which the participants more commonly attend (as with opportunities and encouragements, dilemmas and frustrations, obstacles and rejections, and the like) as they work their way through the situations at hand.

Examining the "what" and "how" (vs. why) of involvements and focusing on the histories or careers of people's participation in particular situations, a process-oriented approach to people's involvements not only provides a great deal of insight into particular realms of activity but also better enables researchers to appreciate the nature of people's experiences in those settings more specifically.

Because virtually everyone is apt to be involved in multiple subcultural life-worlds on both a simultaneous and sequential basis, it is important to attend to the multiple, shifting, and potentially incompatible nature of people's subcultural participation.

Nevertheless, people's careers of involvement in each arena may be envisioned with respect to four somewhat interrelated processes: *initial involvements, continuities, disinvolvements,* and *reinvolvements.*[5] It might be noted, too, that just as people need not become involved in particular subcultures, they also need not continue these activities for any appreciable period of time. In addition, once involved in particular subcultures, people need not become disinvolved from these associations during their lifetimes. If they should become disinvolved from some subcultural endeavor, they may, but need not ever, become reinvolved in these or similar ventures. While this chapter gives more sustained attention to initial involvements, it will only briefly consider continuities, disinvolvements, and reinvolvements. These latter processes will be addressed more completely in later chapters.

INITIAL INVOLVEMENTS

As a first step in comprehending people's fuller participation in specific activities, events, relationships, and the like, this discussion considers the ways in which people enter into these situations. Although not all of the things that people do entail direct interchanges with others, the material introduced here attends to people's entries into group-related activities as well as to those involvements that people may initiate on a more singular or individual level.[6]

It should be noted that this statement differs from the ways in which involvements are generally approached in the social sciences. First, in contrast to the structuralists and others who ask why people do things or what causes or makes them do things, the emphasis here is on the ways in which people engage situations *as agents*. This means attending to people as minded, reflective, acting, and interacting entities. In addition to recognizing people's capacities for devising and selectively pursuing lines of action for themselves, this standpoint also acknowledges people's abilities to shape one another's participation in situations; to influence and resist one another by adopting tactical positions with respect to one another.

Second, in contrast to those who presume that one is either involved in something or not, the material introduced here examines initial involvements in *process terms*. Approached thusly, people's involvements not only may be partialized and tentative in many cases, but also multifaceted in their flows or development. Likewise, whereas people's participation in some situations may be more irretractable and effectively lock people into certain roles or circumstances, other instances of involvement may entail multiple points of engagement, withdrawal, and vacillation, even at more preliminary levels.

The present statement also is attentive to the matters of people *fitting in* with others in the setting and *engaging subcultural roles* in meaningful, adjustive manners. Newcomers sometimes have preexisting contacts (as in friends, supporters, and other previous associates) in the setting who explain aspects of the subculture to them, introduce them to others, and show them ways in which to more effectively engage in the activities at hand. Still, those who participate in almost any realm of group life (deviant or otherwise) are apt to find that they are more or less continuously involved in fitting in with the people in the setting and learning the ropes. This refers to the matters of people experiencing, interpreting, and adjusting to those whom they encounter as well as trying to find ways of pursuing their interests within the particular subcultural life-worlds in which they find themselves.

Clearly, the situation is not the same for all who venture into particular subcultures. Given people's past experiences, some may be comfortable with many aspects of the setting while others may be struck by its apparent strangeness. Likewise, some may have developed proficiencies that enable them to engage in subcultural activities in much more direct and effective manners, whereas others may experience considerable difficulties with the more rudimentary practices that characterize particular realms of group life.

Goffman (1961) uses the term "presenting culture" to refer to people's earlier lifestyles, including their circumstances, resources, activities, experiences, and senses of self. In addition to their physical appearances, habits, abilities, interests, objectives, and other things that people bring into particular situations, we might also acknowledge the limitations, concerns, dilemmas, fears, anxieties, priorities, and external commitments that they carry into those settings. In these respects, newcomers would seem differentially advantaged with respect to one another even as they enter into associations with others.

As well, there is the matter of being accepted by others in the setting. This also is problematic, for potential associates may be screened as well as tested for acceptability to others in the group. Depending on the viewpoints of existing subcultural participants and the particular situations in which those people find themselves when they make contact with particular newcomers, people may be welcomed or resisted based on the qualities (e.g., resources, appearances, skills, potentialities) that members of the receiving group associate with them.

With notions of these sorts in mind, six aspects of people's initial involve-ments in situations are outlined: *being recruited, pursuing intrigues, attending to instrumentality, experiencing closure, managing reservations,* and *acknowl-edging inadvertency.*

Although it is unlikely that people would experience all of these matters in any single instance of involvement, these dimensions or themes should not be seen as mutually exclusive with respect to people's involvements in specific situations. People may attend centrally to one or other of these matters in particular cases, but people's involvements often reflect more than one of these themes.

Being Recruited

The term recruitment refers to the efforts of others (as agents or tacticians of sorts) to involve people (targets) in certain situations. Recruitment draws attention to some of the orientational, guided, encouraged, negotiated, and impositional features of people's entry into situations. Although a seemingly simple concept, a closer examination of this realm of influence work suggests several noteworthy analytical subthemes. While first attending to the situa-tions of those involved in recruiting others into particular ventures, this state-ment also considers the ways that targets engage the recruitment process.[7]

First, people may endeavor to involve specific (identified) targets in situations or they may pitch their efforts more broadly (directing their messages to cer-tain categories of people or more highly diffuse audiences within the wider community). Second, recruiting agents may pursue these endeavors on a more solitary basis or agents may encourage target involvements in conjunction with others (i.e., as collective ventures). Third, while some of these efforts may be intended to involve targets on more enduring and/or broadly encompassing bases, other recruitment endeavors may be envisioned as highly situated and/or sharply focused in scope.

Fourth, recruitment endeavors may be more singular or unilateral in thrust in some instances but denote considerable mutuality of emphases in other cases where the parties at hand more or less simultaneously intend to involve each other in the setting. Likewise, although some recruitment efforts may be di-rected toward anyone in the setting, agents may be much more exclusive or exacting in the criteria they establish for recruiting others. In these latter cases, targets may be screened more thoroughly and/or subjected to extended realms and occasions of testing. Relatedly, while some recruiters may focus on pre-existing target qualities, others may place more emphases on people's abilities to learn appropriate viewpoints, practices, composure, and the like.

In addition to their more direct target concerns, agents also may attend to the positions and practices of others who appear to contend for the attention of the same targets. In some cases, competitor interests in targets may be strik-ingly similar to one another but, in other instances, the competition may come from people endeavoring to involve the same targets in notably different realms of endeavor. Whenever recruiters envision competitors as threats to their enterprises, they are more apt to monitor competitor activities and adjust their own practices with respect to the targets under consideration.

People attempting to involve others in specific situations also may utilize wide varieties of tactics in pursuing their objectives. These may include (a) various allures, inducements, and other attraction-oriented appeals to targets' interests, as well as (b) assortments of threats or treatments of an intendedly negative nature.[8] However, agents also may (c) attempt to convince targets of the instrumental or rational implications of particular involvements, emphasizing target advantages of participation and/or the necessity of targets becoming involved as broader matters of principle or obligation that may extend beyond immediate target interests. Still, at other times, agents may (d) involve targets in situations without prior target awareness or consultation. Thus, agents may impose treatments on others or otherwise "enroll" targets in situations in ways that preclude active choice on the part of targets.

As an extension of their own activities, agents also may (e) seek assistance from third parties in their broader recruitment efforts.[9] Sometimes, third parties may assist agents by identifying viable prospects for tactician agendas. At other times, however, third parties may more directly encourage targets to pursue agent-related positions. As well, agents may seek the support of particular third parties who already are thought to be trusted by particular targets. It might be noted too, that even more generalized displays of support and vague endorsements of the agents (i.e., tacticians) on the part of third parties may be adequate to encourage target involvements in some cases.

Further, although many recruitment endeavors may be intended to (a) advantage agents in certain ways, it should be acknowledged that agents attempting to involve others in particular ventures also may act (b) primarily in the interests of the targets or (c) on behalf of other third parties whose interests, likewise, may assume a range of dimensions. Thus, in addition to their own interests, people may attempt to involve targets in situations from which they believe targets would derive enjoyment or other benefits. Likewise, tacticians may adopt the viewpoint of third parties who have interests in fostering certain target involvements and proceed to act on behalf of those third parties.

As well, whereas agents may encourage others to do things in a great many ways, recruiters may also try to *discourage* targets from participating in particular situations. In addition to (a) the dissuasion associated with denunciations and other denigrations of potential target involvements (as with devalued or inappropriate settings, practices, associates, or groupings), agents also may attempt to prevent target involvements in other ways. When agents serve as gatekeepers to certain realms of endeavor, they may (b) veto or otherwise prohibit admission. Likewise, agents may (c) set up obstacles of various sorts to keep targets from becoming involved in particular situations.

When one adopts the *viewpoint of people (as agents)* trying to affect the involvements of others in particular situations, it is important to consider (a) the bases on which agents take particular interest in the things that others do; (b) those who become defined as the targets of influence work; (c) agent attempts to persuade targets to embark on certain activities; (d) agent efforts to dissuade targets from doing certain activities; and (e) agent attempts to obtain third-party assistance in their recruitment endeavors. These are outlined here:[10]

Developing Interests in Target Involvements
> Pursuing agent (organizational, personal) objectives
> Attending to target interests and dependencies
> Acknowledging third-party viewpoints on target involvements

Identifying the Targets of Influence Work
> Defining appropriate targets
> Focusing on specific (target) persons
> Pitching to specific groups or associations
> Addressing people in the community more generally

Encouraging Target Involvements in Specific Situations
> Considering and selecting influence tactics
> Initiating influence work with targets
> Monitoring target activities
> Encountering receptivity from targets
> Dealing with resistance from targets or others
> Making strategic adjustments to targets
> Monitoring and adjusting to competitors

Discouraging Target Involvements in Specific Situations
> Defining particular situations as inappropriate for targets
> Defining targets as inappropriate for particular involvements
> Restricting target access to specific situations
> Monitoring developments involving targets
> Making tactical adjustments regarding targets

Involving Third Parties in Recruitment Endeavors[11]
> Consulting with others about targets
> Seeking third-party assistance in dealing with targets
> Developing networks of (agent) supporters to deal with targets
> Embarking on collective recruitment ventures involving targets

When one assumes the *viewpoint of targets* subject to influence work by others, a related, somewhat parallel set of processes is consequential. Notably, however, the situation assumes more fortuitous dimensions. As the focal points for other people's pursuits, targets are more dependent on (a) the initiatives of specific others who direct influence work toward those targets and (b) the more specific ways that these people endeavor to frame or shape target experiences.

Still, this should not obscure (c) the variable interpretations (and reinterpretations) of the situations that targets may invoke on both a more immediate and subsequent basis,[12] (d) the earlier efforts that targets may have (tactically) assumed in reference to those who now are endeavoring to recruit them, or (e) target capacities for resisting unwanted involvements and related opportunities. Thus, not only may targets interpret the situations they encounter in ways that differ substantially from those intended by the agents at hand, but targets may also assume active roles in anticipating and shaping the initial efforts of recruiting agents as well as encouraging, resisting, and reformulating encounters with tacticians.

Notably, too, although attending to people's overall senses of receptivity and resistance to others (both in terms of initial contacts and preliminary engagements), it should be appreciated that people also may have more nebulous, if not more distinctively mixed, concerns about contacts with particular people or categories thereof. Thus, while not all of the following processes will be invoked in every situation, people envisioned as targets may engage in activities of the following sorts:[13]

Anticipating Encounters with Others
　　Acknowledging possible encounters with others
　　Preparing oneself for contact with others
　　Pursuing access to others
　　Indicating receptivity to others
　　Encouraging initiatives from others
Encountering Initiatives from Others (as agents)
　　Attending to others
　　Defining and assessing agent initiatives[14]
　　Expressing receptivity to agents
　　Accommodating agent initiatives
　　Negotiating the terms of involvement
Averting Contact with Others
　　Striving to be inaccessible
　　Disattending to others
　　Displaying disregard for others
　　Adopting hostile postures toward others
Resisting Initiatives from Others (as agents)
　　Resisting agents on one's own
　　Seeking third-party advice on dealing with agents

Seeking supporters to deal collectively with agents

Resisting agents through collective ventures with others[15]

Pursuing Intrigues

The term *intrigue* acknowledges the attractions, enjoyments, allures, fascinations, or mystiques that people may associate with particular involvements.[16] It is worth noting at the outset that people may develop and seek particular allures on their own as well as within collective (i.e., group, gathering, subcultural) contexts.[17]

Like recruitment, people's intrigues not only may vary greatly in intensity, but also assume several dimensions. First, although some intrigues may become more widespread among certain communities or subgroups therein, people (as self-reflective entities) may also develop fascinations or allures more exclusively on their own.

Second, because any involvement normally implies several things (e.g., physical settings, activities, emotional sensations,[18] risks, outcomes, associates), it is essential that analysts be mindful of the specific things that people find alluring about the situation at hand. Thus, whereas some prospective participants may be intrigued by seemingly all aspects of the immediate situation, others may not only be much more selectively focused in their fascinations in that arena but may also experience disaffections with other aspects of these same realms of involvement.

It also should be appreciated that in addition to their own, more personal or self-situated intrigues, people also may become fascinated with things that pertain to other people's experiences. Thus, beyond (a) any allures that more directly and exclusively involve themselves, people may attend to the desired self-feelings or emotions that they experience when certain kinds of things happen to (b) specific other people or (c) certain groups, collectivities, or kinds of people. People also appear to have capacities for developing somewhat parallel fascinations with (d) the fate of other things (e.g., animals, art forms, realms of scholarship, and religions).

On a more basic level, thus, people may take delight in the good things experienced by those people (or other objects) for whom they have affection and find somewhat parallel satisfaction in the misfortunes of those for whom they have developed disaffections. Relatedly, people also may consider pursuing lines of action thought (justly or deservedly) likely to contribute to other people's experiences in these regards.

Further, since there are at least two interrelated, developmental aspects of involvement entailed in pursuing fascinations, it is most instructive to ask (1) when and how people *develop intrigues* with (one or more features of) particular situations, and (2) when and how people *act on*, cultivate, or otherwise engage these intrigues. Although very much interlinked in actual practice, the points articulated here suggest lines of inquiry pertaining to each of these subprocesses.[19]

Developing Particular Intrigues

    Being encouraged to appreciate specific things by others

    Viewing instances of other people's allures as relevant / desirable

    Attending to specific things on one's own

    Articulating definitions of specific things as noteworthy / desirable

Engaging Fascinations

    Contemplating particular intrigues on one's own

    Seeking out opportunities for particular involvements

    Discussing intrigues with others

    Attending to opportunities provided by others

    Encountering obstacles in pursuing fascinations

    Making adjustments mindful of one's intrigues

Attending to Instrumentality

As used herein, instrumentality refers to the practice of doing things as a means of pursuing particular interests, objectives, tasks, benefits, advantages, gains, conveniences, competencies or other ends that people deem appropriate in some way.[20]

Although people may invoke some instances of instrumentalism with respect to (a) specific suggestions or encouragement that people encounter from others (recruitment); (b) fascinations that people develop (seekership); and (c) the particular obligations that people experience (closure; discussed later), instrumentalism also includes (d) any other means-ends considerations to which people may attend as they contemplate particular lines of action.[21]

In addition to invoking an instrumentalist stance in pursuing a variety of externally oriented tasks or objectives (as with work, hobbies, driving, or helping others, for instance), people also may pursue situations that they think might enable them to achieve desired aspects of self (as in questing for imaged, expressive, affiliated, and proficient notions of self; see Prus, 1997:169–187).

Implying a purposive or minded means-end orientation, instrumentalism, thus, draws direct attention to the goals, objectives, or other concerns that people anticipate being able to achieve as a consequence of particular involvements. Denoting ways of pursuing interests, achieving objectives, or "doing better," instrumentally oriented involvements may be intended to directly enable participants to engage the situation at hand in more appropriate, effective, or desired manners, as well as to enhance people's abilities to do well in other theaters of operation.

From an instrumentalist perspective, people engage situations in order to achieve specific objectives or better accomplish things in some way. From this viewpoint, specific involvements represent enabling mechanisms of (more specific and more generalized) sorts.[22] At the same time, however, there is no assumption that people will act effectively or make viable inferences between interests, activities, and outcomes. Instead, the emphasis is on attending to the ways that people envision and invoke purposive behavior.

Instrumentalist involvements may vary considerably with respect to scope, duration, completion, consequences, and the like. Thus, a great many of the things people do may imply comparatively minor or temporary changes in people's practices, techniques, objects used, associates, locations, and the like. However, other involvements may denote more extensive or enduring changes in people's life-worlds.

As minded or self-reflective beings, people may monitor and reconsider their involvements even as they pursue particular lines of action. This enables them to terminate, postpone, continue, intensify, or otherwise adjust their practices. Relatedly, it should not be assumed that changes that appear inconsequential or highly consequential to outsiders would be envisioned in these terms by people engaging the situations at hand.

Although notions of instrumentality may suggest that analysts adopt an extended or centralizing "means-ends-alternatives" calculus, wherein people more or less continuously envision, weigh, approach, and adjust their involvements in ways that maximize their (externally oriented) outcomes, this approach is unwarranted. Our rejection of an external or objective motivational calculus does not deny people's concerns with rationality (i.e., activity as purposive). However, we observe that people may (a) work with *multiple senses* of rationality in a given setting (Schutz, 1964: 64–88; Garfinkel, 1967: 262–283; Prus, 1989b: 133–200) and (b) invoke widely varying notions of rationality amidst wide assortments of perspectives and objectives. Thus, rationality is not a singular or an objective state of affairs. Rather than a quality of an act or actor, rationality is something to be worked out in process terms. Rationality is achieved as people interpret situations, formulate lines of action, monitor and access their activities and the ensuing circumstances, and make subsequent adjustments.

Further, because people (c) are so dependent on others (to confirm the rationality, wisdom, or correctness of their choices and activities) in direct and more nebulous terms, rationality-in-practice denotes a distinctively sociological as opposed to a more singularly psychological or logical-deductive process. Although people may try to anticipate others, there is no guarantee that these others will acknowledge these viewpoints (and activities) as viable.

In very basic terms, rationality is much more multifaceted, situated, emergent, and negotiable than implied by any overarching calculus. Thus, rather than assume a rational-economic formulation of some sort that "drives" human behavior or presumes that people's activities are determined by generalized rational models or specific instances of calculation, rationality is to be studied as "something in the making."

This means acknowledging (1) the viewpoints that the participants adopt as they contemplate or otherwise engage the situations at hand; (2) the ways that people implement and adjust these viewpoints and procedures as they work their way through those instances; and (3) the ways that people attend to associates and significant others of various sorts within particular contexts.

Because people's initial involvements often entail sets of subactivities on the part of those engaging in some situation, themes of the following sort are especially relevant to instrumentalist-oriented involvements:

Acknowledging Specific Concerns, Interests, or Objectives
  Identifying particular concerns, interests, or objectives
  Deciding to pursue one or more of these matters
Considering Means and Options
  Defining possible lines of action
  Contemplating outcomes associated with specific activities
  Assessing comparative advantages and feasibilities of options
  Discussing options with others
  Dealing with reservations / Rejecting particular options
Engaging Situations at Preliminary Levels
  Initiating activities
  Seeking third-party assistance in implementing activities
  Assessing preliminary developments
  Making adjustments within situations
  Disengaging from situations
Anticipating Future Involvements
  Defining objectives
  Assessing experiences and present circumstances
  Formulating plans and making adjustments

Experiencing Closure

As used herein, the term "closure" signifies a version of an instrumental orientation, but one that is more pointedly intensified by matters of urgency, desperation, and limited choice.[23] Closure refers to instances in which people envision themselves to be "forced into" or having little choice about doing specific things because of pressing requirements or obligations.

In addition to (a) any activities that people may pursue only as last resorts for pursuing their personal intrigues, it is important to recognize (b) the limited options that people associate with the desires or requirements of others they may be attempting to satisfy or help, as well as (c) the restricted ranges of options that people may associate with the roles or duties of particular positions or offices to which they aspire or have assumed.

As reflective entities, people may assign variable senses of urgency or obligation to the specific circumstances in which they find themselves. However, others (as recruiting agents) also may contribute to people's heightened *and* lessened senses of obligation, urgency, or desperation.

When people associate greater urgency with particular objectives, they seem more apt to focus on "quick fixes" or short-term solutions than would likely be the case otherwise. Assuming stances such as "desperate times warrant desperate measures," or engaging in what they envision as "last resorts" (Emerson, 1981), people experiencing closure may opt for lines of activity that they find more costly over the long run.

Likewise, because some choices and commitments that people make preclude other options and effectively lock them into certain lines of action, it is important to appreciate that some choices denote "points of no return." For better or worse, people who have made certain commitments often are in for the duration of the event and whatever may happen along the way.

Although the wisdom of people's choices is best known "after the fact," the following themes focus on choices, obligations, and commitments as these pertain to people's preliminary involvements:

Attending to Pressing Requirements / Obligations

    Experiencing urgency regarding one's own interests

    Encountering encouragements from others

    Fulfilling obligations of position (or grouping)

Minimizing Obligations

    Recontextualizing situations on one's own

    Encountering neutralizations from others

Focusing on Specific Lines of Involvement

    Envisioning means-ends linkages

    Defining alternatives as unfeasible

    Dealing with reservations

Making Commitments to Particular Involvements

    Making more totalizing commitments

    Maintaining disengagement (exit) options

    Negotiating for release from commitments

Monitoring and Assessing Lines of Action

    Encountering points of no return

    Dealing with losses and successes

Managing Reservations

Although some aspects of people's reluctances or hesitations to act have been suggested in the preceding considerations of recruitment, fascinations, instrumentality, and closure, it is important to acknowledge people's reservations on a more explicit level.[24] While people's concerns with things such as physical well-being, economic implications, moral viewpoints, effects on others, and personal preferences and disenchantments may vary extensively, people's reservations are noteworthy because of their potentially inhibiting effects.

People's hesitations to pursue particular lines of action may reflect (a) any general cautions to which they may attend, (b) earlier related personal experiences, (c) concerns about the viewpoints and reactions of others, and (d) more situated deliberative processes.

In addition to invoking cautions that they may have learned from others or considering generalized stocks of knowledge with respect to the situation at hand, people also may draw linkages with past experiences pertaining to their own similar matters, applying these notions more specifically to the particular situations in which they find themselves.

Still, many reservations that people experience revolve around other people in somewhat more direct terms. Thus, beyond any direct communications from others, people may explicitly ask themselves about the ways that others (generally and specifically) might view these involvements and act toward people who do things of a certain sort.

In a related manner, prospective participants may ask themselves about the likelihood of "others finding out" about certain (e.g., potentially disreputable) involvements and whether they might be able to conceal or otherwise manage these situations without others learning of their involvements. Hence, even when dealing with situations more entirely on their own, people may invoke reference points of these sorts.

Further, as with the other features of involvements to which prospects may attend, it should not be supposed that people experience reservations on a singular or uniform plane. People sometimes attend to particular hesitations on a more sustained basis, but they also may consider reservations on a more fleeting or intermittent basis. Likewise, prospective participants may consider single risks or dilemmas in some instances, they may emphasize (or dispense with) multiple reservations in other cases.

Acknowledging (1) reservations of the preceding sort that people experience, we also consider (2) the ways that they minimize the relevancy of these hesitations for the situations at hand and (3) deal with various, potentially unsettling concerns as they engage specific situations in both the shorter and longer terms.[25] The list following addresses the ways that people deal with reservations more generally:

Experiencing Reservations
  Attending to general cautions or rules of thumb
  Reflecting on past experiences with related matters
  Envisioning potential problems
  Anticipating oppositionary viewpoints from others
  Encountering discouragements from others

Neutralizing Reservations

    Pursuing organizational objectives

    Focusing on the obligations of one's position

    Attending to encouragements from others

    Having confidence in others (especially leaders, partners)

    Envisioning other participants as successful

    Anticipating support from others

    Viewing self as invincible or immune to injury or loss

    Dismissing risks as inconsequential to self

    Taking precautions to minimize risks

    Invoking supernatural aids or protections

    Concentrating on self-fascinations

    Perceiving oneself as having nothing to lose

    Being distracted from reservations by other matters

Living With Reservations

    Hedging bets (strategizing to minimize risk)[26]

    Experiencing closure (urgency to act)

    Acknowledging and accepting points of no return

Acknowledging Inadvertency

In contrast to instrumentalist considerations of all sorts, wherein people knowingly contemplate and embark on lines of activity, inadvertent involvements refer to instances in which people find themselves unwittingly or accidentally involved in situations. Typically, this reflects events of which people were unaware or unable to control. This would include things such as natural disasters, accidents, illnesses, forgetfulness, misjudgments, and circumstances generated more exclusively by others, and unanticipated outcomes of all sorts.

In addition to various aspects of fortune and misfortune that befall people through no intent or failing of their own, one also may acknowledge events and outcomes that reflect people's efforts in some partially related manner, as well as fully intended activities that result in outcomes quite different from any anticipated by the participants. Because of the unwitting and comparatively unexpected nature of these eventualities, people typically learn of their participation in these matters only when the situation is defined as one in which they "are now involved." The emphasis, thus, shifts from people's considerations of involvement to the tasks of (a) making sense of and (b) adjusting to the comparatively new features of their current situations.

Still, because people routinely live with ambiguity, we may step back and ask if people (c) do specific things in order to alter (decrease or increase) the likelihood of experiencing certain "uncontrollables" or (d) anticipate and prepare themselves (in some ways) for certain kinds of outcomes even though they cannot foresee these in direct, experiential terms (e.g., consider particular occurrences, specific outcomes, and the actual timing of events).

As well, whether people are more prepared for the particular eventualities that come their way or find themselves more extensively taken by surprise, there is still the matter of people coming to terms with the very specific situations in which they now find themselves. Thus, the analyses of unwitting or unanticipated involvements is apt to be most instructive when researchers attend to (a) the participants' (subsequent) definitions of the direction and relevance of specific events and (b) the ways in which the participants engage those situations. The themes following suggest some lines of inquiry pertinent to people's encounters with inadvertent events:

Living with Ambiguity (and inadvertency)
    Attending to generalized uncertainties
    Contemplating uncertainties on one's own
    Discussing uncertainties with others
Acknowledging Situated Unpredictability
    Identifying specific risks in particular situations
    Minimizing (more predictable) risks and losses
Defining Inadvertent Events as More Consequential[27]
    Encountering personal limitations, obstacles, and losses
    Acknowledging definitions of inadequacy from others
    Attending to enhanced abilities and opportunities
    Receiving heightened recognition from others
Dealing with Unexpected Losses or Gains
    Making short-term adjustments
    Encountering assistance/Seeking help
    Acknowledging long-term experiences

CONTINUITIES, DISINVOLVEMENTS, AND REINVOLVEMENTS

Although the preceding statement on initial involvements covers a considerable range of people's routings into activities and life-worlds, it presents only a partial picture of people's participation in situations. Thus, we turn to the interrelated processes entailed in continuities, disinvolvements, and reinvolvements.

Sustaining and Intensifying Involvements

Insofar as they perceive advantages in remaining members in good standing, a practical concern for all participants becomes one of "fitting in" with the other people in the setting. The matter is further complicated because people not only enter groups with varying levels of interests and background experiences, but they also may do so with differing senses of purpose, expectations, and patience. As well, it is not uncommon for people to redefine their group experiences and their own senses of self in notably different terms as they deal with particular insiders and relate to an assortment of outside associates.

Although people's involvements in particular situations may vary greatly in duration and intensity, we still may ask when and how people are more likely to sustain, if not also intensify, their participation in particular subcultural life-worlds. Additionally, despite seemingly common tendencies to assume that people are either involved in something or not, it should be acknowledged that people may not only experience considerable vacillation in interest, activities, contacts, and commitments but also may engage particular group-life-worlds in a plurality of terms (as in perspectives, identities, emotionalities, and relationships).

Quite directly, those who intend more adequately to comprehend people's involvements in subcultural contexts, deviant and otherwise, would likely find it helpful to consider several dimensions of people's involvements in these settings (Prus, 1997:60–61). Particularly consequential in these regards are the matters of people (1) acquiring perspectives; (2) achieving identity; (3) accomplishing activities; (4) making commitments; (5) developing relationships; (6) acquiring linguistic fluency; (7) managing emotionality; and (8) participating in collective events.[28] The processes entailed within these aspects of subcultural life will be examined in more detail in chapters 7 and 8, but readers may appreciate the many dimensions that people's overall careers of participation assume in subcultural settings. Involvements, thus, are most centrally signified by people's activities, but much more is involved than the precise things that people do, especially in a physiological or behaviorist sense.

The matter of acquiring *perspectives* draws attention to the somewhat unique shared sets of meanings that people normally develop in the course of association with others in the group. In some cases, newcomers to the group already may have developed similar or somewhat compatible viewpoints through earlier associations with others. However, newcomers typically acquire fuller comprehensions of the orientational frameworks of the group at hand only through more intimate and sustained interaction with those peoples.

As with other objects to which people give meanings, members of the group also seek to make sense of one another as well as an assortment of outsiders. Because people's *identities* suggest and qualify ways of relating to others and oneself, the actual terms of reference and the specific definitions that people assign to existing members, newcomers, former associates, outsiders, and themselves become consequential both to the group generally and to individual members more specifically.

Since all groups are involved in *activities* of some sort, and people activities are central to any group's existence, the things that people actually do in subcultural arenas are important for people's continuities in those settings. Insofar as members consider the activities in which the group is engaged to be viable in meeting their interests, they seem much more likely to continue these involvements. Likewise, as members become more accomplished performers in these arenas, they are apt to encounter more encouragement to continue from others in the group.

Because group life not only depends on people doing things, but also implies a sense of dedication to matters pertaining to the group, people's *commitments* to the group (as in investments made, obligations to, loyalties toward, and concerns about) seem pivotal to their own continuities within. Relatedly, people also seem likely to continue to participate in situations when they see no viable options or alternatives to their present involvements. Thus, where people are unaware of or have neglected other options (as in knowledge, skills, and contacts), they may feel more compelled to remain in specific group settings.

The matter of people developing *relationships* or affiliational linkages with others in the group also appears central for their continuity in those settings. Because of their other intrigues, objectives, or commitments, people sometimes sustain group involvements even when they define themselves as having more extensive difficulties with their associates. Nevertheless, where people experience closer affinities with others in the group, they seem more likely to remain in those settings even when they become more notably disenchanted with other aspects of the setting.

Although often taken for granted, the matter of developing *linguistic fluency* (as in terminology, apparent direction or precision of thought, interpretive abilities, and other adequacies of speech) represents another highly consequential dimension of group life. Somewhat relatedly, groups may vary extensively in the ways in which they express *emotionality*, as well as their tolerances for individual variations of expression within. Still, people who find their desired affective states and expressivities compatible with those of their associates seem more apt to continue their involvements with these others.

In addition to activities that people might do more generally as participants in particular subcultures, it is important to acknowledge people's *participation in collective events* (such as celebrations, assemblies, contests, and confrontations) because these shared focal points frequently represent matters of intense, often multifaceted relevance to the participants. Thus, people's participation in collective events is often interfused in consequential manners with their notions of viable perspectives, identities, relationships, emotional experiences, and so forth.

Becoming Disinvolved

Although the topic of disinvolvement is given extended attention in chapter 13, it is important to comment on disinvolvement or disengagement as a social process within the broader context of a career contingency model. Whereas continuity and disinvolvement are often envisioned as distinctive and possibly contradictory notions, a closer examination of people's careers in deviance (as well as other kinds of activity) indicates that the two processes are much more closely connected than is commonly supposed. Indeed, continuity and disinvolvement are best understood within the very same parameters of people's involvements in situations. Hence, if we return to the notions of perspectives, identities, activities, emotionalities, linguistic fluencies, commitments, relationships, and participation in collective events that were introduced with respect to continuities (and intensifications) of people's involvements in particular situations, we find that the very same matters are directly relevant for understanding the disinvolvement process.

There will be some occasions in which continuities and disinvolvements are more notably or more clearly distinct, but one often encounters considerable vacillation in people's thoughts and activities with respect to particular role involvements. As well, people's senses of continuity and detachment commonly vary along the several dimensions of subcultural involvements (e.g., perspectives, identities, activities, and relationships) discussed earlier.

Thus, just as people may find themselves more comfortable in particular subcultures in various ways, so also may participants find their present involvements inadequate or troublesome with regard to such things as appropriateness of group viewpoints and objectives, congruity of definitions of self and others, competence in central activities, assessments of the relationships that they have with others in the setting, and the nature of their participation in collective events. In these respects, it seems common for people to question the viability of one or other features of the subculture at hand as well as their own abilities to deal with certain aspects of that situation.

While recognizing that people's experiences with, and assessments of, the various components or dimensions of their role involvements are apt to vary considerably, it appears that the more extensively people organize their lives around particular sets of involvements (thereby fostering success within the group), the more difficult it will be for them to become disengaged from the setting. Indeed, the very things that enable people to achieve success as participants in a particular subculture (as in the acceptance of group perspectives, developing competence in group activities, and developing more viable relationships with other members, and the like) commonly make it more difficult for people to disentangle themselves from those social life-worlds even when they might very much desire to do so.

Still, people who have maintained earlier options or envision viable opportunities to pursue their interests in other settings appear much less likely to remain in particular settings when they run into difficulties in those areas. Likewise, other people (as insiders and/or outsiders) may actively encourage and/or discourage the participation of particular individuals in these and other settings.

Becoming Reinvolved

Although people's reinvolvements in situations may be considerably less common than their disinvolvements from those same arenas, reinvolvement is very much a part of the broader process of involvement. Like initial involvements, continuity, and disinvolvement, reinvolvement is best comprehended as a multidimensional process of human group life. Clearly, not everyone who becomes disinvolved from a particular realm of activity will reengage that forum at a later point in time. However, even when detachments are more distinct and people wish to avoid earlier types of situations, they may still be involved in those life-worlds in other ways.

Consequently, we become attentive to the *partial, often incomplete* nature of disinvolvement as it is humanly experienced. Hence, even when people are no longer able to participate in certain subcultural contexts, they may still maintain some sympathies of perspectives, share some former senses of group identity, retain memories of valued emotional experiences, and the like. As well, while some people very much intend to distance themselves from former life-world involvements, there still may be numerous occasions in which they desire to reengage aspects of those situations.

In some respects, it may be easier for people to reinvolve themselves in former situations than to begin new sets of involvements. Thus, for instance, former participants may feel comfortable with the viewpoints and practices of others in the setting. They also may have retained some skills in the specific activities of the group as well as maintained congenial relationships with others in the setting. Further, they may now define themselves or others as having changed in ways that would make reinvolvements more viable at these later points in time.

Nevertheless, as with their initial involvements and subsequent continuities, people's abilities to access and maintain associations with particular groups of others are also contingent on the willingness of these others to accept those who desire membership back into their midst. In this sense, as well, it becomes strikingly apparent that people's careers in subcultural life-worlds cannot be explained by reference to their individual qualities.

Whereas chapter 6 has addressed a series of processes central to people's participation in any realm of community life, the matters of initial involvements, continuities, disinvolvements, and reinvolvements receive further attention in subsequent chapters. Attending more directly to the multiple realms of involvement that subcultures entail (chapter 7) and the ways that people form, consolidate, and work within group-based associations (chapter 8), we begin to see how the careers of the various people who participate in particular subcultural ventures overlap with one another. By examining subcultural life-worlds as enacted theaters of operation, we develop a fuller appreciation of how these people's lives become entangled and interwoven with one another as they

engage the unfolding instances of the here and now in which they find themselves.

NOTES

1. For a more extended consideration of subcultural mosaics and career contingencies, see Prus (1997).

2. In some ways, too, the broader communities (e.g., cities, states, or nations) in
which smaller subcultures are embedded also may be seen as subcultures of sorts with
respect to those who approach these latter units on an overarching basis (i.e., as cities
within provinces or states; as states within nations; or as nations within international
reference points).

3. Whereas many ethnographies address aspects of insider-outsider relationships
and other matters of group life, the following ethnographies more directly portray the
interlinkages of a multiplicity of subcultures within communities: Anderson's (1923)
The Hobo; Cressey's (1932) *The Taxi-Dance Hall*; Wiseman's (1970) *Stations of the
Lost*; Lesieur's (1977) *The Chase*; Prus and Irini's (1980) *Hookers, Rounders, and Desk
Clerks*; Prus's (1989b) *Pursuing Customers*; and Wolf's (1991) *The Rebels*. For an extended consideration of subcultures, the variants that develop therein, and the ways in
which the concept of subcultures (or subcultural life-worlds) lends itself to sustained
research across the broader parameters of the human community, see Prus (1997).

4. Consider the subcultures that develop around activities such as medical school
training (Becker et al., 1961; Haas and Shaffir, 1987), racetrack (Scott, 1968; Lesieur,
1977) and card (Hayano, 1982) gambling, mountain climbing (Mitchell, 1983), magic
(Prus and Sharper, 1991), shuffleboarding (Snyder, 1994), ballet (Dietz, 1994), musical
performances (Becker, 1963; Faulkner, 1971; MacLeod, 1993), politics (Grills, 1994),
television soaps (Harrington and Bielby, 1995), restaurant cooking (Fine, 1996), and
high school debates (Fine, 2001).

5. Readers interested in ethnographic depictions of deviance that illustrate the career
contingencies concept are apt to find the following studies particularly valuable: Shaw's
(1930) study of street delinquents; Cressey's (1932) examination of the taxi-dance hall
world; Sutherland's (1937) account of professional thieves; Becker's (1963) consideration of jazz musicians and drug users; Lofland's (1966) and Van Zandt's (1991) studies
of religious cults; Bartell's (1971) depiction of sexual swingers; Lesieur's (1977) statement on gambling; Prus and Sharper's (1977) account of card and dice hustlers; Prus
and Irini's (1980) study of a hotel community; Sanders's (1989) examination of the
tattoo subculture; Wolf's (1991) account of outlaw biker gangs; Harrington and Bielby's
(1995) consideration of television soap fans, Karp's (1996) study of depression, Ekins's
(1997) research on transgendering, and Jacobs's (1999) study of drug dealers.

6. This material represents a much needed elaboration of the "initial involvement
process" that is notably underdeveloped in other statements I had prepared on career
contingencies (see Prus, 1996b, 1997)—RP.

7. For ethnographies that focus more directly on the recruitment process, see: Lofland's (1966), Prus's (1976), Van Zandt's (1991), and Jorgensen's (1992) examinations
of religious recruitment; Prus and Sharper's (1977), and Prus and Irini's (1980) considerations of hustlers and thieves; Wiseman's (1970) account of skid row control agencies;
Rock's (1973), Prus's (1989a, 1989b), Prus and Frisby's (1990), Sanders's (1989), and

Prus and Fleras's (1996) portrayals of marketplace activity; Dietz and Cooper's (1994) study of college athletic recruiters; Wolf's (1991) depiction of outlaw bikers; Karsh et al.'s (1953) study of union organizing tactics; Grills' (1994) examination of a political party; Bartell's (1971) research on mate-swapping; Wolf's (1994) portrayal of feminist involvements; and Prus and Irini's (1980), Stebbins's (1990), Prus and Sharper's (1991), and MacLeod's (1993) studies of entertainers. The recruitment process also is evident in studies of drug users and drug dealers (Brown, 1931; Becker, 1963; Adler, 1985; Biernacki, 1988; Faupel, 1991; and Jacobs, 1999) and homosexual life-worlds (Reiss, 1961; Warren, 1974; Humphreys, 1975; Ponse, 1978; Newton, 1979; Correll, 1995).

8. In addition to pitching to (a) targets' own interests and aversions, tacticians also may appeal to target concerns about (b) the well-being of others (as in family members, friends, organizations, or matters pertaining to the community at large) and (c) inflicting loss or injury on particular parties with whom targets are disenchanted.

9. For some ethnographic materials that consider third party involvements in the recruitment process, see studies of thieves and hustlers (Sutherland, 1937; Prus and Sharper, 1977; Prus and Irini, 1980), salespeople (Prus, 1989a, 1989b; Prus and Frisby, 1990; Prus and Fleras, 1996), and "blue-chip" athletes (Dietz and Cooper, 1994).

10. A more extended theoretical consideration of the processes, practices, and problematics of influence work (and resistance) is available in Prus (1999).

11. Clearly, third parties can interfere with (resist, obstruct) the recruitment process as well as adopt standpoints and practices favorable to agent agendas.

12. It should be appreciated that people need not define themselves as targets. Likewise, people unknowingly may be targets of other people's endeavors. Still, one does not become a target in a more comprehensive sense until one adopts the viewpoint of a target; i.e., envisions onself as the intended recipient of some treatment on the part of some agent.

13. Ethnographic considerations of target roles (and experiences) can be found in studies of consumers (Blumer, 1933; Blumer and Hauser, 1933; Sanders, 1989; Prus, 1994; Harrington and Bielby, 1995; Holyfield, 1999; Jonas, 1999), "blue-chip" athletes (Dietz and Cooper, 1994), people using drugs (Brown, 1931; Ray, 1961; Becker, 1963; Ingraham, 1984; Biernacki, 1988; Faupel, 1991) and consuming alcohol (Rubington, 1968; Spradley, 1970; Prus, 1983; Ingraham, 1984), depictions of religious seekers (Lofland, 1966; Van Zandt, 1991; Shaffir, 1993, 1995), and those experiencing "treatment programs" (Brown, 1931; Ray, 1961; Roth, 1962; Davis, 1963; Wiseman, 1970; Schneider and Conrad, 1983; Charmaz, 1991; Anspach, 1993; Horowitz, 1995; Karp, 1996).

Prus (1999) provides a more extended theoretical consideration of the ways that people may experience (and engage) an assortment of "target roles."

14. Notably, too, people may adopt target roles by inferring or assuming certain activities or intentions on the part of agents, even if these are not actualized or so intended by these others. Practices and tendencies of these sorts seem somewhat commonplace in casual contexts, wherein people sometimes invoke fears and anxieties or simply misread the intentions of their associates. As well, viewpoints of this type may be explicitly encouraged by third parties who try to generate distrust and animosity between others. Exchanges of these latter sorts might take place between individuals and some third person or between groups or sectors of the community and reflect the polarizing initiatives of agitators of parallel sorts.

In discussing paranoia as a social process, Lemert (1962) provides a particularly instructive account of the ways in which mistrust, animosity, and exclusion may become more enduring features of particular relationships that people have with others.

15. The reference here is to group-based resistances of sorts, wherein two or more targets band together in some way or involve others as allies, supporters, spokespeople, and the like.

16. Although intrigues presume a positive evaluation of something about the situation under consideration, it should be appreciated that people need not be particularly or consistently pleased with themselves for having developed these interests. Indeed, some may view these as notable drawbacks. See, for instance, research on people involved in the drug subculture (Brown, 1931; Ray, 1961; Biernacki, 1988; Faupel, 1991; Jacobs, 1999), heavy drinking (Spradley, 1970; Wiseman, 1970), transgendering (Kando, 1973; Ekins, 1997), and heavy gambling (Lesieur, 1977).

17. For some ethnographic materials that focus more directly on the ways that people develop and pursue fascinations in both more solitary and collective ways, see Lofland's (1966) and Van Zandt's (1991) depictions of religious seekers; Scott's (1968), Lesieur's (1977), and Hayano's (1982) considerations of gamblers; Bartell's (1971) research on mate-swapping; Kando's (1973) and Ekins's (1997) studies of transgendering; Sanders's (1989) work on tattoos; Prus and Sharper's (1991) statement on magic; Prus and Dawson's (1991) inquiry into people's shopping practices; Roebuck and Frese's (1976), Prus and Irini's (1980), and Prus's (1983) materials on bar life; Wolf's (1991) consideration of outlaw bikers; Mitchell's (1983) examination of mountain climbing; Blumer's (1933), Blumer and Hauser's (1933), and Harrington and Bielby's (1995) studies of movie and television soap opera fans; Becker's (1963, 1967), Ingraham's (1984), and Faupel's (1991) depictions of drug users; and Reiss's (1961), Warren's (1974), Humphreys' (1975), Ponse's (1978), Newton's (1979), McNamara's (1994), and Correll's (1995) accounts of people's involvements in various homosexually focused arenas.

18. People's experiences with emotionality are given further consideration in chapters 8 and 9.

19. Seemingly, a similar set of processes would be relevant to the matters of developing disenchantments with certain things and engaging these disaffections. Those interested in either fascinations or disenchantments would benefit greatly by examining these affective tendencies and their associated behaviors in conjunction with one another.

20. We would be remiss were we not to acknowledge a conceptual indebtedness to Aristotle (especially *Nicomachean Ethics* and *Rhetoric*) in developing this material on instrumentalism more directly and the present discussion of initial involvements more generally.

21. While virtually all ethnographies presume purposive behavior on the part of those being studied, those that focus more directly on the production of activity best illustrate an instrumentalist emphasis. See, for instance, studies of drug use and drinking (Becker, 1963; Rubington, 1968; Spradley, 1970; Prus, 1983; Ingraham, 1984; Faupel, 1991; Kotarba and Rasmussen, 1996), religious recruitment (Lofland, 1966; Prus, 1976; Van Zandt, 1991; Jorgensen, 1992), hustlers and thieves (Sutherland, 1937; Maurer, 1955; Prus and Sharper, 1977; Prus and Irini, 1980; Steffensmeier, 1986), drug dealing (Adler, 1985; Jacobs, 1999), the marketplace (Prus, 1989a, 1989b; Sanders, 1989; Prus and Frisby, 1990), police work (Bittner, 1967; Rubinstein, 1973; Sanders, 1977; Charles, 1986; Meehan, 1992), factory workers involved in deviance (Bensmen and Gerver, 1963), gamblers (Scott, 1968; Lesieur, 1977; Hayano, 1982), musicians (Becker, 1963; Faulkner, 1971; MacLeod, 1993), students (Albas and Albas, 1984; Haas and Shaffir, 1987), outlaw bikers

(Wolf, 1991), high school debaters (Fine, 2001), mate-swapping (Bartell, 1971), and transgendering (Kando, 1973; Ekins, 1997).

22. Because money (Aristotle, *Nicomachean Ethics*, 1133a–1134a, 1257a–1258a; Simmel, 1907) allows people to obtain an exceedingly wide variety of goods and services, the matter of "making money" may be seen to epitomize the generalized (enabling, tool-like) instrumentality of people's involvements as broadly as any other. Accordingly, people commonly involve themselves in particular situations in order to obtain a medium that allows them to pursue a wide range of other interests. Still, money represents only one (instrumental) device and people may become involved in specific situations in the pursuit of wide ranges of other interests (e.g., convenience, prestige, mobility, espionage, salvation, productivity, entertainment).

23. The term *closure* was introduced to the sociological literature by Edwin Lemert (1953) in his discussion of naive check forgers. These are people who, in the face of pressing financial problems, knowingly write unredeemable checks, but make no particular effort to conceal their identities or places of residence. For some ethnographic materials that address people's experiences with pressing obligations or other senses of unavoidable urgency, see Cressey's (1953) study of embezzlement, Lesieur's (1977) work on racetrack gamblers, Prus and Irini's (1980) study of the hotel community, Albas and Albas's (1984, 1993, 1994) considerations of university students engaging exams, Kando's (1973) and Ekins's (1997) research on transgendering activity, Anspach's (1993) examination of life-choices in intensive care nurseries, and Karp's (1996) depiction of people experiencing depression.

24. Some insightful materials on the ways that people deal with reservations can be found in ethnographic studies of drug users and jazz musicians (Becker, 1963), factory workers engaging in deviance (Bensmen and Gerver, 1963), deep-sea divers (Hunt, 1995), people in religious cults (Lofland, 1966; Van Zandt, 1991), hustlers and thieves (Prus and Sharper, 1977; Adler, 1985; Jacobs, 1999), bar life (Roebuck and Frese, 1976; Prus and Irini, 1980), gamblers (Lesieur, 1977), multiracial couples (Rosenblatt et al., 1995), divorce (Waller, 1930; Vaughan, 1986), mate-swapping (Bartell, 1971), and transgendering (Kando, 1973; Ekins, 1997).

25. Even when people recognize the possibility of certain kinds of risks or losses, they often minimize these by relegating these to lower order probabilities. Thus, with respect to legalistic concerns, they may anticipate (in turn) avoiding detection, averting prosecution, escaping guilt judgements, and avoiding or receiving minimalist penalties. Similarly, people may knowingly enter situations involving higher levels or physical risk, but anticipate good fortune or only minor difficulties.

26. For some ethnographic materials on people dealing with reservations by "hedging their bets," see Lesieur (1977) and Prus (1989b) wherein racetrack gamblers and company buyers (retailers and manufacturers), respectively, invoke a variety of tactics intended to improve their chances of success.

27. Some of the most instructive literature on people's definitions of, and experiences with, inadvertent events can be found in ethnographic research on illness. See, for instance, Davis (1963), Roth (1962), Schneider and Conrad (1983), Sandstrom (1990), Charmaz (1991), and Anspach (1993). Smith and Belgrave's (1995) account of people's experiences with a hurricane is instructive here as well.

28. While addressing these processes in notably variable terms, several ethnographies provide considerable insight into continuities (and intensification) of people's involvements in disreputable life-worlds. These include studies of hobos (Anderson, 1923);

delinquents (Shaw, 1930); taxi-dance hall participants (Cressey, 1932); hookers, strippers, and bar staff (Roebuck and Frese, 1976; Prus and Irini, 1980); hustlers and thieves (Sutherland, 1937; Maurer, 1955; Letkemann, 1973; Ditton, 1977; Prus and Sharper, 1977; Prus and Irini, 1980; Adler, 1985; Steffensmeier, 1986; Shover, 1996; Jacobs, 1999); cults (Lofland, 1966; Van Zandt, 1991; Jorgensen, 1992); gamblers (Lesieur, 1977; Hayano, 1982), gangs (Thrasher, 1927; Keiser, 1969; Wolf, 1991); mate-swapping (Bartell, 1971); multiracial couples (Rosenblatt et al., 1995); homosexual life-worlds (Reiss, 1961; Warren, 1974; Humphreys, 1975; Ponse, 1978; Newton, 1979; Correll, 1995); and transgendering (Kando, 1973; Ekins, 1997).

7

Engaging Subcultures
Interactive Life-Worlds

People will often hang out at a bar. They'll just hang out there. You know 20 or 25 people are going to be regulars. Like, I've been hanging out at the Jubilee, for two and a half years . . . I'm a regular there. On my days off, I'm there all the time. During the days, if I've got time off, often by the time the bar opens, I'm there drinking with the boys. . . . The Jubilee's my bar. I live there. It's my hangout. And the regulars feel that way. The regulars are regulars, and nothing is going to stop them. Like, Wilson has been a regular there for 18 years. I've been a regular for two and a half years. No matter what happens, I'm going to be a regular there. I love the bar. (patron) (Prus and Irini, 1980:194–195)

While denoting groups of people who do things and interact with one another amidst a sense of some distinctiveness (via insider and/or outsider definitions) within the broader community, only some subcultures may be envisioned as having deviant motifs or qualities. Still, subcultures are essential for the understanding of deviance because it is in specific group settings that people work out a great many facets of their lives. It is here, in these associational contexts or arenas, in which people engage one another in more direct, immediate, and enacted terms, that things come together or are accomplished within the course of community life.

Indeed, if the students of the human condition are to move beyond vague references to "society" or the community at large, it will be necessary for them to attend to the smaller human groupings in which people develop activities mindfully of and through direct interchange with others. Likewise, if social scientists are to advance theory beyond references and speculations pertaining to factors, variables, contexts, and the like, it will be necessary for them to examine instances of group life in the making and to develop concepts that reflect the actualities of human interchange as this takes place.

Outsiders often are quick to define subcultures or other associational configurations around particular themes and typically envision these groupings in rather singular and unified manners. However, as Simmons (1969) observes, subcultures also are subject to considerable internal flux, ambiguity, inconsistency, and confrontation.

Likewise, while some may be inclined to dismiss subcultures as inconsequential, superficial, or simplistic occurrences, these associations are as authentic and pertinent to the participants as any other realms of human endeavor. Indeed, although people vary in the emphasis that they place on any set of relationships and activities, there is no meaningful life beyond the associations that we have with others. For scholars of deviance or any other realm of human behavior to disregard or trivialize associations of these sorts would be an error of the first degree. Moreover, whereas many subcultural associations are fleeting and may be comparatively undeveloped, it should be appreciated that other subcultural associations may be highly enduring and remarkably complex in constitution. Further, while outsiders may focus on particular (often troublesome or unusual) features of those groups or associations that they have designated as deviant in some way, typically this is at the cost of ignoring the much fuller range of activities that take place within all subcultural arenas.

Thus, regardless of whether people in particular subcultures operate in more formal or more casual manners or their associations are more or less enduring in essence, people's involvements in particular activities (deviant or otherwise) effectively can be understood only by examining the specific, interactionally accomplished life-worlds in which these people operate. Representing the focal points at which, and through which, group life "comes together" and "takes place," subcultures are best studied in process terms, as *formulative instances* of human interchange.

It is in this respect that we attend to the matters of people (1) *acquiring perspectives*, (2) *achieving identity*, (3) *doing activity*, (4) *making commitments*, (5) *managing relationships*, (6) *developing linguistic fluency*, (7) *experiencing emotionality*, and (8) *participating in collective events*.[1]

Because these processes pertain to the more particular groups or life-worlds in which people find themselves, each of these dimensions enables us to more fully appreciate the ways in which people experience subcultural involvements. Only by working with notions of these sorts are we able to move past vague notions of "conformity," "peer pressure," and the like to more directly examine the multidimensional, enacted essences of community life.

Still, while we will be discussing each of these subcultural processes in more focused terms, these processes are very much interconnected in ongoing group life. Indeed, it is virtually impossible to discuss any one of these features of human group life without referencing or presuming aspects of the others. However, each theme is not only somewhat unique but each also is highly enabling. For this reason, each of these processes merits extended attention on the part of social scientists.

ACQUIRING PERSPECTIVES

Although the perspectives or viewpoints that any group of people adopts on things are apt to be only partially distinct from the standpoints assumed by other groups in the broader community, the unique features of each group's perspectives serve to differentiate those groups from other groups in the broader community.

No less importantly, the perspectives (also worldviews, frames of reference, ideologies, or orientational frameworks) that particular groups develop provide interpretational standpoints for members of those groups, thereby enabling the people participating in those groups to make sense of the things that they encounter from the perspectives of those groups.

Relatedly, whenever people locate things within a particular group's framework, this suggests ways that participants might approach and engage those objects within their theaters of operation. Not only do the perspectives that people invoke include people's conceptions of *what is* (i.e., that which is acknowledged as existing in some way) and *what is not*, but also notions of how one might *act* toward and *assess* all things of relevance to the group at hand.

Since it is the people in specific settings who (a) establish [particular things] as focal points; (b) imbue recognized objects with certain kinds of meaning and relevance; and (c) define appropriate ways of acting toward things, it is essential that students of deviance attend to these meaning-making processes.

Thus, things (e.g., activities, appearances, thoughts, products) that may be considered deviant or reprehensible in one group may be defined as entirely acceptable or even highly desirable among those adopting different viewpoints on these things. As Blumer (1969) emphasizes, it is only through a process of communication and interpretation that the meanings of things are carried into, engaged, and modified within, interactional contexts.

Notably, too, the viewpoints that particular groups adopt on things are apt to undergo change, sometimes quickly and dramatically, as the particular people involved do things and adjust to the situations (and other people) that they encounter. People also objectify or imbue their own viewpoints with meanings that are considered special, unique, or more realistic in some way.

Newcomers, thus, are encouraged to learn about and accept prevailing group standpoints. Somewhat relatedly, existing members who fail to subscribe to these notions are often viewed with distrust and disaffection. As well, participants may be openly sanctioned or excluded for failing to respect things considered important to the group.

As indicated elsewhere (Prus 1996b: 151–152), the matter of acquiring perspectives is best viewed in processually enacted and experienced terms. Thus, newcomers, as well as current members of groups, typically: (1) encounter definitions of reality from existing members; (2) find themselves assessing group perspectives relative to other viewpoints; (3) develop images of objects pertinent to group perspectives; (4) learn group-related ways of dealing with objects; and (5) define the situations that they encounter in ways that are mindful of these notions.

However, subcultural participants often find that group notions of things are inadequate in some way, contradict one another, or are subject to challenge by others. Thus, those examining the ways in which people acquire group perspectives should also attend to the ways that participants: (6) experience ambiguity in the particular instances of situations that they encounter; (7) attempt to resolve contradictions and dilemmas relative to group perspectives; (8) extend and otherwise revise existing group viewpoints; (9) promote and defend group viewpoints to others; (10) reject or become more distant from formerly held perspectives; and (11) attend to and deal with current and emergent group viewpoints.[2]

ACHIEVING IDENTITY

Although we have dealt with identities at some length in chapter 5 (labeling deviants), it should be appreciated that the matter of assigning identities (as in labels, definitions, and reputations) is highly consequential to all realms of group life. Thus, we reengage the topic of identity within a somewhat broader context.

Since people act toward objects in terms of the meanings that they have for those things, the ways that people define themselves and others are highly consequential for all manners of human association. Like other objects of their awareness, people attach names and meanings both to other people and to themselves. As with other objects, the names and associated meanings that people attach to others and to themselves also suggest ways that people might act toward these essences.

Although people's identities can only be understood within the perspectives of the groups that constitute the reference points that people invoke in making sense of the particular individuals or groups under consideration, it also should be recognized that people's identities, like other objects of people's awareness, commonly undergo transformation in meaning. This occurs as people test out their ideas about things (including people) in the course of performing activities and/or learn about things (and people) by watching and listening to others. Thus, it is not at all unusual to find that people revise their own understandings of people and other things, as well as promote certain meanings and names of specific people and other things to others in the community. Likewise, people not only may assess, but also resist and contest the names and meanings assigned to people and other objects by others.

However, in addition to acknowledging the roles that people may assume in drawing attention to, and shaping definitions of, particular objects for one another, it is essential that analysts also attend to people's capacities as "objects unto themselves" (Mead, 1934). It is this ability to envision oneself from the standpoint of the other that allows people to *present* themselves and others in more desired fashions (Goffman, 1959; Klapp, 1964) as well as *resist* definitions of self and others that they consider inappropriate in some way (Goffman, 1963; Prus, 1975b).

Since each group or subculture to which people are exposed offers members somewhat particularized frameworks for interpreting themselves and others, each new group that people encounter is apt to suggest variations, if not more extensive shifts, in the definitions that people might assign to themselves and others. Quite directly, then, earlier definitions of self and other may be adjusted, ignored, or pointedly rejected as people move from one group to another, even within the same community. Like the formulation of group perspectives, the development, assignment, and application of people's identities are best seen in processual, enacted terms.

The process of achieving identity, thus, involves finding a place for self and other within the various contexts in which people engage one another in specific life-worlds (and the activities within). Although they may vary greatly in the direction, clarity, intensity, and consistency of the references they make to one another, people typically assist one another in defining persons of mutual awareness. Still, two or more people in any group may have very different ideas of the ways in which particular people should be seen. And, definitions of particular targets that some people in a setting envision as desirable or appropriate may be viewed as highly threatening, offensive, or otherwise troubling by others.[3]

The following processes (from Prus 1996b: 152–153) are particularly consequential for examining identity work or the ways that people develop definitions of self and definitions of others. When people *attend to themselves as objects of definition,* themes of the following sort are apt to be invoked: (1) encountering definitions of self from others in the setting; (2) assigning definitions received from others to oneself; (3) assessing incoming and earlier definitions of self for comparative viability; (4) contesting undesired definitions; and (5) selectively conveying or presenting information about self to others.

When people *develop definitions of others,* matters of the following type become more consequential: (1) obtaining information about others; (2) privately assigning or attributing identities to others; (3) more openly or publicly designating others as specific kinds of people; (4) encountering resistance of designations assigned to targets from others; and (5) reassessing and possibly readjusting identities imputed to others.[4]

DOING ACTIVITY

Although all of the processes considered in reference to subcultures in this chapter (as in acquiring perspectives, achieving identities, developing linguistic fluency, and so forth) presume some activity, enterprise, or deliberative behavior on the part of the people involved in the setting, we may focus somewhat more directly on two kinds of activity: (a) instrumentalist or task endeavors and (b) persuasive interchange or influence work.

These two sets of activities may be largely synonymous in some occasions, especially since all instances of influence work are instrumentalist in emphasis.

Still, the matter of the "getting something done" often is notably different from that of "persuading others to do things." Thus, whereas people may pursue particular objectives alone and/or in conjunction with others, and many of the same processes may be involved, the matter of influencing others adds another highly consequential dimension to the study of activity as something in the making. Thus, influence work will be given some additional attention as an instrumentalist process unto itself.

Because people do things in *instrumental* terms, in order that they might accomplish other things or attain certain objectives, it is important to consider the ways in which members of particular subcultures pursue activities that they consider relevant to the situations they encounter.

While it is not assumed that people will act wisely or responsibly on either their own terms or from the viewpoints of any others who may assess their goals and practices, it is essential that social scientists focus on the things that people do as minded (i.e., as knowing, intentioned, deliberative) agents. Accordingly, the emphasis is on developing an analytical scheme that would allow researchers to examine exactly what people do in this and that set of instances and how they proceed from there.

Examining instances of activity in process terms,[5] we may consider the ways and extent to which people in one or other subcultural arenas attend to the matters (as suggested in Prus, 1996b: 157) of: (1) developing preliminary plans of action; (2) getting prepared for particular lines of action; (3) dealing with fears and reservations, if any; (4) pursuing competencies, resources, and viable applications; (5) implementing activity in specific instances; and (6) monitoring and adjusting one's behaviors in the process of developing particular lines of action.

Also noteworthy in these regards are the activity-related processes signified by (7) coordinating events with others when this is desired or otherwise thought appropriate; (8) dealing with ambiguity, obstacles, and resistance of various sorts; (9) displaying competence, as in ability and composure; (10) dealing with competition or opposition that may be encountered; and (11) making ongoing assessments and adjustments to one's activities as situations or events unfold.

Because many instances of activity require the cooperation or deliberative participation of others, it is important that the researchers attending to people's experiences in subcultures be mindful of the ways in which people engage others in *persuasive interchange*. While not providing a sustained consideration of influence work in the present statement,[6] we can highlight some processes that are central to influence work from the point of view of the tacticians involved.

Although people may engage the role of tacticians in a great many ways, the following themes (see Prus, 1996b: 158) represent common features of strategic interchange: (1) formulating preliminary plans for engaging the other; (2) attending to the role or perspective of the other; (3) promoting interests in one's objectives on the part of the other; (4) encouraging or generating trust on the part of the other; (5) proposing specific lines of activity for the other to pursue; (6) encountering resistance from the target or others; (7) neutralizing or minimizing obstacles and resistances; (8) considering, offering, and acknowledging concessions; (9) confirming agreements between oneself and the other; and (10) monitoring self and others, assessing outcomes, attending to failures, and recasting plans.[7]

MAKING COMMITMENTS

Whereas the major objective of influence work is that of obtaining cooperation and related commitments from others, it is important to consider the ways in which people (both as targets of influence work on the part of others and willing initiators on their own) make commitments or otherwise obligate themselves to the group or subculture at hand.

In some cases, the commitments or obligations that people make to the group at hand may be dramatic, if not also substantial. In other instances, the commitments involved may be seen as minimal or inconsequential to the people involved. Likewise, although some commitments may be more enduring, possibly entailing extensive as well as long-term involvements, others may be fleeting or highly situated.

Rather notably, though, whenever subcultures survive for longer periods of time, subcultures normally achieve some longevity because certain people have made fairly substantial commitments to the group. Clearly, members of groups may vary greatly in the extent to which they are willing to dedicate themselves to the subculture at hand. However, people can and do organize their lives around particular subcultures at times and it is important to acknowledge the subactivities associated with the commitment-making process.

Drawing on an earlier statement (Prus, 1996b: 158), several subprocesses are deemed central for understanding people's commitments in subcultural settings. These are: (1) considering and assessing one's alternatives within and across settings; (2) attending to and dealing with earlier commitments one may have made; (3) avoiding undesired commitments; (4) minimizing risks or diversifying investments in the situation at hand; (5) more fully organizing routines around subcultural activities; and (6) disregarding outside options (thereby experiencing closure within by default).

Still, other features of the commitment-making process appear pertinent for comprehending people's involvements in subcultural arenas. These include the matters of (7) making irretractable or irretrievable investments, wherein the things under consideration may not be withdrawn by the member making the commitment; (8) making more enduring commitments, wherein people are obligated to the group over longer, possibly lifelong terms; and (9) attending to obligations that others (as in teammates, managers, accomplices, allies, and the like) have made or presumed on one's behalf; and (10) dealing with limitations and other restrictions imposed on individuals or groups by other people.

Although people may make a great many commitments in more knowing terms, it also should be recognized that (11) any obligations that people assume with respect to some particular group or subculture may take the participants in directions that may be quite different from any that they had earlier anticipated. Because of their commitments (and the related bonds or relationships that these people develop with others), participants may find themselves engaged in situations and activities that are far removed from things they would have intended. Indeed, people's continuity as members in good standing may require that the participants forgo wide ranges of self-interest as a consequence of the commitments they earlier had made to the group, even as the group itself undergoes change in composition and/or emphases.[8]

MANAGING RELATIONSHIPS

Because human group life is constituted only as people come together and associate with others, the practices of developing, managing, severing, and renewing relationships represent fundamental features of human community life.

Although people often take other people's affiliations and bonds for granted or envision these in more singular and undifferentiated terms, the people actually involved in particular groups or subcultures are apt to be attentive to the problematic, uneven, and changing nature of their own relationships with others as well as disruptions and transitions in the relationships involving other members of the same group.

As with other instrumentalist and persuasive activities in which they engage, people also may be seen to approach and relate to specific sets of others in meaningful, reflective, deliberative terms. Similarly, they may be seen to adjust their own behaviors relative to their associates as well as assess the activities of others with respect to their own interests.

Like people's activities more generally, there is no presumption that people will act wisely with respect to the relationships that they develop with others or that they will enter relationships in ways that effectively maximize longer-term, desirable end-states of some particular sort. Although not precluding possibilities of these types, the emphasis, more generically, is on the ways in which people engage specific sets of others over the course of association with these people. Of particular consequence, thus, is the matter of what particular people represent to one another over time and how they deal with one another within the particular interactional theaters in which they find themselves.

Approaching relationships in process terms, one may delineate a series of subprocesses that appear pivotal to understanding the ways in which people in subcultural groupings of all sorts develop relationships with others in those settings. On a broader basis, it appears instructive to acknowledge three features of the relationship process: anticipating encounters with others; attending to particular relationships; and dealing with distractions and disaffections. Incorporating these notions with some earlier material from Prus (1996b: 159), we may begin to envision the relationship process in terms of the following sort.

Anticipating encounters with others would include such things as (1) getting prepared for encounters with people more generally; (2) envisioning oneself as available for association with others; (3) defining particular others as potentially desirable associates; (4) approaching potential associates and/or receiving indications of receptivity from others; (5) encountering and indicating acceptance and resistance with respect to other associates; and (6) assessing self and others as viable associates for desired relationships.

As people begin *attending to particular relationships*, we may expect that their associations would assume a somewhat more distinctive cast, reflecting processes of the following sort: (1) developing styles of interaction unique to each situation; (2) managing openness and secrecy in associations with the other; (3) developing shared understandings, joint preferences, and loyalties to the association at hand; and (4) intensifying closeness (as through expressing affection, developing dependencies on others, fostering reliance of self by others, embarking on cooperative ventures, and collectively dealing with threats and opposition).

Following the overall relationship along, it also is instructive to ask about the ways that people *deal with distractions and disaffections*. This means examining: (1) the kinds of things that participants define as problematic or that emerge as points of contention among the participants; (2) the ways that people attempt to deal with these troublesome situations; (3) when and how these episodes continue, intensify, dissipate, and possibly become renewed and extended among members of the group; (4) when and how other people (other insiders or outsiders) become involved in these interchanges, and what sorts of directions the ensuing interchanges may take; and (5) how these interchanges are worked out with respect to any longer term relationships between the members of the particular group under consideration.[9]

Still other aspects of people's relationships are evident in the following discussions of developing communicative fluency and experiencing emotionality.

DEVELOPING LINGUISTIC FLUENCY

Because human activity encompasses speech or language as well as other enacted features of the local human condition, activity may be seen to transcend the human animal more completely than does language on its own. Still, because it is language that enables people to communicate or share meanings with one another (i.e., achieve intersubjectivity with the other), it is the capacity for sustained symbolic interchange that most uniquely defines the human community and most centrally enables individual members of the human community to invoke agency in meaningful terms; to act in deliberative manners or to do things with particular senses of purpose.

Nevertheless, and possibly because language is so basic to the human condition, the relevance of language for explaining human group life generally and for examining subcultural life-worlds more specifically, largely has been ignored by social scientists in the quest to find the structures, factors, or variables that they have deemed to be responsible for certain human states (i.e., behaviors, outcomes, conditions). Thus, although ethnographers are very much aware of the fundamental human dependence on speech for people's survival, activities, and moral orders, the centrality of speech as *an enabling device* has yet to be adequately appreciated with respect to research and analysis of human life-worlds.

As a set of symbols that allows people to achieve intersubjectivity or establish a sharedness or mutuality of meanings with a set of others, it is language that most fundamentally enables people to attain a more unified or centralized community-wide culture. Somewhat ironically however, it is the same human capacity for speech that allows people to develop and sustain subcultures that may become highly diverse in their emphases.

Thus, the very features of community life that enable people to come together and associate with one another in meaningful terms also provide the very basis on which people may develop life-worlds that become increasingly distant from, and incomprehensible to, people who earlier had shared a broader linguistic affinity with those embarked on particular subcultural ventures.

Interestingly, because people are differentially involved in the comprehension, use, and promotion of, particular linguistic expressions, even within the same "society," language represents a "subcultural realm of involvement" in its own right. Virtually everyone becomes involved in perpetuating, employing, and resisting variants of a still emergent linguistic base.

Like other subcultural instances, thus, we can ask about (1) people's careers as users of, or participants in, particular realms of language, speech, or symbolic interchange; (2) the particular terms, concepts, and expressions that people invoke in this or that subcultural arena; and (3) people's perspectives on that language, as well as the ways in which their identities, activities, relationships, and senses of emotionality are interwoven into the use of that language.

Although it is only with the possession of an earlier (intersubjectively accomplished) language of some sort that one may engage other people and other things in meaningful fashions, each set of activities in which people participate represents another realm around which extensions or variants of that linguistic base subsequently may be developed. Thus, researchers may expect to find that each group or subculture of some duration will develop a language that is somewhat unique unto itself. This is clearly evident in studies of hobos (Anderson, 1923), hustlers and thieves (Sutherland, 1937; Maurer, 1955; Shover, 1996; Jacobs, 1999), gamblers (Scott, 1968; Lesieur, 1977), musicians (Becker, 1963, 1967; MacLeod, 1993), drug users (Brown, 1931; Becker, 1963; Biernacki,

1988; Faupel, 1991), biker gangs (Wolf, 1991), police dispatchers (Manning, 1988), mountain climbers (Mitchell, 1983), mate-swappers (Bartell, 1971), comedians (Stebbins, 1990), shuffleboarders (Snyder, 1994), religious cults (Lofland, 1966; Van Zandt, 1991; Jorgensen, 1992), high school debaters (Fine, 2001), depression (Karp, 1996), and transgendering (Kando, 1973; Ekins, 1997).

Relatedly, as well, it is through extensions of linguistic expressions that people generate in more specific settings that the language of the broader community typically becomes diversified, expanded, and readjusted. As in the development of a shared language more generally, this presumes some ongoing, if only sporadic, association between members of particular subcultural life-worlds and the others in the community.

Whereas a great many communications are apt to be taken for granted by the participants in any life-world, there will be times that communications take on heightened relevancies with respect to the continuity and effectiveness (as in being able to coordinate activities) of the subculture as well as fostering the interests and understandings of the particular people involved in those communications. Conversely, people's failures to generate clear messages and/or adequately comprehend messages that others in the subculture generate may on some occasions have dire consequences for the group at large or certain members more specifically.

For reasons of these sorts, it is important that scholars give close attention, not only to (a) the chronological or sequential development of specific forms or expressions of language (how these variants are transmitted, consolidated, used, disregarded, and discontinued over time) within particular subcultural setting, but also to the ways in which people in subcultures (b) achieve shared meanings with one another in specific instances (as in generating, interpreting, and confirming messages); (c) invoke, deploy, and adjust linguistic communications relative to the particular sets of activities in which they engage; and (d) engage, sustain, and disengage from, particular communication technologies (devices and procedures) within their life-world settings.

EXPERIENCING EMOTIONALITY

Denoting affective dispositions or self-feelings (involving bodily states and related sensations) that people attribute to themselves and others,[10] one finds considerable variation across communities more generally and subcultures more specifically regarding the ways in which people manage and express their emotions as participants in those life-worlds.

Because people (a) have capacities for exceptionally wide ranges of emotional experience (as in love and animosity, generosity and greed, calm and anger, sadness and joy, fear and courage, and pride and shame), (b) often attach considerable significance to particular emotional states, and (c) act toward others and themselves in emotionally meaningful terms, it is essential that scholarly examinations of people's experiences in subcultures not overlook this aspect of human association.

As well, although emotionality is often envisioned as an individualistic or psychological phenomenon, it may be appreciated that people's experiences with emotionality, like other realms of human endeavor, become meaningful in a broader sense only when people achieve (linguistically enabled) intersubjectivity with others in the community. Further, consideration should be given to the ways that others intensify, neutralize, and redirect people's experiences with emotionality, as well as instruct people on aspects of emotionality.

Indeed, whereas some subcultures may discourage overt expressions of emotionality, and others may strive for moderation in such matters, still other subcultural groupings (and the participants within) may place great emphasis on specific forms of emotional expression. Further, although considerations of emotionality may have rather marginal consequences for the study of certain activities in which people engage (apart from matters of dedication, sincerity, composure, boredom, situated disaffection, and the like), some associations may be centered more extensively around the pursuit of intense, often overt, emotional experience and expression (as in celebrations, excitement, euphoria, anger, and violent protest).

As implied in this broader consideration of subcultural life, notions of experiencing emotionality not only (a) presume that people will acquire perspectives on what emotionality is and how people's affective experiences might be expressed, assessed, and controlled in particular group settings; but also reflect (b) people's identities, as in who is and who is not emotional in this and that way, and how people might deal with those who express emotionality in various manners; (c) people's activities (as in expressing emotionality in certain behavioral terms and in specific situations, or in encouraging others to adopt one or other emotional standpoints or expressivities); (d) commitments (as in anxiety and/or excitement about objectives, options, and long-term obligations); and (e) emergent relationships (as in people expressing affection, concern, or disenchantment with respect to particular others). No less fundamentally, emotionality is (f) a linguistically achieved essence.

Further, even though people may experience aspects of emotional expression in solitary (i.e., more private, reflective) manners, most of the instances of emotionality that people experience revolve around an attentiveness to others. These reflect (a) interchanges people have with others, (b) initiatives and reactions of others to self, (c) assessments of earlier events involving others, and (d) anticipations of subsequent encounters with others within certain contexts.

Whether people experience, invoke, engage, or attempt to shape instances of emotionality on their own or in conjunction with others, *each episode* represents something to be accomplished. Although people sometimes have very clear ideas of the emotional expressions that they intend to achieve, as well as notions of how this might be done, the dynamics of human interchange frequently introduce complexities that render earlier anticipations and preparations inappropriate. Thus, as the interactants say or do particular things along the way, and these are interpreted from one or other frameworks (also objec-tives and interests) that others may invoke, people's abilities to predict and manage emotionality in the "here and now" often become compromised in the course of ongoing interchange.

PARTICIPATING IN COLLECTIVE EVENTS

Acknowledging people's participation in assemblies, episodes, occasions, and other instances of focused association, collective events draw attention to more situated or immediate instances of mutuality or sharedness of human inter-change that may be overlooked when analysts limit themselves to the preceding features of subcultural life.

As readers may appreciate, any interchanges involving two or more people may be seen to constitute a collective event. Because so much human activity involves exchanges with others, only some instances of joint interchange are apt to be given further attention on the part of the participants. Thus, although collective events are best understood as instances of human interchange more generally, we will concentrate on those events that stand out to one or other participants as somehow special, dramatic, or recollectable for one or other reasons.

Attending to the ways that people engage or participate in collective events, we may acknowledge a wide range of grouping contexts or occasions such as festivals, concerts, assemblies, confrontational episodes, contests, honorific cere-monies, and responses to emergency situations on the part of two or more people.

Sometimes, the people assembled in these settings may be members of a single subcultural grouping, but the people involved in other episodes may be much more diverse (as in multiple, possibly competing groups, comparative strangers, and other assortments of participants). Likewise, collective events may be highly routinized, semi-structured, or highly emergent in develop-ment.

Collective events also may be quite fleeting in duration or last over extended periods of time, as well as take place on a more sporadic or intermittent basis. Similarly, people may participate in any specific event in a great many ways. This may range from those who assume roles as central, active, and enthusiastic promoters and participants in the event at hand to people who are only involved in highly reluctant or inescapable manners to people who are inadvertent wit-nesses of various sorts.

What is essential, though, is that the participants, regardless of their inter-ests, intentions, and involvements, have a common focus or point of reference; a jointly acknowledged set of experiences that tie people, in meaningful ref-erential terms, into a particular occasion or event. Clearly, those in the setting may experience any event in vastly different ways. Still, there is a sense of sharing (however unevenly and partial this may be in its development) this event with others in the setting.

Although collective events are important to students of community life in many respects, as in understanding the ways that people do things in political, military, religious, and entertainment arenas as well as in other fields of endeavor, collective events also are fundamental for understanding people's experiences in subcultures more generally.

Whereas members of subcultures often assemble together around task-related activities, they also commonly participate in collective events as modes of entertainment, celebration, and internal contests. As well, members may participate in wide ranges of collective encounters with outsiders. Events involving outsiders might include such things as forming alliances, targeting outsiders for specific kinds of treatment, being the targets of outsider treatment, and confronting outsiders in more direct terms.

Some collective events, such as those involving internal confrontations or leadership contests, may be comparatively disruptive for both the subculture and its members. However, other collective events, such as internal celebrations or confrontations with outsiders, may be used in attempts to generate extended levels of internal cohesion.

Building on Prus (1997: 131–136), we may ask about the various roles that people assume in the developmental flow of collective events. Indeed, if we are to develop a fuller appreciation of subcultural life-worlds, it will be necessary to consider the ways in which members of groups engage in collective events both within their own groupings and in conjunction with an assortment of outsider participants (as with allies, competitors, opponents, curious onlookers, and disinterested parties). Notably, a fuller appreciation of the activities involved in collective events would include: (1) becoming aware of, and involved in, collective events; (2) coordinating and sustaining collective events; (3) making sense of collective events; (4) becoming caught up in collective events; (5) assuming more central roles in collective events; (6) avoiding, and withdrawing participation from, collective events; (7) resisting collective events or components thereof; (8) concluding collective events; and (9) reviewing, reliving, redefining, and readjusting to collective events.[11]

Focusing on the ways that subcultures become constituted and the people in these settings engage one another as well as an assortment of outsiders, chapter 8 extends this consideration of people's participation in collective events.

NOTES

1. This chapter benefits extensively from an earlier statement on generic social processes (Prus, 1996b) and extended consideration of subcultural life-worlds (Prus, 1997).

2. While virtually all ethnographic studies provide some insight into particular and often multiple worldviews, as well as the ways that people acquire, maintain, protect, and promote particular viewpoints, some ethnographies are particularly effective in

depicting the processes just referenced. These include Anderson's (1923) study of hobos; Shaw's (1930) consideration of street delinquents; Blumer's (1933) and Blumer and Hauser's (1933) examinations of young people's encounters with the movies; Sutherland's (1937), Maurer's (1955), and Prus and Sharper's (1977) accounts of professional thieves; Lofland's (1966), Van Zandt's (1991), and Jorgensen's (1992) studies of religious cults; Spradley's (1970) and Wiseman's (1970) examinations of skid row drinkers and control agencies; Bartell's (1971) depiction of heterosexual swingers; Rosenblatt et al.'s (1995) account of multiracial couples; Reiss's (1961), Warren's (1974), Humphreys' (1975), Ponse's (1978), Newton's (1979), and Correll's (1995) depictions of homosexual life-worlds; Ekins's (1997) examination of transgendering; Lesieur's (1977) and Hayano's (1982) considerations of gamblers; Prus and Irini's (1980) research on a hotel community; Rubinstein's (1973), Sanders's (1977), Charles's (1986), and Meehan's (1986, 1992) studies of police work; Evans and Falk's (1986) and Evans's (1994) inquiry into the life-worlds of deaf children; Davis's (1961), Schneider and Conrad's (1983), Charmaz's (1991), and Anspach's (1993) portrayal of illnesses; Karp's (1996) work on depression; Mitchell's (1983) account of mountain climbing; Ingraham's (1984) consideration of enlisted military men; Wolf's (1991) study of outlaw bikers; Becker's (1963), Faulkner's (1971), and MacLeod's (1993) research on musicians; and Fine's (1983, 1987, 1996, and 2001) studies of role-playing games, little-league baseball, kitchen work, and high school debating, respectively.

3. Although those defining other groups as "deviant" commonly think of members of those groups as stigmatized by more conventional sources, it should be recognized that the members of discredited groups also may engage in somewhat parallel discreditation practices. Thus, whereas Becker's (1963) jazz musicians may be stigmatized by their families and others for not living more conventionalist lives, those jazz musicians who endeavor to be more conventionalist in their approaches to things are apt to be stigmatized by other jazz musicians. Somewhat similar observations may be made about outlaw bikers (Wolf, 1991) who have little respect for those bikers who are more conventional in other ways. Here, we start to see the complex issues of identity that emerge with respect to people's interactions with multiple audiences, each of which may assume roles as moral entrepreneurs (Becker, 1963) in defining (and proscribing) people's involvements in other settings.

4. Identity work is given more attention in chapter 5 of the present volume. Among the ethnographies that address identity in more direct terms are Anderson (1923), Davis (1961, 1963), Bartell (1971), Warren (1974), Prus and Sharper (1977, 1991), Ponse (1978), Prus and Irini (1980), Schneider and Conrad (1983), Charles (1986), Haas and Shaffir (1987), Sanders (1989), Sandstrom (1990), Blum (1991), Charmaz (1991), Wolf (1991), Anspach (1993), Harrington and Bielby (1995), Karp (1996), Ekins (1997), Paterniti (2000), and Fine (2001).

5. For a fuller appreciation of the pervasive relevance of activity to an ethnographic research agenda for the social sciences, see Prus (1997). Ethnographies that deal with activity in more explicit manners include studies of street people and service agencies (Anderson, 1923; Spradley, 1970; Wiseman, 1970), drinking and drug use (Becker, 1963; Rubington, 1968; Prus, 1983; Ingraham, 1984), hustlers and thieves (Sutherland, 1937; Maurer, 1955; Letkemann, 1973; Prus and Sharper, 1977; Jacobs, 1999; Hochstetler, 2002), homosexual involvements (Humphreys, 1975; Newton, 1989; Correll, 1995), entertainers (Becker, 1963; Prus and Irini, 1980; Stebbins, 1990; Prus and Sharper, 1991; MacLeod, 1993), participation in disreputable adult recreational arenas (Cressey, 1932;

Roebuck and Frese, 1976; Prus and Irini, 1980), mate-swapping (Bartell, 1971), marketplace exchanges (Prus, 1989a, 1989b; Sanders, 1989; Prus and Frisby, 1990; Prus and
Fleras, 1996), people living with illness (Davis, 1963; Schneider and Conrad, 1983; Charmaz, 1991), religious leaders and their followers (Lofland, 1966; Prus, 1976; Van Zandt,
1991), control agents (Emerson, 1969; Sanders, 1977; Charles, 1986), enlisted soldiers
(Ingraham, 1984), deep-sea divers (Hunt, 1995), insurance adjusters (Ross, 1970), gangs
(Thrasher, 1927; Keiser, 1969; Wolf, 1991), transgendering (Ekins, 1997), fantasy role-
playing games (Fine, 1983), and high school debating (Fine, 2001).

Insofar as adolescence introduces another set of lived experiences and activities for
people making the transition to adulthood, some readers may be interested in examining
a process-oriented conceptual statement that links adolescents and deviants (Prus,
1996a). For some ethnographic research that focuses more specifically on adolescents,
see Shaw (1930), Blumer (1933), Blumer and Hauser (1933), Reiss (1961), Fine (1987,
2001), Dietz (1994), Dietz and Cooper (1994), Horowitz (1995), and Adler and Adler
(1998).

6. Prus (1999) provides an extended analysis of influence work (and resistance)
across the fuller range of humanly engaged theaters.

7. Although these subprocesses are extensively detailed in an ethnographic analysis
of sales activity (Prus, 1989a, 1989b), the following studies also provide instructive
depictions of the persuasion (influence and negotiation) process: Shaw (1930), Cressey
(1932), Sutherland (1937), Roth (1962), Festinger et al., (1956), Lofland (1966), Emerson
(1969), Ross (1970), Wiseman (1970), Bartell (1971), Prus (1976, 1983), Prus and
Sharper (1977, 1991), Sanders (1977), Prus and Irini (1980), Hayano (1982), Fine (1983,
2001), Adler (1985), Charles (1986), Sanders (1989), Van Zandt (1991), Wolf (1992),
Jorgensen (1992), Anspach (1993), MacLeod (1993), Dietz and Cooper (1994), Grills
(1994), Wolf (1994), Holyfield (1999), and Jacobs (1999).

8. For book-length ethnographies that attend more centrally to the (variable) commitment-making process in more problematic or disreputable contexts, readers are referred to examinations of people's involvements in religious cults (Festinger et al., 1956;
Lofland, 1966; Van Zandt, 1991; Jorgensen, 1992), the thief subculture (Sutherland,
1937; Maurer, 1955; Letkemann, 1973; Prus and Sharper, 1977; Prus and Irini, 1980;
Shover, 1996), drug dealing (Adler, 1985; Jacobs, 1999), gambling (Lesieur, 1977), mate-
swapping (Bartell, 1971), multiracial couples (Rosenblatt et al., 1995), homosexuality
(Warren, 1974; Ponse, 1978; Newton, 1979), feminism (Wolf, 1994), tattoos (Sanders,
1989), outlaw biker gangs (Wolf, 1991), television soaps (Harrington and Bielby, 1995),
and transgendering (Kando, 1973; Nanda, 1990; Ekins, 1997). Focusing on medical students, salespeople, and high school debaters, respectively, Haas and Shaffir (1987), Prus
(1989a, 1989b), and Fine (2001) provide some instructive ethnographic parallels in less
stigmatized contexts.

9. There are several ethnographies that address the development, maintenance, and
severance of relationships in some detail. See studies of heterosexual relations (Waller,
1930; Hunt, 1966; Bartell, 1971; Prus and Irini, 1980; Vaughan, 1986; Rosenblatt et al.,
1995), homosexual relations (Reiss, 1961; Warren, 1974; Humphreys, 1975; Ponse,
1978; Correll, 1995), religious cult involvements (Lofland, 1966; Van Zandt, 1991; Jorgensen, 1992), hustlers and thieves (Shaw, 1930; Sutherland, 1937; Maurer, 1955; Letkemann, 1973; Prus and Sharper, 1977; Adler, 1985; Steffensmeier, 1986; Shover, 1996;
Jacobs, 1999), bar life (Roebuck and Frese, 1976; Prus and Irini, 1980); the marketplace
(Prus, 1989a, 1989b; Prus and Frisby, 1990), fantasy role-playing games (Fine, 1983),

musicians (Faulkner, 1971; MacLeod, 1993), outlaw bikers (Wolf, 1991), and the tattoo subculture (Sanders, 1989). Lemert's (1962) analysis of "paranoia and the dynamics of exclusion" remains one of the best accounts of the disruptive potential of interpersonal distrust and disaffection for people's ensuing relationships.

10. It should be appreciated that all human activities (including talking, listening, watching, and thinking) are biologically (and sensory) enabled. Still, sensations are not inherently meaningful and, in themselves, do not constitute emotions or other aspects of meaningful human realities.

While people routinely disregard a great many of the sensations that they (as biological essences) may have at any given point in time, people also have the capacity to attend to particular sensations in much more focused terms. Although people may designate some of these bodily states as "emotions" (as in notions of fear, anger, embarrassment, happiness, and love), it should be emphasized that sensations have no meaning apart from the labels, definitions, expectations, and enactments that people associate with (assign to) these matters. In other words, people's experiences with emotions are socially constituted syntheses of sensations, linguistic definitions, and activity.

As meaningful essences, emotions are brought into existence and take shape as people make linguistic references and develop other lines of action pertaining to particular variants of bodily states and sensations. Focusing attention on certain matters, these applications of knowing and acting, thereby sensitize (and desensitize) people to categories and instances of bodily states or feelings. People's emotional experiences, thus, reflect their interaction with others, their stocks of knowledge, interpretations, activities, adjustments, and habituation (or stabilization). In many ways, too, people's experiences with emotionality parallel (where they do not more directly overlap) their experiences with deviance as realms of meaningful activity.

To emphasize the socially constituted base of emotionality is not to deny the sometimes profound bodily sensations that people associate with emotionality. Clearly, people may become captivated or highly intrigued with certain bodily sensations. They also may become thoroughly disgusted, deeply embarrassed, deathly fearful, incapacitatingly anxious, and so forth. Relatedly, in addition to any present experiences of emotionality, people also may reflect on their past emotional experiences and anticipate future emotional states.

On occasion, as well, people may become so intensively focused on achieving, attending to, or avoiding particular bodily states and sensations that they may forgo typical group perspectives (thereby also losing familiar reference points for understanding their own situations) for shorter or longer periods of time. When emotional focusing takes place on a shared basis (as within subcultural contexts), people's experiences become normalized (even if in disreputable manners) within particular social life-worlds. However, when people intensively engage in selective focusing of this sort more exclusively on their own, they lose some intersubjective connections with their associates and (should they persist in this area) risk further detachment from the group at hand. Also, when people pursue (or avoid) specific emotional states more entirely on their own, they may have considerable difficulty articulating experiences that transcend their existing (group-based) vocabularies.

Although people sometimes invoke supernatural motifs (as in spiritual possession or mystical intervention) when particular people's bodily sensations become centering points for their own life-worlds, the contemporary Western tendency is to define these people's situations in biomedical terms. Still, it is inappropriate to reduce people's emotional experiences to spiritual or biomedical matters. This is not to deny either the strong, sometimes uncontrollable sensations that people experience or the potential of medications or other treatments to provide emotionally entrenched individuals with opportunities to transform or break earlier patterns of dealing with certain kinds of bodily sensations. However, if these people's experiences are to be understood by, or made comprehensible to, others in more direct (as in interactional, interpretive versus imputational) manners, it will have to be within the broader cognitive (linguistic) parameters of the group(s) in which these people are situated.

Interestingly, some of the most insightful analyses of the formulation of emotional experiences have been developed in interactionist considerations of the nature of drug-related experiences (Brown, 1931; Ray, 1961; Becker, 1963, 1967; Biernacki, 1988). For some other ethnographic research that addresses emotionality in more sustained terms, see: Blumer's (1933), Blumer and Hauser's (1933), and Harrington and Bielby's (1995) studies of people's experiences with the media; Evans and Falk's (1986) and Evans's (1994) examination of people learning to be deaf; Lofland's (1966) and Van Zandt's (1991) studies of religious cults; Roebuck and Frese's (1976) and Prus and Irini's (1980) accounts of bar life; Bartell's (1971) work on mate-swapping; Rosenblatt et al.'s (1995) account of multiracial couples; Reiss's (1961), Warren's (1974), Humphreys' (1975), and Ponse's (1978) depictions of homosexual relations; Davis's (1963), Schneider and Conrad's (1983), Charmaz's (1991), and Anspach's (1993) studies of illness; Haas's (1972, 1977) study of high steel ironworkers; Lesieur's (1977) examination of gambling; Wolf's (1991) account of outlaw bikers; Waller's (1930) and Vaughan's (1986) depiction of marital dissolution; Lemert's (1962) study of paranoia; Rubinstein's (1973) and Charles's (1986) examinations of police work; Dietz's (1994) consideration of people's involvements in ballet; Karp's (1996) research on depression; Ekins's (1997) inquiry into transgendering; Holyfield's (1999) and Jonas's (1999) study of people's experiences in white-water rafting; and Fine's (2001) study of high school debaters. Prus (1996b) provides a more sustained interactionist consideration of emotionality on the part of people at large and ethnographers in the field more specifically. Aristotle's observations on emotionality in *Rhetoric* (Prus and Prus, 2000) and *Nicomachean Ethics* also are most instructive.

11. Prus (1997:134–136) provides a more detailed consideration of the subprocesses assumed in each of these features of collective events. While all ethnographies dealing with human interchanges (between two or more people) address collective events in some ways, the following sources deal with instances of people's mutual (not necessarily equal or symmetrical) participation in process terms: Thrasher (1927), Cressey (1932), Sutherland (1937), Maurer (1955), Becker (1963), Lofland (1966), Emerson (1969), Keiser (1969), Ross (1970), Bartell (1971), Faulkner (1971), Warren (1974), Prus and Sharper (1977, 1991), Sanders (1977), Ponse (1978), Newton (1979), Prus and Irini (1980), Hayano (1982), Ingraham (1984), Charles (1986), Prus (1989a, 1989b), Wolf (1991), Jorgensen (1992), Meehan (1992), MacLeod (1993), Dietz (1994), Dietz and Cooper (1994), Grills (1994), Harrington and Bielby (1995), Holyfield (1999), Jacobs (1999), and Fine (2001).

8

Subcultural Ventures
Forming and Coordinating Associations

The majority of gangs develop from the spontaneous play-group. . . . (I)n the course of business or pleasure, a crowd, in the sense of a mere gathering of persons, is formed. (25) . . . On this basis of interests and aptitudes, a play-group emerges. . . . Such a play-group may acquire a real organization. Natural leaders emerge, a relative standing is assigned to various members and traditions develop. It does not become a gang, however, until it begins to excite disapproval and opposition, and thus acquires a more definite group consciousness. (26) . . . This is the real beginning of the gang, for now it starts to draw itself more closely together. It becomes a conflict group. (27) . . . The ganging process is a continuous flux and flow, and there is little permanence in most of the groups. New nuclei are constantly appearing and the business of coalescing and recoalescing is going on everywhere in the congested areas. Both conflict and competition threaten the embryonic gangs with disintegration. . . . Some new activity of settlement, playground or club frequently depletes its membership. (31) (Thrasher, [1927] 1963:25–31)

Albeit one of the earliest considerations of delinquency and people's involvements in street gangs in the social sciences, Frederick Thrasher's (1927) *The Gang* represents a highly compelling account of people's experiences in group settings.

For Thrasher, the labeling of both "gangs" as entities and "individual participants" as delinquents or gang members is not something to be understood in the abstract, but rather represents a series of processes that take shape as people assemble and do things mindfully of others in the setting.

Attending to the definitions of both the insiders who form associations of sorts and the outsiders who attend, assess, and react to these groupings, Thrasher envisions gang contexts as settings in which people develop meaning for life-worlds in association with others. Although individual participants may acquire a variety of insider and outsider definitions, any of which may serve to foster or discourage certain kinds of behaviors on their part and relations with specific (inside and outside) others, Thrasher also acknowledges the images that become associated with specific groups and the implications of these images for people's reactions (as both insiders and outsiders) to these associational networks.

Rather than viewing gangs as collectivities of "disturbed personalities," Thrasher observes that the gang provides a setting in which people may work out a variety of interests in conjunction with others. Approaching gangs in this manner, Thrasher draws attention to the *meaningful* and *enabling* features of group life. Thus, Thrasher clearly envisions groups as offering participants ways of achieving freedom, pursuing entertainment, attaining new experiences, expressing romantic motifs, and developing and maintaining a sense of self (as somebody) in the community.

Importantly, too, an attentiveness to the "grouping phenomenon" further indicates the practical limitations (and conceptual folly) of trying to explain people's involvements in deviance by virtue of individualistic qualities of one or other sorts. Relatedly, whereas outsiders may view certain groups as deviant, dysfunctional, and the like, this should not obscure the more fundamental pragmatic or enabling elements of groups for those studying these enterprises. Indeed, this sociological awareness is a central element, not only for permeating the deviant mystique, but also for comprehending people's involvements in groups (and deviance) at a most fundamental level.

Although neither Lincoln Keiser (*The Vice Lords*; 1969) nor Daniel Wolf (*The Rebels*; 1991) appears familiar with Thrasher's work on gangs, their ethnographic accounts of city street and outlaw biker gangs resonate extensively both with Thrasher's materials and the subcultural themes articulated in the previous chapter of the present volume.

Thus, for instance, one notes strikingly parallel participant perspectives across these studies with respect to gang members' concerns with freedom and autonomy, adventure, territory, and violence. Likewise, one finds extensive concern with achieving identity or being somebody in both a collective and a more personal basis; as evidenced through various group identity tags, such as gang names, insignias, attire, and expressions.

To be a member in good standing also requires that participants directly and extensively immerse themselves in the activities of the group, that they display competence in group-based realms of endeavor and show commitment and courage to the group in the process. Many other parallels run through these studies, but our more immediate emphasis is on the ways in which subcultures are developed and sustained as collectivities.

Consequently, whereas chapter 6 focused primarily on people's careers of participation in subcultural settings, and chapter 7 emphasized a series of generic social processes that cut across people's involvements in subcultures in a more situated or here-and-now sense, the present chapter considers the ways in which people form, implement, and sustain the associations in which subcultural ventures take place.

Beginning with a consideration of (1) the grouping process, this chapter subsequently focuses on the matters of people (2) establishing or generating associations, (3) objectifying or achieving viability of those groups in the community, and (4) dealing with outsiders as members of specific associations.

Although frequently overlooked by those attending to deviance, these associational processes are fundamental for comprehending *all* realms of community life (and interpersonal exchange). Deviance is no exception.

THE GROUPING PROCESS

Given the typically individualistic and structuralist approaches that analysts have employed in explaining deviance, the exceedingly consequential matter of people *getting together* and *doing things in conjunction with others* has been largely neglected by scholars focusing on deviance. This disregard of meaningful, coordinated enterprise has significantly obstructed scholars in the quest to develop more effective linkages or connections between social theory and human activity.

While often neglected by students of deviance, the interactionist literature provides some particularly valuable accounts of the processes through which groups become constituted, are sustained, and attempt to manage their presence in the broader community. In addition to the works of Thrasher (1927), Keiser (1969), and Wolf (1991), just cited, other consequential ethnographic studies of the grouping process include studies of hustlers and thieves (Sutherland, 1937; Prus and Sharper, 1977; Prus and Irini, 1980), alcohol and drug-related associations (Becker, 1963; Rubington, 1968; Prus, 1983; Ingraham, 1984; Adler, 1985), religious social movements (Festinger et al., 1956; Lofland, 1966; Van Zandt, 1991; Jorgensen, 1992), political organizations (Grills, 1989, 1994), and musicians (Becker, 1963; MacLeod, 1993).

As "social processes and social products" that are more or less continuously in the making, subcultures have a rather precarious existence amidst an assortment of relationships, activities, and exchanges involving *both* insiders and outsiders.

Because research on subcultural deviance normally requires that scholars immerse themselves in disreputable, shifting, and often potentially dangerous arenas of human activity for extended periods of time, this also is one of the more challenging realms of inquiry. However, sustained examinations of these human interchanges are essential if social scientists hope to understand the considerable amount of deviance that takes place in group settings.

Although our emphasis is on those associations that develop around people's notions of deviance, most of the processes outlined here are basic to *all* realms of human organization (e.g., religion, politics, entertainment, trade). The most consequential differences for deviant subcultures, thus, revolve around the elements of disrespectability associated with deviance and people's (insiders and outsiders) adjustments to those definitions. Each group ("deviant" or "otherwise") may develop notions that are somewhat unique with respect to content, but this does not invalidate process-based comparisons across broader fields of endeavor.

As indicated in chapter 7, if scholars are to achieve more viable understandings of people's experiences in subcultures, it is essential that they attend to matters such as acquiring perspectives, achieving identities, doing activities, making commitments, managing relationships, experiencing emotionality, developing communicative fluency, and participating in collective events.

Still, while representing key features of the subcultural puzzle, an appreciation of both the developmental flows of people's participation or careers within subcultures (chapter 6) and the generic social processes that constitute subcultures in the making (chapter 7), even when taken together, provide only a partial picture of the larger subcultural process. Thus, it is necessary to more directly examine the matters of people developing and maintaining subcultures as particular or distinctive groupings within the broader communities in which these associations are located.

Some associations may achieve considerable prominence and mystique in the larger community, but other groupings may be much less obvious and, perhaps, fail to attain any noteworthy sense of existence on the part of others in the community.

Still, regardless of whether particular ventures are developed more fully, achieve greater senses of success, or endure for longer periods of time, three subprocesses seem especially consequential for understanding the grouping process. These are *establishing associations; objectifying associations*; and *encountering outsiders*. These three topics form the basic emphases of this chapter.

ESTABLISHING ASSOCIATIONS

Regardless of whether the association at hand is envisioned as a relationship, team, side, agency, organization, gang, committee, department, office, crew, mob, band, tribe, cult, coalition, network, or other category of affiliation, the matter of establishing associations cuts across *all* realms of human association (e.g., work, recreation, friendship, education, religion). By no means, thus, is the grouping process somehow limited to "deviant subcultures" or unique to groups that others define as deviant in some manner.[1]

Indeed, because definitions of deviance always denote audience viewpoints rather than inherently discreditable qualities of the act or actor under consideration, once one looks past the attributions of respectability or deviance associated with particular realms of human endeavor, it becomes apparent that those involved in deviant and conventional endeavors do things in ways that strikingly parallel one another.

Since people routinely develop particularized viewpoints, preferences, practices, modes of interchange, and the like, within group contexts, all of these aspects of group life represent reference points for defining membership status. While those who do not share these notions may be seen as outsiders of various kinds, the people within these associations also are apt to view those insiders who fail to maintain these group viewpoints and practices as less central to the group, if not more threatening in other ways as well.

Although people who are rejected by particular groups sometimes develop other associations (wherein "deviants" interact with one another somewhat by default), it is also the case that people deliberately may embark on (and sustain) deviant activity within particular associational contexts. Thus, whereas some groupings take more distinctive shape (as in membership, emphasis, and activities) only somewhat haphazardly as the people assembled therein pursue an assortment of interests with others in the setting, people also may form groups in much more intentional, direct and specific terms. Some of these focused pursuits may involve things that are considered more acceptable within the community, but people also may knowingly and specifically form and maintain associations in order to pursue activities that others view as "deviant."

Organized around the subheadings of *forming groups* and *engaging the membership*, the following notions are especially pertinent for understanding the emergence and development of subcultures. People involved in more fleeting alignments may circumvent or truncate some of the processes outlined here. However, those involved in longer term ventures seem likely to pursue broader sets of activities along these lines. Since those entering into associations with one another are apt to be variably concerned about these notions, researchers and analysts would want to be mindful of both when the participants consider matters of these sorts and the ways in which they deal with them.

Forming Groups

Although groups may take shape in various ways and often reflect some preexisting associations and contacts, groups may be seen to come into being whenever two or more people begin to attend to one another in some manner. Further, while people may be thrust into one another's presence in some cases, if groups are to achieve some viability as interactive entities, it will be necessary that one or more parties in the setting takes some initiative in establishing the association. Relatedly, some enterprise on the part of one or more of the participants in the setting, along with some cooperation from the other(s), is essential for the development and continuity of the group at hand.

It should not be assumed that the people in the situation at hand are equally interested in associating with one another or that they will maintain these interests over time. Likewise, the people in the setting at hand may envision the immediate association, as well as one another, in quite different terms. Thus, even when two or more people are interested in associating with one another in some manner, it should not be assumed that their interests are similar or even compatible.

Six realms of enterprise that enable groups to come into being in a more complete sense may be delineated (see Prus, 1997:71–72). These subprocesses are: (1) anticipating the value of a particular association; (2) attempting to involve others in the association or venture; (3) providing justifications or rationale for the association; (4) identifying or defining the participants in the association at hand; (5) arranging for subsequent communications between (earlier and potential) members of the association; and (6) pursuing or contributing resources (as in money, time, associates) that would allow the group to operate.

Interestingly, one of the most explicit illustrations of the grouping process can be found in a study of the formation of bottle-gangs on the part of skid row alcoholics by Earl Rubington (1968).[2] Among other practices that these people have developed to deal with their circumstances, the formation of bottle-gangs enables hard-core drinkers to maintain some level of intoxication. The groups take shape as two or more people acknowledge one another, pool resources, send someone to purchase a bottle of wine, and take turns consuming liquor in a reasonably orderly and congenial fashion. When the bottle is finished, the participants may become involved in the formation of another bottle-gang with the same or other participants, or they may pursue other matters (as in panhandling or obtaining a meal) and reengage the bottle-gang process at a later point in time.[3]

Although this practice is among the lesser preferred modes of accessing alcohol, it does provide the participants some contact with a highly desired substance. Some rule violations do occur, as when people trusted to "make the run" (purchase a bottle) fail to return to the group or people take advantage of their associates in other ways. Still, Rubington's statement effectively illustrates the abilities of people who often are considered to be immoral, irresponsible misfits not only to form associations among themselves in pursuing coordinated activity but also to define, sustain, and regulate their own notions of moral order. Indeed, as Rubington's work indicates, the same people also are actively involved in the next aspect of the grouping process, that of engaging the membership.

Engaging the Membership

Whereas the preceding set of processes deals with the formulation of the group in more foundational terms, the subprocesses following address some additional activities associated with maintaining a more viable membership.

Although these subprocesses may seem particularly relevant to larger associations, the same considerations also are pertinent to dyadic and triadic relations. Like the processes just referenced, the following themes also lend themselves to sustained analysis on the part of those who might intend to better comprehend the ways in which specific groups or subcultures within the broader community deal with matters of membership and social order within their own groupings

Following Prus (1997:72), one may identify processes of the following sort as integral to the matter of enabling the group to maintain viability:

(1) arranging for member contacts or assemblies; (2) providing stocks of knowledge or instruction for group participants; (3) observing or monitoring member activities, lifestyles, and the like; (4) assessing or evaluating member activities against prevailing (insider) group standards; (5) emphasizing or recognizing the group venture in more explicit terms; (6) motivating and regulating members and their activities; and (7) rejecting troublesome members and reinstating members who earlier had been disqualified in some way.

While the preceding processes focus more directly on things intended to enable groups to operate more effectively within, the following themes acknowledge the more disruptive, and sometimes terminal, features of particular instances of group life.[4] These processes (also from Prus, 1997:72) include: (8) encountering and dealing with internal disruptions; (9) attending to more generalized disinterest on the part of the membership at large; (10) experiencing fragmentation of the association; and (11) encountering resistance in attempts to reintegrate or revitalize associations.

OBJECTIFYING ASSOCIATIONS

Although the preceding practices may be seen as consequential in displaying or indicating the reality, existence, or presence of some particular group or subculture, analysts also may attend to another set of processes that serve to *objectify* (Berger and Luckmann, 1966) or establish groups as more explicit, authentic, consequential, or noteworthy associations with respect to both the participants within these groupings and the members of the larger community in which these groups are located.

Here, we acknowledge that insiders as well as a wide assortment of outsiders may be involved in defining or depicting particular groups or associations as more distinct, enduring, or consequential entities within the community.

It also may be noted that regardless of whether people's references to particular groups are intended as positive, negative, or even neutral in emphasis, each time that people acknowledge (a) some particular group, (b) the people associated with that group, or (c) the activities, appearances, or other qualities attributed to that group, those significations foster objectification of that group on the part of those who attend to these matters.[5] Although their efforts may overlap in certain regards, it is instructive to attend somewhat more precisely to the ways that insiders and outsiders contribute to the viability or realism of particular groups in the community.

Insider Practices

When we discuss objectification practices on the part of insiders, it should not be assumed that this is a significant concern for all group participants. Thus, many insiders may have little interest in perpetuating or consolidating those

associations. There also are associations in which at least some of the participants expressly hope that no one would draw attention of any sort to the
involvements they may have had with certain people. Still, there are many
cases in which people, as insiders, intend to give greater emphasis or credence
to particular associations and it is to this matter that we now turn. Even here,
however, it is instructive to delineate two sets of the emphases that insiders
may pursue.

First, insiders may attempt to achieve a compelling presence for those within
the association. To this end, insiders may attempt to generate images of importance, relevancy, prestige, and exclusivity of the group for its own membership. Second, insiders also may attempt to establish a more public
prominence or presence within the community. This may involve many of the
same practices that members use to enhance the group for insiders, but the
emphasis here is on drawing attention to the association on the part of outsiders. Commonly, this involves insider-initiated tactics of display, publicity, proselytization, explicit claims-making endeavors, overt challenges, and other
realms of participation in public forums.

Because higher community profiles are often seen as important for attracting
new members, raising funds, and generating more enjoyable, productive operations, even groups that see themselves as vulnerable to outsider condemnations
(possibly related to their agendas, members, lifestyles, or specific practices) may
still quest for greater public presences.

Given the potential gains associated with the broader awareness of their
presence on the one hand and concerns with condemnation and control on the
other, groups who envision themselves to be viewed as deviants in some respect
are apt to experience a variety of dilemmas. These tactical uncertainties are
often accompanied by debates and fragmentation within, as members consider
the ways in which they could or should present themselves to others in the
community. Still, four sets of tactical concerns on the part of insiders may be
delineated: promoting internal viability, achieving a pronounced public identity,
gaining public acceptance, and engaging in protective practices.

When attempting to promote a greater sense of *vitality within the association*, group members may attend to such things (Prus, 1996b: 162) as:
(1) encouraging group identities through the use of names and other markers;
(2) articulating and expressing justifications for the group and its practices;
(3) establishing identity markers or tags for members of the association; and
(4) fostering selectivity or a sense of exclusivity through language, practices,
and codes. Relatedly, (5) group members may also emphasize the centrality of
the group for the well-being or success of the members within and (6) engage
in collective (insider) celebrations of the group's existence and achievements.[6]

To achieve a more *distinctive public identity*, insiders may embark on activities and displays that not only (1) distinguish them from other groups in the
community but also (2) impact on other people in more central manners. However, should insiders see these activities as more extensively interfused with

notions of disrespectability on the part of others, group members may decide
to act in ways intended to (3) invoke moral condemnations from and/or
(4) prompt fear on the part of other people.

Should groups wish to attain higher levels of *public acceptance*, then we also
may expect to find members (Prus, 1996b: 162): (1) encouraging a more pronounced presence of the association in the community (as through display,
proselytization, and rallies); (2) seeking or portraying public acceptance or endorsements of the association (as in seeking acknowledgements, charters, sponsors, and public concessions); and (3) establishing more visible, regularized
locations in which the association may meet and act. As well, groups desiring
more favorable public receptions may (4) visibly embark on public services or
contribute to more notable causes; thereby attempting to establish themselves
as "good citizens." In these, and other possibly more covert manners, group
representatives may attempt to foster lines of dependency and indebtedness to
their association on the part of potential supporters.[7]

Still, where groups feel vulnerable to outsiders more generally but still require contact on the part of more selective categories of outsiders, we expect
to find insiders engaging in *protective practices* of the following sort: (1) living
double lives or assuming secret (deviant) identities on a personal basis;
(2) taking greater care to engage in group practices on a secretive basis when
around outsiders; (3) making pledges and commitments to one another to
maintain loyalty to the group; (4) developing and maintaining organizational
fronts or facades for (insider) group activities; (5) studying outsiders for both
sympathetic practices and particular points of vulnerability; (6) testing outsiders for tolerance and receptivity to insider practices; (7) relying on gradual
disclosures about (insider) group activities when dealing with outsiders;
(8) developing and invoking linguistic subterfuge (double-talk) when communicating with other insiders in the presence of outsiders.[8]

Outsider Objectifications

Whereas insiders may develop a variety of standpoints and practices for
representing themselves (and their groups) to outsiders, outsiders are apt to be
even more diversified in the ways that they envision and act toward these
groups.

Ranging from supporters and sympathizers to competitors and opponents,
as well as informers, mediators, entertainers, consumers, and disinterested parties, particular outsiders (individuals or groups) may do a great deal or virtually
nothing to establish a public presence for any particular group.

However, regardless of their moral viewpoints, interests, or modes of involvement, whenever outsiders talk about and/or act toward particular groups
in more singular or explicit terms, those outsiders foster a sense of realism or
authenticity pertaining to the target group that may go well beyond anything

that the insiders would have been able to achieve along these lines on their own.

In discussing the ways that outsiders may contribute to the identities of particular groups, it is important that we not become caught up in the media mystique any more than the deviant mystique. Thus, rather than envision the media as the central force in the identity-making process for any group or set of groups, it is essential to first consider when and how people assign meanings and other relevancies to particular groups (and their realms of activity). Without these preliminary definitions, there would be no direction (as in condemnation, praise, or entertainment) for any media messages to assume.

Particularly consequential in this regard (see Prus, 1996b: 162) are the matters of specific people (as outsiders): (1) identifying a particular group as distinct from others in the community; (2) attaching specific names and other markers with the group being referenced; (3) assigning specific qualities, properties, activities, and evaluations to the group being referenced; (4) more extensively discussing the group being referenced with others in the community; and (5) making more explicit and sustained efforts to deal with the group in some selective manner.

Also relevant, in some cases, are attempts on the parts of outsiders to (6) access (insider) groups or spokespeople in order to obtain more revealing information on those groups and (7) use those materials to inform others about things that insiders would prefer to maintain as secretive. As well, while insiders might prefer that outsiders represent insider associations in more positive or enabling terms, insiders are apt to find that (8) outsiders who learn or presume to know about insider situations may interpret, use, and convey this information in any ways that suit the outsiders' own purposes.

Although practices of these sorts are commonplace community occurrences, the range and rapidity with which images of particular groups may be transmitted across the broader community can be greatly enhanced through the use of one or other forms and applications of the media.

As noted earlier (see chapter 3), people involved in generating, presenting, and consuming media materials represent consequential participants in the theaters of operation in which deviance and the deviant mystique take shape. However, far from representing a single-minded agent or force of some sort, the media is a vast array of social processes and social products. The media is not one thing in composition, expression, emphasis, or content. Instead, the media represents a broad set of communication options and processes that people may invoke in this or that instance to suit their objectives and interests. Like other instances of human communication, the media is as diversified as the various people involved in its production, distribution, and consumption (and related interpretation, implementation, and adjustment).[9]

With respect to the objectification of particular groups in the community or the more public identity-formation process, the media may be used in several ways. These include: (a) third-party outsiders who attend to certain groups or subcultures as sources of information or entertainment to be conveyed to others through some communicative forum; (b) third-party outsiders who use whatever topics that seem popular to promote their products in some aspect of the media; (c) insiders who employ particular print or electronic mediums as resources with which to facilitate the interests of their associations; and (d) outsiders who use specific media venues to control or endorse certain forms of deviance and/or the people involved therein. As well, an almost endless set of (e) consumers may engage any of the many forms, forums, and instances of media communications in highly diversified manners.

Further, lest some people be inclined to assume that media messages have clear, singular effects on recipients, it should be appreciated that those who encounter messages from others may interpret and engage these communications in highly diverse fashions. Not only may eventual recipients attend unevenly to any messages to which they may be exposed, but these people also may interpret these in manners quite different from that intended by senders, both on their own and through association with others. As well, the recipients may subsequently recall and/or transmit any portion of these messages, accurately or otherwise, with wide ranges of redirection, dramatization (enhancement or denigration), minimization, and omission.

The linkages of media messages and particular lines of activity are even more problematic. Thus, in what still remain the two most insightful and sustained examinations of young people's experiences with the media, Blumer (1933) and Blumer and Hauser (1933) not only found that (a) the effects of media messages were far from uniform in any direct sense, but also that (b) people commonly engage the media in selective terms and (c) may incorporate very different aspects of particular materials into their own cognitions and activities. In addition to acknowledging the highly compelling ways in which media materials may be developed (as in vivid dramatizations, empathetic communications, and heightened emotional sensations), as well as people's capacities to relate to particular media materials in intense, emotional, and action-oriented manners, these studies indicate the importance of analysts attending to the ways in which people interpret the media messages that they encounter with respect to their existing stocks of knowledge, the interactional contexts in which they find themselves, and the situations in which they develop particular lines of activity.

This is not to discount the vast array of communicative forums and instances that people may use in attempting to draw attention to particular subcultures or promote particular notions of deviance and morality, only to demystify the media in certain respects. Denoting instances of technologically enabled communication, people using variants of the media have the potential to reach larger, more diverse audiences than one might access through ordinary talk. Further, more focused and sustained communications encourage a greater sense of awareness of specific groups and practices on the part of audiences thusly exposed. Although the effects of the exposure are apt to be far from uniform, groups that receive greater media attention are apt to be enshrouded with mystique (as in prominence, honor, condemnation, and fear) where this higher level of exposure does not also lend itself to a subsequent sense of banality or comparative disregard of those groups and their pursuits on the part of some audiences.

Given the endless, perpetually emergent assortment of issues to which people in any community may attend, the public prominence or recognition accorded any particular group or subculture is problematic. Thus, as other focal points are introduced, fostered, and disengaged as themes of community relevance, so we may expect that the attention given to any particular subculture is apt to diminish over time, amidst the competition of other matters to which people in the community may attend. In this regard too, the people involved in producing and consuming the media are apt to find that most groups (and their activities) fade into the background of their collective consciousness as other issues, events, and groups receive attention.

For any particular group desiring or receiving outsider attention, the crucial matter is not whether people attend to the media, but *when* and *how* people attend to any messages pertaining to that particular group as an entity in the community. Thus, much more consequential than insider concerns with particular levels of media exposure are the matters of what messages people receive, how they interpret the materials they encounter, and how they incorporate the ensuing notions into their viewpoints and activities with respect to the group at hand.[10]

ENCOUNTERING OUTSIDERS

As the preceding considerations of objectifying associations suggest, people participating in subcultural deviance also face the task of managing relations with outsiders. Although some outsiders may be (variously) disinterested in, receptive to, supportive of, or fascinated with aspects of the subculture at hand, others represent more notable challenges and possibly devastating threats to particular subcultures. Likewise, whereas some outsiders may be of little or no interest to members of particular subcultures, other outsiders (as individuals and/or groups) may be seen as sources of intrigue, support, or entertainment, as well as the embodiments of stress, trouble, animosity, and threat.

Because any group of people may become objects of disaffection on the part of others in the community, people who believe that they (as individuals or as a group) are or could become targets of more pronounced condemnation and hostility face an additional set of dilemmas pertaining to the matters of disclosure and discovery. These concerns seem intensified when particular outsiders are thought to have the potential to disrupt insider activities and life-worlds.

Where outsiders are unaware of the disreputable involvements of subcultural participants, the insiders may be seen as "secret deviants" relative to these outsiders or live "double lives" (Goffman, 1963) of sorts. As long as they are regarded as "normals," these people may experience considerable latitude in their relations with these outsiders.

However, as a consequence of member concerns with discovery (and related sensitivities to some of the viewpoints and activities of the outsiders they encounter), practitioners still may experience some apprehension or vulnerability with respect to these outsiders. As well, even if subcultural participants have not been identified as deviants, these (covert operators) may still be concerned about maintaining secrecy as well as displaying loyalty to their subcultural associates.

Should outsiders learn of their involvements in deviance, the subcultural participants who encounter outsider negativities while on their own may feel very much like solitary deviants (chapter 9). Still, some differences may be noted. Thus, in addition to knowing that "there are others like me," identified members of subcultures also may anticipate that their (insider) associates would be sympathetic to their predicaments.

Those engaged in subcultural deviance also may be "prepped" by insiders about their discreditable status as well as instructed on how to deal with outsiders should their disreputable involvements be discovered at some point in time. Likewise, group members who have maintained integrity in the face of outsider adversity may anticipate some eventual recognition when their activities become known to their own (insider) groups.

However, as a consequence of their subcultural ties, those involved in group-related activities may feel obligated to promote their particular subcultures in more direct manners (e.g., defending the subculture from opponents; proselytizing on behalf of the subculture; and confronting, sabotaging, or terrorizing opponents) with respect to others in the community. Participants sometimes justify these activities by claiming that their reactions are the results of stigma or other negative treatments that they have experienced. However, group members may very well engage in activities along these same lines in attempts to pursue objectives particular to their own interests and those of others in the group.

Some important aspects of people's encounters with outsiders were introduced in the earlier discussion of managing relationships in chapter 7, but the matter of dealing with others from within a subcultural context also presupposes a more specific series of practices. These include things such as: (1) distinguishing outsiders from insiders and distinguishing outsiders from one another; (2) articulating perspectives (including images, explanations, and histories) for dealing with different kinds of outsiders; (3) developing practices (as in rules, strategies, and resistances) for dealing with various kinds of outsiders; (4) representing association interests and objectives in dealing with outsiders; and (5) protecting the association from outsiders.[11]

Specific subcultures (respectable and deviant) may be interfused with one another in a great many ways (e.g., as in cooperation, conflict, compromise, distancing, and both knowing and unwitting disregard), but all realms of human involvement are to be appreciated within the interactive realms of the larger community in which they are embedded. Thus, rather than shroud particular subcultures in mystiques of sorts, it is important that those who wish to understand deviance at a humanly enacted level examine the grouping process in more direct and fundamental enacted terms.

Whereas chapter 9 deals more directly with solitary deviance, readers will find that the materials developed in chapters 6, 7, and 8 are central for achieving a fuller appreciation of what often seems to be isolated instances of deviance.

NOTES

1. Because associations, even of the most extensive and formalized sorts, are but variations of the relationship process, chapter 8 can be seen to extend the materials on relationships developed in chapter 7.

2. Since they are more or less continuously active in forming new groups for the purposes of financial gain, road hustlers (Prus and Sharper, 1977), hookers (Prus and Irini, 1980), salespeople (Prus, 1989a, 1989b; Prus and Frisby, 1990), musicians (Faulkner, 1971; MacLeod, 1993), and drug dealers (Jacobs, 1999) also provide instructive depictions of the grouping process. Some other informative material on the formation and maintenance of groups can be found in studies of mate-swapping (Bartell, 1971), fantasy role-playing games (Fine, 1983), military barracks life (Ingraham, 1984), political organizations (Grills, 1994), biker gangs (Wolf, 1991), and feminist associations (Wolf, 1994).

3. For some other instructive accounts of skid row life, see Anderson (1923), Bittner (1967), Spradley (1970), Wiseman (1970), and Snow and Anderson (1993). Roebuck and Frese (1976), Prus and Irini (1980), Prus (1983), Ingraham (1984) present ethnographic materials that deal with drinking activities in other settings.

4. Beyond Thrasher's (1927) classic statement on gangs, some other studies that deal more directly with fuller sets of processes entailed in "engaging the membership" include Lofland (1966), Keiser (1969), Roebuck and Frese (1976), Prus and Sharper (1977), Prus and Irini (1980), Van Zandt (1991), Wolf (1991), MacLeod (1993), Grills (1994), and Harrington and Bielby (1995).

5. Clearly, some groups very much desire to become well known in the broader community. Among the ethnographic studies that depict instances of group-based quests for recognition in the broader community are: Lofland's (1966), Prus's (1976), Van Zandt's (1991), and Jorgensen's (1992) research on religious organizations; Wiseman's (1970) examination of skid row control agencies; Prus's (1989a, 1989b), Smith's (1989), Prus and Frisby's (1990), and Prus and Fleras's (1996) inquiries into marketplace activity; Sanders' (1989) depiction of tattoo artists; MacLeod's (1993) statement on club date musicians; and Holyfield's (1999) and Jonas's (1999) work on commercialized white-water rafting. However, others such as professional thieves (Sutherland, 1937; Maurer, 1995; Prus and Sharper, 1977) and upper-level drug dealers (Adler, 1985) very much try to maintain covert operations (and identities). Still other groups of people, such as those featuring "adult" entertainment (Cressey, 1932; Roebuck and Frese, 1976;

Heyl, 1979; Prus and Irini, 1980) and outlaw biker gangs (Wolf, 1991) may strive for more selective or guarded levels of public awareness. Notably, one may encounter much more variation in openness among individual participants (and embedded subcultures) within larger subcultures. This is especially evident among those involved in homosexual life-worlds (Reiss, 1961; Warren, 1974; Humphreys, 1975; Ponse, 1978; Newton, 1979; McNamara, 1994; Correll, 1995) and transgendering (Kando, 1973; Ekins, 1997), for instance.

6. Wolf's (1991) depiction of the activities of outlaw bikers addresses collective expressions in very direct terms, but also see Lofland's (1966), Van Zandt's (1991), and Jorgensen's (1992) accounts of those involved in cultic ventures.

7. Studies of religious cults by Lofland (1966) and Van Zandt (1991) address concerns with public acceptance at some length, as also does Grills' (1989, 1994) work on political parties.

8. Matters of managing discreditable identities are discussed in some detail in Goffman (1963), but are ethnographically illustrated in studies of hustlers and thieves (Sutherland, 1937; Prus and Sharper, 1977; Prus and Irini, 1980; Adler, 1985; Steffensmeier, 1986; and Jacobs, 1999), people with chronic illnesses (Davis, 1963; Schneider and Conrad, 1983; Charmaz, 1991), depression (Karp, 1996), mate-swappers (Bartell, 1971), multiracial couples (Rosenblatt et al., 1995), and those involved in homosexual life-worlds (Warren, 1974; Humphreys, 1975; Ponse, 1978; Newton, 1979) as well as transgendering practices (Kando, 1973; Ekins, 1997).

9. Although it is well beyond the scope of the present project, one could embark on an analysis of the media that parallels the present text on deviance. Thus, in addition to permeating the "media mystique" and all of those who participate in the media-making process, one could consider people's careers in the media, the subcultures that develop around people's attempts to engage the media (as technologists, producers, sponsors, promoters, and consumers), people's attempts to regulate (and resist regulatory endeavors) the media, and so forth.

10. Relatedly, even if particular groups actually receive as much media attention or other public awareness as they might at some point desire, a particularly telling question for any group is, What is life like afterward for the group or subculture under consideration? There is no guarantee that existing members will be happier or even remain with the group for longer periods of time should they achieve higher levels of public attention. Thus, even when exposure is not more disruptive or disabling in more distinctively negative terms, increased attention may still result in popularizations, imitations, and banalities that threaten the more unique, seemingly more vibrant or vital nature of earlier subcultural life.

11. For some ethnographic research that considers the ways in which people in subcultures make contact with and relate to outside parties, see studies of drug users (Brown, 1931; Ray, 1961; Becker, 1963; Biernacki, 1988; Faupel, 1991), entertainers (Cressey, 1932; Becker, 1963; Prus and Irini, 1980; MacLeod, 1993; Dietz, 1994), human service workers (Emerson, 1969; Wiseman, 1970), the police (Rubinstein, 1973; Sanders, 1977; Charles, 1986; Meehan, 1992), religious cults (Festinger et al., 1956; Lofland, 1966; Van Zandt, 1991; Jorgensen, 1992), hustlers and thieves (Shaw, 1930; Sutherland, 1937; Maurer, 1955; Prus and Sharper, 1977; Adler, 1985; Steffensmeier, 1986; Jacobs, 1999), mate-swappers (Bartell, 1971), multiracial couples (Rosenblatt et al., 1995), street and

biker gangs (Thrasher, 1927; Keiser, 1969; Wolf, 1991), homosexual life-worlds (Reiss, 1961; Warren, 1974; Humphreys, 1975; Ponse, 1978; Newton, 1979; Sandstrom, 1990; McNamara, 1994; Correll, 1995), and transgendering (Kando, 1973; Ekins, 1997). Prus (1999) provides a more comprehensive consideration of relations between insiders and outsiders with respect to influence (and resistance) work.

9

Solitary Deviance
Alone with Others

One might define "solitary deviance" as wrongdoing or disrespectability that
one experiences on one's own, on a more private or isolated basis. However,
when one begins to sort out the various aspects of solitary deviance, the issues
become much more complicated. Not only are many things *not* as solitary
(private or isolated) as they first seem, but definitions of deviance inevitably
take us into the realm of the other. Solitary deviance, thus, offers social scientists a perplexing challenge, a topic that appears intriguingly individualistic
on the surface and yet can be meaningfully comprehended only within parameters of group life.

Further, although often overlooked in sociological considerations of community life, solitary deviance also represents a consequential, if not essential,
component of the sociological study of the human community. As well, in
contrast to those who assume (a) that one theory is required for "group or
subcultural deviance" and one for "solitary deviance," or (b) that separate theories are required for the "deviants" and "the normals," the interactionists
(c) work with one theory of human association. The interactionist approach
not only encompasses this fuller range of human knowing and acting but it
also enables researchers to attend to the ways in which these matters overlap
or become interfused with one another.

Recognizing that notions of deviance are only consequential when they are
invoked, and that nothing is inherently deviant, people participating in the
activities of any sort may view these endeavors very differently from those of
their audiences. Thus, while participants may accept other people's notions of
deviance, they also may disattend to, or reject, the designations of deviance
proposed by others prior to, during, or following the completion of their activities. As a realm of human endeavor, solitary deviance, thus, represents another instance in which social scientists should recognize "the deviant
mystique" and be prepared to put their own notions of morality and normality

in suspension, lest they, too, unwittingly contribute to the objectification of deviance (and in the process obscure comprehension of this phenomenon).

While only some activity may be envisioned as deviance (and this will vary from audience to audience), any activity defined as deviant still *is* activity in a most fundamental and consequential sense. Hence, before embarking on a consideration of solitary deviance, it is essential to consider the production of human activity more generally. Only, first and foremost, by envisioning deviance as *activity* may social scientists establish a viable foundation for comprehending behavior that may be considered deviant. This means, too, that we have to be careful to distinguish imputations of deviance from the activities so defined. It also is essential that analysts be mindful of exactly whose behaviors they are trying to explain (i.e., that audience viewpoints, definitions, and other reactions not be confused with the behaviors of the presumably focal actors).

ACKNOWLEDGING SOLITARY ACTIVITY

One finds little "sociological theory" that explicitly recognizes the human capacity for solitary activity,[1] but it is apparent that people do a great many things on their own. Accordingly, if we are interested in the study of human behavior in a more thorough sense, we have an obligation to engage this phenomenon in more direct terms.

Interestingly, while the interactionists have steadfastly refused to reduce human behavior to individual qualities or factors ("personalities," "attitudes," "background characteristics") as is done by most psychologists and many sociologists, this does not mean that the interactionists have disregarded people's capacities to act in more independent manners. Indeed, the interactionists have been among the major proponents of notions of *human agency* within the social sciences. By building on interactionist conceptualizations of community and human agency in grappling with the essences of solitary deviance, we can achieve better understandings of both solitary activity *and* deviance.

We begin with a basic interactionist (Mead, 1934; Blumer, 1969) recognition that (a) all things, including human behavior (and expressions, thoughts, appearances) are *meaningful only* because of viewpoints that people develop on these things through association with others, and (b) that the meanings assigned to objects are developed, shared, and altered by means of language. It is only when people possess a language in common that they may be able to engage (i.e., comprehend and act mindfully of) the standpoint of the other. And, it is only in acquiring the standpoint of the other that people develop frames of reference for making sense of any objects (including themselves) to which they may attend. The acquisition of *language* (or sets of group-based symbols or representations), therefore, is essential for enabling people to think about things, to imagine, to anticipate, to initiate, to monitor, to assess, and to adjust their own behaviors in ways that are mindful of the situations in which they find themselves.[2]

As people acquire language (allowing mindedness and a sense of self), they become capable of embarking on and sustaining a variety of meaningful activities in the relative absence of others. There is *nothing inherently deviant* about solitary behavior. Indeed, from very early ages, people are encouraged to develop cognitive and physical competencies (and related senses of independence) that enable them to do things on their own.

This does not mean that everything that people do on their own will be subject to approval. Notably, those overseeing people's early socialization typically discourage as well as encourage certain kinds of behavior. In addition to selectivity fostering and discouraging specific kinds of activities (and expressions) on a more immediate basis, those concerned about developing (futuristic) independence on the part of those being socialized are also apt to communicate principles, guidelines, or rules of thumb that these targets are expected to apply in the situations they subsequently experience, often in highly autonomous manners.

Although people's encounters with "the generalized other" (Mead, 1934) are by no means limited to close associates, these primary group associations (Cooley, 1909) represent people's most rudimentary exposure to notions of deviance and morality. Indeed, it is only in *taking the role of the other* (Mead, 1934) that people acquire senses of morality or reference points for making judgements about the desirability or undesirability of the behaviors (and circumstances) of self *and* others.

At the same time, it is essential to appreciate some variability of people's definitions of things even in seemingly homogeneous groups. Although some definitions may be widely shared in the community, people commonly encounter multiple images of objects both through association with particular others in the community and as they (reflectively) experience specific situations on their own. As well, there is no guarantee that people will comprehend the viewpoints presented to them in the ways in which others may have intended, even when instruction appears both explicit and extensive to others.

Because people can converse with themselves, adopting a variety of standpoints (often oppositionary) in the process, it is instructive (as Shibutani [1961] suggests) to envision (linguistically enabled) individuals as "societies in miniature." People's abilities to invoke multiple standpoints and multiple senses of self (i.e., to assume multiplistic, group-like stances on a solitary basis) have generally been overlooked by social scientists.

Further, as people acquire reflectivity or become objects of their own awareness (and attain related capacities for observation, instruction, or playfulness), they also may begin to selectively present (emphasize, minimize, disclose, and conceal) things to others. While often envisioned in terms of influence work (and tactical considerations of others), people's abilities to shape the images (of things) that they convey to self and others (see Goffman, 1959; 1963) represents another important theme for understanding solitary activity and people's participation in deviance more generally.

QUALIFYING SOLITARY DEVIANCE

Although the term "solitary deviance" is useful in some respects, solitary deviance is far from being one thing. Indeed, the very same people, engaging in (seemingly) identical behaviors, may find themselves experiencing respectability and disrespectability in different ways. Consequently, we acknowledge (a) the differing and multiple definitions that people assign to things; (b) the overlap of subcultural and solitary activities; and (c) people's encounters with emotionality.

Differing and Multiple Definitions

Because deviance achieves its essence only as particular audiences define and act toward specific situations or persons in negative or disrespectable terms, it is vital that analysts recognize the assortment of audiences that may be pertinent to instances of the "here-and-now" circumstances in which people find themselves. Indeed, much of the ambivalence (and anxiety) that people experience as solitary deviants reflects problems that these people have in adjusting to the variable definitions and treatments that they encounter (or anticipate) as they move from audience to audience.

Beyond the diversity of standpoints associated with different audiences, it should also be noted that specific audiences may adopt a variety of viewpoints on the same situation or target, more or less simultaneously or over time. As with other audiences, participants also may define their own situations in multiple manners as they, themselves, invoke different viewpoints on more fleeting, sustained, or sporadic bases.

Regardless of whether people do things more entirely on their own or are involved with some group of others, people who are envisioned as normal or respectable members (of the group at hand) typically have substantial advantages over those who have become suspect or more explicitly identified as deviants in the setting. Because they are treated as normals, the "merely discreditable" generally experience greater freedom, opportunities, and acceptance than those who are already discredited.[3]

Until they are tagged as deviants of some sort, an endless variety of people will be considered among the normals. This includes those who (a) unwittingly (accidentally, inadvertently) do things that others might construe as deviant were they to learn of these, (b) knowingly pursue particular activities but do not anticipate that others would define these as deviant, and (c) those who anticipate that others would find particular pursuits objectionable, but nevertheless knowingly engage in those activities.

Of these three categories of involvement, *the self-acknowledged disrespectables* are particularly noteworthy, for although all are potentially discreditable and, thus, may eventually merit attention as solitary deviants, those in the last set of circumstances are aware of their more precarious status. Because of this, they are more apt to experience some secondary dilemmas as well as develop practices, or make adjustments that are mindful of the moralities of others. Accordingly, while the longer-term experiences of all of these people are best comprehended within a broader interactive context, this subset of people is particularly consequential for the present analysis.

Subcultural and Solitary Involvements

When discussing deviance, it is important to distinguish people who do things more exclusively on their own from people who are more involved in settings as subcultural participants. However, while *solitary operators* (SOs) may be contrasted with *subcultural participants* (SCPs), the two forms of participation are *not* as exclusive as might first seem. Indeed, much solitary deviance can only be appreciated relative to a subcultural backdrop, whereas various aspects of subcultural deviance also are best understood mindfully of people's solitary endeavors. Thus, it is important that analysts attend to the similarities, contrasts, and interlinkages across these two broader realms of deviance.

Likewise, while analysts may overlook solitary deviance within subcultural contexts, it is instructive to recognize that subcultural participants sometimes experience deviance on a more singularistic basis. This seems especially apparent when (a) SCPs encounter imputations of deviance from outsiders on a more isolated basis (i.e., when separated from subcultural associates). However, SCPs may also envision themselves as solitary deviants *within* deviant subcultures when (b) they view themselves as more reluctant participants in specific group settings or (c) consider themselves thought of (and treated) as marginal, undesirable, oppositional or disloyal by others in the subculture.[4]

Beyond those SCPs who become more marginalized or discredited on an isolated basis, people doing things more entirely on their own (i.e., as SOs) still may develop associations of sorts as they pursue particular realms of deviance in more implicit, auxiliary, or vicarious manners. Not only may SOs attend to a wide variety of role-models (fascinating people or "kindred-types" that they notice around them or through the media), but they also may pursue specific partners, services, and products through contacts with other people (in and outside of any marketplace exchanges). In some cases, these associates may knowingly and eagerly provide supports of sorts for these activities, but in other instances they may have little personal interest in the activities of the solitary operators or only most reluctantly become involved with these people. With these interlinkages of solitary and subcultural involvements in mind, we turn to a third aspect of people's experiences with deviance.

Acknowledging Emotionality

As noted in chapter 7, people's experiences with emotionality represent a consequential feature of subcultural life. This seems no less central for solitary deviance and, in many respects, people's emotional experiences may be particularly important for comprehending their involvements as solitary deviants.[5]

Envisioning emotionality as a linguistically mediated attentiveness to bodily states and sensations (see chapter 7), it is essential that we acknowledge the emotional states that people associate with (a) personal designations as deviants (i.e., stigma, embarrassment, shame, fear, indignation, nervousness) and (b) any other treatment that people encounter as deviants (as in pain, anxiety, disaffection, frustration, and anger). However, it also is important that scholars attend to the emotional states that people experience with respect to (c) their involvements in specific activities, (d) an awareness that the things they are doing could result in condemnations from other people in the community, and (e) particular evaluations of self (as in pride of accomplishment or personal resourcefulness, shame in a religious or moral sense, disappointment with oneself for stupidity or carelessness, and frustration over not managing oneself more effectively).

As well, we should appreciate that people may embark on certain activities as expressions of particular emotional states (as in notions of jealousy, greed, anger, or hatred) wherein specific kinds of emotions are seen as providing (f) justifications or motivations for (pursuing or avoiding) particular lines of action.[6]

Notably, too, people may define (g) emotional states as particular ends (as with people seeking happiness, excitement, affection, and the like) to which other activities should be directed. Here, desired emotional states, as goals or objectives, may provide the basis for wide varieties of pursuits (and, relatedly, involvements, continuities, disinvolvements, and reinvolvements from particular lines of action; see chapter 6).

Viewed in these terms, we may recognize several realms of emotionality that people experience as agents acting on their own and in conjunction with others. Some related aspects of people's experiences with emotionality are considered elsewhere (defining deviance in chapter 4, attending to deviant identities in chapter 5, initial involvements in chapter 6, emotionality as a subcultural component in chapter 7, and encountering treatment in chapter 13). However, the more immediate emphasis is on those experiences with emotionality that people find particularly disconcerting in more isolated senses, as potential instances of solitary deviance.

The interlinkages of emotional states of these sorts and deeply troubled senses of self are notably evident in studies of chronic physical illness (Davis, 1963; Schneider and Conrad, 1983; Charmaz, 1991), paranoia (Lemert, 1962), and depression (Karp, 1996) as well as in research on divorce (Waller, 1930; Vaughan, 1986), gambling (Lesieur, 1977), stuttering (Petrunik, 1974; Petrunik and Shearing, 1984), drug use (Becker, 1963, 1967), and transgendering (Kando, 1973; Ekins, 1997), among others.

Because people's sensations and activities are so closely interfused with their cognitive-linguistic notions of emotionality, emotionality cannot be meaningfully experienced except as a sensory-enabled activity.[7] As well, since people's encounters with bodily states and sensations can be comprehended only in linguistic terms, and people acquire notions of emotionality through symbolic interchange with others in the community (including the particular perspectives, terms of reference, practices, and evaluations that people develop over time in group contexts), there are group-based limits to the things that people commonly recognize and acknowledge as constituting viable (as in meaningful, comprehensible, and consequential) emotional states.

Although groups of people may categorize various bodily related states (and sensations) in different ways, they also (collectively) define the parameters with which associated emotional states may be invoked. Thus, group-based variations are apt to emerge with respect to such things as (a) who may experience particular emotional states, (b) in what contexts they may do so, (c) with what intensities they may experience those states, and (d) which objects represent viable emphases for particular kinds of emotional sensations.

These group-based or objectified definitions of emotionality do not prevent people from attending to sensations that fall outside the recognized parameters of the group nor do they preclude people from linking certain sensations with things that may be at variance from more typical or preferred community practices. However, when people encounter exceptions of these sorts, they are apt to (a) be more uncertain about what is happening to them and/or (b) experience senses of marginalization or distancing from others in the community. Although sensations of this sort often are overlooked as insignificant or dismissed as odd or unusual in more fleeting senses, these matters are apt to become more consequential when they (a) seem more intense, (b) occur more frequently, (c) become associated with stronger affections (or disaffections), (d) assume more noteworthy enabling (or disabling) dimensions and (e) are thought to be more disreputable in the community.[8]

Still, regardless of whether their experiences seem only unusual or both strange and subject to condemnation, people in these circumstances almost inevitably lose some ties to "the sensibilities" of the community in which they are embedded.

While some people may consult with existing associates or specialists of sorts in attempts to retain or regain normalcy, others will keep these incidents more entirely to themselves. Some may attempt to distance or detach themselves from particular kinds of emotional episodes by restructuring their situations (as in associations, activities, circumstances) and/or seeking emotional experiences that more adequately fit with group practices and preferences.[9] Others, however, may find these sensations intriguing in certain respects and pursue these emotional states in an assortment of clandestine manners. These latter endeavors may be exclusively solitary in development, involve some very specific confidants or other associates, or take place in broader subcultures that have developed around people with related intrigues or difficulties. As with people's other involvements, we may expect that those caught up in unsettling emotional states commonly would experience cycles of disinvolvement and reinvolvement with respect to these endeavors (especially see chapter 13).

Although we cannot begin to specify the great variety of emotional motifs (and related sensations) to which people may attend in particular instances,[10] people's emotional experiences denote an important aspect of human group life. However, because emotionality represents a socially constructed realm of endeavor, it is essential that scholars maintain a particularly concerted focus on language, activity, and the dynamic and interactive nature of the human group when considering any linkages between emotionality and people's involvements in deviance. Thus, while acknowledging various ways that people's emotional experiences may be connected with attributions of deviance, we put the focus more directly on the ways that people engage activities on a more solitary basis.

EMBARKING ON SOLITARY PURSUITS

Despite its seemingly individualistic base, a closer consideration of solitary involvements suggests that people become involved in solitary deviance in ways not so different from that characterizing group-based deviance. Thus, although some instances of solitary deviance may come about *inadvertently* (e.g., stuttering, nervousness) or may be *imposed* (e.g. accidents, illness) on people in some other cases, people also become involved in solitary deviance through *instrumentalism, seekership, recruitment,* and *closure.* Denoting "minded" involvements, this latter set of routings are particularly consequential for comprehending people's participation in both solitary and subcultural deviance.

People may pursue activities that they consider useful or enabling in some respect (i.e., instrumentally advantageous), or find appealing, fascinating, intriguing, and such (i.e., seekership). As well, people also may have been encouraged to pursue these interests by others (i.e., recruitment) at earlier points in time. Likewise, to the extent that people engage in (otherwise undesired) activities as a means of dealing with particularly pressing concerns or obligations, they may be said to experience closure.[11]

Because we are dealing with matters of *human agency* with respect to instrumentalism, seekership, recruitment, and closure, we also should be attentive to any reservations (e.g., fear, costs, immorality) that participants might associate with certain activities. Since people may attend to a variety of concerns (both generally and over time), some may experience extended senses of freedom from restraints regarding certain kinds of involvements. In other cases, we would want to ask when and how people overcome any situated or more enduring reservations that they associate with particular endeavors as well as when they are unable to do so. Minimally, it should be emphasized that people contemplating particular lines of action may envision the activities (and any reservations they might have) at hand in manners quite differently from the ways these activities are viewed by outsiders (analysts included).

In contrast to instances of involvements in deviance of a subcultural nature in which group members may have developed more extensive justifications for engaging in certain practices and encounter situated encouragements (and neutralizations) from others, solitary operators are faced with the prospects of dealing with any reservations they may experience more exclusively on their own. Still, in both contexts, an attentiveness to people's reservations helps researchers understand the disjunctures between people's inclinations and their activities more generally.

For people knowingly participating in what others (and what they, themselves, may) consider deviance, deviance definitions add complexities to their lives. In addition to the matter of accomplishing particular sets of activities and dealing with any allures or excitement they may associate with these involvements, those knowingly engaging in deviance also typically face the task of managing (variously) discovery and disrespectability, impugned identities, and other negative treatments that they may encounter from others.

Generally speaking, subcultural participants are advantaged over those doing things more exclusively on their own. Although not all matters involving groups will have been extensively worked out by the current participants (or their predecessors), subcultural participants typically can obtain some assistance from at least one other person.[12]

Because solitary practitioners generally are faced with the tasks of establishing their own techniques, implementing their activities on their own, and dealing with any difficulties they may encounter on their own,[13] SOs often find their activities both more challenging and more difficult to sustain than those involved in subcultural ventures.

As well, whereas those involved in both solitary and subcultural deviance may be concerned about averting detection and avoiding related unpleasantries, SOs have no one to help protect them from discovery, and, if discovered, SOs may have no one to help them minimize undesired treatments from others. For these reasons, it is typically more difficult to sustain involvements on a highly solitary basis (Cressey, 1953; Lemert, 1967:109–134; Prus and Sharper, 1977:21–23; Ekins, 1997).[14]

Since sociologists have largely disattended to solitary deviance, at least in a more focused sense, there is comparatively little literature that directly attends to the enacted features of disrespectability on a more solitary basis. Still, some valuable insight into the definitional, experiential, and enacted features of people's solitary (albeit inevitably interspersed with subcultural involvements) encounters with trouble can be found in considerations of embezzlement (Cressey, 1953), check forgery (Lemert, 1967), gambling (Lesieur, 1977), drug use (Brown, 1931; Ray, 1961; Becker, 1963, 1967; and Biernacki, 1988), tattoos (Sanders, 1989), transgendering (Kando, 1973; Ekins, 1997), suicide (Douglas, 1967; Henslin, 1970; Atkinson, 1971), violence (Athens, 1980, 1997; Dietz, 1983), obesity (Himmelfarb and Evans, 1974; Millman, 1980), stuttering (Petrunik, 1974; Petrunik and Shearing, 1983), studying for tests (Albas and Albas, 1984), paranoia (Lemert, 1962), mental illness (Herman, 1994, 1995), depression (Karp, 1996), cognitive limitations (Edgerton, 1967), and people's encounters with physical illnesses and afflictions (Davis, 1961, 1963; Roth, 1962; Schneider and Conrad, 1983; Sandstrom, 1990; and Charmaz, 1991).

Building on this and the related interactionist literature, we have delineated a set of processes involved in initiating and sustaining solitary activities. It is hoped that this frame may suggest some subsequent realms of inquiry as well as provide a base for assessing, synthesizing, and adjusting conceptualizations of enacted solitary deviance with subsequent research in the field.

At the outset, it is essential to appreciate that solitary deviance is *not* a single act but rather entails a *series of activities or processes*. This may be more evident with respect to subcultural deviance but it is no less consequential for people's solitary involvements. People need not engage in all of the subactivities outlined here (they may, for instance, experience no sense of closure or have no reservations about engaging the activity at hand), but this broader set of (sub)activities seems relevant to a wide range of solitary involvements.

Similarly, while we have given these activities a flow for presentational purposes, participants may attend to these subactivities on partial, intermittent, concurrent, or repetitive manners, as well as in sequences quite at variance from those implied herein, as they work their ways through instances of solitary activity and concerns with deviance.

Although people's solitary involvements are located within the career contingency concept (i.e., initial involvements, continuities, disinvolvements, and reinvolvements) introduced in chapter 6, explicit attention is given to the matter of people *implementing instances of activity*. Thus, in addition to acknowledging the histories or overall sequencing of people's involvements over time, the focus is on the more situated or enacted realms of "the here and now" in which people do things. Indeed, as suggested in the listing following, it is only within "instances of the humanly engaged present" that careers of participation derive their essences:

Becoming Initially Involved in Solitary Activity (and Deviance)
 Experiencing inadvertent (accidental, unwittingly) involvements in activities
 Having situations imposed on self by others (involvements by default)
 Developing interests in particular lines of activity
  Encountering encouragements from others (recruitment)
  Anticipating involvement-related advantages (instrumentalism)
  Developing fascinations with particular involvements (seekership)
  Envisioning activities as solving pressing problems (closure)
 Dealing with preliminary reservations (if any)
  Attending to reservations or hesitations
  Overcoming personal (self-defined) reservations
  Disattending to, dismissing, or neutralizing potential reactions from others
  Contemplating ways of concealing activities from others

Implementing Instances of Activities[15]

    Envisioning opportunities for particular activities

    Initiating activity (physically engaging in situated events)

    Monitoring emergent behaviors and situational effects

    Experiencing concerns about performing successfully

    Making situational commitments or investments

    Encountering "points of no return"[16]

    Experiencing emotionality (e.g., fun, excitement, boredom, fear, frustration)

    Working one's way through the (implied) sequence of subactivities

    Encountering difficulties, close calls, trouble

    Attempting to extricate oneself from the situation at hand[17]

    Concluding instances of the activity at hand

    Resuming normal (regular) stances (and involvements)

    Assessing particular events (and earlier instances)

    Anticipating subsequent endeavors/Making adjustments

Continuing Solitary Involvements

    Defining experiences as relevant to present interests

    Pursuing emergent interests in the setting

    Achieving proficiencies in the activities at hand

    Making commitments to specific involvements

    Organizing routines around specific involvements

    Perceiving no viable alternatives

Disengaging from Solitary Involvements[18]

    Becoming distracted by other interests and opportunities

    Experiencing pronounced disappointments (or frustrations) in the setting

    Defining one's interests as fulfilled or no longer consequential

    Defining anticipated losses (costs, risks) as untenable

    Lacking opportunities (e.g., autonomy, time) in which to pursue focal activities

    Becoming more concerned (anxious) about detection (and ensuing treatment)

        Being discovered[19]

        Receiving treatment[20]

    Encountering opportunities to pursue existing interests in other ways

Renewing Solitary Involvements

    Experiencing fascinations, encouragements, or closure regarding reinvolvement[21]

    Neutralizing reservations about reinvolvement

    Dealing with sporadic involvements (vacillations)

    Making more enduring (lifestyle) commitments in the setting

RELATING TO OTHERS

Although people embarked on more solitary lines of action may have certain degrees of freedom or unencumbered involvements because they do things more extensively on their own, solitary operators lack many of the intersubjective and interpersonal supports associated with subcultural involvements. This means that SOs may be able to avoid some confrontations with others about appropriate ways of doing things, but lacking others with whom to more readily identify or offer support and encouragements, SOs also seem more likely to feel strange, isolated, and anxious than their subcultural counterparts.

As well, some of people's solitary activities may spill over into, or become interfused with, their associations with others. Given SO concerns with secrecy, their practices may become the site of some distancing and exclusion, if not more troubled, distrusting, and hostile relations. When this happens, some notably different types of behavior may become blended or intertwined with one another, often to the point that the people (analysts included) involved may have great difficulty separating people's deviant involvements from more protective, secondary adjustive practices.

Thus, even if SOs are more successful in concealing disreputable activities from others, the SOs involved may make a series of adjustments that inconvenience or create some other difficulties (e.g., financial, unusual routines) for others; things that may generate some annoyances on the part of, or distancing from, these others. Should this happen, these SOs are faced with the task of managing relations and emotionality within the group at hand while also maintaining secrecy regarding their disreputable activities.

Should the others more pointedly decide that "some problem" exists (possibly linking this more directly to some undesired activity on the part of the SO), then a secondary set of issues revolving around such matters as controlling or eliminating the behavior in question, dealing with the stigma associated with deviance, and managing subsequent relations tend to become more consequential. In this way, a second, potentially diverse series of interpersonal difficulties, sensitivities, and reactions may become intermeshed with practices that had been contained as solitary activity.[22]

At present, we have very little research that examines the ways in which matters of these sorts are worked by the parties involved. One of the best statements in this area is Edwin Lemert's (1962), "Paranoia and the Dynamics of Exclusion."[23] Here, Lemert examines the interpersonal relationships of some people who had become defined as "paranoid."

After talking to the central parties and their associates, Lemert takes issue with those who consider paranoia as an internal quality of the individual. Instead, he finds that the people who are defined as paranoid develop styles of dealing with others that are characterized by heightened levels of *mutual* distrust, distancing, and artificiality. Examining the processes by which the people involved work their ways through their "troubles," Lemert emphasizes the importance of envisioning disturbances of these sorts in relationship terms, as social processes that encompass people's attempts to deal with ambiguity, disaffection, distrust, distancing, and exclusion within ongoing associational contexts.

Rather than view people's viewpoints and practices in medical or psychological terms, the implication is that *all* situations in which people encounter problems (bigger and smaller) in dealing with others would lend themselves to considerations along these lines. When the parties involved seek reconstitutive arrangements and are prepared to engage one another in more open and sincere terms, earlier problems may be minimized. As well, too, some intensely troublesome relationships (and personal difficulties) may be avoided (i.e., curtailed) because people are able to "walk away" or disengage themselves from other unpleasant situations and exchanges.

Still, when people see themselves as more isolated and stigmatized relative to their activities amidst more enduring sets of associates (e.g., co-workers, neighbors, relatives, friends), they not only seem more inclined to attribute distancing (i.e., rejecting, exclusionary) motivations to others, but also appear more likely to distance themselves from others on the basis that their overtures would not be well received.

No less importantly, SOs and their associates may deny themselves or one another opportunities to "check things out with each other." Not only may they be less understood by the others as a result, but they also are apt to be less understanding of the others. Sometimes, too, it is only after people envision themselves as having "taken all that they can" that they (then in self-defined states of moral indignation) engage others in more aggressive terms, possibly saying and doing more than even they later may have thought appropriate.

Because people engaging in confrontational interchanges often involve themselves with one another in more complete senses (as in bodily states, senses of self, intensity, and expressions of negativity), confrontations frequently result in other sensitivities, fears, senses of distrust, and the like. These events readily lend themselves to more dramatized anticipations of (unpleasant, possibly escalating and uncontainable) future exchanges. Consequently, even when confrontationists continue to associate with one another, their relationships may be characterized by what Lemert terms *spurious communication*, wherein interaction is characterized by insincere, often sarcastic, but more generally ineffective and distancing sets of interchanges.

In other instances, too, having taken all they can, people may become increasingly reclusive. This may result in people more extensively detaching themselves from others and losing shared reference points as well as interest in participating in the life-worlds of the other. As well, we may expect shifts on the part of all disaffected parties, between states of indignation and confrontation on the one hand and isolation and exclusion on the other.

Sometimes apologies, explanations, and other attempts at amends may be effective in restoring relations between the parties involved. At other times, these *remedial interchanges* (Goffman, 1971) denote only temporary fixes and people may reengage one another along similar, possibly more intense lines. Likewise, should people invoke recollections of earlier confrontations and isolations, these earlier episodes (denoting "build-ups" of sorts) may contribute notably to people's subsequent senses of indignation, distance, and frustration. Then, the participants may be even more hesitant to reengage one another in open and trusting manners. Relatedly, when people operate within the context of sensitivities and suspicions, innocent and even benignly intended activities may be construed as negative or malicious in character.

Where situations of these sorts persist over longer periods of time, the parties involved are apt to become increasingly estranged from one another and matters of disaffection and distrust are apt to be intensified. Likewise, they are apt to lose mutuality of relevancies and other shared reference points, as they move into realities that the others can less fully comprehend and engage. Thus, regardless of the base on which their problems may have begun, one or more parties in the setting may increasingly envision themselves as solitary deviants in a more intense and enduring sense.[24]

CONCEPTUAL PROBLEMATICS

As the preceding material suggests, solitary deviance is a multifaceted phenomenon. Even if one focuses on activities in which people engage entirely (and secretly) on their own, one may still ask about the processes by which people acquire particular interests, when and how they pursue, implement, and sustain the activities that reflect their definitions of the world, amidst concerns with potential discovery or other reservations. Should others learn of these activities, people's involvements typically assume a series of other dimensions (possibly quite dramatic) as the (now identified) deviants attempt to come to terms with subsequent statuses (identities and treatments).

For many other participants, solitary deviance may be only partially "solitary" at best. Although these participants may seem to operate alone, closer examinations of their situations reveal that people's solitary enterprises often involve others in capacities as (a) suppliers of goods and services; (b) activity-related associates, partners, or assistants; (c) models or reference points; (d) sources of encouragement and/or provocation; (e) confidants and sources of personal support; and (f) targets of various sorts. Under these conditions, solitary deviance (even if undetected by most others) assumes some subcultural dimensions and should be studied in ways that are mindful of participants' involvements with these other people.[25] This would seem to hold for a number of activities that people might engage while on their own, such as drinking, smoking, using drugs, and stealing.

Many of these activities may be implemented on a more solitary basis, and occasionally may be first attempted on one's own. However, people commonly learn about these activities through association with others and may first try out these activities in the company of close associates (certain friends and family members). As well, where people have relational ties to others, they may have considerably greater support (from these others) for pursuing these activities than appears on the surface.

In approaching the study of solitary deviance, it is especially important that analysts be attentive to the risks of becoming caught up in the deviant mystique. Indeed, because people's solitary ventures lack a more explicit subcultural base they are more apt to be seen as unusual or strange.

Notably, too, since many deviants are encountered on a more isolated basis by families, associates, control agencies, and researchers, there is a common inclination to (a) attribute causality to individual qualities of identified deviants. These more isolated encounters also may partially account for the tendencies on the part of many to (b) invoke psychological or personality explanations when dealing with solitary deviants; (c) focus on the more unusual or consequential features of people's activities rather than the ways that people accomplish the activities in question; (d) ignore the reflective and processual nature of solitary deviance; and (e) disregard all of the subactivities entailed in envisioning, implementing, concluding, and assessing instances of solitary deviance. The sometimes related tendency to view solitary deviants as (f) "sick," "pathological," or "disturbingly evil" has only added to these analytical flaws.

It is essential that social scientists not become caught up in notions of the preceding sort or become mystified by (seemingly) bizarre, injurious, or irrational features of solitary deviance. This means focusing instead on the ways in which people define, implement, and experience activities and adjust to the situations in which they find themselves.

Reviewing the materials presented in this chapter, we may identify several consequential features of solitary deviance. First, there are the more generic matters of when and how people (a) become involved in situations, (b) implement the activities entailed therein, (c) sustain and intensify involvements in the situations at hand, (d) become disengaged from particular situations, and (e) become reinvolved in situations of that sort (on either a more isolated or subcultural basis).

Second, in drawing linkages between people's activities and inferences of deviance, it is important to ask when and how those participating in these activities define these endeavors with respect to morality and deviance. This means attending to the ways that the participants view (a) these activities, (b) themselves, and (c) others pertinent to the setting.

Third, when practitioners envision their activities as morally poblematic in some way, we may ask when and how they (a) attempt to conceal their situations from others and/or (b) engage in other practices intended to maintain or enhance personal respectability within their theaters of operation.

Although solitary practitioners may avoid detection for extended periods of time, we may ask when and how (a) others learn about these involvements, define these situations, and act toward those (targets) so involved; (b) practitioners (as targets) encounter definitions of disrespectability and deal with these definitions and the treatments they receive from others, both in the short run and over the long term; and (c) those who become implicated in deviance manage their relationships with others in both shorter and longer term respects.

Because humans are both enabled by the group and can (once so enabled) act independently of others in a variety of meaningful manners, the deviance phenomenon cannot be understood without examining solitary deviance along the lines developed in this chapter. Still, this chapter provides only a partial analysis of solitary deviance. Thus, whereas the preceding materials on defining deviance (chapter 4), defining deviants (chapter 5), and subcultural involvements, participation, and association (chapter 6 through 8) are essential for comprehending solitary deviance, the following chapters on regulation (10 through 12) and disinvolvement (chapter 13) also are consequential for understanding people's experiences in more solitary aspects of community life.

NOTES

1. Notably, for instance although Durkheim (1897) directly addresses suicide, he does not examine this phenomenon in *enacted* terms. See Douglas (1967) for further commentary on this topic.

2. However, language is itself a social product and a social process (i.e., a meaningful realm of activity). Language provides people with starting points and the foundations of intersubjectivity, but symbolic interchange, itself, is subject to various uses, modifications, and extensions (as it is subsequently invoked by those who engage in communicative practices, with others and oneself). Linguistic representations are social objects and, as such, are open to sense-making activity and interpretation. As much as some might wish to treat language as though it is inherently meaningful, language is an intersubjective, activity-based accomplishment (also see Mead, 1934; Evans and Falk, 1986; Evans, 1987, 1988, 1994).

3. This is not to deny certain fascinations, opportunities, or freedoms that people (as participants or audiences) sometimes associate with specific deviant involvements or advantages that may accrue to people identified as certain kinds of deviants.

4. Somewhat parallel notions of isolation may be experienced by people who envision their groups or collectivities to be more extensively discredited within some larger community. As with individuals who (a) may struggle with matters of morality, disrespectability, and undesired treatments in their minds and (b) may have difficulties relating to their associates (see Lemert, 1962), we may acknowledge the "paranoid relationships" that develop between members of particular subcultures and others in the broader community, as evidenced by more extended instances of denigration, exclusion, distrust, spurious communication, and volatile exchanges.

5. In developing this statement on emotionality, we have benefited particularly from the work of Goffman (1959, 1963), Lemert (1962), Lesieur (1977), Prus and Irini (1980), Petrunik and Shearing (1983), Schneider and Conrad (1983), Evans and Falk (1986), Evans (1987, 1988, 1994), Charmaz (1991), Wolf (1991), Karp (1996), and Ekins (1997),

as well as a wide variety of ethnographic research and interactionist analysis that deals with matters of emotionality in one or other ways (also see Prus 1996b: 173–201).

6. Although emotional sensations do not dictate particular lines of activity, people frequently associate particular emotional conditions with certain kinds of activities (including other emotional states). Thus, in developing certain perspectives or conceptual standpoints (by "taking the role of the other" [Mead, 1934]) on defining and dealing with particular emotional states, people not only learn ways of making sense of particular situations (and sensations) but also manners of acting toward themselves and other people once they have defined themselves (and/or others) as being in certain emotional states. Still, because people also are reflective entities, these group-based linkages of activities and emotional states are far from automatic or singular in application. Thus, even when working with reference points that they share with others, people are faced with the tasks of interpreting, defining, and developing ways of dealing with particular emotional experiences in the instances in which these are experienced both in the presence of others and on their own. In short, people engage emotional states in ongoing, adjustive manners.

7. Once emotionality is viewed as activity, we also may consider people's careers of involvement (see chapter 6) within particular emotional states. Approaching emotionality in process terms, we not only may ask when and how people first become involved in particular emotional states, but also consider the conditions under which particular emotional states or emphases are sustained and intensified, the ways in which people become disinvolved from particular realms of emotionality, and the ways in which people reengage emotional matters of similar sorts.

People seem to learn viewpoints on emotionality in much the same way that they acquire other notions of reality. Thus, we may appreciate that some notions of emotionality are apt to emerge and take shape in what Mead (1934) terms the "play stage" (wherein people begin to adopt particular or more singular role viewpoints as they focus and articulate their activities in meaningful, linguistically enabled manners) and are sharpened in the "game stage" (wherein people engage or act mindfully of, and adjustively to, a more diverse set of others) of childhood.

Whereas people's experiences with emotional states are subject to wide ranges of control efforts (as instruction, direction, and sanctions) from others, and are often mixed with shifting sets of opportunities and limitations, aspects of people's childhood emotional experiences may persist indefinitely. Thus, some emotional residues pertaining to matters such as shyness and embarrassment, fear and disgust, jealousy and excitement, anger and distrust, and the like, may be extended (with variable intensities and situated relevancies) throughout people's lifetimes as they recall or otherwise attend to particular kinds of sensations from the past.

Because people's notions of emotionality begin to develop somewhat concurrently with the acquisition of language, childhood encounters with emotionality are apt to be particularly elusive for researchers (studying people of any age) to trace in people's recollectable consciousness. Still, it would be advantageous for researchers to be mindful of any long-standing concerns and intrigues that people develop with respect to particular sensate experiences and to ask when and how people attend to these matters as well as the ways in which they deal with these and other aspects of emotionality in the situations at hand.

Focusing on sexuality (as a socially constituted, physiologically enabled essence) more specifically, Manford Kuhn (1954) develops an interactionist (Mead, 1934) viewpoint on sexuality (and gender) that very much parallels the present analysis of emotionality. Cooley's (1922) concept of "the looking-glass self" (wherein people imagine how they appear to others, how others assess them, and some subsequent feelings of self assessment) also is relevant to the present consideration of emotionality.

Notably, although people may have sensations that they find strange, inexplicable, or unsettling in more substantial manners, this need not prevent them from assuming roles as competent actors in other respects. Thus, like other discreditable people (see chapter 5), those who conceal their disreputable emotional states may maintain identities as normals within their respective communities on an indefinite basis.

9. Some may define this practice as "sublimation," wherein less desirable tendencies are substituted for more socially acceptable ones. Thus, some people who enjoy the emotional sensations associated with intimidating, embarrassing, or discrediting others may find that roles as lawyers enable them to pursue and achieve related emotional states in more socially acceptable and financially advantageous terms. Therapists, counselors, clergy, and other control agents working with deviance, likewise, may appreciate the opportunities that these roles provide for a range of voyeuristic and vicarious emotional experiences. Relatedly, too, other people may seek out disreputable emotional sensations in the media as consumers, artists, and authors, as well as through wide ranges of interpersonal exchange (as in jokes, stories, personal revelations, and gossip). Still others may emotionally engage aspects of the deviant mystique in roles as researchers, instructors, students, and so forth.

Although neither invoking Freudian assumptions nor viewing these emotive tendencies (in themselves) as adequate explanations for explaining people's involvements in specific roles or situations (even when particular activities are deliberately pursued for their sublimating qualities), the more fundamental point is that no speech-enabled member of the human community is exempt from matters of curiosity, sensation, marginalization, or the moral viewpoints that inform the deviant mystique. Quite directly, people are physiological essences and it is important to consider the ways in which people come to terms with any sensations to which they attend in meaningful (linguistically and action-enabled) terms within the context of ongoing group life.

10. While more sustained ethnographic research may enable scholars to better articulate the conceptual dimensions of people's emotional experiences (also see Prus 1996b), it would be impossible to identify all the possible sources of sensation that people might incorporate, in one or other ways, into their notions of emotionality. In addition to all sorts of circumstantial exposures to situations, more spontaneous bodily processes, definitions and impositions encountered from others, activities jointly developed with others, and people's more solitary activities, we also may recognize the emotional states (and sensations) that people derive from (the comparatively random, but still cognitively configured sensations associated with) sleep-related dreams and (people's more consciously engaged) daydreams.

11. The relevance of closure for solitary deviance is evident in studies of naive check forgers (Lemert, 1953), embezzlers (Cressey, 1953), "suicidees" (Jacobs, 1967, 1970; Henslin, 1970), depression (Karp, 1996), and transgendering (Kando, 1973; Ekins, 1997). It also seems that a great many instances of intentional deception (e.g., lying, cheating) reflect somewhat situated senses of desperation. Although other cases may denote planned, if not systematic, ventures, it is worth asking how people overcome any reservations about dishonestly, deceptive activities, and possible sanctions.

12. Those who engage in disreputable activities in small teams provide an instructive comparison point with respect to those who engage in deviance more exclusively on their own. Still, while members of teams may be highly concerned about detection (and condemnations) and often assist one another with concealment, anxieties, and a wide range of other difficulties and challenges, teams also introduce dilemmas, diversions, and vulnerabilities that people operating on their own may be able to avoid. Studies of professional thieves (Sutherland, 1937; Maurer, 1955; Prus and Sharper, 1977) who work in small groups are illustrative here, as is research on couples involved in mate-swapping (Bartell, 1971) and multiracial cohabitation (Rosenblatt et al., 1995). See Goffman (1959) for a valuable consideration of teamwork and related matters of secrecy, trust, and vulnerability.

13. This does not mean that solitary operators may not encounter some outsiders (relative to SO activities) who are willing to help them in some regard, but it should be recognized that these outsiders, however benignly intended they may be, may be unable to relate to the SOs in the same (intimately knowledgeable) ways that insiders in a subculture might be able to do. This does not mean that the subcultural insiders are always benignly concerned about the long-term future of other members, but it is important to acknowledge some insider affinities that outsiders may be unable or unwilling to appreciate. Brown's (1931), Ray's (1961), Biernacki's (1988), and Faupel's (1991) studies of the problematics of disinvolvement from drug use are instructive in these respects.

14. A consideration of the vulnerability of the solitary performers involved in "close-up magic" (as compared with group-facilitated card and dice hustling) is illustrative here (Prus and Sharper, 1991).

15. People's careers as (solitary deviants) would normally involve a set or series of situated engagements in particular activities. Although these often become blended in people's memories (and careers as practitioners) over time, specific episodes may be quite consequential for people's continued involvements in these realms of endeavor.

16. While people may later redefine the significance of various "points of no return," these encapsulating or funneling events are consequential because, on those occasions or instances in time, the participants feel "trapped" or "locked into" the flow of the situation; they cannot readily turn back to the point of merely contemplating the activity. They may try to disengage themselves from the activity at hand or opt to continue, but they realize that, somehow, they have to deal with a presently uncompleted episode or instance of activity. For example, readers may appreciate the differences between someone purchasing a marked deck of cards with the intention of cheating one's associates and actually putting that deck into play. Although the purchase need never be discovered, once one puts that deck into an actual game situation, one's fate as an honest player may more readily be subject to question. Similarly, a shopper who puts an item into a pocket or purse has placed himself or herself into a rather different situation from simply aspiring to own the object, holding it in one's hands, or even contemplating ways in which one might steal that object. People may be able to extricate themselves from these and similar commitments on many occasions, but their fates become much more dependent on the observations, reactions, and good will of others. In addition to (a) situations that they initiate on their own, people may sometimes experience points of no return as a consequence of (b) being incorporated into, or implicated by, the actions of others or (c) being unexpectedly discovered (as in, "being caught with one's hands in the cookie jar").

Relatedly, although people who undergo full-scale sex transformation (usually male to female) may try to readopt former male roles at times, the transsexual operation (see Kando, 1973; Ekins, 1997) represents a powerful illustration of people encountering points of no return. Also consider those who attempt suicide (see Douglas, 1967; Jacobs, 1967, 1970; and Henslin, 1970) or people who make life-and-death decisions in intensive care nursery settings (Anspach, 1993).

17. This is related to notions of "points of no return," but more specifically draws attention to the problematics of disengagement or disentanglement from aspects of the situation relative to the (anticipated) completion of the activity at hand.

18. Although disengagement may be abrupt and total in some cases of solitary deviance, it is essential to recognize the tendency for people to vacillate rather unevenly between solitary deviance pursuits and periods of inactivity with respect to those endeavors (see chapter 13).

19. Notably, discovery may result in dramatic disengagements in some cases. In other cases, however, formerly secret deviants may sustain or even pursue their involvements more extensively and openly in other cases after being discovered. It is necessary, therefore, to attend to discovery as an interpretive, interactive, and adjustive process. Clearly, "discovery" (and its aftermath) does not have uniform implications across cases (also see chapter 13 on treatment).

20. Whereas the matter of "receiving treatment" may be voluntarily sought out in some instances (likely reflecting some variety of the other themes listed in this section), it may also be imposed by outsiders who learn about or suspect particular (undesired) involvements. Treatments may vary greatly in formality and emphasis, but rather importantly they thrust the (formerly) solitary deviant into one or more subcultural settings or realms of experience. In some cases, these new (treatment) realms of interchange may still be experienced by recipients on a more isolated or singularistic basis, but at other times people may be put in direct association with like-situated recipients. In these latter cases, people who may have done things more on their own now find their activities are located more directly within subculturally shared contexts (and possibly much more experienced associates, collectively developed rationales, and such).

21. People's stocks of knowledge, interests, contacts, and senses of obligation may change notably over time, as may any reservations that they might associate with particular lines of activity, but the processes pertinent to "initial involvement" also are relevant to reinvolvements.

22. Although Lemert (1951, 1967) largely disregards activities that are not more pointedly designated as deviance ("primary deviation" in his terms), his work provides a valuable exposition of "secondary deviance" (which emerges in response to the reactions of others) to identified instances of deviance.

23. Somewhat parallel processes are evident in the often secretive, emotionally laden experiences associated with considerations of divorce (Vaughan, 1986), depression (Karp, 1996), and transgendering (Ekins, 1997).

24. This may also account for the sometimes surprising (to others) abilities of "troubled individuals" to connect effectively with people who are outside of the particular settings (in which certain disruptive practices seem so clearly established).

25. Concerns with discovery and discreditation are also generally prominent and consequential for this set of actors. In addition to frequent attempts to keep suppliers,

partners, and targets separate from other associates (i.e., minimizing disclosure by maintaining dual world separations), these solitary deviants may also experience heightened
senses of vulnerability as a consequence of these "shared secrets." See Goffman (1963),
Schneider and Conrad (1983), Herman (1994), Karp (1996), and Ekins (1997) for materials that address matters of these sorts.

Part IV

Regulating Deviance

10

Encountering Trouble
Handling Deviance Informally

> One of the waitresses [working in a rough bar] was saying that if there is any trouble,
> the staff usually sticks together and helps one another out. She also said that the
> regulars were pretty helpful in that sense too, they would pitch in and help out if
> you got into trouble. She added that the reason she thought the regulars got involved
> was because it was their bar and they felt that things like that didn't belong in the
> place, which is in a sense like their home. (notes) (Prus and Irini, 1980:163)

Having considered the ways in which people define deviance and deviants, as
well as the ways that people become involved in a variety of deviance-related
ventures on both a subcultural and more solitary basis, attention is now directed at the ways in which people attempt to deal with situations that they
consider troublesome or bothersome in some way.

Although discussions of regulating deviance often conjure up images of formal control agencies, such as the police, courts, and rehabilitative facilities, it
is advisable to distinguish formal control agency work from more casual or
informal attempts of members of the community at large to deal with those
whose behaviors they consider deviant or otherwise troublesome. Still, before
one divides regulatory attempts within the community too sharply along these
lines, it should be noted that both "citizens" and "control agents" frequently
act in ways that blur these distinctions.

In actual practice, thus, a great deal of deviance encountered both outside
and inside control agencies is handled informally.[1] Likewise, even those involved in more casual instances of deviance regulation may attempt to for-
malize, legitimate, or objectify aspects of the situations in which they operate.
Hence, people dealing with family members, friends, and other associates may
establish rules or other explicit definitions of trouble as well as particular procedures or shared understandings of the practices that they might invoke to
deal with instances of trouble in those settings.[2]

These latter practices need not be endorsed by any "official" agencies in the
community, but the citizens involved may reach understandings with others
that effectively establish the integrity of the definitions and other practices that
they may (righteously) invoke in the subsequent instances of trouble that they

encounter. As well, whether others in the setting agree with them or not, people often attempt to deal with situations that they define as troublesome from one or other standpoints.

On another level, it is ironic that even though most deviance is encountered, experienced, and handled informally, most of the literature on people's responses to deviance has focused on formal control systems, such as the police, courts, and psychiatric facilities. Formal control agencies are important elements in the "law and order" theme and may handle a large percentage of the "heavy" cases. Still, many cases may become consequential or distressing primarily because of agency involvements. Some other instances become more intense essentially because of the heightened public attention that they receive.

Even when considering the more disruptive and life-threatening events that people encounter, however, it should be noted that most of these instances are still *first* experienced by people on their own or in small group settings. In most of these cases, as well, those encountering situations that they define as troublesome have few, if any, of the organizational resources, preparations, or support systems that characterize control agencies.

Thus, although some highly threatening instances of trouble are first encountered by control agents (and even these agents may be taken by surprise by the instances in which these actually occur), control agents most often learn of trouble after cases are brought to their attention by those more directly involved at the outset (as victims, witnesses, or perpetrators thereof). Fortunately, from the viewpoint of citizens at large, most of the trouble they encounter is apt to be comparatively nonthreatening in essence (although even seemingly simple or fleeting things may assume significant proportions).

In some instances, control agencies may explicitly assume roles of monitoring and initiating contact with troublesome cases. However, as research on both the "referral process" (Ennis, 1967; Block, 1974) and the field responses of police officers to complainants suggests, citizens play central roles (both through their decisions to actually report crimes and their relative preferences for legal action as complainants) in determining what will be processed as crime at a formal or official level.[3]

Quite directly, many things that people consider deviant (and criminal) go unreported, and, even when people report instances of trouble to control agents, those reporting these instances may prefer not to push for prosecution or other more severe sanctions. Much trouble, thus, is subsequently ignored or handled in other, comparatively informal and often minimalist manners.

Also of relevance are the informal ways in which much of the deviance encountered by formal control agencies is handled. Proportionately little deviance is referred to, or discovered by, formal control agencies, and even then, the chances that it will be handled informally in those settings are much greater than would seem from examining formal control agency mandates.[4] However, since we will be examining control agencies in more detail later (chapters 11 and 12), the more immediate focus is on people's attempts to deal with deviance without recourse to those people who work more specifically as control agents.

DEALING WITH TROUBLE

The problem is not just the disruptive student on his or her own, because if they want to waste their own time, there's not much I can do about that. The problem comes when they waste my time and take the other students away from what they are supposed to be learning. That's the real problem with disruptive students. You'd just like to get rid of them. Get them out of your classroom for good! The problem is, where do you send them? They just pull everybody down. That's one of the really frustrating aspects of teaching and nobody really seems to care about that. . . .

What do I do? Well, you try everything you can. You try to ignore it. Sometimes, you try to reorganize your lessons or change the way you do things to get this person involved or maybe to isolate him. It's not always a him, of course. . . .

What else? You can give them that look, where they can or should be able to tell that you are onto them. If that doesn't work, you tell them to be quiet or try talking to them after class. Maybe take an interest in them sometimes, but that usually doesn't work that well either . . .

Sometimes, you just end up yelling at them, which isn't good, but you do it because you get so frustrated! You might try making them look foolish, sometimes, hoping that that will help. Then, there's detention, after class, or sending them to the office. But you don't like doing that, sending them to the office, all that often because then you start to look like you can't handle your own class. So that's not good. . . .

Sometimes, you laugh, too, because they might do something that's actually funny to you, too, or maybe they'll do or say something that's just so stupid that you can't help but laugh because they are so incredibly stupid! . . . A lot of times, you really can't do much because they've been doing this for years and you just happen to be the next in line and then, if they pass, the next teacher gets this pain in the neck and it just seems to continue. But nobody seems to care, other than the teacher that's having the problems at the time. (teacher, female, 45)

Rather than approach trouble as a discrete or objective event or circumstance, each instance of trouble will be envisioned in "career" terms, as having a developmental flow or history unto itself. The process begins when people define particular situations as troublesome and then act mindfully of these definitions.

Many things may be quickly dismissed as inconsequential or possibly as inferences that were mistaken or unfounded in some way. When things are thought more significant in some respect, those first invoking definitions of instances as troublesome may disclose these to others or deal with these matters more exclusively on their own.

Should the people involved reflect further on these instances on their own or in conjunction with others, they subsequently may attach different kinds of interpretations and levels of significance to the particular events under consideration. Thus, things thought less consequential earlier may be envisioned as more troublesome at later points in time, whereas matters initially deemed highly bothersome may be dismissed or allowed to fade in prominence at later times.

Further, although people may deal with some instances of trouble on a more solitary or unilateral basis, those defining situations in troublesome terms also may talk with, consult with, or otherwise attend to the inputs of the (alleged) perpetrators and/or other parties at a variety of points in the process.

Notably, too, instances of trouble may range from fleeting and short-lived concerns to more sustained and highly consequential sources of difficulty for the involved parties. Further, while much trouble is envisioned and approached in more singular or isolated terms, those encountering specific instances may relate (assess, compare, contrast) these occurrences with other earlier experiences or more prototypic images (as in common variants) of trouble.

Indeed, it might be appreciated that not only do people develop *memories* of what they (and often others) have experienced and done over time, but their regulatory efforts frequently also assume *adjustive* (though not necessarily more effective) qualities. Thus, when dealing with repeated instances of trouble involving the same person, people may employ similar and differing tactics in dealing with successive instances. Likewise, people who encounter certain kinds of situations involving different participants on a more recurrent basis may alter their responses from one time to the next even though the instances may be quite similar otherwise.

Relatedly, while those defining situations as troublesome may become increasingly bothered by, frustrated with, or indignant about having to deal with the same problem (with the same or different sources), they also may resign themselves to what seems a fairly common, possibly inextinguishable, pattern on the part of one or more people.

The ensuing analysis is divided into three parts: *defining situations as troublesome, responding to deviance,* and *contending with target associates.* Focusing on these three themes, we not only may achieve a better understanding of the ways in which people deal with deviance informally, but also may be able to suggest some lines of inquiry for subsequent research and analysis of the informal regulation of deviance.

DEFINING SITUATIONS AS TROUBLESOME

Because deviance is not a quality of an act or actor, people may define virtually *anything* as troublesome. As well, they also may define *anyone* (strangers, acquaintances, group members, or oneself) as the particular source(s) of the difficulties at hand.

Still, regardless of the focal points or targets associated with the deviance at hand, we may begin to articulate the processes and contingencies that people take into account in arriving at the particular notions of trouble with which they work. In this respect, it is instructive to consider people's (1) judgmental standpoints, (2) tendencies to define things as troublesome, and (3) attributions of culpability to those associated with trouble.

First, since nothing is inherently deviant or troublesome, it is essential to recognize that the definitions of deviance that people invoke reflect judgmental standpoints or frames of reference. Although people may implement an unlimited array of viewpoints in defining instances of deviance, five judgmental standpoints are especially noteworthy. These pertain to the matters of people (a) applying generalized group standards to the instances at hand; (b) assuming positional stances; (c) claiming rights within the group; (d) pursuing or accomplishing particular activities; and (e) attending to personal interests and disaffections.

Those applying generalized group standards to the situation at hand may not only reference one or more viewpoints of the broader community (ranging from generalized notions of civility and manners to more precise religious and legal codes, to concerns with threats to the group whose standards are being invoked). People also may define things as deviant by referencing viewpoints and understandings that are more unique to specific organizations or groups within the broader community.

Those invoking positional stances in defining trouble may be seen to attend to the particular concerns or obligations of their statuses or roles within the broader community or more specific associations within. Thus, for instance, political leaders, religious leaders, and parents may have very different notions of responsibility, trouble, and fun from members of their respective associations. However, as with people's tendencies to invoke generalized group standards, we also may expect wide ranges of positionally defined notions of deviance in actual practice.

When considering the standpoints that people may engage in defining trouble in group settings, it is important to recognize the claims that people may make as members of particular groups and how people invoke these claims in defining instances of trouble or deviance. The stances that people adopt on their rights may be somewhat specific to the positions they hold or the arrangements they have worked out in particular groups, but other claims may reflect more general, comparative notions of equality, fair play, and justice. From this broader viewpoint as well, others who receive greater shares or advantages of things within the group, compared to oneself or other deserving persons, may be subject to negative imputations. Likewise, those who are seen to distribute advantages unfairly (relative, variously, to people's desires for unqualified equality, distributive justice, or privileged rights of position) within group settings also may be sources of considerable disenchantment.[5]

However, because people's activities represent the most central means by which they are able to achieve particular objectives or ends, anything that is seen to interfere with their activities may become the focus of people's disaffections with others. In addition to those who may be seen to frustrate people's activities in more immediate respects, people also may resent those who may interfere with their abilities to accomplish certain things over the longer term. Thus, insofar as other people are envisioned to interfere with their abilities (physical, mental, technological, or managerial) to achieve their objectives, these people may become targets of considerable disaffection from those concerned about pursuing particular activities.

Other definitions of deviance may reflect people's more personal preferences and disaffections. Even here, however, while appreciating the more ideographic nature of deviance definitions that people may develop as self-reflective entities, it is important to be attentive to the ways in which these more particularized notions of deviance may be expressed, assessed, accepted, resisted, moderated, dismissed, and possibly more firmly entrenched or institutionalized within the group at hand.

Although people may invoke these and other judgmental standpoints in defining particular things as deviant, a related question revolves around the matter of when people are likely to implement these judgments. Given all of the things that people potentially could define as troublesome in one or other respects, it may be appreciated that people routinely overlook a great many things that they could find bothersome from one or other standpoints. Thus, we ask when people are more apt to attend to more specific things as instances of trouble.

Further, while people may experience somewhat vague senses of discomfort in particular situations, deviance becomes more consequential when certain activities or outcomes seem more intrusive or become highlighted in some way. Thus, people frequently *define things as instances of trouble* after observing that (a) some injury, damage, injustice, impropriety or other loss has occurred, particularly when they define those outcomes as more relevant or substantial in effect. Still, in addition to things that have already occurred, people may define things as troublesome when they are seen as indications of inappropriate present practices and undesired future states. Notions of trouble, accordingly, may be extended to include people who (b) are presently engaged in undesired, possibly dangerous activities; (c) are seen to disrupt, disturb, or influence others in ways that could become troublesome; and (d) display undesired or inappropriate appearances, viewpoints, attitudes, or emotional stances thought symptomatic of troublesome behavior in the future.

As well, in addition to things that people may observe on their own and the viewpoints that they may invoke in defining the significance of the things they notice, it also should be noted that (e) people's associates may draw attention to various matters that people might have overlooked as instances of deviance or trouble had they been on their own at the time (also see Emerson and Messinger, 1977).

The third process involved in defining situations as troublesome is that of assigning culpability to people in the situations at hand. Activities of the sort listed here tend to be more central to people's definitions of blame: (a) identifying perpetrators (through one's own observations, third-party testimony, or perpetrator revelations); (b) assessing perpetrator knowledge and anticipations of effects, responsibilities, common practices, and intentionalities; (c) encountering perpetrator-expressed sympathies, apologies, or restitution; (d) attending to and discerning of the relative relationships of multiple participants in the setting; and (e) being distracted by, or diverted from, concerns with assigning culpability on the part of targets by other matters.[6]

RESPONDING TO DEVIANCE

While people's definitions of deviance (as in invoking judgmental standpoints, articulating instances of trouble, and assigning responsibility) are foundational to people's responses to trouble, the emphasis here is more directly on the things that people do once they have defined particular events as instances of trouble.

Notably, too, just as people give meanings to the things that they encounter, so also may they give meanings to the things *they do* in dealing with troublesome situations. As Emerson (1981) observes, people may attach quite different meanings to particular strategies of regulation (be these formal or informal), both from one person to another and from one instance to the next. While people may develop customary and/or preferred ways of dealing with trouble with the same people or others more generally, they may use other modes of response only as "last resorts"; as tactics to be employed only when other things have proved ineffective or are discarded as inappropriate.

In discussing the informal regulation of deviance, five means of responding to deviance by concerned parties can be delineated, along with some of the contingencies affecting their usage. People encountering troublesome situations may *do nothing, alter their own behaviors, attempt to change other people, seek third-party assistance,* and *develop collective responses to the problems at hand.*

Although these options have somewhat different emphases, it should be appreciated that tacticians may employ wide ranges of strategies in dealing with others on a concurrent as well as a sequential basis. They also may do so in more mixed, partial, and tentative terms.

Doing Nothing

While people may assume inactive states on things because they are inattentive to (or unaware of) things in the setting, the emphasis here is on people who have knowingly defined things as troublesome but decide, for one or other reasons, not to engage the situation in more direct, open, and possibly confrontational manners:

One of the things I didn't like about the department store was that if the customers didn't like something or something was wrong with it, they could bring it back. No problem! You always were to be cheerful. The customer is always right! . . . That bothered me a lot because you're there working and doing your best, and here comes the customer and takes advantage of the store. Of you too, because you and the other people who work there, you have to work harder to make up for the loss that that person caused the store, by their stupidity, their carelessness in the way they treated the item. (dept. store) (Prus, 1989a:190)

While "doing nothing" or refraining from overtly responding to the perpetrators may seem to be the least consequential overall tactic that people may employ, this strategy need not be less effective than other tactics. Likewise, although not a preferred strategy in many cases, this tactic may offer people a great many advantages over more overt responses.

Because doing nothing enables people to remain more anonymous or unencumbered, it may free people from further, possibly difficult entanglements with troublesome individuals and/or their supporters.[7] Frequently also, not responding allows people to maintain viable relations with troublesome parties and others. As well, troublesome persons sometimes discontinue bothersome activities on their own. Given advantages of this sort, doing nothing may well be the most common way that people deal with troublesome situations. Still, we can ask when people are more or less likely to refrain from engaging targets in more direct terms.

Generally speaking, people seem less likely to engage targets when they: (1) consider the activities in question to be more inconsequential; (2) perceive themselves as having more pressing interests and/or obligations; (3) perceive target activities as less likely to persist; (4) anticipate that doing something would be personally more costly or risky than doing nothing; and (5) are more uncertain about how to appropriately respond to the situation.

People also seem less likely to adopt interventional stances when they (6) are more concerned with maintaining congenial relationships with the "troublemakers" and/or their supporters; (7) are personally more sympathetic to the activities under consideration; and (8) anticipate less success in their attempts to remedy the troublesome behavior.

Conversely, people seem more likely to take action when they (1) become morally incensed (i.e., experience righteous indignation) over an activity;[8] (2) believe that overlooking an activity may have more significant negative, longer-term consequences; (3) perceive themselves more accountable for upholding principles or rights that the activity is seen to jeopardize; or (4) envision themselves as obligated to act in the best interests of others (possibly including the troublesome persons) in the setting.

When doing nothing is viewed as untenable, four broad realms of remedial interchange become consequential: altering one's own behavior, trying to change other people, involving third parties, and developing collective responses.

Altering One's Own Behavior

People changing their own behavior in response to troublesome others have three major options. First, as a general tactic, people may endeavor to avoid those whom they envision as sources of difficulty. Second, and particularly in cases where people are concerned about sustaining congenial relationships with troublesome others (or feel dependent on their continuing good will), people may adjust their own behaviors in ways that are intended to accommodate (or minimize the consequence of) troublesome activities on the part of others.

Third, when people define certain kinds of situations as likely to recur with the same or different people, they may begin to develop practices or routines that are intended to minimize particular types of episodes. To this end, people may attempt to restructure situations in various ways. This may include the use of physical props and barriers, restricting modes and kinds of access to others, establishing certain kinds of responses to people's requests, or attempting to set the emotional tone of subsequent encounters with potentially troublesome others.

Although strategies of these sorts often have the effect of altering the behavior of the other, they focus on things that people can do somewhat more directly on their own. The following quote from an exotic dancer is illustrative here:

Sociability is a problem, because if you are too distant from the people, they won't treat you very well when you are on the stage, and you can't afford that. One of the things you might do if they say, "Hey, come and join us," or whatever, you say, "Fine, I will be there, but I have to get changed." You just never make it back down. You only choose the people you want to sit down with and you have to judge by sort of looking at them and just seeing how they treated you at first, who's decent and who isn't. Like some of them, you can see from a mile away that they are noisy or rowdy, by the way they're treating other people, or they are yelling or whatever, and they're the sort of people I try to avoid. (dancer) (Prus and Irini, 1980:99)

Trying to Change Other People

The third mode of dealing with deviance revolves around the matter of engaging troublesome persons in more direct terms. Typically, this means embarking on some form of influence work that is intended to change other people's activities in desired manners. In their attempts to change the other, people may embark on a wide variety of tactics, both on a more or less simultaneous basis and in sequences and repetitions of all sorts. Notably, too, some of these control efforts may result in entanglements with other people in the setting that are quite unanticipated and often, as a consequence of subsequent interchange, entail undesired outcomes.

The analysis of people's attempts to reshape or transform other people's behaviors is a multifaceted phenomenon. In engaging the other, regulators may bring a variety of aspects of self and other into play. Thus, once people have more overtly intervened in situations as regulators, their targets may assume opportunities to act back on those attempting to regulate their (target) behaviors. Once this occurs, both the "regulators" and their "intended objects of change" may assume roles as targets and tacticians on a sequential, if not also simultaneous, basis.

Although regulators do not always take this possibility into account, the anticipation of targets' reactions may represent an important consideration in people's decisions to do nothing or to alter their own behaviors in a great many cases. Still, people may persist in attempts to shape the activities and experiences of others even when they anticipate substantial difficulties along the way. Indeed, they may so much desire a resolution to the problems at hand that it may be exceedingly difficult for them to withdraw even from what they may anticipate is likely to be a costly failure.

If the people targeted for change are perceived to merit more considerate treatment, attempts may be made to explain and justify alternatives that the troublesome target might pursue. Likewise, targets defined as more reasonable may be given new chances or offered alternative lines of action (albeit possibly with the overriding threat of sanctions).

Those assuming stances as agents of control also may endeavor to educate or rehabilitate troublesome targets by invoking treatments (e.g., embarrassing, criticizing, punishing, counseling, therapy) designed to draw attention to undesired target behaviors, if not more directly intended to alter target behaviors in more specific ways.

In dealing with deviance, those who attempt to control other people's behaviors enter into the realm of influence (and resistance) work in a very fundamental sense. Accordingly, once one permeates the deviant mystique, people's attempts to regulate deviance may be envisioned within the more general context of influence endeavors (see Prus, 1999). Relatedly, we may ask when and how tactics intended to influence others are envisioned, implemented, assessed, extended, modified, or discontinued by those people who attempt to shape or redirect the activities of others.

Among the more noteworthy change-oriented tactics that people employ in their attempts to regulate deviance are the following: (1) providing instruction; (2) invoking inducements, threats, and treatments; (3) negotiating with perpetrators; (4) restructuring relationships with perpetrators; and (5) monitoring situations and preventing trouble.

Providing instruction entails things such as (a) defining behavioral guidelines and indicating acceptable limitations; (b) expressing explicit and subtle disapproval; (c) generating remedial (postbehavioral) definitions of propriety; and (d) indicating (also providing, enhancing, justifying) alternatives.

Using inducements, threats, and treatments encompasses the matters of (a) appealing to perpetrator interests and vulnerabilities and (b) administering (any form of) treatment. Although some treatments may be highly unilateral (as in sanctions), those using inducements, threats, and treatments (like those providing instruction) are highly dependent on target acknowledgments and cooperation. Accordingly, these efforts often result in more explicit target-tactician interchange and compromise.

Whether it is the eventual product of earlier attempts on the part of regulators to direct target behavior through inducements, threats, and treatments, or the more immediate and explicit position adopted by the involved parties at some point in time, the related notion of *negotiating with perpetrators* (and perpetrator representatives) generally involves things such as (a) attending to perpetrator activity (behaviors, targets, occasions); (b) focusing on perpetrator responsibilities and treatments; (c) offering concessions and special arrangements; and (d) defining options and justifying limitations.

In addition to other modes of affecting people's behaviors, tacticians also may attempt to *restructure relations with troublesome parties*. Thus, regulators may attempt to (a) calm others down and (b) cultivate more congenial relationships with troublesome parties, as well as (c) promote distancing between themselves and others and (d) deliberately antagonize or provoke certain targets.

When people attempt to "cool out," placate, or calm the other down, they may engage in practices such as (a) sympathetically minimizing the relevancies of target anxieties, fears, or losses; (b) generating diversions that targets are likely to appreciate; (c) offering apologies and restitution; and (d) providing reassurances and hope to targets.

Cultivating (more obligatory) relationships with perpetrators may involve activities such as (a) doing things for the other; (b) getting the other to do things for self; (c) displaying sacrifices made for the other; (d) indicating interest in the other; (e) acknowledging and otherwise attempting to ingratiate oneself with the other; and (f) assuming friendship positions with the other.

By contrast, regulators also may embark on explicit distancing practices. These may be invoked on a more unilateral basis or represent negotiated understandings about restrained or limited forms and arenas of contact (as in divisions or other arrangements of places, times, and possessions).

Although a great many efforts that tacticians make in dealing with others may be intended to foster smoother, more peaceful, or cooperative arrangements with targets, this is not always the intention of the people defining trouble in the setting. In some instances, thus, tacticians may knowingly and deliberately attempt to provoke or antagonize their targets. This might involve things such as belittling matters thought consequential to the target (as in viewpoints, concerns, relationships, activities, and the like) and frustrating the target from attaining things to which the target may aspire. In cases of this sort, tacticians may well "look for instances of trouble" as a basis on which to engage targets in more sustained confrontations.

The last set of practices considered here, *monitoring and assessing developments*, draws attention to people's attempts to anticipate and avert troublesome behaviors on the part of others. Among the more noteworthy themes here are (a) generating and/or sustaining surveillance in the setting; (b) defining particular people (individuals or groups) as more unpredictable or untrustworthy; (c) looking for indicators of potential trouble; (d) attempting to detect patterned or escalating conditions of concern; and (e) defining others as assuming inappropriate emotional stances (as in being rude, uncaring, vindictive, envious, or untreatable). The emphasis here is on minimizing trouble through earlier and/or selective intervention in the lives or situations of troublesome individuals.

Regulator intentions aside, it should not be assumed that any tactic or set of tactics will be successful in remedying particular sets of difficulties. Accordingly, regulators often *vacillate* both in the specific strategies that they use in attempting to come to terms with troublesome targets when problems persist over time and their hopes of finding effective ways of dealing with particularly troublesome situations. As well, whereas people often find that they are unable to manage their own behaviors in desired ways,[9] those attempting to manage other people's activities are apt to fare considerably less well than those trying to change their own routines.

Although people sometimes impose themselves on those they wish to control in highly unilateral fashions, the vast majority of people's attempts to regulate deviance occur *within dynamic, interactive theaters*. This has important implications for those studying the regulatory process. First, people's situations and concerns often *change* over time, thereby rendering some practices and objectives somewhat ineffectual or irrelevant on a more natural basis. Secondly, people trying to influence the behaviors of troublesome targets are dealing with objects that can knowingly *acknowledge* and *cooperate* with them as well as *resist* and *act back* on them in various ways. Notably, should the "deviants" define the "regulators" as the sources of trouble and attempt to direct and sanction the regulators, then both parties may engage roles as agents of control and targets.[10] Thus, while people often envision deviance and control as two separate realms of activity, these two roles are much more intertwined and interchangeable than might first seem. The interactive theater of operations becomes yet further extended when regulators involve third parties or collectively engage in attempts to deal with troublesome targets.

Seeking Third-Party Assistance

Another way that people attempt to control the activities of others is by involving other people in the regulatory process. Although this may be a last resort in some cases, it is quite apparent that other people may become involved in the regulation of trouble at various points in time. Third parties may, thus, be involved from people's first suspicions and throughout people's involvements in particularly troublesome situations. In some instances, too, people may begin to consider particular situations to be bothersome or somehow undesirable only after some third party has defined the instance as troublesome for the parties involved.[11]

Because we will be focusing on the collective responses to deviance that people develop as part of a group in the next section, the present discussion attends more directly on those third parties whom tacticians envision as outsiders to the situation rather than those with whom they would establish associations for dealing with troublesome others in more direct terms (as in teams or coalitions). Still, there may be some overlaps here, as well, because tacticians and other third parties may combine their efforts in a wide variety of manners.

In general, people (as tacticians) seem more likely to seek assistance from third parties when the tacticians (1) perceive third parties as (a) more accessible, (b) more ready to believe their accounts, and (c) more likely to act in their interests; (2) view troublesome situations as (a) more identifiable, (b) more persistent, (c) more offensive, (d) more threatening, and (e) more difficult to control; (3) consider revelations of trouble to be less personally costly (e.g., reputation, friendship);[12] (4) hold targets in lower esteem (disclosers are less concerned about any subsequent costs targets may incur as a result of the revelations); and (5) envision disclosures as opportunities for injuring particular targets.

Those seeking (or accepting) third-party involvements often anticipate direct and beneficial assistance in dealing with troublesome others. However, the results of third-party involvements are frequently much more uneven and mixed in effect, if not more singularly counterproductive at times.

In some cases, third parties may suggest that the concerned people "do nothing" about the situations at hand, possibly minimizing or defining the trouble away for the concerned parties (e.g., as needless, unfounded, mistaken, or unduly costly concerns). Likewise, third parties may suggest that troubled parties adjust their own behaviors in dealing with difficult situations or that the people intending to change the activities of troublesome others do so more exclusively on their own.

Third-party contact may result in people viewing and dealing with particular instances of trouble in ways that might be quite different from those they had anticipated, but third parties need not extend the options considered to this point. As well, some third parties only reluctantly may become involved or intend more entirely to avoid fuller participation (as in "doing nothing"). Still, by opening themselves to third-party counsel, people normally forego some control over the ensuing directions of the situations at hand.

Once contacted, too, some third parties may take charge of situations in much more direct and complete senses. In some cases, the original party may have little subsequent input into the outcome of the situation or sharply limited contact with the target. Even in those instances where third parties assume consulting, adjudication, or mediation roles, those seeking third-party assistance may find that they have much less impact on the ensuing situation than they may have anticipated.

Somewhat ironically, too, regulators opening themselves to third-party intervention also may find that they, themselves, become focal points of trouble from third-party standpoints.

Developing Collective Responses

Four young Mexicans were very noisy and were told to leave [the bar]. As they were leaving, one of the hookers was using the pay phone in the lobby and one of these guys grabbed her hair. She started screaming. The bouncer came up and started fighting with these guys. As the fight progressed, it went back into the bar and at this point a number of staff members became involved. Eventually, they threw these four guys out. They were beaten up pretty badly and were covered with blood. But once outside, they then started yelling and kicking at the door from the outside, and one came rushing back in. The bar people were just waiting, and when he came in, one of the waiters grabbed him and started hitting him in the face. The manager started hitting him in the back. The man went limp, but they just kept kicking him. At that point, I called the cops. A few minutes later, the manager came up and told me that I had better call the cops, to get this guy out of here. The police arrived, and by then the four guys were all outside, in very bad shape, bleeding extensively. The police called the ambulance and it took them away. The police talked to the manager a little. The manager was quite upset because the door had been battered. (notes) (Prus and Irini, 1980:162–163)

So far, we have discussed the informal regulation of deviance in ways that are largely consistent with people engaging troublesome situations on a solitary basis or with some (typically distinctive) third-party assistance. The notion of people developing collective responses to deviance builds on much of this earlier material (as in deliberations and tactics), but acknowledges some of the other practices that are open to people who encounter and attempt to regulate deviance.

Although the preceding extract about a bar fight indicates how quickly collective responses to trouble may develop and subside, other instances of collectively developed responses may entail extensive planning, recruitment, consultation, negotiation, confrontation, and extended sets of adjustments as the parties involved (targets included) engage the situations in much more sustained terms.

The emphasis here is on the alignments that people develop with others as they jointly attempt to deal with troublesome others in some comparatively focused, coordinated, or team-like fashion. In contrast to situations in which people singularly deal with troublesome others or refer targets to more independent third parties, those embarking on group-based ventures are apt to find themselves engaged in establishing, coordinating, and sustaining associations with others as well as dealing with the problematics of working out particular lines of action on a collective basis (as in defining, planning, negotiating, assessing, and adjusting activities) to be directed toward troublesome targets. Consequently, while people acting in groups may benefit from loyalties, resources, and an often greater sense of righteous indignation (via expressed sentiments, rationales, and consensus), those dealing with deviance in conjunction with others may find themselves drawn into situations, dramas, roles, positions, and associations that they might have preferred to avoid.

While focused on regulatory concerns, it may be appreciated that these collective endeavors very much reflect the grouping processes discussed in chapter 8. Thus, the very same processes pertinent to the development of subcultures or associations that are centered around deviant activities also are relevant to the development of groups or associations of people who assume the objective of regulating troublesome behavior on the part of some targets.

This would include the matters of participants (1) becoming aware of focal points and involved in collective events; (2) coordinating and sustaining collective events; (3) making sense of collective events; (4) becoming caught up in collective events and assuming more central roles; (5) withdrawing from or resisting collective events; (6) concluding collective events; and (7) reviewing and readjusting to collective events.[13]

Although we have focused on those attempting to manage deviance in the preceding collective ventures, it is important to acknowledge another set of participants who may enter into the broader regulatory theater of operations.

CONTENDING WITH TARGET ASSOCIATES

Another element that complicates tactician attempts to regulate deviance revolves around third parties of another sort; those who collectively participate in specific situations with targets or otherwise associate with the targets toward whom control efforts are directed. Here, somewhat like salespeople trying to deal with groups of shoppers (Prus, 1989a), tacticians who attempt to regulate deviance involving groups of people are apt to find these situations much more challenging than one-to-one encounters.

Not only may participants feel less culpable for things that they might do in group settings, but they often are more easily distracted by their associates and may be encouraged to persist in activities that they might have forgone on their own. As well, participants in groups also may experience obligations to defend one another's viewpoints and practices to any outsiders who might challenge them.

Even when target associates do not directly engage in troublesome activities with targets, they may still interfere with tactician attempts to deal with troublesome targets. In addition to (a) representing alternative reference points to which targets may attend (even in the absence of particular associates), target associates also may (b) ridicule or otherwise denounce tactician viewpoints and practices, (c) encourage targets to maintain or intensify practices deemed troublesome by the tactician, (d) confront tacticians on behalf of targets, and (e) attempt to sabotage tactician ventures in other ways. It might be appreciated as well, that tacticians need not be aware of the interchanges that take place between targets and their associates. Relatedly, even when tacticians are aware of target-associate interactions, tacticians seldom are well informed about the specific contents of these interchanges.

Target associates need not be effective in nullifying tactician efforts in all cases, but these third parties often represent extended sources of difficulty and frustration for those trying to regulate deviance. In the longer term, target associates may discourage tacticians from attempting to deal with the same or other targets in regulatory manners, but these third parties also may generate greater hostility between particular tacticians and their targets.[14] Thus, where targets assume more liberties (act with greater impunity) in the future as a consequence of third-party involvements, tacticians may become increasingly frustrated in their efforts to deal with these more elusive targets (and their associates). When matters intensify along lines of this latter sort, tacticians seem more likely to seek outside third-party assistance in dealing with what, for them, may have become unmanageable problems.

Although much overlooked by students of deviance, target associates represent pervasive sources of struggle for those attempting to regulate deviance in both informal and formal (see chapters 12 and 13) contexts. Indeed, virtually every parent or other person who assumes responsibility for maintaining the moral order of a particular setting or life-world can testify to the additional difficulties that arise when one attempts to deal with specific targets amidst their associates.

Because of the comparatively limited attention given to the informal regulation of deviance in the social sciences, much of the material introduced in this chapter is suggestive rather than definitive in emphasis. Nevertheless, it points to the importance of examining people's definitional practices and other regulatory endeavors in direct and sustained interactional terms. As chapters 11 through 13 illustrate, the ambiguous, reflective, tactical, and adjustive features of the regulatory endeavors are far from unique to citizens at large. Indeed, despite the more formal arenas in which control agents work, we find that a great deal of their activities also revolve around the matter of "handling deviance informally."

NOTES

1. The informal regulation of deviance received some groundbreaking conceptual attention from Emerson and Messinger (1977). These authors consider not only the problematics of defining "trouble" or "troublemakers" in everyday contexts, but also examine strategies for informally dealing with disruptive behavior and the roles that third parties may play in the "micro-politics of trouble." Ethnographic materials that

consider the ways in which disruptive behaviors are handled in more informal manners in family settings include Jackson's (1954), Wiseman's (1991), and Asher's (1992) analyses of family reactions to drinking problems; Waller's (1930) and Vaughan's (1986) work on marital dissolution; Fishman's (1990) study of prisoners' wives; and Davis's (1963), Schneider and Conrad's (1983), Blum's (1991), and Charmaz's (1991) considerations of families dealing with polio, epilepsy, Alzheimer's, and other debilitating illnesses.

For some materials dealing with the informal regulation of trouble in the workplace, see research on factory work (Bensmen and Gerver, 1963); truckers (Ouellet, 1994); work incentive programs (Miller, 1983, 1991); tuberculosis clinics (Roth, 1962); institutions for deaf children (Evans and Falk, 1986; Evans, 1987, 1988, 1994), caregiving agencies for the elderly (Gubrium, 1975; Lyman, 1993) and people with AIDS (Kotarba and Hurt, 1995); gynecological examinations (Emerson, 1970); classrooms (Hargreaves et al., 1975; Martin, 1975; Emerson, 1994); insurance claims adjustment (Ross, 1970); religious leaders (Lofland, 1966; Prus, 1976; Van Zandt, 1991; Shaffir, 1993, 1995); salespeople (Prus 1989a, 1989b); hustlers and thieves (Sutherland, 1937; Prus and Sharper, 1997; Prus and Irini, 1980; Alder, 1985; Steffensmeier, 1986; Jacobs,1999).

Although often interrelated with people's work roles, one may also ask about the regulation of deviance with respect to settings that are somewhat more distinctively recreational in emphasis. Here, one may acknowledge studies of drinking and drug use (Becker, 1963; Rubington, 1968; Prus, 1983; Ingraham, 1984; Faupel, 1991); gang life (Thrasher, 1927; Keiser, 1969; Wolf, 1991); fantasy role-playing games (Fine, 1983); pre-adolescent culture (Adler and Adler, 1998), high school debaters (Fine, 2001), little-league baseball (Fine, 1987); ballet (Dietz, 1994), women's college basketball (Scott, 1981); women's college hockey (Theberge, 2000); homosexual life-worlds (Reiss, 1961; Warren, 1974; Humphreys, 1975; Ponse, 1978; McNamara, 1994; Correll, 1995), nudism (Weinberg, 1970); entertainers (Becker, 1963; Prus and Irini, 1980; Newton, 1979; MacLeod, 1993); and places featuring heterosexual entertainment (Cressey, 1932; Roebuck and Frese, 1976; Heyl, 1979; Prus and Irini, 1980; Irini and Prus, 1982); mate-swapping (Bartell, 1971), and transgendering (Kando, 1973; Ekins, 1997).

Lemert (1962) provides an instructive depiction of the ways in which troublesome interpersonal relations may intensify in his examination of paranoid relationships. Focusing on depression, David Karp (1996) generates a particularly valuable consideration of people's experiences with a troublesome (i.e., troubled) self. In addition to depicting a wide variety of ways in which people attempt to remedy personal senses of depression on their own (as in doing nothing, altering their own behavior), Karp also indicates how these people consult with third-party others in more casual as well as more formalized control settings.

2. When members of groups, such as families, recreational associates, and coworkers embark on collective definitions of trouble, they may be seen to operate as microcosms of the larger community. Thus, in defining trouble, people in smaller groups are apt to be involved in processes somewhat parallel to those outlined in chapter 4 (e.g., see the discussion of "social problems as collective behavior").

3. Although there are few sustained ethnographic studies of either the referral process or the ways that police officers deal with these cases, the following materials are among the more informative: Parnas, 1967; Black, 1970, 1980; Black and Reiss, 1970; Lundman et al, 1978; Davis, 1983; Charles, 1986; Meehan, 1992; and Lundman, 1996.

4. For some indication of the ways in which deviance is handled informally in control agency settings, see studies of the police (Bittner, 1967; Parnas, 1967; Rubinstein, 1973; Davis, 1983; Charles, 1986; and Meehan, 1992); parole and probation officers (Emerson 1969; McCleary, 1975, 1983; and Prus and Stratton, 1976); the military (Ingraham, 1984), and other human service workers (Daniels, 1970; Wiseman, 1970; Gubrium, 1975; Emerson, et al., 1983; Hall, 1983; Miller, 1983, 1991; Wharton, 1989, 1991; Broadhead and Fox, 1990; Warren, 1983; Lyman, 1993; Horowitz, 1995; and Kotarba and Hurt, 1995).

5. This analysis has benefited from Aristotle's *Nicomachean Ethics*. The notions of unqualified equality suggest that all people are equally meritorious irrespective of who they are, what they do, or whether they have contributed to anything. Distributive justice refers to the notions of equality that reflect the ratio of people's activities and other contributions to their rewards they receive (i.e., on a comparative, regulative basis). Privileged justice recognizes the differential positions (e.g., citizen-noncitizen, parent-child) from which people may claim certain advantages.

6. While this discussion deals with people's notions of culpability more generally, Garfinkel's (1956) consideration of successful degradation ceremonies also is relevant here.

7. Although troublesome people often act in more solitary fashions, it might be appreciated that other people (as in friends, family, and other associates) may take up their defense and/or attack (in various ways) those who might try to deal with the target as a source of trouble. Sometimes, the targets will seek out the assistance of these other people, but these other parties may enter into confrontational settings even when the targets have not invited them to do so.

8. Relatedly, it should not be assumed that "doing nothing" represents the easiest way in which to deal with all situations that people may encounter. Indeed, on some occasions, those refraining from taking direct action against perpetrators may be subject to considerable criticism from third parties.

9. As Goffman (1959, 1963) emphasizes with respect to impression management, the matter of "managing oneself" is of pervasive relevance for comprehending people's activities (and applications within). Although this task may be particularly troublesome for those experiencing physically debilitating illnesses (see Davis, 1963; Schneider and Conrad, 1983; Sandstrom, 1990; Blum, 1991; Charmaz, 1991; Lyman, 1993) and people implicated in deviant life-worlds (especially see chapters 5 through 9 and 13) more generally, the matter of managing oneself extends across wide domains of community life. Bernstein's (1972), Haas and Shaffir's (1987), and Albas and Albas's (1994) studies of students managing their studies is illustrative here, as are Prus's (1989a) consideration of people attempting to achieve and sustain enthusiasm in sales settings, Karp's (1996) study of people's encounters with depression, and Fine's (2001) account of high school debaters.

Although people who have difficulties managing any realm of activity may experience some disrepute as a consequence of inadequate performances, those involved in ventures that are more distinctively defined as deviant or criminal have yet more to lose should their performances fail to provide the cover necessary to avoid detection and any ensuing responses from others. See Sutherland (1937), Bartell (1971), Prus and Sharper (1977), Prus and Irini (1980), Steffensmeier (1986), Ekins (1997), and Jacobs (1999) for some indication of the ways in which concerns with disrespectability and/or illegality enter into people's endeavors.

10. A more comprehensive analysis of influence (and resistance) work across an extended range of humanly enacted settings is available in Prus (1999).

11. In addition to Emerson and Messinger (1977) who deal with the role of third parties in the regulation of trouble, readers also may find Simmel's (1950) statement on triadic relationships instructive more generally. For considerations of the roles that police officers assume as third parties (between complainants and their targets), readers are referred to Bittner (1967), Black (1970, 1980), Black and Reiss (1970), Parnas (1967), Rubinstein (1973), Lundman et al. (1978), Davis (1983), Charles (1986), Meehan (1992), and Lundman (1996). Ross's (1980) work on insurance claims adjustment also is instructive here as is Emerson's (1994) study of high school discipline officers.

12. In some cases, these disclosures (truthful or otherwise) may be very productive for the "troubled" individuals, enabling them to restore or achieve esteem by indicating the obstacles they have encountered, their suffering, their relative innocence in the venture, and the like.

13. See Prus (1999:261–265) for a fuller elaboration of the variable roles and processes entailed in people's participation in collective events.

14. Third parties thought to interfere with target-tactician relations also are apt to become focal points of tactician disaffection.

11

Organizational Agendas
Maintaining Control Agencies

In contemporary society, the formal regulation of deviance is exemplified by the practices of a large variety of control agencies (e.g., police, prisons, regulatory agencies). Although control agencies may be "one-person operations" in some instances, they are more apt to be group endeavors of sorts and frequently become complex organizations. At the same time, however, it is instructive to recognize the processually engaged features of control agencies. As associations that are more or less continuously in the making, control agencies are ultimately contingent on the ways in which they are represented, engaged, and integrated into the community through human interchange. We will be considering the roles of those working in control agencies more directly in chapter 12, but it is most instructive to attend to the ways in which control agencies take shape and are maintained within the community context. It is to this latter set of issues that this chapter is directed.

Control agencies may be developed in a variety of ways. Sometimes, agencies emerge from occasional informal control endeavors that eventually become routinized and consolidated within the community. Control agencies also may develop within the context of other groups, agencies, or governmental departments that (in one or other ways) begin dealing with certain kinds of cases, only to become more distinctively known as agencies for particular realms of deviance. In other instances, agencies are created more directly and specifically in response to particular "social problems" (either by interested people within the broader community or by those envisioning themselves as mandated in some respect to protect the public interests).

Minimally, though, the establishment of a control agency implies some enterprise (and coordination), if only to the extent of conceptualizing an agency or office of some sort that would attend to an agenda of control in some arena, encouraging this arrangement as an acceptable practice within the community, obtaining funding (facilities, supplies, etc.) for sustaining the program, and locating and instructing personnel. Clearly, these latter matters assume greater consequence if the agency or office is to achieve some uniformity and continuity in implementation (i.e., transcend the efforts of isolated individuals). Attending to issues of the sort just delineated, this chapter addresses a set of concerns to which those involved in control agencies (particularly as coordinators) are likely to attend on a day-to-day basis.

Notably, thus, there is an overarching concern with *maintaining the agency* if not also expanding the jurisdiction, scope, prominence, and centrality of the agency within a competitive arena involving other control agencies. It also should be appreciated that control agencies represent the sites within which coordinators and other staff develop workplace careers. Agent viewpoints and practices may vary considerably, but office holders typically try to achieve personally viable workplaces within these settings. This is often reflected in quests for job security, lightened workloads, more recognition, greater workplace autonomy, and greater control over the day-to-day tasks in which the staff, themselves, engage. These latter concerns will be addressed more centrally in chapter 12, however, the immediate focus is on the activities entailed in maintaining control agencies.

To this end, consideration is given to the tasks of *achieving support; accessing cases; classifying cases; emphasizing treatment; restoring justice*; and *pursuing internal order*. As will become quickly apparent, these matters not only involve agent-case relationships but also, almost inevitably, locate agency concerns and activities in a much broader community context.

ACHIEVING SUPPORT

If an agency is to regulate deviance on any large scale, a fundamental concern is that of achieving public awareness and support. Not all agencies are dependent on government funding, but some degree of community acceptance is essential if the agency is to become influential in its regulatory endeavors. Not only does public acceptance provide legitimation, but it also establishes a basis on which to obtain both the funding and the cases necessary to keep the program viable. Promotions or public relations work may assume a variety of forms, and may be sufficiently effective to convince the community that the agency (e.g., police, courts, mental hospitals) is an essential element of community life.

As Hawkins and Tiedman (1975) suggest, "controlling deviance is big business." Operations may range from educational programs, counseling services, social work programs, and other community assistance projects to prisons, mental hospital, and other "total institutions" (Goffman, 1961). In each case, however, and regardless of whether the agency approaches deviance from a legal, medical, psychological, welfare, or religious perspective, agencies seem obligated to make some claims about their validity.

To the outside public on which they are dependent for support, the agencies endeavor to appear expert, effective, and trustworthy.[1] If there is sharp competition in dealing with particular types of deviance, agencies may endeavor to indicate that they are not only more knowledgeable and reliable than their competitors, but that their programs also are more economical, humane, or otherwise more desirable. Agencies may seek out deviants as "grist for the mill," but agencies also recruit support for their programs. Agencies' publicly expressed philosophies may represent ineffectual indications of their actual operations, but to the extent that agencies are perceived as representing desired community objectives, these images may serve as a basis for generating community support (and funding) as well as client referrals.

ACCESSING CASES

Although some of the deviance that control agencies encounter comes about as a result of agency surveillance routines (e.g., police patrol; see Bittner, 1967; Rubinstein, 1973; Black, 1980; Charles, 1986; Meehan, 1992) and more intensive purging activities (e.g., Erikson, 1966; Connor, 1972), a great deal of the deviance coming to the attention of formal control agencies reflects citizen activities (complaints, inquiries, and referrals).

Citizens may be somewhat skeptical of the effectiveness of control agencies (Ennis, 1967), but perhaps out of senses of desperation, desires to follow procedures, attempts to restore order, or achieve retribution relative to offenders, many people will contact, consult, or inform agencies regarding troublesome situations. In general, and in spite of indications that lay referrals and inquiries constitute the bulk of agency-encountered deviance, it is also apparent that citizens handle a great deal of the deviance they encounter without recourse to agency intervention. Consequently, extensive promotions work (e.g., the marketing of legal, medical, or welfare programs) may be conducted to increase the likelihood that any given instance of trouble will be referred to this or that control agency.

As well, although other people (as individuals or groups) may endeavor to access and deal with troublesome cases that might fall under the purview of particular control agencies, these efforts need not be appreciated by those representing those agencies. Thus, people thought to "take matters into their own hands" (or to presume other state-sanctified agency objectives, as in practicing medicine, psychiatry, or law without appropriate certification) are often viewed as vigilantes or lawbreakers of sorts. Despite possible support or encouragement for these external efforts by other people in the community, those representing affected agencies may treat these "helpers" in ways that are more severe than the treatments they might direct at their allegedly primary target cases.

CLASSIFYING CASES

Once contact is made with troublesome cases, agencies typically require that those they encounter be sorted into agency-specific categories (e.g., particular legal or psychiatric categories) before they are processed further. This is not to imply that these categories are objective or are consistently and accurately applied. Research suggests that agency categorizations (see the labeling process in chapter 5) are perspectival, negotiable, and may be assigned on the basis of little (and sometimes conflicting) evidence.[2] Formats may vary extensively across agencies and, in some cases, targets may have neither the desire nor the opportunity (or resources) to resist labels being affixed to them.

In general, target designations are likely to reflect agent perceptions of standardized agency case dispositions and tend to be affixed in the most expedient means available.[3] Expediency seems particularly likely to be emphasized when control agents (1) hold targets in lower esteem, (2) envision themselves as less accountable to targets, (3) anticipate lower levels of subsequent interaction with targets, and (4) perceive a larger number of cases to be processed.

As Burkholdt and Gubrium (1983) note, typings also seem influenced by (5) perceived concerns of audiences to whom agents consider themselves accountable, (6) attempts to appear competent, and (7) particular instances of target sympathy. Emerson (1983b) further suggests that agent processing of individual cases reflects (8) the judgements of particular cases relative to the other cases under consideration at the time; (9) the resources available to treat particular types of cases at that time; (10) the immediate implications of increased numbers of particular kinds of cases relative to agent concerns with outside evaluators; and (11) concerns with establishing particular patterns (e.g., precedents, examples to others) in the cases processed.

Where agents sense less accountability to the agency (or others), the labels they assign to others are particularly likely to reflect their personal styles and preferences. However, to the extent that (12) targets and/or others (including control agents promoting other programs) interested in the target's future are able to intervene in the definitional process, the resulting typings are more likely to be negotiated and, as such, are less apt to reflect the interests of the agency or the preferences of the agents at hand than would otherwise be the case.

EMPHASIZING TREATMENT

Regardless of whether agency programs are directed toward the society at large, particular groups of people, or specific individuals, the matter of effecting change or doing something about the problem is the primary, publicly expressed directive of control agencies.

It is because of community faith in agency claims to be able to do something positive about undesired situations that control agencies are supported. Whether their objectives are preventative, educational, deterrent, rehabilitative or punitive in central thrust, the claim is that these pursuits or "treatments" will be effective and beneficial to the community on whose support the agency is dependent.

Good intentions aside, the task of achieving treatment objectives becomes highly elusive when people are involved (as is the related matter of program evaluation). There are genuine incentives (agency maintenance, career advancements, ideological commitments) on the part of staff people to selectively define, portray, and embellish images of their programs and their successes. However, as indicated in chapters 12 and 13, there is very little research that directly examines the ways in which people in human services work tactically promote change on the part of others.

In what follows, consideration is given to the treatment-related matters of *assessing change; evaluating programs; displaying competence;* and *acknowledging limitations.*

Assessing Change

To date, the predominant strategy for assessing change has been to compare variants of "before" and "after" (treatment) measurements of attitudes and behaviors pertaining to deviance. These comparisons may appear fairly straightforward on the surface, but the task of evaluating change or treatment effects has also become the locus of extended debate and enterprise in itself.

First, although agencies sometimes selectively screen their clients or define successes in manners that tend to inflate their programs' effectiveness, more open inquiries indicate that most remedial programs are nowhere as successful as anticipated or claimed by the agencies promoting these programs.

Second, most attempts to ascertain success have been rooted in quantitative analysis. Typically, "before" and "after" treatment rates are compared, with any gains in success attributed to that specific treatment program. Changes may be measured by attitude scales or behavioral indices of some sorts but the comparisons are generally made in global terms. Control groups (comparable, but untreated populations) may or may not be used as reference points. When treatment groups score higher than untreated populations, this is usually taken as an indication of the program's effectiveness. However, agencies also develop standardized sets of justifications for offsetting disappointing results (see Cressey, 1958).

Other problems exist. When evaluations are conducted by insiders, these are often suspect of motive. However, when outside evaluations reflect poorly on the agency in question, agency personnel typically claim that these outsiders are insensitive to the situations at hand.

In general terms, as well, it is not apparent that doing nothing (i.e., relying on informal, casual, or spontaneous improvement in untreated cases) is less effective overall than are most treatment programs. Thus, although some people may change as a consequence of their participation in this or that program, rates of success for treatment programs generally are not substantially greater than those for similar groups of untreated populations in the community.

If one were to ask whether control agencies are able to effect change on the part of the people they treat, the best answer may be, "Yes, somewhat, but likely nowhere as much as control agencies claim or anticipate; and probably not much more effectively than doing nothing."

Agencies generally claim to provide effective sources of treatment and one encounters some scholarly attempts (e.g., see Andrews et al., 1990; Andrews and Dowden, 1999 on correctional reform) to reestablish respectability and optimism for rehabilitation programs as well as neutralize those they define as detractors of these programs. However, other scholars surveying the field have been struck by the relative *inability* of agency programs to distinguish themselves as sources of effective treatment. The reviews of Logan (1972), Martinson and Wilks (1975), and Walker (1989) in the area of correctional reform are typical in this regard. Although most programs may help some people and many achieve better "success rates" than do people who are left on their own, there is limited overall optimism for any agency claims about running highly compelling or particularly effective treatment programs.[4]

There is another often overlooked, but basic issue at stake. Thus, regardless of who gathers and analyzes the data or how carefully designed particular statistical studies may be, people who emphasize the outcomes of treatment programs miss the actual lived experiences (interpretations, practices, adjustments) of both the staff and the clients involved in these programs. Quite directly, one cannot claim to know how agencies function on a day-to-day basis or how clients experience and attend to treatments without sustained ethnographic inquiry (and this type of research has been notably absent in most evaluative research).

In the interim, however, government agencies feel pressured (desperately in some cases) to provide indications that they are doing something consequential about certain problems. Thus, governments remain viable targets for those promising panaceas in the treatment and prevention of deviance.[5]

Evaluating Programs

Although people administering funds (to support control agencies) often are aware of the vested interests of control agencies and may be cognizant of some of the shortcomings of quantitative research, they nonetheless tend to insist on efficiency reports. Despite the problems associated with assessing treatment programs, a great deal of emphasis has been placed on evaluation research and conveying images of success. Since administrators are accountable to other publics for their decisions to fund particular programs, they often use statistical reports as "quick-fix" justifications for supporting certain programs over others. Notably, as well, the emphasis on program evaluation within the funding sector has created additional analytic problems for scholars attempting to comprehend agency routines and assess treatment programs.

In response to concerns with program evaluations on the part of both funding sources and control agencies, a major industry has developed around the business of program assessment. Addressing and emphasizing "the desirability, feasibility, and benefits of program evaluation," program assessment has become big business. Ironically, while promising a viable technology of assessment, those in program evaluation have developed a sophisticated, but elusive rhetoric of competence.

Traditionally, program evaluations have been rooted in positivist conceptions of cause and effect (see Rossi and Freeman, 1989, as a contemporary exemplar), but these quantitative modes of evaluation have encountered some resistance in the field (see Patton, 1981; 1982). While some (minor in impact) of the criticism has centered around the failure of these emphases on measurements of success to depict actual program practices on a day-to-day basis (Loseke, 1989), quantitative evaluations have been more centrally opposed by those running various programs because seldom have these studies supported the success claims that control agencies wish to make in pursuing private and public funding.

However, because program evaluation provides administrators with a set of shorthand images (accurately or otherwise) of particular programs, evaluation research has become entrenched in human services work. Indeed, evaluations typically are mandatory elements for agencies attempting to obtain and maintain (and pursue more) government funding.

Displaying Competence

Those working in control agencies, thus, generally see program evaluations as unavoidable and have sought to make these intrusions as "agency friendly" as possible. Consequently, not only may programs be set up explicitly with the intention of maximizing favorable evaluations, but efforts also may be made to maintain practices that contribute to images of success (regardless of their implications for actually changing the target population). Whether agencies do or do not achieve their alleged objectives, they recognize that it is important to "look good" or maintain a "cloak of competence."[6]

These two objectives of "assessing effectiveness" and "looking effective" have resulted in some consequential schisms in the field of program evaluation. Thus, in addition to those who continue to do more conventional statistical comparison studies (and occasionally supplement these with qualitative research), program evaluation has moved in some new, agency (and consultant) serving directions. In the pursuit of research contracts, some of those whose livelihoods depend on program evaluation have become highly attentive to matters of agency preservation and enhancement.

Indeed, program evaluation (see Patton, 1981, especially pp. 180–193) is so diffused, multifaceted, and politically compromised (emphasizing benign images and funding potential) that it may be viewed as "agency serving" rather than focused on assessing change. Whereas many evaluators genuinely still subscribe to the task of assessing change (treatment effects) in programs, other outside evaluators (most of whom also do quantitative work) have been assuming "fronting" or "cloaking" roles, effectively serving as agents (claiming expertise, invoking mystifying rhetoric, and creating illusion and misdirection) for the agencies presumably being assessed.[7]

Acknowledging Limitations

Because they work with people, human service workers lack the sort of "quality control" that people may achieve when working with aluminum or plastics, for example. As minded beings, humans not only may interpret particular things in a great many different ways, but they also can act back on those attempting to work with them. Thus, in addition to having to contend with legal rights and humane treatment concerns, as well as dealing with diverse and complex "materials," those engaging in people-work also deal with objects that can act back on and attempt to shape worker behaviors and experiences (see Goffman, 1961; Emerson, 1969, 1994; Spradley, 1970; Wiseman, 1970; Gubrium, 1975; Hall, 1983; Miller, 1983, 1991; Lyman, 1993; Horowitz, 1995).

Agent attempts to influence targets (via justification, benign intentions, instruction, ingratiation, threats, sanctions, and negotiation) become even more problematic when it is recognized that the targets may (a) not want to change (or be changed); (b) not trust the agents working with them; (c) not value the particular orientations promoted by the agent; (d) not consider agent viewpoints relevant to the "real world;" and (e) encounter considerable opposition to agency positions among other targets receiving agency treatment as well as outsiders with whom targets have contact.

Although longer and more intensive programs are likely to result in targets being more knowledgeable about agency life, the problematics of accomplishing people-work and dealing with target resistance tend to render rehabilitation ineffective. Not only may the clients with whom control agencies deal not be interested in changing their lifestyles, but even when they intend to pursue agency programs, the clients are apt to find that this is much less readily accomplished in practice than they had anticipated.

Whereas those engaging the role of "reformed sinners" commonly encounter some distrust and exclusion on the part of "straight society," these clients often find that they miss aspects of their former lifestyles (as in perspectives, identities, activities, and relationships). As well, clients frequently encounter encouragements from former associates to revitalize their involvements in those subcultural (deviant) pursuits. As a consequence, reinvolvements in deviance and subsequent vacillations between deviant and straight involvements tend to be commonplace occurrences in rehabilitation programs, even when clients indicate strong desires to disengage themselves from their deviant life-styles (see chapter 13).

Although many programs are designed to foster change by removing targets from particular situations and/or providing them with opportunities to pursue alternative lifestyles that agency personnel consider more appropriate, sur-prisingly little attention has been directed toward examinations of what staff people or their clients *actually* do (think, experience, act, interact) in these programs.

This discussion does not deny the "good intentions" or the sincerity of those working as control agents, but it does indicate that success is an elusive concept. In addition to (a) whatever conceptual and practical limitations particular pro-grams and agency personnel may represent for dealing with the situation at hand, success is further compromised by (b) the abilities of the targets of vari-ous remedial programs to resist undesired changes, and (c) the roles that former and current (nonstaff) associates play in the deviance-making (and rehabilita-tion) process. It also would be erroneous to assume (d) that all of these working as control agents fully endorse and support agency-expressed objectives.

When matters of these sorts are taken into account, it becomes apparent that one cannot develop an appreciation of the complex social processes involved in attempts to implement and sustain rehabilitative treatment through quanti-tative research. Nor will this be achieved through program evaluations, given agency concerns with maintaining cloaks of competence in their quests for funding.

If social scientists intend to learn just what goes on in particular control agencies and how successes are defined and attained in practice, it will be nec-essary to embark on extended ethnographic research in these settings. Only in this way may scholars learn (1) what agents actually do and how they go about their activities (including both their adjustments to the clients they encounter and their attempts to negotiate their routines with other control agency per-sonnel); (2) how agency targets experience these treatments (their definitions of staff programs and practices, their perceptions of the relevance, desirability, and feasibility of attending to these matters, and their ways of dealing with these treatment programs); and (3) the ways in which agency targets and their broader set of associates within the community define and act toward each other before, during, and after agency contact.

Rather than assume that control agents are effective implementers of change and that the clients are relatively mindless, passive targets whose behavior will be reshaped in desirable directions by exposing them to some treatment pro-gram, the suggestion is that rehabilitation work be envisioned as a negotiated enterprise in which *both* the clients and the staff may attempt to adjust to, influence, and resist one another on an ongoing, day-to-day basis (Goffman, 1961; Ray, 1961; Roth, 1962; Irwin, 1970; Wiseman, 1970; Carroll, 1974; Miller, 1983, 1991; Peyrot, 1985; Wharton, 1989, 1991; Loseke, 1992; Prus, 1992a; Horowitz, 1995; Owen, 1998).

RESTORING JUSTICE

Regardless of their effectiveness in achieving change on the part of their targets, control agencies serve another basic social function, that of restoring moral order or community notions of justice.

Agency practices and styles of "realignment" vary extensively, as do the philosophies underlying their implementation. Agency reactions are often linked to the definition of trouble, wherein religious organizations handle "sinners," courts handle "criminals," and the like. Still, multiple programs may be applicable to the same instance of trouble and, in some cases, agencies may very directly compete for the same targets. "Violent offenders," thus, may not only represent candidates for court, but also may be referred to, or sought out by, control agencies with a religious or psychiatric flavor. Somewhat relatedly, regardless of its orientation, any "well-intentioned" agency may serve to neutralize deviance (and the hostility directed towards the "culprits" involved) within the community.

As "something is being done," those concerned with troublesome cases can return to life as usual. Justice is restored (for the time being) as a consequence of agency intervention. However precarious or superficial agency practices may be, the restoration of moral order represents a major function of control agencies; that they serve as "buffers between offenders and victims" (or other concerned parties), thereby neutralizing troublesome situations. This is where "punishment," to the extent it restores "social regulation" (Durkheim, 1897), wherein people are rewarded (or punished) in proportion to their conforming behavior, serves to quell injured and otherwise indignant parties.[8] Likewise, "requiring that deviants receive remedial treatment" (suggesting that they were not fully responsible for their actions) also serves to validate the existing moral order.

One may argue that control agencies are only partially successful in restoring moral order by settlement, confinement, punishment, and the like. However, once one moves past this "justice maintenance" function, and examines other control agency roles (e.g., rehabilitation, deterrence), agency effectiveness becomes even more questionable. Further, these other "objectives" often become secondary to a fifth task, that of keeping order within the agency.

PURSUING INTERNAL ORDER

Although the problematics of achieving internal order becomes especially evident in instances such as prison riots and "unnatural institutional deaths," it is apparent that the problem of achieving peace or coherence within also has major implications for agency maintenance, access to targets, classification schemes, images of competence, and styles of restoring justice. Space prohibits a more developed statement, but it should be noted that concerns with "internal order" are operative on a number of levels ranging from inter-staff policies and

practices and staff-target interchanges, to exchanges between targets or between targets and outsiders.

Further, whereas one might expect to find integrated systems of control
agencies (e.g., criminal justice system, welfare programs) with each component
working toward a larger system goal, and agents coordinating their activities
with those of the other subsystems in such a way as to best handle the cases
they encounter, this does not happen in practice. Even those agencies that seem
highly dependent on one another (e.g., police, courts, prison, parole) generally
compete for budgets, as often do divisions within.

Concerned with varying objectives, agencies also utilize different indicators
of "successful activity" and agents may deliberately block and stall progress in
other agencies as they attempt to pursue their own goals in the midst of over-
lapping interests and cases. Also, agents in subsystems tend not to be well
informed, or even concerned, about the daily operations of related function-
aries. Upper-level directors may meet to discuss "system integration and operations," but the actual people-work is typically done at a very different level.
These conditions are further complicated by a lack of consistency and cooperation among those working within specific programs.

As Freidson (1966), Stoll (1968), Prus and Stratton (1976), Hall (1983), and
Horowitz (1995) note, the models of control employed by agents within the
same system may vary considerably from one agent to the next. Whenever
agents use different paradigms to explain "how human behavior comes about"
or decide "what causes people to act in certain ways," one may expect to encounter different interpretations of target activities and different responses to
these activities.

Agents viewing deviance as "self-willed" or "subject to conditioning," for
instance, may be more prone to using punishment as a means of rehabilitation
than those perceiving troublesome behavior as "illnesses," the "fault of society," or "situational occurrences." Not only may particular agencies assume
varying, and if not more contradictory, policies and practices, but agencies often
vacillate in their positions over time. Still, even sharper differences may emerge
across control agencies. Thus, for example, police officers may work with different notions of causality and culpability than do probation officers, psychiatrists, and religious leaders.

One consequence of this lack of consistency within and across agencies may
be that each of the subsystems may be rendered less effective in practice. Rather
than being "changed" or rehabilitated, those being processed frequently become more adept at adapting to a variety of perspectives. Relatedly, and with
concerns for assessing the general effectiveness of treatment programs, it would
be useful to direct more attention to "what various programs and agencies
represent to the people being processed therein" (also see chapter 13).

As well, there is an administrative concern about maintaining relative har-
mony within particular agencies or subdivisions within. Thus, it is both embarrassing and frustrating for administrators who claim to offer effective

treatment programs to simultaneously acknowledge more pronounced conflicts and other divisions among staff who are alleged to pursue the agency's dominant agendas in consistent, cooperative, and competent manners.

Concerns with internal order also extend to appropriate supervision of the clients under agency charge. In particular, it is expected that agency clients would not disturb or threaten outsiders or unduly injure one another, themselves, or agency staff. The concessions required to achieve client cooperation in these manners may take agencies some distance from their avowed treatment programs, but this allows agencies to maintain the impression that, minimally, they have things under control in their own arenas. Relatedly, it is important to observe that agencies also vary in the extent to which their contacts with targets are more fleeting or extensive. Typically, agencies dealing with voluntary and short-term cases tend to be less concerned with the matters of confinement than are agencies who deal with involuntary and long-term cases, particularly those thought disruptive in other ways. Notably, whenever containment concerns become more prominent, other objectives (e.g., rehabilitation, humane treatment) generally become less consequential to the daily routines of the staff.

IN PERSPECTIVE

While we have some insightful material on the problematics of agency life and routines,[9] those interested in deviance regulation need to more fully and specifically examine the ways in which those involved in agency routines (1) seek and achieve community support; (2) access prospective deviants; (3) classify targets; (4) emphasize treatment; (5) restore justice; and (6) pursue internal order. It is strikingly apparent that a great deal of ethnographic research is required if we are to better understand the operations of control agencies and the roles that "those being processed" play in the process.

This discussion of regulating deviance has been left toward the end of this volume, but it may be important to emphasize the interlinkages of the various deviance-making processes examined in this chapter with other aspects of ongoing community life. Regulatory endeavors may be informed and affected by (a) the ways in which people define deviance and identify deviants and (b) the ways in which people become involved in, and do, deviance in both solitary and group contexts. However, people's regulatory practices (formal and informal) also have important implications for (c) the ways in which people define deviance and identify deviants as well as (d) the ways in which people become involved in, and do, deviance.

Indeed, the deviance-making process might be viewed as a set of ongoing interpretations and interactive adjustments to the shifting sets of realities that people develop and share with one another in varying degrees within the broader community in which they find themselves. Approached in this manner, deviance is not a subjective phenomenon or an objective phenomenon; it is an intersubjective process rooted thoroughly and fundamentally in ongoing community life. Hopefully, this elaboration of the various concerns that coordinators and staff may have with "maintaining the agency" will suggest some instructive avenues of inquiry. No less consequentially, though, an appreciation of these organizational agendas helps define the theaters of operation in which control agents (chapter 12) and their targets (chapter 13) engage one another on a day-to-day basis.

NOTES

1. Insofar as actual levels of effectiveness are difficult to measure with high degrees of accuracy or validity, agencies that present themselves (Goffman, 1959, 1961; Stanton, 1970) as effective or otherwise essential tend to fare better. The widespread tendency to use statistics as indicators of effectiveness becomes readily suspect when one investigates "how rates are obtained" (see, for example, Rubinstein, 1973; Prus and Stratton, 1976; Black, 1980; Meehan, 1986, 1992; Lundman, 1996). Cressey (1958) provides a particularly insightful discussion of the dilemmas of evaluative research and accounting strategies. Although Cressey speaks most directly to correctional programs, his statement has much more general relevance. Goffman (1961) presents an illustrative analysis on the attempts of total institutions to "manage impressions," during tours, visits, and the like. Scott (1969) provides valuable insight into the operations of agencies intended to assist the blind, while Stanton (1970) deals with agency practices on a more generic level. Because it attends to an extended assortment of agencies and their clients, Wiseman's (1970) ethnographic depiction of skid row life is particularly instructive.

2. Considerations of psychiatric practice by Jewell (1952), Scheff (1964), Stachnik and Ulrich (1965), Daniels (1970), Szasz (1970), Rosenhan (1973), and Karp (1996) attest to these points. So does research by Bittner (1967), Black (1970), Black and Reiss (1970), Rubinstein (1973), Charles (1986), and Meehan (1992) on the police. Similar trends are evidenced by court materials gathered by Newman (1956), Reiss (1960), Sudnow (1965), Blumberg (1967), and Wiseman (1970). Materials on probation and parole by Emerson (1969), McCleary (1975; 1983), Prus and Stratton (1976), and Spencer (1983) further indicate the extent to which target definitions are problematic, as does research on emergency wards (Sudnow, 1970; Roth, 1972), and coroner assessments of death (Atkinson, 1971).

3. For more contextualized statements on the typification tendencies of control agencies, see Scheff (1963; 1964; 1966), Bittner (1967), Daniels (1970), Connor (1972), Prus and Stratton (1976), Sanders (1977), Emerson et al. (1983), Spencer (1983), Warren (1983), Charles (1986), and Meehan (1986, 1992).

4. These reviews are essentially abstract and quantitative in emphasis and give little attention to actual treatment programs. More instructive materials on the practical limitations of "success" rates and institutional objectives can be found in the prisons and parole literature (e.g., Cressey, 1958; Emerson, 1969; McCleary, 1975; Prus and Stratton, 1976). Indeed, because agents and agencies are attentive to the importance of success rates for the future of their programs and careers, there often is considerable incentive to ensure that clients are protected from revocation, relapses, and other difficulties in ways that extend far beyond any recognized program "treatments." Comparable populations on their own seldom have access to comparable ("nontreatment")

resources. The elusiveness of success is also evident in the treatment of mental illness (see Goffman, 1961; Scheff, 1964; Stachnik and Ulrich, 1965; Daniels, 1970; Rosenhan, 1973; Karp, 1996). Also relevant are ethnographic studies of agencies that attempt to treat people with drug addiction (Brown, 1931; Ray, 1961; Peyrot, 1985), heavy drinking (Wiseman, 1970), and gambling problems (Lesieur, 1977) as well as deal with workplace training (Miller, 1991), domestic violence (Loseke, 1992), and teenage welfare mothers (Horowitz, 1995).

5. Those interested in a review of the literature on the history of corrections (pertaining to practices, philosophies, debates, and research) in western Europe and America are apt to find Blomberg and Lucken (2000) a valuable resource.

6. The term, "cloak of competence" was first used by Edgerton (1967) in his study of the mentally retarded, but was subsequently employed by Haas and Shaffir (1987) in their research on medical students. See Goffman (1961, especially pp. 321–386), Stanton (1970), Wiseman (1970), and Meehan (1992) for instances of "fronting" activities in control agency settings.

7. Ironically, even when outside evaluators attempt to be helpful, these people often spend so little time in the settings under consideration that the recommendations that they offer may generate more difficulties for workers pursuing the objectives of the program than any inadequacies evaluators attempt to solve. However, because outside evaluators generally are seen as impartial experts in the area by upper-level administrators, there is often considerable pressure on the part of the agency or division being assessed to endorse and implement evaluators' proposals even when insiders more familiar with the day-to-day operations of the agency define these recommendations as clearly disadvantageous to the objectives of the program over the long term.

8. Readers familiar with classical Greek scholarship will recognize that somewhat parallel notions of justice and regulation are discussed at length by Plato (*Laws, Republic*) and Aristotle (*Nicomachean Ethics, Rhetoric*).

9. For a fuller appreciation of people-work in rehabilitation agency settings, see Goffman's (1961) analysis of total institutions, Roth's (1962) depiction of a tuberculosis facility, Scott's (1969) account of agencies for the blind, Irwin's (1970) and Carroll's (1974) analyses of prison life, Wiseman's (1970) work on agencies for skid row alcoholics, Emerson's (1969), McCleary's (1975, 1983), Prus and Stratton's (1976), and Spencer's (1983) discussion of probation and parole officers, and Gubrium's (1975), Hall's (1983), Lyman's (1993) and Kotarba and Hurt's (1995) portrayals of frontline institutional workers.

12

Assuming Office
Control Agents at Work

Whereas chapter 11 focused on control agencies as organizational entities, the present chapter examines the activities of the people involved in control agency work. Given its location in the text, this chapter extends the conceptual agenda of this volume by attending to the life-worlds of the people (agents, tacticians) involved in regulatory practices. However, in a way that parallels the experiences of those in deviant subcultures, this chapter considers the ways in which staff members act and survive within regulatory subcultural contexts.

As used herein, "control work" or "deviance regulation" includes (a) all manners of rule-making, monitoring, and assessing activities, as well as (b) practices designed to deter or prevent deviance, and (c) activities intended to correct, sanction, or rehabilitate those involved in undesired kinds of situations.[1] As well, unless indicated otherwise, both paid and volunteer workers will be subsumed by the term control agent. Somewhat relatedly, the term target (also client, case) refers to those who are acted toward or are the intended recipients of some action or outcome indicated by control agents. However, it should be noted that control agents also may represent targets for the activities of others, including supervisors, coworkers, cases, and third-party outsiders. Readers, therefore, should be prepared to adjust to situated use of target as a more generic term of reference.

For many readers, this chapter means overcoming another series of mystiques. In addition to dealing with the more obvious and central mystique that thematizes popular considerations of deviance, this chapter (like chapter 11 to some extent) entails a neutralization of the more exotic or emotive images that sometimes people associate with control work.

Whereas some people may view control work as mundane or clearly disdainful activity, it is not uncommon to find that others have developed certain allures or intrigues with the lifestyles, practices, and personas that they associate with control agents. For some people, fascinations of this latter sort may be associated with the deviants with whom control agents work. For others, it may denote the more heroic, crusader-like, or salvationist auras that they attribute to those involved in the pursuit of morality, justice, and the alleviation of suffering and loss amidst the forces of destruction and evil. Likewise, whereas some people have considerable confidence in the viability of the treatments associated with particular agencies, others are highly cynical of any agent intentions, applications, or effectiveness.

Although outsiders and insiders may view control agents and their activities in highly diverse, often judgmental terms, we attend more directly to the ways in which control agents engage their roles. Further, while some people may be inclined to focus on either the general practices of agents within organizations or the individual qualities of control agents, the emphasis here is on the ways that people implement their roles as control agents. This is not to deny the importance of particular organizational motifs or the implications of more individualized agent viewpoints and practices, but rather to focus on control work as realms of activity that are developed within collective, interactive, and adjustive sets of regulatory arenas or theaters of operation.

Mindful of issues of these sorts, this chapter addresses five themes pertinent to people's roles in control agencies. These are *acknowledging organizational objectives; learning the ropes; maintaining order; engaging targets;* and *sustaining presence.* Although these matters overlap in several respects, each points to a somewhat unique set of concerns that agents address as they implement their roles as officeholders.

ACKNOWLEDGING ORGANIZATIONAL OBJECTIVES

Given the prominence (and proliferation) of control agencies in contemporary society, it may be tempting to speak of an integrated "control agency venture." However, as noted in chapter 11, it should not be assumed that all of those who engage in control work are of one viewpoint or that those involved in regulatory pursuits are concerned about cooperating with one another, especially on a more sustained basis.

Thus, for example, although some may view "the criminal justice system" as an integrated unit in a given state, region, or community, it seems more accurate to see those working within each control agency (e.g., police, courts, probation office) as involved in their own "sets of games" (with their own objectives, rationales, practices, budgets, *and* internal factions). Indeed, there are apt to be major rifts and divisions within this broader field of operations. The agents from each of these and other control agency sectors may cooperate with agents from other units in certain respects when it seems practical to do so, but it does not seem uncommon for workers in particular agencies to knowingly disregard the objectives and concerns of the other agencies as they deal with particular cases at hand.

Despite some tendencies toward (a) a mutuality of objectives (e.g., "law and order"), (b) sympathetic understandings revolving around control work,

(c) upper level interagency linkages, and (d) situated interdependencies, the people working within each operational unit (agent, division, or agency) are likely to (e) pursue greater levels of autonomy over their own more immediate operations within the broader community.

Thus, while generally aware of broader organizational agendas (chapter 11), such as achieving support, accessing cases, classifying cases, emphasizing treatment, restoring justice, and pursuing internal order, agents tend to be more concerned about their immediate situations and work roles within.

LEARNING THE ROPES

Learning the ropes or becoming socialized into the role of control agent refers to the practice of people developing familiarity and fluency in the viewpoints, general techniques, and situated operating practices of the control agency workplaces in which they find themselves.

Developing competence as a control agent is not a simple matter of attending to manuals, organizational charts, formal duties, assigned tasks, or obtaining instruction from management. Indeed, in order to engage the role more effectively, people typically learn that the formal features of the organization at hand are to be selectively interpreted, differentially emphasized, and frequently disregarded in pursuing the many tasks and obstacles their work roles entail. As suggested in the ethnographic literature on police work (e.g., Bittner, 1967; Rubinstein, 1973; Sanders, 1977; Davis, 1983; Charles, 1986; Meehan, 1986, 1992; and McNulty, 1994),[2] learning one's role as a control agent is an emergent, enacted, negotiated, and ongoing adjustive process.

Normally, this involves people acquiring (and distinguishing) both formal and informal guidelines regarding work (and related activities) in the setting at hand. Learning the ropes, likewise, is not synonymous with people becoming ideal agents or achieving formally articulated organizational objectives. Instead, it refers somewhat more basically to people fitting in with coworkers, clients, and others and finding ways of effectively doing things on an ongoing basis within the work setting. Rather centrally, despite the more formal or official appearances of control agencies, the people involved in these settings (not unlike street gangs or other groups of deviants) constitute *subcultures* within the larger community.

The associations that workers in control agency contexts generate may differ from those developed in deviant subcultures by virtue of their particular objectives and the greater respectability or community support normally associated with control agency enterprises. However, once one puts matters of deviance and regulation aside, the materials that deal with subcultures (chapters 6, 7, and 8) become directly relevant to considerations of "organizational subcultures" (see Trice, 1993; Trice and Beyer, 1993; Prus, 1997, 1999) within the control agency setting.

Irrespective of the typically more overt formal or official emphases that characterize regulatory settings, matters of perspectives, identities, activities, emotionalities, communicative fluency, and the like, are no less consequential here than they are in other settings. Indeed, these subcultural elements are relevant to the full range of official *and* informal sets of group relations that one finds in control settings.

In somewhat related terms, people's careers of participation in control agencies seem highly parallel to people's involvements as deviants in other subcultural settings. Not only do control agents deal with an assortment of others (insiders and outsiders) whose careers and activities intersect with their own on an ongoing basis but, like those in other subcultures, control agents are apt to encounter shifting sets of opportunity contexts. Thus, agents' earlier and current associates may significantly affect the ways that agents encounter and experience their work roles.

It also should be noted that control agents operate within at least three subcultural fields on a more or less simultaneous basis. Hence, in addition to the life-world that revolves around policy, assessments, and other matters of formal organization, it is important to recognize the subcultures that develop among control agents and other staff in the setting as well as those that develop between agents and the clientele with whom they work. Further, because their work roles often spill over into their personal lives, agents also find themselves dealing with aspects of their work roles with people outside of the agency context.

Interestingly, too, although control agents generally are more esteemed than those with whom they work, control agents also may experience senses of the disrespectability (by virtue of their subject matters and activities) that parallel the "stigma" (Goffman, 1963) encountered by those with whom they work.

At a most fundamental level as well, control work not only is a collective endeavor, but it also takes place in settings in which individual agents routinely experience conflicting demands and interactional cross-pressures. There may be some cases in which control work is highly unilateral (i.e., agents experience high autonomy, minimal accountability) in thrust or when agents feel highly isolated in dealing with the cases at hand, but regulatory activity is generally best envisioned within the interactive (insider and outsider) theaters of operation in which agents work on a more or less concurrent basis.

Not only may each context or setting in which they work require some reorientation on the part of the agents involved, but each of the parties (e.g., managers, coworkers, clients) with whom agents associate in each arena typically have somewhat different ideas of how agents should frame and engage their activities in those settings.

Because all meaningful human activity is developed in the more situated instances of the here-and-now and entails some focusing of effort, it is most unlikely that agents will simultaneously attend to all of the (multiple) frames of reference that they might deem relevant more generally. Thus, some notions of control that could pertain to particular cases may never be invoked, and other standpoints may be considered only prior to, or after, other particular themes are given priority in an enacted sense.

Indeed, agents who attempt to incorporate all potentially relevant viewpoints in dealing with the cases at hand may find themselves greatly impeded in getting things done amidst a diverse, often contradictory set of operational frameworks (and expectations). Thus, agents concerned with the matter of accomplishing particular tasks within the practical limitations of office often feel compelled to compromise organizational agendas and directives.

Relatedly, it is essential that we acknowledge the often diverse assortment of others (e.g., clients, coworkers and support staff, supervisors) with whom agents work. Control agents and their associates may be "of one mind" on some occasions, but they may actively strive to persuade and resist one another in other instances. Hence, although it may be tempting to envision agents as assuming more singularistic tactician roles, it is much more productive to view agents as both tacticians and targets in their dealings with clients and others in the organizational setting at hand.

Learning the ropes, thus, represents a multifaceted, adjustive process, wherein agents more or less continuously build up, test out, and adjust their conceptual frameworks across an assortment of interactional theaters. Consequently, the following considerations of maintaining order, engaging targets, and sustaining presence are best seen within this shifting, experiential base.

MAINTAINING ORDER

As people become more involved in their roles (i.e., work "in the trenches"), they are apt to find that both the organizational objectives of particular agencies and their own (more personal) ideals become compromised by the practical demands (e.g., time, secondary organizational policies and concerns, and cooperation problems involving clients and coworkers) of their situations.

Accordingly, the matters of keeping order and maintaining appearances of control (over their own affairs and those of any associates for which agents may be responsible) assume an importance or centrality that agents may not have anticipated. Part of learning the ropes, thus, involves some recognition of a "negotiated order" wherein concerns with expediency and impression management, along with agents' ongoing adjustments to the unexpected, often assume greater prominence for the ways that agents deal with the situations at hand than any formal agency objectives or personal agent ideals.

Two ethnographic studies of policing activity by Bittner (1967) and Meehan (1992) pointedly illustrate agent concerns with expediency and images. Whereas Bittner focuses on police work with skid row drunks and Meehan attends to the regulation of teen-related disturbances, both studies indicate how formal concerns about enforcing the law, achieving justice, and respecting citizen rights give way to (a) the practice of dispensing with trouble informally and (b) doing so in ways that foster public appearances of social order. It is not the case that the officers involved are unaware of, or unconcerned about, "the law on paper," but they also realize that peacekeeping often is better accomplished in more casual ways. Indeed, attempts to "go by the book" in many cases would reduce peacekeeping to the level of absurd inefficiencies. Similar practices are evident in studies of quality control in an airplane factory (Bensmen and Gerver, 1963), probation and parole officers (Emerson, 1969; Prus and Stratton, 1976), agencies catering to skid row alcoholics (Wiseman, 1970), and hotel security staff (Irini and Prus, 1982).

These and other ethnographic studies suggest a general irony in the organizational features of community life. Organizations whose public front is one of relative order and competence often involve much more uncertainty, negotiation, and disorder than is portrayed, while settings taken to be less ordered are often much more organized in essence than one might initially presume. Relatedly, although control agents may work in "ordered" settings where the front stage typically is marked by formalized organizational policy, elaborate job descriptions, highly specified institutional procedures, and well-defined caseloads, the task of sustaining order in the face of the actual cases and events at hand along with the competing demands that workers encounter is apt to render formal work roles highly problematic if not also extremely perplexing at times. The following discussions of engaging targets and sustaining presence shed more light on the practical limitations of formalized role expectations.

ENGAGING TARGETS

Although not attending to all of the things that agents do as they deal with clients in control contexts, the matters of *encountering targets, assessing target situations, providing treatment, managing relations with targets,* and *contending with target associates* are especially consequential for understanding control agent work roles.

Encountering Targets

Because agents may come into contact with clients in a wide variety of ways and pursue as well as juggle diverse sets of objectives, it is instructive to acknowledge the sorts of control mandates with which agents may be working as well as the major ways in which agents make contact with actual cases. Control work may be most evident when agents engage targets in more direct and immediate terms, but contact seldom occurs as a completely random event.

Generally speaking, agents receive direction from supervisors or other administrators on whom to target and how to deal with those people. Agents sometimes assume more central roles in defining the control programs that they plan to engage. However, even those who intend to deal with targets in more unilateral fashions may still seek approval of their plans from those in positions of relative authority.

As well, regardless of the sources of the control agenda and any compromises or adjustments that may be made along the way, it is generally anticipated that those operating as control agents would be prepared to act. It is presumed that agents would be available, ready, and able to attend to the control mandates at hand.

When considering agent contact with targets, four means of learning about cases may be distinguished. First, agents may assume more active roles in seeking out or pursuing certain kinds of targets for purposes of control. Agents adopting these mandates may pursue targets on a more intense or concerted basis, possibly embarking on focused campaigns on a longer-term basis. However, programs of this sort also may assume shorter term, possibly sporadic or only occasional, qualities. Likewise, these agendas may be invoked in more overt or clandestine manners. Still, these constitute notably more intrusive pursuits.

In a related, second variant, agents may assume surveillance roles wherein they attend to the possibility of encountering troublesome targets of one or other sorts while in some setting. Although surveillance activity may assume more sustained or more sporadic dimensions, those involved attend more centrally only to those cases that appear overtly troublesome.

A third contact routing involves third-party referrals. Although this may be a common means of learning about trouble in many settings, it should not be assumed that agents uniformly desire outsider involvements or referrals of these sorts. Likewise, once they learn about cases from third parties, some agents may encourage those reporting these matters to them to assume more active roles in dealing with the targets at hand while others may actively discourage third parties from any further participation in the regulatory process.

Finally, agents also may encounter people who make self-referrals; people who turn themselves over to control agents more or less on their own initiative. Whether these people desire help, experience guilt, acquiesce to the desires or pressures of their associates, or seek attention of some sort, self-referrals are important for appreciating the fuller range of agent-target contacts.

Although the matter of first learning about trouble represents an important aspect of control agent work, for most agents this generally is only the beginning. Thus, we turn to the matter of agents assessing the cases that they encounter in one or other ways.

Assessing Target Situations

Not unlike those handling deviance informally (chapter 10), control agents who learn of trouble face the task of evaluating the instances, situations, or cases at hand and selecting from various lines of activity available to them. However, because control agents deal with certain kinds of trouble on a more recurrent basis, they not only develop more standardized ways of approaching these situations but also build up additional resources with which to handle particular kinds of cases.

Here, the matter of learning the ropes implies a familiarity with certain operational guidelines or rules of thumb that agents implement in dealing with more stereotypic or routine cases. Thus, although agents may be expected to invoke (formal) agency policy in dealing with the cases at hand, agents in the field commonly develop their own criteria for dealing with those they encounter.

As indicated in studies of police (Bittner, 1967; Rubinstein, 1973; Davis, 1983; Charles, 1986; Meehan, 1992), probation and parole officers (Emerson, 1969; McCleary, 1975, 1983; Prus and Stratton, 1976; Spencer, 1983), physicians in institutional settings (Roth, 1962), human service workers dealing with people with disabilities (Gubrium, 1975; Lyman, 1993) and skid row clients (Wiseman, 1970), and discipline officers in high schools (Emerson, 1994), agency policy is often overshadowed by concerns with expediency (as in convenience, time pressures, and image concerns).[3] In addition, however, there will be cases that agents view in more particular, often mixed, and perhaps more puzzling, terms.

As well, because control agents seldom have the time to examine each case they encounter in more comprehensive analytical terms, agents generally try to envision or define the instances they encounter within more routine sets of agency categories, qualifying these somewhat relative to their own experiences or stocks of knowledge in this arena. In the process, agents develop notions of "normal" or routine categories of the cases they confront.

Relatedly, because agents are expected to deal with the cases that they encounter in some way, agents tend to be concerned about developing more viable tactics for handling subsequent cases of similar or related sorts in more expedient terms. Each instance, accordingly, may provide agents with opportunities of sorts to learn more about the nature of control work.

Still, given the (highly variable) human subject matter with which they work and agents' inabilities to access the minds of those they encounter in more open, complete, and predictable manners, agents are apt to find that the matter of assessing cases remains somewhat problematic, if not clearly perplexing, at times. The task of sorting out particular instances is apt to become more challenging when agents intend to be more precise and thorough and/or encounter targets and third parties who misrepresent situations or are evasive in other ways.

Like people encountering trouble in more casual settings, control agents may decide to "do nothing" about certain cases or instances in the shorter or longer terms; change their own behaviors in attempts to accommodate the case(s) at hand; attempt to alter other people's behavior in certain ways; refer cases to third parties for assistance or other kinds of processing; or develop collective ventures in dealing with particular targets.

While each of these options warrants extended attention on behalf of those who intend to understand control work more generally, the material following focuses more directly on agents attempting to *alter the behaviors of troublesome parties* by administering "treatment." Relatedly, whether agent categories are accurate or otherwise, these definitions become important with respect to the subsequent disposition and treatment of cases.

Providing Treatment

Although agents may be assigned roles that clearly are more focused on monitoring and screening practices, a great many agents find themselves in the position of trying to alter other people's situations (e.g., experiences, dispositions, behaviors) in some ways. Accordingly, as used herein, the term *treatment* refers to any activity in which control agents engage with the intention of realigning target behaviors and experiences in some respect.[4]

We will be considering target experiences with treatment more directly in chapter 13, but because treatment reflects agent initiatives, the present consideration of agent viewpoints and practices also is highly relevant to the understanding of target experiences with treatment. Especially central in these respects is an appreciation that treatment *is a definitional, enacted, and pluralistically experienced social process.*

While treatment is often considered the central ingredient in regulating deviance, comparatively few outsiders know what treatment actually entails in control agency work. Relatedly, insiders (as control agents) may know what they do, but often become so concerned about "getting their jobs done" (as in learning the ropes, keeping order, and dealing with other pressing matters) that they may have little opportunity to engage in more careful, sustained examinations and analyses of their own treatment-related practices. This appears to hold not only for people involved in newer and more "exotic" control programs, but also for those involved in the seemingly most common instances of treatment (e.g., confinement, counseling) administered in control settings.

Three things compound the general lack of awareness of what treatment is all about. First, treatment programs are apt to be much more variable (inclusive, diminished, selective, erratic, and ambiguous) in implementation than might first seem on the surface. Second, we have very little (ethnographic) research on how those involved in "administering treatment" actually go about their activities on a moment-to-moment, day-to-day basis. Third, treatment cannot adequately be understood apart from the definitions and other experiences of those targeted for "treatment." And, as indicated in the next chapter, little sustained ethnographic attention has been given to people's experiences, as targets, within treatment programs.

Generally speaking, outsiders do not seem especially interested in "what actually goes on" in treatment contexts. Instead, citizens typically are more concerned about receiving reassuring answers to questions of the sort, "Does

it work?" "Is it humane?" and "What does it cost?" Likewise, despite their lack
of awareness of treatment as a socially engaged experience, outsiders seem to
assume that treatment is a "good thing" for both the community at large and
for the specific people to whom these treatments are directed.

Though outsiders sometimes become intrigued with certain issues, situations, and controversies, the regulation of deviance more generally entails a
massive set of policies, practices, and processes. Few people have the interest,
capacity, or opportunity to learn about treatment or its limitations in any careful, systematic, and sustained manner. In this sense, there is often more emphasis on ensuring that people "get treatment" than attending to the ensuing
matter of "what treatment entails" from the viewpoint of either the control
agents or the targets involved.

Accordingly, and somewhat regardless of agency practices and accomplishments (see chapter 11), those providing treatment of any sort normally try to
convey the impression that the treatments they provide are efficient, humane
by the standards of the day, and comparatively cost efficient. To do otherwise,
could jeopardize the support accorded to the agency at hand as well as invite
undesired criticism and related disruptions.

Because treatment presupposes intentional human enterprise, it is most instructive to consider the ways in which agents (as tacticians) view and invoke
inducements (threats and promises) and other treatments. The issues of
whether treatments employ deception or not, are voluntary or imposed, or are
more "physically" (physiologically or materially) or "symbolically" oriented,
are much less consequential than the meanings that tacticians and targets assign
to these phenomena.

Similarly, while some treatments may be more extensively intended as preventative practices, and others may be invoked as remedial (e.g., restitution,
retribution, resocialization) devices, the emphasis here is more directly on the
ways that treatments are experienced by *all* of the parties involved in the
situations under consideration.

There is no assurance that treatments will be interpreted as intended or that
any of the people (tacticians, targets, or others) involved will continue to view
the "same treatments" the same way over time. Relatedly, our concern is not
whether treatments are successful or not, or whether agents should redefine
their agendas and practices. More centrally, as indicated in chapter 13, the
emphasis is on the ways that agents and targets approach, define, interpret,
and adjust to agency treatments and how the agents and targets involved in
instances of treatment relate to one another more generally. Notably, the matters of agents managing relations with targets and dealing with target associates
also enter consequentially into treatment considerations.

Managing Relations with Targets

While often overlooked by outsiders, client-agent associations are often
considerably more extensive than that implied by agency notions of "making

contact" and "administering treatment." In actual practice, a great deal of control work requires considerable client cooperation *and* ongoing client-agent interaction. These matters often extend well beyond and may modify, if not more directly contradict, formal control mandates (and formal treatment programs).

Thus, in addition to the sorts of affinities and disaffections that commonly develop between people who are thrust into one another's presence, possibly for extended periods of time, agents faced with the task of working directly with clients generally become aware that they are dependent on their clients for managing their tasks on a day-to-day basis. The result normally is a set of working concessions (e.g., see Roth, 1962; Bittner, 1967; Parnas, 1967; Emerson, 1969, 1994; Wiseman, 1970; Prus and Stratton, 1976; Davis, 1983; Meehan, 1992), wherein agency objectives frequently are compromised for smoother relations among the parties in the setting at hand.

Further, although some treatments may be administered in more isolated or highly unilateral manners, many other treatments can only be implemented and understood within the more pervasive set of relations (and interchanges) in which agents and clients are involved. Likewise, although the focus of treatment is normally on "troublesome targets," those working as control agents also are subjected to treatments of various sorts by those (clients) with whom they work. Indeed, it is not uncommon to find that control agents define themselves as requiring outside treatment as a consequence of the stresses associated with their own work roles.

It should not be assumed that agents actively support, or even adequately comprehend, the treatments mandated by the agencies in which they work. Nor should it be assumed that agents like the work roles (as in settings, associates, activities) in which they are situated. Thus, despite some initial allures of control agency work and some sustained interests in pursuing regulatory activity, many control agents also may see themselves as "doing time" and experiencing treatment in the regulatory setting at hand.

Contending with Target Associates

Whatever relations control agents may develop with their clients (targets), the impact of agency treatment is often moderated, if not rendered more completely ineffective, as a consequence of the other people with whom targets may be involved.

One sometimes encounters references to inmate subcultures in analyses of people's experiences in prisons (Irwin, 1970; Owen, 1998) and other total institutions (Goffman, 1961; Roth, 1962), wherein a more sustained subcultural underlife is seen to coexist with that intended by the control agency under consideration. Still, the notion of target subcultures is relevant to a seemingly endless array of agency contexts. Thus, regardless of whether targets are kept in one another's co-presence for extended periods of time and are subject to centralized programs, rules, and procedures (as in total institutions; Goffman, 1961; Carroll, 1974; Gubrium, 1975; Owen, 1998) or whether targets have more situated and fleeting contact with agency personnel and other agency targets (e.g., Bittner, 1961; Wiseman, 1970; Meehan, 1992), it is important to recognize the existence of target subcultures and to ask when and how agents experience these associations in light of the goals and activities that agents pursue with particular targets.

Beyond the more general realms of target-agency contact and target-agent relations more specifically, it is useful to distinguish two other broad sets of target associations. One set of associations involves insiders, people who experience (parallel) agency treatment. The second set of target associates is somewhat more diverse and may include people who have little or no agency contact (as in family, friends, and coworkers) as well as those who may deal with agency targets on a more explicit interventional basis (as in legal counsel, social workers, and psychiatrists). These two sets of target associates may interact with one another at times, just as they may have contact of varying sorts with agency personnel.

Although unevenly concerned and/or informed about target-agency matters, both insider and outsider target associates frequently provide agency clientele with definitions of (a) agency programs, practices, and personnel; (b) agency targets; (c) focal targets and target life-worlds; and (d) alternative involvements for targets to pursue. Targets' associates also may provide targets with information, advice, and other resources that targets might invoke in their dealings with control agents. This information may be intended to help targets achieve agency objectives, satisfy target interests, or pursue the goals of those giving targets advice. Given the diverse interests and wisdom of their associates, targets may have difficulty discerning the viability of any information and advice or other assistance that they receive from their associates.

For agents dealing with targets, and by extension their associates, the experience may be somewhat like "fighting ghosts." Whatever difficulties and limitations agents may encounter in dealing with specific targets, the matter becomes compounded when agents try to sort out target influences and activities from those of various target associates. Because of these more amorphous interactional contexts, agents are apt to experience considerable frustration at times as they find themselves unable to effectively adjust to, and defend against, both insider and outsider target subcultures.

Whereas target associates sometimes intervene in agent-target relationships in very direct and overt terms, many other matters involving targets and these other people are much less evident to the agents working with those cases. Not only are agents unlikely to know everything of relevance that may have transpired between targets and particular associates in the past, but agents also may not know how these people deal with one another in the present. Further, even if targets seem genuinely intent in following agent advice and other treatments, agents do not know how things will work out between targets and these other people in the future.

Relatedly, each group of people with whom agency clientele associate are likely to have their own notions of morality, trouble, and treatments that they direct toward these targets. Further, these people may engage these targets in ways that are notably less constrained in their practices than are agency personnel. Thus, while agents are commonly limited by agency directives regarding programs, policies, and progress as well as more personal notions of position, professionalism, and performance, the other people with whom targets associate may have comparatively little concern about organizational responsibilities, accountability, or future target states. Pursuing their own interests relative to (agency) targets, these other people may engage targets in highly varied ways.

Likewise, just as agents may be uncertain of how all these other people represent the agency or its personnel to targets, agents also do not know how targets will represent aspects of the agency (including agents' own treatments of, and relationships with, the target) to others. As with their associates more generally, the clients of agency programs are less apt to be constrained in the ways that they refer to agency staff than vice-versa. Further, agents need not be aware of the differing identities that targets may assume (invoke or be assigned) in these other subcultural arenas. Insofar as their associates expect and encourage consistency and continuity on the part of targets within those settings, clients may find it difficult to change in agency-intended manners even if they very much desire to do so.

Interestingly, as well, although few agents appear to anticipate this aspect of their work roles, some of the control agents' more unsettling and intense interchanges may very well involve people other than the (presumably troublesome) clients with whom they work.

SUSTAINING PRESENCE

Beyond the challenges that (a) targets (i.e., clients, cases) and their associates represent, control agents are apt to find that their relations with (b) supervisors, (c) work-role associates, and (d) third-party outsiders have important implications for agents' day-to-day work conditions and their own continuity in that organizational theater.

Matters of these sorts may be taken for granted by outsiders, but worker relations with supervisors, coworkers, and other third parties often are among the most difficult features of office that control agents encounter. Thus, the last part of this chapter considers the ways in which control agents pursue autonomy and continuity amongst concerns with accountability and vulnerability within the interactional arenas in which control work takes place.

Acknowledging Accountability

As officeholders, those involved in control agencies almost invariably find themselves dependent on supervisors for role-related evaluations, promotions, and other continuities of office. Whereas government-sponsored agencies are generally accountable to some political administrative branch, even those whose offices depend on other forms of public or private sponsorship are typically expected to exhibit an acceptable presence (even if more extensive accomplishments seem elusive).

Given the general disjunctures between the formal aspects of office and the things typically required to accomplish their activities, virtually all control agents are apt to experience some, albeit often uneven and sporadic, senses of vulnerability. Most supervisors seem to recognize this and overlook some of the more problematic features of control work. Indeed, given their other administrative responsibilities, most supervisors have no desire to know all of the details of control work. Relatedly, subordinates often feel obliged to convey the message that all is well, thereby ensuring that supervisors are not "implicated" by knowing about the more problematic practices of the agents in their charge.

As well, it is not uncommon for supervisors to try to protect agents from external (or internal) challenges, especially when they have greater confidence in their subordinates. Nevertheless, there are a great many points of potential disparity, disaffection, and disregard. Thus, control agents commonly find themselves seeking ways to minimize accountability (and vulnerability) with respect to administrators.

Interestingly, in assuming the role of targets vis-à-vis administrators, agents find themselves in situations that parallel the clients with whom they work.[5] Thus, the agents envision themselves as subject to supervisory-initiated treatments and may assume a variety of tactics intended to provide themselves with some protection from the treatments they might encounter from their administrators.

Although agents often anticipate that a stronger, longer-term record of performance will shield them from most of the potentially disruptive episodes they may encounter during their careers, agents commonly envision supervisors as uninformed about the specific challenges encountered by agents in the field and disinterested in particular agents' situations except with respect to the broader matters of organizational maintenance and supervisors' own comfort zones and interests.

These viewpoints are likely to assume greater relevance when agents envision little relationship between agent effort and competence and supervisor treatments of those agents. Under these conditions, agents may pursue a variety of other means of protecting themselves from supervisory challenges. Among the more notable tendencies are worker reliance on their coworkers for immediate support and the development of broader insider solidarity. Here, people working in teams or in somewhat parallel work roles in the same setting may exhibit considerable discretionary tolerance of one another as well as provide cover for agents whose activities are more marginal in some way.

Like workers in some other organizations, another mode of protection that control agents collectively may invoke in an attempt to gain protection from administrations is through participation in a unionized workforce. While the day-to-day operations of the union may take workers even further from their formal control mandates, as well as generate some new realms of direction, accountability, and disaffection, agents who consider themselves more vulnerable to administrative concerns may see unionization as an attractive option. Still, agent-administrator relations denote only one potentially hazardous career aspect of control agency work and, of those who encounter substantial problems in the workplace, coworker relations may be much more disruptive than those involving administrators.

Dealing with Coworkers

Although control agents may anticipate some support from staff associates, especially when dealing with negatively defined outsiders (e.g., clients, supervisors, outsider critics), it is important to acknowledge the widely ranging manners in which coworkers deal with one another. Each agency may be seen as a unit unto itself, but closer examinations of specific control agencies often reveal a wide range of internal relations, including some that may be characterized by high levels of overt and/or subterranean animosity between coworkers within the same organization or office. For analysts, it is most instructive to envision control agents as engaged in a series of subcultures (i.e., embedded subcultures within the agency) that are more or less continuously in the making.

Like people in other work settings, control agents may develop various internal alignments in dealing with specific coworkers who, for one or other reasons, are seen as troublesome. While newcomers may be surprised to "walk into" work situations that are characterized by staff factions and conflicts, the novices also are apt to find that they are expected to adjust quickly to local agency routines.

As well, although new agents are sometimes courted (as future allies) by members of one or other of the existing staff factions, new workers often are subjected to distrust and distancing. Because newcomers are more likely to disrupt local practices with their idealist enthusiasm, formal rigidity, critical moral stances, and rather inevitable blunders, they often encounter resistance, disaffection, and distancing from more experienced agents.

Still, coworkers who have been together longer also have opportunities to develop more extended conflicts. Should coworker conflicts become more intense and the agents involved pursue antagonisms on a more sustained basis, these insider exchanges may become highly consequential sources of vulnerability. This not only holds for any particular agents who may be the targets of broader coworker disaffection, but also for other workers in those settings as well.[6]

While acknowledging the advantages of teamwork or coworker assistance, Goffman (1959) addresses the vulnerabilities of the group and its members to other insiders, especially careless, incompetent, and disenchanted insiders. Because insiders often have access to potentially sensitive back region information, and may be involved in wide ranges of performance contexts (challenges, successes, failures, risks, adjustments), the team and people within are vulnerable to all of those who assume roles as team members.

Dependent on member cooperation for achieving group objectives and sustaining images of overall group and individual competency, the well-being of these organizational units generally reflects members' willingness to maintain confidences pertaining to team viewpoints, objectives, activities, and accomplishments. Consequently, team members are apt to become particularly concerned about, distrusting of, and hostile toward, insiders thought more likely to jeopardize the organization or other people's situations within.

Although team members need not create any particular problems for those coworkers whom they view as troublesome in some way, these same team members may be reluctant to help those (troublesome) coworkers deal with challenges from supervisors, clients, or outsiders. Hence, beyond any difficulties that particular agents may have with their work associates, internal assistance may not be forthcoming when those agents may most require, or benefit from, coworker support.

Encountering External Challenges

In addition to any threats associated with people (i.e., clients, administrators, or coworkers) within the agency, control agents also may find that they are the targets of criticism or undesired inquiries initiated by one or more outside sources.

These challenges may be directed, variously, at the control agency more generally, at one or more offices within the agency, at certain workers more specifically, or at one or more of the clients with whom the agency is somehow linked. The outside challenges, likewise, may pertain to things (as in agendas, policies, practices, incidents) done or not done, as well as the ways in which any organizational matters are handled. As with internal confrontations, external challenges also may vary greatly with respect to the accuracy of any claims being made. Still, all challenges suggest denunciations of sorts and, as such, represent matters of potential concern to agency personnel.

For our immediate purposes, seven general points of agency concern on the part of those encountering challenges may be delineated. These are (1) interpreting situations as threatening or challenging; (2) defining the focus of attack; (3) identifying the source of the difficulty; (4) contextualizing the issue;

(5) containing the challenge; (6) maintaining images; and (7) working in knowingly politicized environments. These concerns often overlap with, and qualify, one another in actual instances, but they represent matters that those in control agencies commonly consider, if often only in passing terms.

Whereas some communications directed toward particular agencies (or agents within) clearly may be intended to have negative or destructive efforts on the targets of these attacks, other messages not so intended may still be interpreted as threats of sorts and, in some cases, may be seen to be more consequential than intendedly malicious messages.

We may expect great variability in the ways that particular communications are interpreted, assessed, and dealt with by the people involved. Relatedly, even as agency personnel encounter, interpret, think about, talk about, and act toward particular messages, the threat potential of any communication may be substantially heightened *or* diminished. Thus, an early analytic concern is whether (as in what ways and to what extent) any particular communication is *perceived as a threat* by one or other parties of those involved in the control work setting under consideration.

Although agents (and administrations) may learn of challenges in a variety of ways, most challenges have the potential to implicate more than those at whom specific criticisms or other attacks may be directed. Thus, another early concern is that of *identifying the targets* or focus of the attack at hand and any potentially implicated or otherwise affected others.

Notably, thus, while some attacks may be directed at the agency, others may be focused on the administrators, staff, or the clients with whom agents work. Likewise, whereas some challenges may be oriented toward categories of people, or certain kinds of activities, other criticisms may be targeted at very specific individuals within one or other sectors of the organization. The primary significance of the attack may depend on who or what is the subject of the challenge, but other people who envision themselves as somehow threatened, affected, implicated, inconvenienced, or otherwise vulnerable, also may become concerned about the risks that particular challenges entail.

The significance of the criticism is apt to be moderated by the *source of the attack*. Because agencies and agents are apt to envision themselves as more vulnerable or accountable to certain spokespeople or segments of the community than others, a third concern often revolves around an identification of the source of the challenge and, relatedly, an attempt to ascertain the relevance, credibility, motives, viewpoints, resources, and persistence of those instituting or supporting the challenges at hand.

Although agencies may have difficulty detecting some or all of the sources of the specific challenges they encounter, particularly those involving "behind-the-scenes" interests, it is useful for analysts to acknowledge at least five potentially distinct sources of outsider challenge. These are (a) client supporters (representatives, sponsors, friends, dependents, allies); (b) client detractors (victims, enemies, other disaffected parties); (c) media representatives (who, in varying and mixed degrees, may adopt hostile, dramatic, or informatively curious stances); (d) outsiders whose broader agendas happen to intersect with this setting; and (e) external (agency) regulators. While criticisms that involve multiple and more diverse sources can be particularly devastating to those in office, external challenges that are developed in conjunction with insider (agents, staff) encouragement or assistance tend to be among the most insidious. Not only do these incidents generally imply dissension (and often more pervasive disloyalty) within the organization but they also tend to be among the most difficult challenges for members of organizations to defend against on both individual and collective levels.

Challenges also commonly take agencies and/or agents in a fourth direction, that of *contextualizing* or defining the relevance of the issue for the situation at hand. In addition to concerns with the locus of the challenge and nature of the source(s) of attack, this may involve such things as attempts to reconstruct any events about which allegations have been made. In control settings, this may include questions that go well beyond particular instances to matters of broader policies, practices, and responsibilities. It also may result in inquiries into the reputations, styles, and practices of people even marginally implicated in the challenges.

A fifth concern is that of *containing the challenge* or reducing the present and future threat of the attack at hand. Thus, while members (i.e., supervisors, agents) of agencies sometimes may welcome challenges directed at specific programs or targets that they might like to see removed or sanctioned in some way, a more general emphasis is that of achieving damage control or minimizing the obtrusiveness of issues that (warranted or otherwise) could harm the organization, its programs, or its staff in some way.

Thus, not unlike agents dealing with clients in the field, those (agents and administrators) dealing with third-party challenges also may subscribe to expediency over policy. Mindful of the disruptive potential of challenges, officeholders also may make concessions and compromises that may go well beyond policy or against "their better judgements" in attempts to protect their agencies and their own positions as well as maintain order within the broader community. Common "quick fixes" may include the sacrifices of certain programs, resources, practices, or personnel, even when agency personnel taking these lines of action consider these highly inappropriate from other organizational standpoints.

The matter of *maintaining images* also may be seen as an attempt to achieve longer-term autonomy or damage control. In contrast to the preceding concern about containing particular (existing) challenges, the emphasis on maintaining images also may be invoked in attempts to (a) curtail the pursuit of earlier challenges, as well as (b) minimize the likelihood of future attacks, and (c) decrease organizational vulnerability should any future challenges be encountered.

Once challenges have been made, the organizations and the people more specifically involved are apt to become more attentive to the risks of *working in politicized environments*. This does not necessarily mean that control agents will change their operating procedures in more substantial respects. Indeed, this may be seen as highly untenable.

However, in addition to other procedural adjustments that agents (and administrators) may implement, agency personnel also may take precautions intended to reduce agency, staff, and client vulnerability to outsiders. To this end, those involved in control agencies may try to limit any exposure of third parties to insider practices, construct routinized strategies for managing particular kinds of trouble, encourage greater insider loyalties to the team, and specifically recruit and train team members to deal with these external sources of interference.

As well, as various challenges are encountered and are seen to fall into certain kinds of categories, agents (and administrators) may develop more standardized tactics for neutralizing these attacks. In some instances, specialized personnel may be hired and/or control agencies may be established within control agencies specifically to minimize the organizational impact of disruptions of these sorts. Agency personnel are often well aware that defensive practices of these sorts may detract notably from other agency objectives, but the concern here is to maintain the agency and its personnel amidst the potential hostility of a politicized environment.

IN PERSPECTIVE

Although a great deal of emphasis in this volume is on the viewpoints and practices of "deviants," the materials introduced in chapters 10, 11, and 12 represent essential components in the deviance-making process. Dealing with the informal regulation of deviance, the organizational emphases of control agencies, and control agent work roles, respectively, these chapters address a set of activities that are fundamental to a fuller comprehension and demystification of the deviance-making process. Indeed, without regulatory efforts of some sort (also see chapter 4 on defining deviance), the activities considered deviant would remain inconsequential (beyond their more purely instrumental intentions and behavioral outcomes) for particular arenas of community life.

Still, much more is involved. Thus, chapters 10, 11, and 12 take the study of deviance more directly into the analysis of organizational behavior, occupational roles, management, and political activity. Accordingly, researchers and analysts working in the area of deviance regulation may benefit from examining ethnographic research on these other topics, but so too may those working in these other areas gain from research and analyses in the area of deviance regulation. In these ways, as well, we move beyond the deviant mystique and attend to the more generic features of organizational activity and the ways in which specific organizational units spill over onto, and are impacted by, people engaged in other realms of community life.

However, a consideration of regulatory activity would be most incomplete without examining the ways that people encounter and experience control work as targets of treatment programs. Thus, the next chapter attends to the ways that those identified as deviants experience the treatment process and the linkages of these treatments with the disinvolvement process.

NOTES

1. Among the more relevant ethnographic studies of control agents at work are materials focusing on police work (Bittner, 1967; Parnas, 1967; Rubinstein, 1973; Sanders, 1977; Ericson, 1981; Charles, 1986; Meehan, 1986, 1992; Manning, 1988; Jacobs, 1994; McNulty, 1994; and Mulcahy, 1995); probation and parole officers (Emerson, 1969; McCleary, 1975, 1983; Prus and Stratton, 1976; Spencer, 1983), hotel security staff (Irini and Prus, 1982), educators (Hargreaves et al., 1975; Emerson, 1994), physicians (Roth, 1962), and human service workers (Wiseman, 1970; Gubrium, 1975; Hall, 1983; Miller, 1983, 1991; Wharton, 1989, 1991; Lyman, 1993; Horowitz, 1995; Kotarba and Hurt, 1995).

2. Those interested in research on the police subculture more generally are apt to find Waddington's (1999) review statement a particularly valuable source.

3. Although often taken for granted by insiders, some formal control agents also face the task of dealing with considerable physical danger. Whereas actual role-related injuries are far from constant or even in occurrence, this precarious aspect of control work is notably compounded when people work in arenas in which there is the continued potential for quick, dramatic realization of injury. This is especially true for the police (e.g., Rubinstein, 1973; Charles, 1986) but by no means is it so limited, as indicated in Hall's (1983) and Lyman's (1993) depictions of frontline service workers.

In addition to the more obvious physical threats and injuries that agents may encounter, it should be recognized that control agents often are subject to considerable verbal and other symbolic denigrations as well as other kinds of client-related unpleasantries. Notably, as well, these people often witness injuries and other instances of destruction that particular people have inflicted on specific others or on the community at large. Representing these other people in various ways, agents often experience some indignation and frustration on behalf of those whom the agents envision as the comparatively innocent victims of these transgressions. Although these latter events may not pose distinct physical threats to the agents in the setting, these incidents also may make it difficult for agents to deal with other clients or third parties who may become injured, angered, and otherwise distracted because of the troublesome behaviors perpetrated by particular people. These elements also contribute to agents handling cases with a practical, sometimes abrupt and forceful expediency that those caught up in the more idealistic or purely technical features of regulatory work may find difficult to comprehend and appreciate.

4. This discussion of treatment is informed by a broader consideration of the tactical enterprise associated with influence work (Prus, 1999).

5. Whereas concerns with the task of "regulating the regulators" explicitly can be traced back to Plato (*Laws, Republic*), those interested in the practical features of this

task may find Mulcahy's (1995) depiction of the work worlds of "internal affairs" officers in police departments instructive in this respect.

6. Although it deals with interpersonal difficulties more generally, Edwin Lemert's (1962) depiction of "Paranoia and the Dynamics of Exclusion" (as a social process) is highly pertinent to understanding coworker difficulties in control settings.

13

Experiencing Disinvolvement
The Problematics of Disengagement

Despite the pronounced emphasis that is often placed on people becoming "disinvolved from deviance," one finds very little research that deals directly with people's experiences of becoming disengaged from these realms of activity. Instead, much more attention has been directed toward the identification of factors or variables that are presumed to result (somehow) in discontinuities of people's activities along certain lines and the deployment of treatments (e.g., physical treatments, remedial programs, therapies, counseling) that are thought (often by invoking disease-like metaphors) to encourage deviants to conform to societal conventions. Unfortunately, regardless of their particular configurations, these approaches miss some of the most central features of the disinvolvement process.

Quite directly, approaches that emphasize factors and treatment generally disregard the enacted nature of people's involvements in deviance and control; the associational contexts in which people participate in deviance and control; the ways in which people do and do not become disengaged from particular involvements; and the ways that those targeted for control fit into the community more generally.

By contrast, the approach taken here emphasizes the importance of examining people's disinvolvements in career terms with respect to any participatory theme under consideration. Thus, disinvolvement is envisioned in developmentally engaged terms. Further, because people's involvements in deviance normally represent only one or a few of a much broader series of endeavors in which those people may be involved at any point in time, we acknowledge the multiple realms of community life in which those designated as deviants participate. Thus, even when people engage in deviance in direct and sustained terms, people's involvements in other life-world arenas frequently are interconnected with their involvements in (and disinvolvements from) particular realms of deviance.

It also is important to appreciate that disinvolvement often requires giving up things that the participants might view as important or desirable in some way. Not only may people envision certain activities as the means to achieving particular objectives, but they also may be concerned about relinquishing other things that they have acquired up to that point, including friendships and senses of self as well as other matters that they might enjoy in more sensate or emotive terms.

Still, people can and do become disengaged from a great many forms of deviance. Sometimes, this takes place with considerable ease, clarity, and finality. In many other instances, however, disinvolvement is much less direct, consistent, or effective than the participants and/or others desire. Perhaps, most centrally, disinvolvement should be approached as a *process*, as something in the making rather than something that is signified by a distinct decision, critical event, or the completion of a treatment program.

In an attempt to more fully sort out these and related matters, consideration is given to *involvement processes and contexts; disinvolvement processes; people's experiences with treatment;* and *disinvolvement, ambivalence, and reinvolvement.*

INVOLVEMENT PROCESSES AND CONTEXTS

Although the processes of disinvolvement may seem distinct from those pertaining to involvement, disengagement from deviance is very much interfused with people's initial involvements, continuities, and intensifications of involvements in those roles.

Interestingly, though, whereas much popular and academic intrigue with deviance focuses on the matter of disinvolvement, most of this seems oriented to (a) condemnations of the activities at hand, (b) the pursuit of remedies, (c) the assessments of success rates, and (d) the quest for factors underlying these rates. Little research has been directed toward the ways in which people targeted for disinvolvement actually engage treatment and experience disengagement.[1]

When one examines ethnographic studies of people's experiences with disinvolvement, one of the major findings pertains to the frustration, failure, and vacillation that people experience when they try to detach themselves from particular role involvements.[2]

Further, while the participants may play rather central, reflective, and active roles in "deciding their own fates," deviance involvements (and disinvolvements) are often more multifaceted and complicated than may first seem (especially to those outsiders who might simply intend to eliminate the deviance in question).

It is often easier for people to become disinvolved or disentangled from solitary practices than subcultural involvements, but it is apparent that even activities that people do on their own tend to become incorporated into other aspects of these people's life-worlds. Thus, for instance, even though people often smoke cigarettes, use marijuana, or consume alcohol on a solitary basis, these activities are often integrated into other routines such as reading, eating, driving, and watching television. When people consume these substances in association with others (even in more situated and fleeting instances), these practices often become embedded in, or interfused with, other activities (especially "socializing with others") taking place in those settings (see Becker, 1963; Prus and Irini, 1980; Prus, 1983; Ingraham, 1984; Faupel, 1991).

Further, people's deviant involvements do not exist as exclusively singular or isolated activities even for the most devoted of participants. Thus, it is necessary for analysts to consider the ways in which particular aspects of people's deviant activities (subculturally or solitarily) are tied into other realms of activity in which those people are involved and the ways in which those people experience the problematics of disentanglement with respect to these other settings.

With these notions in mind, we briefly consider the *multiple life-world involvements* in which people find themselves; people's *variable participation* in specific roles or situations; and *subcultural dimensions and dissaffections*.

Multiple Life-World Involvements

The concept of multiple life-world involvements acknowledges the rather inevitable tendency for people to engage a plurality of roles (conventional and deviant) on a sequential and/or concurrent basis. Although seemingly obvious, researchers and analysts typically focus so exclusively on particular aspects of deviance that this consequential feature of human lived experience is generally overlooked.

As well, whereas a great many of the roles in which all people participate seem quite conventional in broader terms (e.g., such as being someone's child, sibling, or friend, having recreational interests, being a shopper, driving an automobile), some other roles or subcomponents thereof (including the matter of having particular associates, being involved in certain activities, purchasing particular lines of merchandise, and so forth) may be defined in distinctively negative or disreputable terms by certain audiences. Like everyone else, deviants find themselves managing or juggling multiple realms of activity. However, they also encounter the matter of managing the reactions from others that are associated with imputations of deviance. Relatedly, because deviance (as activity) is not accomplished in a social vacuum, the other things that these people do may become interfused with their participation in matters defined as deviant.

Further, because people do not become disinvolved from situations into "nothingness," we also want to be attentive to people's former, current, and anticipated involvements in other life-worlds as these pertain to people's detachments from certain lines of activity. While some people (e.g., agents of control, audiences, and some participants) may orient their attention most directly to the mystique that they associate with realms of disrespectable involvement, it is most instructive for social scientists to consider the ways in

which the participants view themselves both within particular subcultural settings and across the multiple realms of activity in which they may be involved.

Variable Participation

Although any number of people may seem to engage in similar ventures or
enter identical life-worlds, their involvements (encompassing perspectives,
identities, activities, relationships, emotionalities, and the like) in particular
roles or situations may be developed in significantly different ways. Notably,
too, individual participants may experience wide assortments of allures and
competencies as well as disaffections and difficulties with their situations on a
sequential and/or concurrent basis. No less importantly, people not only may
sustain their involvements for shorter or longer durations, but they also may
engage particular roles with widely varying levels of intensity, dedication, commitment, and linkages with others in the setting.

These matters may seem inconsequential to outsiders who wish to focus
more exclusively on disinvolvement. But, for the participants, these attractions,
activities, commitments, associations, successes, acknowledgements, obstacles,
failures, troubles, interpersonal difficulties, dilemmas, and so forth, attest to
consequential variations in their experiences and careers of participation in
particular life-worlds.

Relatedly, the things "being left behind" also may be viewed quite differently by the various people considering disinvolvement from specific situations.
Both solitary and subcultural deviants may miss aspects of the situations at
hand, including possessions, sensations, senses of self, skills developed, and
anticipations of the future. When people are involved in subcultural arenas,
the things left behind commonly include shared viewpoints, relationships,
identities, collective experiences, and so forth, as well as any specific benefits
that participants might associate with more immediate and longer-term involvements in particular group ventures.

However, because any activity (group embedded or more solitary in development) entails a number of dimensions of participation, the problems of disentanglement are often more complicated than might first seem. This is
particularly the case when people more fully have organized their lives around
particular realms (solitary or subculture) of activity. Disentanglement from
those situations is apt to be more difficult, even if these are changes that the
people themselves might desire.

Subcultural Dimensions and Disaffections

Given the group-based features of subcultural life and the ways in which
people develop their careers or strands of involvement in particular endeavors
in conjunction with others, it is inappropriate to explain people's initial involvements and continuities by virtue of participants' individual qualities. It is

no less feasible to explain people's disinvolvements from these same theaters of operation on the basis of individual properties.

Although people doing things on their own (as in solitary deviance) sometimes develop highly focused and elaborated realms of activity, people doing things in group settings (particularly when they maintain a collective focus over more extended periods of time) often develop their lines of involvement in more extended and intensively focused manners. It is not the case that people who are involved in group ventures pursue everything with great vigor, clarity, efficiency, or precision. However, when groups of people intensively pursue particular themes, the participants often develop greater specification, sophistication, and devotion than they might on their own.

Conversely, those who intend to become disentangled from group-based realms of activity often find that there are more (and more extensively developed) things from which to detach themselves than those doing things more exclusively on their own. Further, subcultural insiders may assume considerable initiative in dissuading their associates (especially those who seem more desirable in some respect) from leaving that setting. On the other hand, where internal relations become more distant or volatile, participants may be tempted to sever group attachments.

People's departures from subcultures sometimes are both abrupt and extensive. However, just as people's involvements in situations are often partial and rather uneven (both at the outset and along the way), so may people's disinvolvements also assume incomplete and erratic qualities. Relatedly, it is because of the multifaceted nature of subcultural involvements that people frequently continue their involvements in situations even when they experience more acute doubts, disenchantments, or setbacks in certain areas of subcultural life.

Still, because of the disruptive potential of these matters, assessments of the following sorts often seem consequential in people's overall decisions to try to disengage from particular subcultural life-worlds: (1) questioning the viability of subcultural *perspectives* (facing obstacles, dilemmas); (2) reassessing *identity* (noting inconsistencies with desired images) in the setting; (3) finding subcultural *activities* troublesome (boring, unpleasant, cumbersome); (4) experiencing *relational* difficulties with subcultural (insider) associates; (5) defining themselves as unable (or unwilling) to maintain subcultural *commitments*; (6) encountering *emotional* setbacks (e.g., fear, rejection, anxiety) in the subculture; (7) lacking *linguistic fluency* (encountering difficulties communicating with insiders in the subculture); and (8) experiencing disenchantment with *collective events*.

Since these subcultural themes address consequential aspects of people's life-worlds, disinvolvement also seems more likely when people view themselves as (9) free from existing subcultural commitments (i.e., available to "relocate"); (10) rejected by subcultural associates (e.g., conflict, animosity, exclusion); (11) disenchanted with changes occurring within the subculture; (12) encountering opportunities and/or encouragement for alternative involvements;[3] and (13) preparing for new role involvements.

With this conceptual backdrop in mind, we turn more directly to considerations of people's experiences with disinvolvement or disengagement from deviant life-worlds.

DISINVOLVEMENT PROCESSES

Whereas the preceding matters draw attention to some of the major issues around which people may consider disinvolvement, we now acknowledge three routings or modes of disengagement: *voluntary*, *default*, and *treatment-related*. Although not mutually exclusive, each of these routings addresses somewhat different matters. Because the treatment process is much more complicated than is commonly presumed, treatment will be dealt with on its own, after more cursory considerations of voluntary and default disengagement.

Voluntary Disengagement

Voluntary disengagements refer to those situations in which the targets of change embark on some efforts at disinvolvement on a more intentional or self-deliberative basis. There is no requirement that the people involved need initiate these endeavors entirely on their own. They may do so in some cases, but those pursuing voluntary disinvolvement also may be responding to a variety of initiatives, exclusions, and treatment-related threats on the part of others. In more general terms, however, those embarking on voluntary withdrawal from deviance often find themselves in a disentanglement process, of which a particularly perplexing component revolves around relations with other people.

Given the group-based features of subcultural involvements, this is apt to be of particular concern to those involved in subcultural (vs. solitary) deviance. Whether those involved in group-based deviance consider the prospect of withdrawing from the subculture on a secretive or more open basis, voluntary disengagement from group involvements often is more complicated because it involves coordinating the activity of leaving in ways that are mindful of those being "left behind." Further, in addition to whatever concerns that those contemplating departure may have about leaving others behind, people's associates may not appreciate their impending departure and sometimes directly interfere with people's abilities to disengage from those settings.

Mindful of people's enacted life-worlds (and associations therein), our more immediate concern, thus, is much less with any particular sources of motivation associated with voluntary disinvolvements than with the ways in which people engage and experience the disengagement process. Accordingly, much insight into voluntary departures from deviance may be gained by research that focuses on when and how people (1) define disenchantments and difficulties in the setting; (2) develop or attend to external interests or obligations; (3) en-counter outsider encouragements, opportunities, or acceptances; (4) minimize reservations about disinvolvement; (5) assume initiatives or make plans for disinvolvement; (6) coordinate departures and outside engagements; (7) en-counter and deal with insider resistances; (8) avoid subcultural practices, set-tings, and associates; and (9) reengage former roles in one or other respects. Relatedly, as existing ethnographic research on disinvolvement attests,[4] it is essential that social scientists attend to people's roles in managing themselves amidst somewhat concurrent concerns on their parts of influencing others in desired ways and selectively attending to any influence work that others may direct toward them.

Default Detachments

Default detachments or forced disinvolvements assume three basic forms. The first involves instances in which people, through no inclination of their own, are prevented from pursuing particular involvements as a consequence of existing external circumstances (as in limitations pertaining to people's re-sources, opportunities, and obligations).

A second set of default detachments refers to those cases in which subcultural participants find themselves excluded (as in rejected, displaced, ignored, or re-placed) by others in this setting. These exclusionary or distancing practices need not be uniformly implemented or desired by all of the other participants in the subcultural setting, nor need they be sustained over extended periods of time. However, many instances of people's disinvolvements from subcultural deviance come about when relations between insiders become more hostile and/or exclusionary in emphasis.

Third, subcultures of all sorts dissipate or expire over time as the participants depart in one or other ways and/or attend to other intrigues, obligations, and the like, thereby rendering particular groups inconsequential for earlier par-ticipants. Similarly, even when the group persists in one or other forms, insid-ers may introduce agendas, practices, or new members in ways that some earlier participants consider to have destroyed the association "that was" (i.e., from their viewpoint, the group no longer exists).

Like voluntary disinvolvements, default detachments may alert scholars to some of the more tentative and precarious aspects of people's ties with others in the setting. However, whereas those who attempt to become disinvolved on a voluntary basis may encounter some subsequent rejection from former as-sociates (thereby approximating default detachments in some respects), the following processes seem relevant especially to considerations of default de-tachments: (1) defining subcultural life-worlds as inaccessible; (2) being rejected by subcultural others (insiders, members); and (3) finding that the subculture has dissipated or is no longer recognized as a viable essence by earlier partici-pants.

As with voluntary withdrawals, it should not be assumed that default detachments are as comprehensive or as enduring as they might first appear. Thus, in addition to ties of various sorts with former associates, people may reengage earlier or related life-worlds by (1) retaining partial subcultural attachments (as in maintaining contacts, perspectives, memories); (2) attempting to renew earlier subcultural reinvolvements; and (3) seeking substitute subcultural associations in which to pursue certain kinds of activity.

Treatment and Disinvolvement

Although treatment is often presumed to be the key to successful disinvolvement of people from deviance, it must be emphasized that treatment is *not* synonymous with disinvolvement. Treatment and disinvolvement represent two very different sets of humanly engaged processes.

As suggested earlier in this chapter, one of the major obstacles that people encounter, even when they desire to leave certain activities behind, revolves around the matter of disentanglement, or people's attempts to separate themselves more completely and comprehensively from the many features (e.g., perspectives, activities, relationships) of the setting at hand.

Further, while some treatments may be so severe or restricting as to preclude people from engaging in various activities (i.e., disengagement by default), other treatments may be viewed and experienced in ways that are very different from any intended by those implementing particular treatments. Not only may targets ignore some treatments that others deem consequential, but even when treatments are "objectified" or made overtly apparent to the targets and others, the effects of many treatments are far from those desired.

The treatment administered to targets becomes objectified when agents of control more pointedly define (accurately or otherwise) and act toward particular targets as "the sources of difficulty." Although forceful designations often seem desirable to agents of control, the labeling of specific people as deviants and the related dramatization of evil (insofar as it results in targets organizing their routines more fully around particular problematic realms of endeavor) may very well contribute to people's intensified involvements in the very activities that tacticians might wish to avoid. As Tannenbaum (1938) and Lemert (1951, 1967) contend, where the problematic activity is viewed by people more generally as (a) more synonymous with particular targets, (b) more disruptive to the community at large, and (c) more enduring, those defined as targets are apt to find that opportunities (as accorded to them by others) to assume more "acceptable" identities (and activities) are dramatically reduced. Likewise, (d) those more prominently cast into particular deviant roles tend to envision themselves more fully within these terms.

However, before one assumes that people's more intensive involvements in deviance are simply, or even largely, the product of audience rejections or exclusions, it is important to be mindful of (a) people's capacities for knowingly embarking on specific pursuits on their own and (b) the roles that people's other associates (as subcultural insiders) may play in sustaining and intensifying people's involvements in particular realms of deviance. Likewise, because (c) people's careers of participation are constituted through their activities and interactions rather than being the direct products of their attitudes, intentions, or individual qualities, it is essential that those studying disinvolvement attend to the ways that human behavior is developed within the various theaters of operation in which people find themselves.

EXPERIENCING TREATMENT

As used herein, *treatment* refers to efforts on the part of others (i.e., tacticians or agents of control) to alter people's involvements in particular situations. In contrast to chapters 10 through 12, however, which have dealt with regulatory (informal and more formalized) treatments from the viewpoint of the agents of control, the emphasis here is on target definitions of, experiences with, and adjustments to treatment efforts.

Relatedly, we use the term *agent of control* (AC) to refer to the person or tactician who is administering treatment of some sort.[5] Because people can and often do act back on one another, it is inappropriate to maintain distinct or rigid identifications of the participants as targets or tacticians. Still, we will strive for conceptual consistency while acknowledging the fuller range of human association that "treatments" entail in actual practice.

There is no presumption that the treatment implemented in any instance is legitimate, warranted, effective, or desirable. Likewise, there is no requirement that target viewpoints correspond with (or even acknowledge) tactician intentions, nor is any emphasis placed on the desirability of targets seeking, accepting, or resisting any treatment.

Further, treatment is not a "thing" as much as it is a *social process*. Relatedly, whether people willingly enter into or otherwise encounter treatment, they effectively venture into another *subcultural setting*. People experiencing instances of treatment, thus, may be seen to engage particular life-worlds with certain sets of associates, perspectives, identities, relationships, and so forth.

Once treatment is envisioned in processual, enacted terms, matters pertaining to initial contacts between those administering treatment (i.e., ACs, tacticians) and those encountering treatment (i.e., recipients, targets) become consequential, as do any concerns, anticipations, past experiences, preparations, or adjustments to which one or more of the participants (tacticians or targets) may attend. In particular, because people (a) often have memories of past experiences regarding similar or related situations and (b) commonly attempt to shape the future, both through self-directed activities and behaviors intended to affect the ways that others treat them, people's experiences with treatments may assume reflective-adjustive as well as more situated-initiatory qualities.

Targets need not be aware of any or all tactician attempts to shape their experiences (as in definitions, inclinations, and activities). However, even when targets are clearly aware of the viewpoints and practices of tacticians in the settings at hand, targets need not be receptive to, or accepting of, these matters. Thus, even when tacticians intend only to aid or otherwise enhance target experiences, there is no requirement that targets will view these (benign) efforts as desirable. Conversely, there is no requirement that any treatments that tacticians intend as negative experiences for targets will be viewed as such by the targets in question.

Likewise, we should recognize target capacities to question, reject, and resist tactician efforts with respect to their own experiences, as well as target attempts to act back on (and try to influence) the very tacticians that the targets see as trying to influence them. Indeed, as minded beings, those viewed as targets for control on the part of others may themselves assume active, tactical roles in attempts to shape their own circumstances *and* the experiences of those (agents of control) trying to change them in some way.

Viewed thusly, both those who represent the objects or targets of control and the agents of control may assume roles as *tacticians* whenever one tries to change or influence the other. Relatedly, both may become *targets* for the endeavors or objectives of the other.

This *interchangeability of viewpoints and practices* or the capacity for all interactants to assume roles as tacticians *and* targets on a sequential, as well as a simultaneous, basis is fundamental for a fuller appreciation of the control-treatment process.[6] There is no inference that people are equal participants in this process and some people may be clearly advantaged over others in certain respects, but human capacities for (deliberative) influence and resistance work are much more consequential than is implied in most considerations of treatment programs.[7]

As analysts, we also would be remiss were we not to directly acknowledge tendencies on the part of targets to adopt tactician perspectives and cooperate willingly, if not eagerly in some cases. It is to be appreciated, as well, that ACs may envision target viewpoints as highly reasonable on occasion, possibly substituting target viewpoints for their own.

Notably, too, it should be observed that even those who interact with one another around the more formal roles of targets and control agents may develop a variety of other (and possibly, for the participants, more consequential) roles that may take them well beyond conventional images of the treatment process. Thus, one or other of the interactionists may assume roles as educators, entertainers, confidants, friends, intimates, and the like. Although some may be inclined to chastise agents of control on these matters, it is important that scholars be mindful of, and receptive to, the entire range of human association (including any *secondary roles*) that people may develop in "treatment" contexts. Relatedly, it should not be assumed that these secondary involvements render the treatment process less effective than otherwise would be the case.

Some further limitations of more conventional images of treatment become evident when one recognizes that, in addition to any treatments that originate with particular agents of control (ACs), targets commonly encounter a variety of treatments from their other associates.

Because targets are faced with the prospects of coming to terms with the viewpoints of a potentially diverse assortment of others, each of these realms of interchange may serve to contextualize (endorse, redefine, reject, distract) AC treatment. For this reason, it is vital that analysts envision treatment within recipients' broader, often multiplistic theaters of operation.

Mindful of people's capacities for reflectivity and adjustment (as in invoking multiple viewpoints on the desirability of any program or instance of treatment, adopting roles as both tacticians and targets, and attending to a plurality of others in both more immediate and anticipatory manners), we have sketched out a series of processes that are consequential to fuller investigations of target experiences with the treatment process. These are organized around the matters of people *encountering agents of control* (ACs); *minimizing contact* with ACs; *receiving treatment; extending the parameters, maintaining self, sustaining deviant involvements;* and *invoking self-treatment.*

Encountering Agents of Control

As noted in the statements following, those encountering agents of control may make contact with those agents of control through the recruitment efforts of ACs, the recruitment efforts of third parties, or the targets' own initiatives.

In the first instance, targets may become caught up in various monitoring activities that others may invoke in informal or formal manners (see chapters 10 through 12). While subject to any variety of classification practices that these others may invoke, one common contact route takes place as those implicated in these AC frameworks are approached or otherwise acknowledged as problem cases by specific agents of control.

When people (as targets) become aware of agent initiatives, matters of the following sorts become consequential: (a) encountering AC definitions, cautions, and warnings; (b) contesting AC definitions of the situation; (c) attending to AC surveillance; and (d) defining self as being subjected to AC treatment.

Readers may refer to chapter 10 for a fuller discussion of third-party referrals, but it is worth noting here that people may refer targets to other ACs in more direct terms or may do so only after they, themselves, have engaged targets as ACs. When targets encounter ACs through third-party referrals, considerations of the following types are relevant: (a) receiving deviance definitions and other treatments from third parties (initial ACs); (b) being reported to (other) ACs by third parties; and (c) target attempts to resist third-party referrals and claims in dealing with the ACs to whom they have been referred.

Should people engage agents of control through self-referrals, the focus shifts to matters of these sorts: (a) assuming contact initiative (on one's own);

(b) encountering encouragements to contact ACs from others; and (c) overcoming reservations about dealing with ACs. In this third mode of contact, people may seek out treatments that they find alluring in some way or may engage ACs as a means of dealing with pressing problems (obligations, fears, or other troublesome circumstances).[8] Even when AC contacts are voluntary and/or considered highly desirable from target viewpoints, we still may ask whether these people have any reservations about engaging particular ACs and, if so, how they deal with these reservations. In all cases, though, the emphasis is on the ways in which targets experience these contacts. Relatedly, although people often seem to avoid AC contact, it should be acknowledged that people (e.g., see Schneider and Conrad, 1983; Karp, 1996) may actively pursue and sustain, if not maximize, AC contact (and treatment).

Minimizing Contact

The points introduced here focus more directly on those targets who knowingly define AC viewpoints and practices to be at variance from their own interests. Thus, although one major tactic is that of (1) trying to avoid contact with particular ACs, other concerns revolve around people's attempts to (2) minimize the impact of AC contact and (3) avert undesired treatments when caught up in AC activities.[9]

When people attempt to avert detection from agents of control, activities of the following sort tend to become consequential: (a) decreasing involvements in instances of problematic activities; (b) minimizing obtrusiveness of problematic activities; (c) maximizing camouflage of problematic activities; (d) seeking third-party assistance in concealment; and (e) devising agent distractions to cover their own activities.

Should people anticipate that they may be subjected to agent detection and unfavorable treatment thereof, practices of the following sorts become more noteworthy: (a) dealing with apprehensions, anxieties, and distrust; (b) monitoring and adjusting to agent practices; and (c) developing contingency plans and resources in anticipation of detection.

If targeted for treatment, people may still attempt to avoid certain kinds of treatment by resisting agent categories or encouraging agents to make concessions of various kinds. Particularly relevant here are the matters of (a) contesting designations of self as troublesome; (b) negotiating for lesser treatments; and (c) involving third parties as defenders or supporters of sorts.[10]

Receiving Treatment

While not disregarding concerns with treatment effects on the part of agents of control, the material here focuses on target experiences with treatment. In addition to attending to (1) the multiple, potentially conflicting and shifting ways that targets define particular aspects of treatment and (2) the sources of these definitions, it is most important to examine (3) the ways that targets experience treatment in more direct, enacted terms, and (4) the ways in which targets may extend their relations with particular agents of control.

Because treatment is not one thing, people may define and assess treatment with respect to multiple reference points, including (a) the particular instances (and targets) of application; (b) the specific programs being implemented; (c) the expressed objectives of the treatment program; (d) the particular administrators of the treatment; and (e) notions of ideal and probable outcomes of treatments.

Likewise, targets may obtain definitions of treatment not only (a) from tacticians, but also (b) from third parties who may be inside and/or outside the treatment arena, and (c) through considerations of their own stocks of knowledge. Target assessments of treatment also would seem contingent on (d) their past experiences with treatment programs, their immediate circumstances, and their anticipations of the future, along with some sense of developments to date in the more immediate treatment setting.

The somewhat related matter of people engaging treatment seems contingent on people (a) acknowledging and attending to agent viewpoints and practices; (b) distancing themselves (covertly) from treatment; (c) explicitly resisting agent viewpoints and practices; (d) consulting with third parties about the treatment at hand; and (e) embarking on coordinated resistance with others.

As reflective entities with an assortment of interests that they can deliberately pursue in making the best of their situations, targets also may engage the treatment process in ways that extend target-agent relationships well beyond more routine treatment considerations. Thus, we may be attentive to (a) the occasions and ways in which targets accept and resist secondary roles offered to them by ACs in the setting as well as (b) target initiatives and practices in promoting and intensifying secondary realms of involvement with the ACs in the setting.

Extending the Parameters

In addition to the associations that people experience as a direct consequence of AC contact and treatment, it is important to acknowledge the other lifeworlds in which targets participate. Whether these associations consist of other insiders who also are subject to AC treatment or involve people who may be quite removed from the target-AC context, these other associations can be highly consequential for understanding target experiences with the treatment process as well as the disinvolvement process more generally.

While people often are uncertain of their places of self and other within each of these sets of relationships, each of these associations offers reference points that bespeak their own traditions (as in group understandings and agreed-upon practices), wisdom (as in people's earlier practical experiences and stocks of knowledge), and potentialities (as in opportunities for realizing participant interests). Thus, regardless of the viewpoints and practices adopted in these settings, targets often find these associations appealing. More generally, too, even when targets only partially subscribe to aspects of particular subcultures, they still may find it difficult to ignore certain associates and their activities, especially when thrust into their midst.

Should these target associates (insiders or outsiders) reference AC-target treatments in some way, targets very well may receive alternative definitions of the AC, AC treatments, other AC targets, the targets themselves, and any outside activities that targets might pursue. Thus, in addition to representing sources of knowledge, advice, resources, and other modes of support, these other people also represent alternative involvements, diversions, distractions, and sources of disaffection relative to AC agendas.

People in these other subcultural settings also may provide targets with encouragements and opportunities that go well beyond AC-approved involvements. Insofar as these people are familiar to targets and are seen as trustworthy or hold other relevance for targets, these associates may be exceedingly important for understanding people's long-term involvements in AC-defined deviance.

Maintaining Self

Although treatment programs sometimes are so constraining that people have minimal capacity for self-initiated activity, it is important that researchers consider the ways in which people pursue autonomy or find other ways of maintaining desired expressions of self amidst treatment programs.

Regardless of whether people pursue their interests more extensively on their own or in collective associations of sorts, it is important (as Goffman [1961] so effectively indicates) to be mindful of the ways in which people maintain senses of self while undergoing treatment programs. In addition to those targets who (1) envision the treatments promoted by agents of control as personally viable and appropriate, some other modes of maintaining self in treatment contexts may be distinguished. These include (2) withholding cooperation; (3) sabotaging aspects of the treatment situation; (4) managing impressions and engaging in strategic interchange; (5) involving third parties in interventionist roles; (6) making use of the resources found in the setting; and (7) exercising self-reflectivity. Although we have identified some variants of the latter modes of maintaining self, it should be noted that these practices are apt to overlap with one another in actual practice.

In some cases, people may maintain integrity of self by withholding cooperation or refusing to comply with treatment programs in one or other manners. Thus, people may (a) pretend to cooperate with agents of control; (b) cooperate only reluctantly, or with delay, questions, debate, or other less overt forms of resistance; (c) engage in noncompliance through more extensive passive resistance; (d) become openly defiant in refusals to cooperate or in challenges directed toward agents; (e) attempt to incite opposition to treatments, personnel, or programs on the part of others; and (f) participate in collectively developed instances of resistance.

Targets also may attempt to maintain a sense of self-direction by sabotaging or disrupting treatment by (a) disabling or destroying treatment-related materials, (b) creating situated and/or enduring procedural obstructions, (c) denigrating programs, agents, and other targets, and (d) creating embarrassments and other liabilities intended to discredit or nullify aspects of the treatment process.

At other times, however, those targeted for treatment may pursue their own interests by (a) conforming with agents and treatment programs in the pursuit of better short and/or long-term conditions; (b) conveying impressions of compliance with, or appreciation of, treatment programs; (c) embarking on ingratiation tactics directed towards specific agents of control and others considered influential in certain regards; (d) negotiating for privileges or other considerations with ACs and/or others in the settings; (e) interacting with ACs and/or others in more selective, strategic manners; and (f) pursuing activities and interests in more covert, selective, and deceptive ways.

In some instances as well, targets may seek interventionist assistance from third parties within or outside of the treatment context. In addition to (a) seeking more direct personal considerations, targets also may use third-party contacts in attempts to (b) neutralize and/or punish agents of control as well as to (c) challenge, redirect, or eliminate specific treatments or broader aspects of the associations promoting these treatments.

As targets become more familiar with treatment, agent routines, and settings more generally, targets also may (a) redefine and/or reconfigure objects within their situations so that these things become more consistent with their preferences and more useful for their purposes, and (b) take advantage of particular features of treatment programs.

Finally, people may sustain aspects of self through more focused, reflective considerations that allow them to transcend, or shift perspectives within, the treatment context. While notions of these sorts may be invoked in any setting and may involve group interchange (as in reminiscences, comments) at different times, people's capacities for private or covert "mindedness" allows targets to retain some essences of self in even highly constricting treatment conditions.

Thus, by (a) invoking wide ranges of emotional sensations such as spite or affection for ACs, pride or pity with respect to oneself, or despair or hopes for the future, (b) contemplating alternative lines of action on behalf of themselves or others in the setting, or (c) recollecting and reflecting upon an assortment of earlier expressions, people may be able to transcend the more immediate settings in which they find themselves.

Although these methods of maintaining essences of self (especially where they reflect matters of cooperation and resistance) may seem contradictory, we may expect people to assume a variety of tactical stances as they attempt to adjust to the particular situations (short-term and more enduring) in which they find themselves. The following consideration of "sustaining problematic behaviors" addresses a related aspect of people's attempts to maintain self within the context of treatment programs.

Sustaining Deviant Involvements

Because people's participation in problematic activities does not automatically cease once treatment is begun or even completed, it is vital that analysts not lose track of target involvements in deviance in the midst of treatment.

Even when people desire to become disengaged from particular realms of involvement they may have difficulty doing so. However, when their viewpoints are at variance from those of the ACs in the setting, targets may assume considerable enterprise in sustaining and extending these activities (or questing for the best available approximations).

When targets operate in the company of others whose viewpoints openly are at odds with those of the ACs in the setting, targets are apt to experience greater latitude both in ignoring treatment programs and maintaining closer, if not, more intense approximations of earlier realms of problematic behavior.

Although target opportunities for involvements in deviance often are more restricted when undergoing treatment, targets may still look to the future and, thus, maintain a focus conducive to subsequent reinvolvements. Thus, even in those occasions in which a better future seems severely removed, targets may still derive some freedom from AC directives and constraints by reengaging memories of the past.

Accordingly, in considering people's activities that persist through the treatment process, it is important to acknowledge (1) the occasions and ways in which targets actually continue particular realms of activity (as in extended or partialized involvements of identical or similar activities or other approximated alternatives to forbidden activities) while undergoing treatment; as well as attend to the matters of targets (2) encountering encouragement for continuity from others, (3) anticipating opportunities for activities following treatment, and (4) living on memories of earlier involvements.

Invoking Self-Treatment

While people are often reminded of their failings by others and subjected to treatments that others invoke in their attempts to reshape target activities (and experiences), targets also may administer a wide variety of treatments to themselves. As self-reflective entities, people may attempt to improve upon or correct things about themselves that they (or others) might find troublesome.

Like treatments that they might experience from others, the treatments that people direct toward themselves may assume a wide variety of objectives and forms. People's self treatments may represent highly isolated instances of application or they may be located within broader programs or agendas. Similarly, people may embark on self-treatment programs for shorter or longer periods and may mix any assortment of self-directed treatments with treatments administered by others.

Further, whereas some self-directed treatments might be considered acceptable by particular ACs or others in the target's community, certain self-administered treatments may be ones that targets know would be rejected by others. In cases of this latter sort, the particular remedial endeavors that targets invoke may very well take targets trying to manage one set of encounters with deviance into yet other realms of deviance and disrespectability.

As with other treatments, too, those that are self-directed are apt to be far from uniformly successful. Thus, even when "setting one's own agenda" or "trying to manage oneself," targets are apt to encounter distractions, interactions, frustrations, and allures that take them some distance from their "good intentions." Still, social scientists interested in matters of this sort could productively examine the ways in which people who contemplate and invoke instances of self-treatment (1) experience disenchantment with self; (2) set objectives for self-change; (3) initiate and sustain self-treatment; (4) monitor and assess progress of self-treatment; (5) encounter distractions, setbacks, and failures; (6) readjust treatments, objectives, and viewpoints; (7) define success; (8) discontinue self-treatment; (9) seek external treatment (from agents of control); (10) give up on treatment-related objectives; and (11) reengage self-treatment ventures.

Having considered people's experiences with treatment from agents of control and subcultural associates as well as instances of self-directed treatment, we now return to a more explicit consideration of the disinvolvement process and the related matters of ambivalence and reinvolvement.

DISINVOLVEMENT, AMBIVALENCE, AND REINVOLVEMENT

While people frequently envision treatment as the last chapter in disinvolvement, it is much more accurate to view treatment as part of the larger involvement process pertaining to particular realms of people's endeavors. Thus, although some treatments may physically prevent people from engaging in certain kinds of activities, treatment and disinvolvement are two distinct processes. They may overlap in many cases, but the two are far from synonymous.

Outsiders often see disinvolvements from deviance in more singular or exclusive terms, wherein people are thought to be either involved in, or disinvolved from, particular situations, but those caught up in deviance as participants are apt to see things quite differently.

This is not to discount the significance of people's encounters with treatment, particularly people's personal experiences with unpleasant and costly aspects of many treatment programs. Nor, is there any intent to minimize the implications of the designation of people as deviants (which also represents a consequential feature of the broader treatment process). Indeed, those involved in deviance often struggle with the unpleasantries and disabling aspects of treatment as well as the disrespectability associated with deviance.[11] Thus, whereas outsiders may envision treatment as a desirable remedial procedure, those encountering treatment often find that treatment presents sets of obstacles to be endured in addition to their other life challenges.

Like people who have avoided deviant imputations and related treatments, those involved in deviance also are apt to be concerned about matters of freedom and autonomy as well as achieving their notions of happiness in life. Similar to other people as well, those implicated in deviance are apt to develop a variety of interests and intrigues, encounter limitations in achieving their objectives, and contemplate ways in which they might have better lives. For the most part, those implicated in deviance seem to approach their situations in manners that are not so different from the ways in which people consider continuities and disinvolvements in their other activities. Thus, it is important to acknowledge the mixes of allures, disaffections, fears, instrumentalities, boredom, hesitations, alternatives, and urgencies to which people may attend both on a more situated basis and over time.

In these respects, those labeled and treated as deviants may be seen to act with emphases that are not so different from those they may have had prior to their identification as deviants. Like a great many other people, those implicated in deviance learn things along the way and may reconcile themselves to less promising futures. As well, unless they have particular reasons for optimism, those who have experienced treatment (particularly of an externally imposed sort) tend to avoid further deviance-related treatments.

Not only do treatments seldom offer targets the things these people had hoped to achieve, but treatments often take these people further from the things they desire. Unless analysts acknowledge this seemingly obvious point, they will have great difficulty comprehending the disinvolvement process experienced by those encountering treatment programs. Likewise, rather than being grateful to those trying to reform them (and take away from their disreputable pursuits), considerable resentment may be directed toward those administering treatments in these areas or otherwise preventing these people from pursuing personally more desired objectives.

Knowing that others disapprove of their situations does not make people's decisions to disinvolve automatic. However, concerns with disapproval on the part of others may very well generate additional dilemmas for people involved in particular lines of action. Many treatments, thus, are better seen as unwelcome intrusions, interruptions, or complications in continuity than complete or even viable temporary instances of disinvolvement.

Still, because treatments often involve negative sanctions, anxiety, and noteworthy inconveniences, these disruptions (along with any setbacks and disaffections people experience more naturally in deviant life-worlds) may give participants specific occasions in which to more fully assess their circumstances.

Acknowledging the ambiguities that people may experience, both following treatment and independently of any treatment considerations, the following points may help focus research on disinvolvement-related deliberation and choices. Thus, it is important to examine the ways that (and extent to which) people (1) encounter uncertainties, dilemmas, and vulnerabilities in the here-and-now; (2) review their interests and objectives; (3) define and assess their options and limitations; (4) experience closure (as in urgency to act and/or select from highly limited options); (5) attend to input from others (as in encouragements, condemnations, and distractions); and (6) experience failures and successes along the way.

People's uncertainties are by no means confined to their involvements in deviance, but revolve around their participation in two broader (deviant and conventional) life-worlds. Whereas outsiders often expect targets to change substantially (in conventionalized ways) following treatment, virtually all of the involved parties (i.e., control agents, other outsiders, subcultural insiders, and the targets) also know from past experience that this is a problematic assumption.[12] More generally, the implication of a deviance status is that people who have been designated as deviants have not been, and may never be, fully regular members of the community. Thus, even when others attempt to normalize relations with deviants in various respects, this is often accompanied by a skepticism that permeates present and future expectations as well as an appreciation of situated and longer-term target vulnerabilities in this area.

While people may experience personal ambiguity and mixed receptivities with respect to any venture (deviant or otherwise) in which they may embark, people becoming disinvolved from deviance often encounter wider assortments of definitions, expectations, supports, and condemnations from others. In addition to more punitive ACs, one may acknowledge the varying definitions, expectations, opportunities, and resistances directed toward targets by other target associates (including subcultural insiders, family members, friends, co-workers, and supportive service providers). As participants in a plurality of life-worlds, those involved in deviance commonly find themselves caught between differing viewpoints, associates, and opportunities. Few transitions to conventional lifestyles are apt to be free from uncertainty and difficulty. Thus, when things are not going well in more conventional sectors, reinvolvement in earlier realms of deviance may seem appealing.

Experiencing Reinvolvement

Should people find that disinvolvements (however partial these may be) from particular situations are less satisfactory than they had anticipated, they may consider reengaging earlier situations. These reinvolvements may represent alternatives to one or more current endeavors or they may be incorporated (as additional role involvements) into people's present situations. Nevertheless, reinvolvements seem more likely when people (1) envision former situations as ways to obtain desired or required outcomes; (2) encounter or anticipate greater receptivities on the part of former associates; (3) define opportunities for reinvolvements in former situations as more feasible (4) note changes to self or former situations that would justify reinvolvement; and (5) observe that disentanglement from present routines is more easily accomplished.[13]

Still, reinvolvement generally is not the final sequence in people's experiences with particular realms of deviance. Indeed, given the relatively common tendency for people to go through multiple instances of disinvolvement from, and reinvolvement in, particular realms of deviance, analysts sometimes refer to people experiencing "cycles" or "spirals" of abstinence and reinvolvement. While these notions are strikingly apparent in research involving drug users (Brown, 1931; Ray, 1961), heavy drinkers (Wiseman, 1970), and gamblers (Lesieur, 1977), they have a much more general relevance as implied in people's involvements in divorce (Waller, 1930; Vaughan, 1986), depression (Karp, 1996), and a variety of roles in the hotel community (Prus and Irini, 1980).

People who become reinvolved in earlier (or more comparable) situations are often able to make the transition to familiar roles much more easily, quickly, and completely than those first starting out in arenas of those sorts. However, deviant lifestyles can be demanding and highly unsettling. Often encountering difficulties and disappointments similar to those preceding their earlier disinvolvements and reliving incidents of more intense, unsettling sorts, even more experienced participants frequently find that reinvolvements are less viable than they had hoped. Still, the options associated with subsequent disinvolvement often are unsatisfactory as well. Thus, people may vacillate indefinitely between deviance and more respectable involvements, despite various treatment programs, benefactors, and situated optimism regarding a more respectable lifestyle. For some people, too, things just may not go well in any area and they may find themselves bouncing somewhat erratically between two or more sets of associates and their related life-worlds as they try to make the best of precarious, often emotionally troublesome and sometimes physically volatile, sets of practices and interchanges.

Residual Involvements

Regardless of when and how people become disengaged from particular situations, including the most direct, overt, sustained, and comprehensive instances, people's disinvolvements are often more partial than they might like. Thus, well after people have become disengaged from deviance (and clearly detach themselves from former activities, associations, and settings), people's memories, identities, and emotional entanglements (such as sympathies, fascinations, anxieties) still may tie them to former life-worlds.

On some occasions as well, former associates may embarrassingly (and sometimes forcefully) impose themselves on targets. However, other people (who know about people's earlier involvements in deviance) also may remind participants of their earlier involvements (possibly using these occasions to admonish or otherwise sanction targets).

This means that aspects of people's pasts, such as reputations, relationships, and personal recollections may spill over into people's current situations and their plans for the future, even when the former participants might very much wish that this not happen. Thus, although disinvolvement sometimes appears complete, one of the rather inevitable (personal, if not also interpersonal and, sometimes, more public) legacies of being implicated in deviance at earlier points in time is that of being an "ex-deviant."

Although disinvolvement is often seen as the product of individual qualities, structuralist conditions, or treatment programs, the preceding material not only acknowledges the humanly enacted features of disinvolvement, but it also draws attention to the more fully socially engaged aspects of this process. Quite directly, disinvolvement from deviance is to be understood not only with respect to people's broader participation (careers) and situated involvements in specific realms of activity but, like other aspects of people's participation in deviance, disengagement is very much a multifaceted social process.

As in so many other areas subsumed by notions of deviance and respectability, the challenge is to learn more about the disinvolvement as a humanly engaged process. This will require that researchers carefully investigate the many theaters of operation in which matters of treatment, disinvolvement, and reinvolvement are experienced. Mindful of concerns about studying human-lived experience in these and other settings, we consider the ethnographic research venture somewhat more extensively in chapter 14.

NOTES

1. In developing *Becoming an Ex*, Helen Rose Ebaugh (1988) has provided one of the most extended and instructive considerations of the disinvolvement process available in the literature. Focusing on the disengagement process, Ebaugh organizes her discussion around the matters of (a) first doubts, (b) the quest for alternatives, (c) turning points, and (d) creating the ex-role. While the present statement is cast in somewhat different terms, Ebaugh's text is highly recommended to anyone interested in the process of role exit (and managing "ex" roles).

2. Waller's (1930) and Vaughan's (1986) ethnographic considerations of the divorce experience are especially instructive for comprehending the disinvolvement process, as are studies of disengagement from drug use by Brown (1931), Ray (1961), Biernacki (1988), and Faupel (1991). Also relevant are Lofland's (1966) study of a religious cult, Wiseman's (1970) depiction of skid row drinkers, Lesieur's (1977) study of heavy gamblers, Prus and Sharper's (1977) examination of road hustlers, Prus and Irini's (1980) account of disinvolvement activities among an assortment of people whose lives intersect in the hotel community (i.e., hookers, exotic dancers, rounders, and bar staff), and Karp's (1996) depiction of people's experiences with depression. Along with Ebaugh's (1988) statement on disinvolvement, these texts represent the essential base on which this statement has been developed.

3. The matter of "encountering opportunities for alternative involvements" is more consequential for explaining disinvolvements than might first seem. While people appear more willing to entertain alternatives when they find themselves more disenchanted with a current situation, many people may only begin to question their present situations when they see something that appears more advantageous in another sense. As well, whereas the prospects of becoming disinvolved into "nothingness" may foster continuity in a current situation, people representing alternatives (as recruiting agents) may attempt to generate dissatisfaction on the part of subcultural participants with respect to their present circumstances.

4. The works of Waller (1930) and Vaughan (1986) on the divorce experience are particularly instructive with respect to people managing themselves amidst the disinvolvement process, as are Brown's (1931), Ray's (1961), and Biernacki's (1988) work on people becoming disinvolved from drug use and Karp's (1996) examination of people's experiences with depression.

5. As used herein, the term agents of control (ACs) would include not only (a) those who administer treatment in a more formal capacity of control, but also (b) all other forms of influence work in which formal control agents might engage to shape target behaviors (and experiences) and (c) all of the more informal roles that people routinely adopt in trying to shape one another's behaviors or experiences in ways that they (as tacticians or agents of control) deem necessary, moral, desirable, and the like. Children, thus, frequently assume stances as ACs in dealing with their parents, siblings, and peers, for instance, as also commonly do one's friends.

6. See Prus (1999) for a more extensive discussion of target roles and the related potential of all parties to an interchange to assume roles as both tacticians and targets.

7. For some indications of the interpersonal resilience of people who are among the more disadvantaged interactors, readers are referred to Goffman's (1961) account of the underlife of patients in a mental hospital; Edgerton's (1967) study of the lives of those considered to be mentally retarded; Rubington's (1968), Spradley's (1970), Wiseman's (1970) accounts of skid row drinkers; and Evans and Falk's (1986) and Evans's (1994) examination of a residential school for deaf children.

8. Wiseman's (1970) study of skid row drinkers' reliance on service providers is instructive here. Although not a preferred form of existence, skid row drinkers and other street people generally become adept at "working" agencies in their immediate vicinities to maximize personal comforts and interests. For other indications of the resourcefulness of street people, see Anderson (1923), Spradley (1970), Faupel (1991), and Snow and Anderson (1993).

9. Because they not only attempt to minimize AC contact, but do so on a more systematic basis, studies of hustlers and thieves (Sutherland, 1937; Maurer, 1955; Prus and Sharper, 1977; Jacobs, 1999) are especially instructive in these regards.

10. See chapter 5 for a fuller consideration of the labeling (and resisting) process.

11. In addition to Goffman's (1963) groundbreaking statement on people's experiences with stigma, readers may also appreciate the ambiguity and disrespectability pertaining more specifically to the treatment process. See, for example, Goffman's (1961) account of the underlife of a mental hospital, Schmid and Jones's (1991, 1993) considerations of prison experiences, Wiseman's (1970) study of skid row drinkers, Schneider and Conrad's (1983) account of people's experiences with epilepsy, Sandstrom's (1990) depiction of people with AIDS, Herman's (1994, 1995) portrayal of former psychiatric patients, and Karp's (1996) study of people's experiences with depression.

12. Thus, even when people are comparative converts and accept the goals and treatments associated with reformed lifestyles, they still are likely to encounter difficulties and setbacks along the way. "Going straight," "getting religion," and the like, commonly are beset with frustrations and risks within the straight world and distractions and temptations associated with deviant lifestyles and associates. Consequently, in addition to missing the things (people, activities, senses of self) being left behind, those striving for disinvolvement often venture into unfamiliar territories of sorts. Even in the midst of supportive others, the people trying to make the transition to "normalcy" also come to realize that those supporting these involvements generally do not fully understand the problems and dilemmas experienced by those assuming roles as "repentant sinners."

13. Only a few ethnographies have addressed the reinvolvement process. See Waller (1930), Brown (1931), Ray (1961), Wiseman (1970), Lesieur (1977), Prus and Sharper (1977), Prus and Irini (1980), Vaughan (1986), Biernacki (1988), and Karp (1996). Taken together, these studies suggest that vacillation (disinvolvement and reinvolvement) represent commonplace experiences for people involved in, and attempting to disentangle themselves from, troublesome situations.

Part V

In Perspective

14

Studying Deviance
Ethnographic Examinations of Community Life

In developing this text, we have sought to extend the parameters of interactionist theory and research with respect to the study of deviance as a community phenomenon that is more or less continuously in the making.

Focusing on people's involvements in deviance in a more comprehensive sense, central distinctions have been made between people (a) defining, condemning, or attempting to control deviance; (b) doing things that might have been construed as deviant in some way; (c) becoming caught up in the intrigues of deviance (as in curiosities, entertainment, and other attractions); and (d) approaching deviance in a more scholarly fashion. Relatedly, while acknowledging the importance of researchers and analysts attending to the mystiques or auras that people commonly associate with deviance, we have examined deviance primarily as an essence whose instances are accomplished through human activity and interchange.

Following an overview of symbolic interaction in chapter 2, wherein emphasis is on human knowing and acting in direct and engaged terms, chapter 3 acknowledges the many theaters of operation in which people may engage aspects of the deviance process. Not only may people engage deviance in a great many ways, but deviance also is a social essence thoroughly enmeshed in community life.

Addressing some essential features of the deviance-making process, chapter 4 considers the ways in which people define things in negative terms and chapter 5 focuses on the ways in which specific people are identified as deviants. Thus, attention is given to the problematic and negotiated processes through which people's notions of moral order are given expression and particular target identities within are invoked, applied, contested, engaged, sustained, and readjusted over time.

Recognizing the human enterprise involved in the production of particular activities and life-worlds that may be considered deviant in one or other ways, chapter 6 deals with people's careers of participation in subcultural arenas, while chapter 7 addresses people's experiences within the interactive and multidimensional life-worlds that constitute deviant subcultures and chapter 8 considers the ways that people form and coordinate associations and engage in particular collective events. As well, because people may experience deviance more exclusively on their own at times, chapter 9 acknowledges people's experiences as solitary deviants and the ways that people manage their situations when they find themselves more exclusively on their own.

Whereas chapters 6 through 9 primarily attend to the activities and experiences of people caught up in deviance as practitioners of sorts, chapters 10 through 12 focus on those who are involved in the regulation of deviance. Returning to the earlier moral emphases and notions of control introduced in chapters 4 and 5, wherein the people involved in defining deviance and identifying deviants are accorded central stage, chapters 10 through 12 reengage people's concerns about achieving appropriate moral orders with respect to deviance. While chapter 10 attends to people's attempts to restore order on a more informal basis, chapters 11 and 12 consider the operations of formal control agencies and the life-worlds in which the agents working in regulatory environments find themselves.

Examining the processes by which people become disinvolved from disreputable activities and life-worlds, chapter 13 further considers the ways in which deviants and others attempt to pursue their interests with respect to one another. Here, target quests for self-direction become consequential amidst regulator concerns with applying treatments of various sorts to those targeted for change. Acknowledging people's capacities to assume roles as both targets and tacticians in treatment and other associational contexts, people's disinvolvements from deviance are examined mindfully of the shifting arenas in which those designated as deviants find themselves.

In rounding out this text, three additional matters merit our attention. These pertain to the matters of *transcending the deviant mystique, examining deviance in the making,* and *extending the conceptual frame.* Although we will be able to address these matters in more fleeting terms only, it is important to acknowledge some of the problems that researchers encounter in the ethnographic study of deviance and how they try to deal with them. While complicated somewhat by the deviant mystique, most of the matters considered here pertain to the study of human group life more generally.[1]

TRANSCENDING THE DEVIANT MYSTIQUE

A first aspect of moving beyond the deviant mystique is the recognition that deviance does not exist apart from people's moral judgements. Relatedly, deviance is not a simple or a single thing. Whereas the term deviance allows us to acknowledge that various things (as in certain activities, outcomes, actors, and ideas) may be deemed troublesome, disturbing, or offensive in some way, deviance is a social essence and is as multifaceted as any other aspect of community life.

Specific individuals and groups may be identified as deviants and often are viewed as the sources or causes of the problem, but deviance is a much broader, socially constituted phenomenon. Accordingly, deviance cannot be adequately understood in isolation from the ways in which people define, engage, and experience these matters within the context of ongoing group life. Not only do notions of deviance develop within community contexts and find expression in group settings in the practices of identifying, regulating, and adjusting to troublesome persons, but all of people's behaviors are comprehensible only in terms of the communities in which the participants live, think, and act. Although it may be tempting to explain deviance by saying that definitions of deviance are relativistic or reflect audience perspectives, this sociological insight is little more than a starting point for developing more sustained considerations of deviance.

It is essential that social scientists appreciate the relativism of deviance or that people's notions of "what is" and "what is not" considered deviant are apt to vary between and within communities. But, to recognize differences in the ways that people label something or someone as deviant, bad, troublesome, evil, and the like, does little to explain how people actually define, formulate, and deal with the instances at hand. Consequently, the more productive focus revolves around examinations of the ways that people (a) generate and apply notions of deviance to human life-worlds; (b) engage in the activities that somehow are considered to be deviant; and (c) adjust to instances of deviance as these take place in their midst.

Not only do emphases of these latter sorts take scholars more directly and fully into considerations of deviance as a social process, but they also enable researchers and analysts to examine the ways in which people participate in the wide assortment of roles and activities that constitute deviance as something "in the making." Closer study of these matters not only indicates the great many instances, roles, and standpoints that people may develop with respect to deviance over their lifetimes but also attests to the enduring nature of people's concerns with deviance within the human community.

Deviance will not be eliminated by wishing or by invoking policies intended to banish wrongdoing from human existence. It may be possible to lessen and divert certain kinds of activities within particular settings, but this is not synonymous with eliminating deviance in a more comprehensive or sustained sense. Indeed, were deviance to be somehow totally eliminated, so would the very essence of human lived experience (as in meaningful activity, multiple viewpoints, moral assessments, reflectivity, persuasive endeavor, and human relations).

Because deviance is developed on the very same foundations on which people accomplish other activities in the human community, it is essential that analysts not become so enraptured or caught up in intrigues with deviance that they lose focus on the more fundamental essences of community life. Quite directly, if we are to make scholarly progress in the study of deviance, it will be necessary that analysts permeate the deviance mystique in a comprehensive and sustained fashion.

While recognizing that people may become caught up in wide arrays of moralisms and condemnations, remedialism and control, and entertainment and emotional expressivity, it is necessary that researchers examine any and all aspects of deviance in the same way that they might study any other subject matter. Thus, a scholarly analysis would entail an extended openness to the study of anyone doing anything, anywhere, anytime, in any manner, and with any others. For people engaging in field research, this means concentrating on the activities at hand and the central participants involved therein, without invoking or privileging any moral or ethical standpoints to assess (condemn, honor, or promote) the practices of any participants over any others.

Still, even when researchers or analysts put their own moralities in suspension while studying the life-worlds of other people, they commonly encounter morally motivated criticism and restrictions from outsiders.[2] This may include moralists, ethics committees, and other control agents, as well as people who fund research. While typically claiming "good intentions," these outsiders may impose their viewpoints on researchers and analysts, often with diversionary, if not more disabling consequences. Whereas some of these concerns may be directed toward people doing research on any group, these frequently become intensified when the particular subject matters or the people being studied are considered deviant or disreputable in some way.

In addition to criticizing researchers for not pursuing agendas that they consider more appropriate, outsiders also may restrict researcher access to particular groups or attempt to extract information about researchers' sources. As Henslin (1972) observes, outsiders also may implicate researchers (as in images, reputations, and culpability) in any disreputable or illegal activities that those outsiders associate with the group or project at hand. At times, as well, people with other agendas may attempt to censor or obstruct publication and dissemination of scholarly research and analyses.

Another set of resistances that researchers may encounter comes from the members of the groups being studied. Thus, whereas many subcultural participants may be willing to help researchers with their inquiries, others may have little interest in scholarly endeavors of any sorts or may envision researchers primarily as threats to the group's agendas or their more personal interests. As well, some of those involved in deviance may be especially concerned that researchers not jeopardize their immediate activities or their autonomy in the broader community. Notably, too, much like outsiders, insiders also may attempt to use researchers to promote group objectives or their more personal interests.

As a result, it is not uncommon for people doing ethnographic research to find themselves walking a variety of interpersonal tightropes as they try to maintain a more sustained scholarly focus amidst an assortment of outsider and insider cross-pressures. Although these matters may complicate and frustrate any instance of research, they frequently become more pronounced when people embark on ethnographic research in deviance.

Not only do ethnographers typically (and necessarily, if they are to be effective) develop closer and more sustained contact with the people whose life-worlds they are studying, but those studying deviance commonly also face problems pertaining to the disrespectability and possible illegality associated with the activities with which the participants in the setting may be involved. To some extent, both insider and outsider resistances may be overcome when researchers exercise care, sincerity, and confidentiality in their dealings with others, thereby fostering higher levels of trust on the part of others. Still, this is no guarantee that researchers will not become caught between two or more sets of antagonists or encounter people (insiders or outsiders) who define researchers more exclusively in troublesome terms.

Researchers may try to prepare for some contingencies and restrictions by developing straightforward explanations and accounts of their activities, exercising discretion in their treatment of the people they encounter, dealing with the materials that they collect in more circumspect manners, and so forth. However, it is impossible to fully anticipate all of the issues that people might raise from one or other standpoints. Thus, ethnographers often find it advantageous to assume more chameleon-like postures in dealing with others both in and outside of the field and to strive for maximal personal composure in dealing with unexpected events and difficult people.

For this reason, as well, more seasoned ethnographers are generally mindful of the access they might have to particular people within (e.g., contacts, sponsors, and general receptivities on the part of participants) settings as opposed to pursuing more specific intrigues that researchers might have with one or other groups of deviants.

Relatedly, it is important to recognize that careful, detailed, and sustained research on any group (deviant or otherwise) can be exceedingly valuable for comprehending group life more generally. When one focuses on human activities, relationships, identities, and the like, in more generic terms, then virtually any group (deviant or otherwise) may provide researchers with valuable insight into human lived experience. Conversely, when researchers are unable to access particular groups in adequate detail, the ensuing research is unlikely to offer much to the scholarly community.

In addition to developing more viable initial contacts with people in the field, it is important that researchers be able to sustain and develop contacts with those people. Given the extended reliance of ethnographers on the openness and cooperation of their associates, it is crucial that researchers develop trust on the part of the people whose life-worlds they intend to examine. For this reason, it is essential that researchers do as much as they can to ensure that the people helping them with their inquiries are comfortable with the researchers in the setting. It also is important that researchers' own mystifications, awkwardness, or disaffections not be allowed to interfere with the research process. Notably, too, things that researchers initially might define as strange, shocking, or otherwise unsettling, may be viewed as mundane, boring, or desirable by others in the setting. Likewise, things that researchers may be inclined to view as unexceptional, inconsequential, or acceptable, may be seen in very different terms by their associates. As well, participants in the setting at hand generally do not expect researchers to be "just like them," and may resent researchers who more completely attempt to appropriate member roles and lifestyles. However, it is important that differences not be envisioned as threatening by the participants.

While researchers sometimes find themselves in extended agreement with the viewpoints and practices of those whom they are studying, it is important that researchers not allow personal sympathies or moral congruencies to detract from more extended, open examinations of the situation or more generic analyses of the material they collect.

Many of these matters are fundamental to an adequate examination of any realm of endeavor, but those studying aspects of the deviance-making process are apt to be doubly advantaged as well as more extensively challenged because of the deviant mystique. Beyond their opportunities to learn about some focal activity, those studying deviance also are able to examine the ways in which people deal with disrespectability (i.e., the additional sets of activities that people invoke to deal with their more marginalized, if not more distinctively pluralized lives). The task of following and disentangling the multiple activities in which these people are involved introduces a more pronounced set of challenges for those studying deviance in the field, as also does the matter of dealing with notions of morality and disrespectability vis-à-vis one's own role as a researcher.

EXAMINING DEVIANCE IN THE MAKING

Although the deviant mystique is likely to "haunt" ethnographers studying deviance throughout the course of their projects and may affect their own careers in diverse manners, a second, but related task is that of embarking on programs of study that directly, fully, and carefully examine deviance as an emergent essence or something in the making. This means approaching and studying deviance as sets of meaningful, multifaceted, and humanly engaged processes. In Herbert Blumer's (1969) terms, the objective is to establish intimate familiarity with one's human subject matter; to study the enacted features of human lived experience in close, thorough, and highly detailed manners.

In addition to coming to terms with the deviant mystique, viable ethnographic research requires that researchers embark on prolonged, inquisitive interchange, and extended association with the people involved in particular life-worlds. Only in this way, by opening themselves to these others (and assuming roles as students relative to these others), may researchers more adequately learn how these people make sense of the settings at hand and how they develop their lines of activity in conjunction with others in their particular theaters of operation.

The study of deviance as something in the making also requires that researchers exercise great patience in their inquiries. Thus, it is vital that researchers not only attend carefully to the instances in which things occur, but also pursue in-depth understandings of all the matters that people experience along the way. This would encompass participants' interests, intrigues, reservations, fears, hesitations, options, second thoughts, tactics, adjustments, and so forth. It requires an attentiveness to the ways that people define and deal with the various objects of their life-worlds, including themselves and any other people whose lives intersect with their own along the way.

It is important that researchers also be open to the varying ways and points at which those involved in activities deemed problematic attend to and deal with notions of disrespectability (and morality) in reference to themselves and others. Although those implicated in deviance generally do not do things so differently from the ways that other people accomplish their activities, their lives are more complicated as a result of the negativities associated with their situations and the treatments they encounter from others. It is important, therefore, that researchers attend to the ambiguities, contradictions, excitement, and limitations that those viewed as deviants experience as well as the adjustments that they and their associates make to these situations.

While stressing the importance of researchers achieving intimate familiarity with their human subject matters, it may be instructive to indicate a little more fully how this might be accomplished. First and foremost, it is important that ethnographers be patient and prepared to experience a great deal of ambiguity as they attend to the life-worlds and examine the situated activities of the other. Because emergence, uncertainty, and complexity are the constant companions of researchers in the field, it is important that ethnographers readjust their notions of things as they learn more about humanly engaged instances in the setting at hand.

Second, for those who wish to achieve greater familiarity with their human subject matter, it is essential to attend to the full range of activities that take place in particular human arenas and to examine the ways in which people do things on a here-and-now, moment-to-moment basis. The emphasis thus, is on what happens and how people do things or enter into the formulative process; not what should happen or why people do things. Likewise, in developing accounts of people's situations and activities, it is advisable for ethnographers to examine the typical as well as the more exceptional events that they encounter in the field. This means attending to things that people might define as boring, exciting, humorous, threatening, routine, highly unusual, and so forth.

Similarly, rather than forcing the analysis of the things encountered into some overarching model of human affairs such as conflict or cooperation, it is most instructive for researchers to be mindful of the full range of human association and any related senses of self that people experience as they go about their activities and deal with others. When examining the ways in which people engage one another, it is important that researchers be cognizant of people's interests and intentions, the emergent contexts in which these people find themselves, and the situated and more extended interchanges that they develop in conjunction with others. Thus, in addition to examining all instances of cooperation and conflict in collectively enacted, process terms, researchers could productively attend to the processes entailed in instances of compromise, confusion, entertainment, and role reversals, as people engage one another amidst wide ranges of interests, objectives, affections, and animosities.

Third, it is important that ethnographers keep detailed records on as many things as possible. Just as it is challenging for people new to the field to sort out all of the things they encounter (particularly as those in the setting might view those things), it also is difficult to predict which things will be important later on. Indeed, many things develop in ways that even highly knowledgeable participants in the setting would be unable to anticipate. Moreover, when one follows a group of people over time, it also becomes apparent that the participants often assume a variety of roles, activities, and viewpoints; develop different relationships and senses of self; experience and express assortments of emotional states; and participate in arrays of emergent, collective events.

When researchers fail to keep more sustained records on matters of these sorts, a great deal of valuable information is apt to be lost. Sometimes, so much happens in the field that it is impossible for researchers to keep track of all these developments. Still, when they do not maintain detailed records overall, researchers are apt to pass up many valuable opportunities to learn more about particular people and the ways in which they do things.

It also is essential that ethnographers attend carefully to a fourth matter, human agency. While encompassing the anticipations, deliberations, and initiatives that people meaningfully invoke in particular instances, agency also includes people's subsequent attentiveness and adjustments to their earlier and ongoing lines of action as well as their tendencies to monitor and adjust to the circumstances, commentaries, and activities of others.

Acknowledging human agency also means considering the ways in which people knowingly and intentionally engage the causal process. It involves examinations of the ways that people enter into the processual flow of human thought and activity in meaningful, reflective, deliberative, and adjustive manners. It means attending to people as active participants within their respective life-worlds, including the ways that people endeavor to influence and resist one another as well as the ways that people deal with limitations of various kinds (as in cases of physical obstacles, ambiguities, competition, or more direct forms of opposition). A recognition of agency entails a commitment to examining human group life in enacted terms. It means pursuing activities of the following sort: attending, speaking, learning, defining, anticipating, deliberating, consulting, choosing, possessing, implementing, persuading, resisting, assessing, readjusting, discontinuing, remembering, and disregarding things.

By focusing on exactly what people do and more precisely how they do these things (as agents), researchers will be better able to develop a process-based analysis that attends to the developmental flow of events or instances in some realm of endeavor.

As well, while people often focus on (a) the successes that participants have in this or that endeavor, it is important that researchers also attend to (b) people's failures as well as their (c) earlier plans, preparations, and choices; (d) their tentative undertakings, confusions, and frustrations; (e) their interruptions, distractions, limitations, adjustments, terminations of activities; and (f) any redefinitions that people may make (e.g., of activities, objects, or participants) as they deal with matters in this and that setting.

Fifth, people striving for greater familiarity with human lived experience also are encouraged to study human activity in the instances in which human group life takes place. The emphasis is on examining the ways that people accomplish (i.e., anticipate, formulate, enact, resist, and adjust) their activities as they engage these events both on their own and in conjunction with specific other people. This necessitates focusing on specific sequences or emergent flows of individual activities and collectively achieved events over the course of their development.

Sixth, because ethnographers are highly dependent on those they study to reveal and explain their life-worlds to the researchers, ethnographic research requires extended levels of cooperation and openness on the part of those about whose life-worlds ethnographers attempt to learn. Referring to the human capacity to achieve shared awareness or mutuality of understanding with others through extended linguistic (verbal and/or signed) interchange, intersubjectivity is not only a centrally enabling feature of human group life, intersubjectivity also is the primary focus of ethnographic inquiry.

The ethnographic practices of observing others, participating in other people's life-worlds, and opening oneself to extended explanation from, and inquiry of, others are basic to human knowing and acting more generally. However, sustained ethnographic research provides scholars with opportunities to obtain much more systematic, detailed, and thorough comprehensions of the life-worlds of the other than people normally achieve in the course of everyday life.

Still, while representing the essential mechanism or technology that enables researchers to achieve a heightened sharedness of understanding with the other, ethnographic inquiry does not guarantee intersubjectivity in itself. Accordingly, it is most important that researchers striving for greater familiarity with their subject matters endeavor to fit in with their associates throughout the research process. This not only implies a genuine, sustained interest in learning about the life-world of the other on the part of researchers, but that researchers also pursue this objective in ways that the participants would find acceptable and nonthreatening.

On a more ironic note, researchers striving for higher levels of shared awareness with the other may be cautioned about being overly helpful, supportive, sympathetic, emotive, presumptive, or appearing to be too bright or knowledgeable. Because it is so important that participants be allowed to explain their situations to researchers in great detail with a minimum of researcher influence, researchers who are persistently curious, open to wide ranges of possibilities, and seek more complete, detailed explanations of things are apt to derive a greater awareness of the other.

EXTENDING THE CONCEPTUAL FRAME

Although the matters of overcoming the deviant mystique and striving for intimate familiarity with one's subject matter are invaluable in developing instructive descriptive materials, it also is important that researchers take their projects to the next level wherein they indicate what they have learned about human group life more generically from the inquiry at hand.

While not endorsing hypotheses testing in ethnographic research, it is apparent that people require concepts or reference points of some sort if they are to indicate what they have learned from particular ethnographic ventures. The task, in part, is to develop or locate existing concepts that not only address aspects of situations under consideration but that also represent these matters in more direct terms. Likewise, instead of looking for overall confirmations or disconfirmations of particular notions on the basis of specific indicators and abstracted measurements (as one does in hypothesis testing), the emphasis is on examining aspects of the activities at hand relative to one another and assessing the viability of particular concepts in more comparative, grounded, and articulate manners. This requires that one examine specific concepts mindful of the instances at hand with the purpose of learning more about those concepts and their linkages with other aspects of the situation. Effectively, then, each instance of ethnographic research provides opportunities to learn more about certain concepts and hopefully develop increasingly precise and explicit formulations of these concepts for future research and analysis.

Consequently, the overall analytical objective is to develop conceptual schemes that more closely approximate the actualities of human lived experience.[3] This involves questing for terms of reference that would allow researchers in the field to highlight, isolate, address, assess, and clarify various features of deviance as something in the making.

If the concepts selected are to reflect actual instances of human group life as closely as possible, it will be necessary for researchers and analysts to (a) attend to the world as it is known and engaged by the people whose lives and activities are under consideration and (b) more or less continuously adjust their concepts to better approximate the enacted instances of human group life encountered in the field. By focusing on particular subprocesses within the instances of ethnographic inquiry, researchers will better be able to develop analytic comparisons both within specific contexts and relative to other studies that address similar (parallel) features of group life. This entails a concerted focus on comparative analysis, wherein analysts not only examine instances of human group life within particular settings with respect to similarities and differences, but also compare these materials with those gathered in other settings. It means developing specifications, qualifications, and contingencies in attempts to more effectively represent and encompass instances within more general notions of the phenomenon at hand.

Thus, while ethnographers may obtain invaluable assistance in sorting through the complexities of the instances at hand through more sustained inquiry and consultation with participants in the study, much also can be learned by comparing one's materials with that developed in other ethnographic inquiry. Although people often search out literature that deals with particular substantive topics, the more productive analytical practice is to focus on studies that examine any subject matter in conceptually parallel fashions (as in attending to activities, identities, and relationships).

When developing transcontextual comparisons, the most valuable ethnographies typically are those that provide highly detailed participant accounts of people's experiences in particular life-worlds. Working with materials of this sort, researchers and analysts often can derive extended insight into current situations by asking about parallel processes and making comparisons of similarities and differences across two or more fields of human endeavor.

IN CONCLUSION

Rather than view deviance as somehow distinct or separate from the study of everyday life, the approach taken here envisions the study of deviance as an integral part of the study of ongoing community life. The "aura" or "mystique" associated with deviance and control originates not with the specific activities that people do or the particular people who may be involved, but emerges (i.e., is formulated and sustained) as people in the community engage situations involving others in some negative fashion.

An understanding of deviance requires a sustained examination of community life in the making. For researchers, this means attending to all of the things that people do as opposed to studying those identified as deviants in more attenuated or exclusive manners. Without the human community, there is no language, there is no meaning, there is no morality, there is no deviance, and there are no concerns about regulatory activity.

Thus, although people who have been part of, or socialized into, a community can impute notions of deviance to others as well as themselves, they can do so only by adopting the standpoint of the other (see Mead, 1934). Relatedly, the study of deviance is much more a study of ongoing community life than it is the study of particular individuals or intriguing life-worlds. While it is always specific people who become caught up in any and all matters human, researchers and analysts who focus on the qualities of individuals in accounting for deviance will miss almost all of the humanly enacted features of deviance as will those who concentrate on particular allures and disenchantments.

Notions of deviance come into play only when people define some aspect of someone's (or some group's) situation as troublesome, offensive, disturbing, threatening, or as negative in some manner. These definitions (and the interpretive frameworks undergirding their applications) represent the beginnings of the deviance mystique. Thus, the auras that people associate with deviance take shape as people attend to an assortment of others in the community and develop lines of action around these focal points.

In developing this volume, we have been attentive to the collective, interpersonal, solitary, subcultural, and (formal) organizational dimensions of the deviance-making process. Deviance entails multiple versions of reality and wide-ranging variants of the influence process. In addition to pursuing a fuller, community-based appreciation of the ways in which people promote and resist definitions of morality and disrespectability, consideration has been given to the ways in which people become identified or labeled as deviants, as well as people's involvements in, continuities in, disinvolvements from, and reinvolvements in deviance.

Although some deviance takes place on a more solitary or isolated basis, a great deal of the disreputable activities in which people participate take place in subcultural contexts. Denoting somewhat distinctive sets of perspectives, identities, activities, relationships, emotionalities, and linguistic forms, these subcultural life-worlds represent the essential theaters of operation for all manners of human endeavor. Because so much deviance (and control) involves people "doing things" in interactive arenas, consideration was directed to the ways that people engage these life-worlds in practice and the ways in which people's involvements (and activities) intersect with those of others in these settings over time.

Finally, while control agencies may be set up with a wide variety of objectives pertaining to deviance regulation, it is highly instructive to consider the informal, tentative, contradictory, negotiated, and adjustive nature of people's attempts to deal with troublesome cases. Somewhat relatedly, there is a tendency to emphasize treatment-related matters, but this represents only one part of the multiple life-worlds within which both control agents and those targeted for treatment find themselves.

In all instances, it is essential that social scientists retain focus on *the activities* that people do, the ways that people develop these activities, and the array of interchanges in which people engage on a collective, emergent, here-and-now basis. Deviance is a community phenomenon in a most fundamental sense, but deviance is not a single or unitary thing and it is most unproductive to try to explain or study deviance as if it were.

Indeed, if we are to achieve a viable theory of deviance, it will be necessary to consider the many different theaters in which community life takes place and to examine in very direct and focused terms the ways that the participants in these various settings work out their lines of activity in conjunction with one another. In the preceding chapters, we have attempted to take the deviance-making process apart, piece by piece, and present these aspects of human knowing and acting in ways that are more amenable to ethnographic research and comparative conceptual analysis. Only by maintaining a sustained focus on people's activities in ways that permeate the deviant mystique, may we begin to develop theory and research that is more attentive to the humanly engaged realities that constitute community life in the making.

While people may develop concerns and intrigues with an unlimited assortment of topics pertaining to deviance in specific times and places, the emphasis is on developing a more enduring, transsituational comprehension of deviance. To be more worthwhile, a theory of deviance not only has to be able to deal with the specifics of situations as people experience and engage these instances, but it also has to have a thoroughly generic or transcontextual and transhistorical relevance.

NOTES

1. For materials that deal with ethnographic research as a mode of inquiry in more direct terms, see Becker (1970), Bogdan and Taylor (1975), Johnson (1975), Douglas (1976), Lofland and Lofland (1984, 1995), Jorgensen (1989), and Prus (1996b, 1997). Readers are referred to Shaffir, Stebbins, and Turowetz (1980), Emerson (1983a, 2001), Shaffir and Stebbins (1991), and Grills (1998) for instructive collections of articles that discuss people's experiences in the field as ethnographers.

Because it is intended as a pragmatist research agenda for the social sciences, readers may find *Subcultural Mosaics and Intersubjective Realities* (Prus, 1997) a valuable resource for conducting ethnographic research on deviance as human lived experience. In addition to (a) addressing the fundamental features of interactionist analysis, (b) providing a statement on generic social processes, and (c) outlining ways in which scholars may approach a wide range of humanly engaged realms of activity (e.g., developing stocks of knowledge, dealing with objects, achieving mobility, providing person-directed services, encountering the interpersonal other, managing morality, experiencing multiple aspects of the self) as well as citing various ethnographic studies pertinent to these issues, this volume also deals with the matters of (d) pursuing ethnographic research in the field and (e) developing ethnographic research reports.

2. We recognize the inherent moral dimension present in the claim we are making. Clearly, we are proposing a preferred relationship between students of deviance and the people whose lives they hope to engage as researchers and analysts. There is, however, a fundamental distinction to be made between those who approach the study of deviance

for the purpose of promoting a particular morally motivated criticism of the other and those who are committed to the study of human group life in all of its forms.

3. More extended considerations of the task of developing generic conceptualizations of human lived experience can be found in Glaser and Strauss (1967), Blumer (1969), Lofland (1976, 1995), Couch (1984), Strauss (1993), and Prus (1996b, 1997, 1999). Readers also may appreciate that the present text very much engages this task in direct and sustained terms with respect to deviance as a generic, enacted feature of community life.

References

Adler, Patricia. 1985. *Wheeling and Dealing*. New York: Columbia University Press.

Adler, Patricia, and Peter Adler. 1998. *Peer Power: Preadolescent Culture and Identity*. New Brunswick, NJ: Rutgers University Press.

———. 2000. *Constructions of Deviance: Social Power, Context, and Interaction*. 3rd ed. Belmont, CA: Wadsworth.

Albas, Daniel C., and Cheryl Mills Albas. 1984. *Student Life and Exams: Stresses and Coping Strategies*. Dubuque, IA: Kendall/Hunt.

———. 1993. "Disclaimer Mannerisms of Students: How to Avoid being Labelled as Cheaters." *The Canadian Review of Sociology and Anthropology* 30:451–467.

———. 1994. "Studying Students Studying," in *Doing Everyday Life: Ethnography as Human Lived Experience*, ed. Mary Lorenz Dietz, Robert Prus, and William Shaffir. Toronto: Copp Clark Longman.

Altheide, David L. 1996. "Fear and the Ecology of Communication." Paper presented at the Pacific Sociological Association Meetings. March 21–24, Seattle, Washington.

Anderson, Nels. 1923. *The Hobo*. Chicago: University of Chicago Press.

Andrews, D.A., and Craig Dowden, 1999. "A Meta-Analytic Investigation into Effective Correctional Intervention for Female Offenders." *Forum on Corrections Research* 11: 17–21.

Andrews, D.A., et al., 1990. "Does Correctional Treatment Work?: A Clinically Relevant and Psychologically Informed Meta-Analysis." *Criminology* 28: 369–404.

Anspach, Renee R. 1993. *Deciding Who Lives: Fateful Choices in the Intensive-Care Nursery*. Berkeley, CA: University of California Press.

Aquinas, Thomas St. [1225–1274c.e.]. *Summa Theologiae* (Latin text and English translation). 60 Vols. Reprint, New York: McGraw-Hill, with Blackfriars and Eyre and Spottiswoode of London (1964).

Aristotle. [c384–322b.c.e.]. Nicomachean Ethics, in *The Complete Works of Aristotle*, ed. Jonathan Barnes. Princeton, NJ: Princeton University Press (1984).

———. Poetics, in *The Complete Works of Aristotle*, ed. Jonathan Barnes. Princeton, NJ: Princeton University Press (1984).

———. Rhetoric, in *The Complete Works of Aristotle*, ed. Jonathan Barnes. Princeton, NJ: Princeton University Press (1984).

Arluke, Arnold. 1991. "Going into the Closet with Science: Information Control among Animal Experimenters." *Journal of Contemporary Ethnography* 20: 306–330.

Asher, Ramona M. 1992. *Women with Alcoholic Husbands: Ambivalence and the Trap of Codependency.* Chapel Hill, NC: University of North Carolina Press.

Athens, Lonnie H. 1980. *Violent Criminal Acts and Actors: A Symbolic Interactionist Study.* Boston: Oxford University Press.

———. 1997. *Violent Criminal Acts and Actors Revisited.* Urbana, IL: University of Illinois Press.

Atkinson, J. Maxwell. 1971. "Societal Reactions to Suicide: The Role of Coroners' Definitions," in *Images of Deviance,* ed. Stanley Cohen. Baltimore: Penguin.

Bacon, Francis. 1605. *The Advancement of Learning and The New Atlantis,* ed. Arthur Johnson. New York: Oxford University Press (1974).

Ball, Donald. 1970. "The Problematics of Respectability," in *Deviance and Respectability,* ed. Jack Douglas. New York: Basic.

Bartell, Gilbert. 1971. *Group Sex.* New York: Signet.

Becker, Howard S. 1963. *Outsiders: Studies in the Sociology of Deviance.* New York: Free Press.

———. 1967. "Social Bases of Drug Induced Experiences." *Journal of Health and Social Behavior* 8: 163–176.

———. 1970. *Sociological Work: Method and Substance.* Chicago: Aldine.

———. 1986. *Doing Things Together.* Evanston, IL: Northwestern University Press.

Becker, Howard, Everett Hughes, Blanche Geer, and Anselm Strauss. 1961. *The Boys in White.* Chicago: University of Chicago Press.

Belasco, James A., and Harrison M. Trice. 1969. *The Assessment of Change and Training in Therapy.* New York: McGraw-Hill.

Bensmen, Joseph, and Israel Gerver. 1963. "Crime and Punishment and the Factory: The Function of Deviancy in Maintaining the Social System." *American Sociological Review* 28: 588-598.

Berger, Peter, and Thomas Luckmann. 1966. *The Social Construction of Reality.* New York: Doubleday-Anchor.

Bernstein, Stan. 1972. "Getting it Done: Notes on Student Fritters." *Urban Life and Culture* 2: 275–292.

Best, Joel. 1989. *Images of Issues: Typifying Contemporary Social Problems.* New York: Aldine de Gruyter.

———. 1995a. *Images of Issues: Typifying Contemporary Social Problems.* 2nd ed. New York: Aldine de Gruyter.

———. 1995b. "Lost in the Ozone Again: The Postmodernist Fad and Interactionist Foibles," in *Studies in Symbolic Interaction,* ed. Norman K. Denzin, vol. 17. Greenwich, CT: JAI.

———. 1998. "Too Much Fun: Toys as Social Problems and the Interpretation of Culture." *Social Problems* 21: 197–212.

Best, Joel, and David Luckenbill. 1982. *Organizing Deviance.* Englewood Cliffs, NJ: Prentice-Hall.

Biernacki, Patrick. 1988. *Pathways from Heroin Addiction: Recovery without Treatment.* Philadelphia, PA: Temple University Press.

Bittner, Egon. 1967. "The Police on Skid Row." *American Sociological Review* 32: 699–715.

Black, Donald J. 1970. "Production of Crime Rates." *American Sociological Review* 35: 733–747.

———. 1980. *The Manners and Customs of the Police.* New York: Academic Press.

Black, Donald J., and Albert J. Reiss, Jr. 1970. "Police Control of Juveniles." *American Sociological Review* 35: 63–77.

Block, Richard. 1974. "Why Notify the Police: The Victim's Decision to Notify the Police of an Assault." *Criminology* 11: 555–569.

Blomberg, Thomas G., and Karol Lucken. 2000. *American Penology: A History of Control*. New York: Aldine de Gruyter.

Blum, Nancy S. 1991. "The Management of Stigma by Alzheimer Family Caregivers." *Journal of Contemporary Ethnography* 20: 263–284.

Blumberg, Abraham. 1967. "The Practice of Law as a Confidence Game: Organizational Cooptation of a Profession." *Law and Society Review* 41: 15–39.

Blumer, Herbert. 1928. Method in Social Psychology. Ph.D. diss., University of Chicago, Chicago, IL.

———. 1933. *Movies and Conduct*. Reprint, New York: Arno Press, (1970).

———. 1960. "Early Industrialization and the Laboring Class." *Sociological Quarterly* 1: 5–14.

———. 1969. *Symbolic Interaction*. Englewood Cliffs, NJ: Prentice-Hall.

———. 1971. "Social Problems as Collective Behavior." *Social Problems* 1: 298–306.

Blumer, Herbert, and Philip Hauser. 1933. *Movies, Delinquency and Crime*. Reprint, New York: Arno Press (1970).

Bogdan, Robert, and Steven J. Taylor. 1975. *Introduction to Qualitative Research Methods: A Phenomenological Approach to the Social Sciences*. New York: Wiley Interscience.

Broadhead, Robert, and Kathryn J. Fox. 1990. "Takin' it to the Streets: AIDS Outreach as Ethnography." *Journal of Contemporary Ethnography* 19: 322–348.

Brown, L. Guy. 1931. "The Sociological Implications of Drug Addiction." *Journal of Educational Sociology* 4: 358–369.

Burkholdt, David, and Jaber Gubrium. 1983. "Practicing Accountability in Human Service Institutions." *Urban Life* 12: 249–268.

Carroll, Leo. 1974. *Hacks, Blacks and Cons: Race Relations in a Maximum Security Prison*. Lexington, MA: Lexington Books.

Chambliss, William J. 1964. "A Sociological Analysis of the Law of Vagrancy." *Social Problems* 12: 67–77.

Charles, Michael T. 1986. *Policing the Streets*. Springfield, IL: Charles C. Thomas.

Charmaz, Kathy. 1991. *Good Days Bad Days: The Self in Chronic Illness and Time*. New Brunswick, NJ: Rutgers University Press.

———. 1995. "Between Positivism and Postmodernism: Implications for Methods," in *Studies in Symbolic Interaction*, ed. Norman K. Denzin, vol. 17. Greenwich, CT: JAI.

Cicero [c106–43 B.C.E.]. *Brutus*, trans. G.L. Hendrickson. Cambridge, MA: Harvard University Press (1962).

———. *Orator*, trans. by H.M. Hubbell. Reprint, Cambridge, MA: Harvard University Press (1962).

Cohen, Albert. 1959. *Deviance and Control*. Englewood Cliffs, NJ: Prentice-Hall.

———. 1974. "The Elasticity of Evil: Changes in the Social Definition of Deviance." *Oxford University Penal Research Unit*. Occasional Paper Number Seven. Oxford: Basil Blackwell.

Cole, G.D.H. 1959. *A History of Socialist Thought*. London: Macmillan.

Connor, Walter D. 1972. "The Manufacture of Deviance: The Case of the Soviet Purge, 1936–1938." *American Sociological Review* 37: 403–413.

Cooley, Charles Horton. 1909. *Social Organization: A Study of the Larger Mind.* New York: Shocken.

———. 1902. *Human Nature and the Social Order.* Reprint, New York: Shocken, (1922).

———. 1926. "The Roots of Social Knowledge." *American Journal of Sociology* 32: 59–79.

———. 1928. "Case Study of Small Institutions as a Method of Research." *American Sociological Review* 22: 123–132.

Correll, Shelley. 1995. "The Ethnography of an Electronic Bar: The Lesbian Cafe." *Journal of Contemporary Ethnography* 24: 270–298.

Couch, Carl. 1984. "Symbolic Interaction and Generic Sociological Principles." *Symbolic Interaction* 7: 1–14.

———. 1995. "Oh What Webs Those Phantoms Spin." *Symbolic Interaction* 18: 229–245.

Cressey, Donald. 1953. *Other People's Money. A Study in the Social Psychology of Embezzlement.* Glencoe, IL: Free Press.

———. 1958. "The Nature and Effectiveness of Correctional Techniques." *Law and Contemporary Problems* 23 (3): 754–771.

Cressey, Paul. 1932. *The Taxi-Dance Hall.* Chicago: University of Chicago Press.

Cullen, Francis T., and John B. Cullen. 1978. *Towards a Paradigm of Labeling Theory,* no. 58. Lincoln, NB: University of Nebraska Series.

Daniels, Arlene Kaplan. 1970. "The Social Construction of Military Diagnoses," in *Recent Sociology,* ed. H.P. Diretzel, no. 2. New York: Macmillan.

Davis, Fred. 1961. "Deviance Disavowal: The Management of Strained Interaction by the Visibly Physically Handicapped." *Social Problems* 9: 120–132.

———. 1963. *Passage through Crisis.* Indianapolis, IN: Bobbs-Merrill.

Davis, Philip. 1983. "Restoring the Semblance of Order: Police Strategies in the Domestic Disturbance." *Symbolic Interaction* 6: 261–278.

Dawson, Lorne, and Robert Prus. 1993a. "Interactionist Ethnography and Postmodernist Discourse: Affinities and Disjunctures in Approaching Human Lived Experiences," in *Studies in Symbolic Interaction,* ed. Norman K. Denzin, vol. 15. Greenwich, CT: JAI.

———. 1993b. "Human Enterprise, Intersubjectivity, and the Ethnographic Other: A Reply to Denzin and Fontana," in *Studies in Symbolic Interaction,* ed, Norman K. Denzin, vol. 15. Greenwich, CT: JAI.

———. 1995. "Postmodernism and Linguistic Reality Versus Symbolic Interactionism and Obdurate Reality," in *Studies in Symbolic Interaction,* ed. Norman K. Denzin, vol. 17. Greenwich, CT: JAI.

Denzin, Norman. 1970. "Rules of Conduct and the Study of Deviant Behavior: Social Relationships," in *Deviance and Respectability,* ed. Jack Douglas. New York: Basic.

Dewey, John. 1910. *How We Think.* Reprint, Amherst, NY: Prometheus (1975).

———. 1977. *The Middle Works, 1899–1924,* ed. Jo Ann Boydston. Carbondale, IL: Southern Illinois University Press.

Dietz, Mary Lorenz. 1983. *Killing for Profit: The Social Organization of Felony Homicide.* Chicago: Nelson-Hall.

————. 1994. "On Your Toes: Dancing Your Way into the Ballet World," in *Doing Everyday Life: Ethnography as Human Lived Experience*, ed. Mary Lorenz Dietz, Robert Prus, and William Shaffir. Toronto, ON: Copp Clark Longman.

Dietz, Mary Lorenz, and Michael Cooper. 1994. "Being Recruited: The Experiences of 'Blue Chip' High School Athletes," in *Doing Everyday Life: Ethnography as Human Lived Experience*, ed. Mary Lorenz Dietz, Robert Prus, and William Shaffir. Toronto, ON: Copp Clark Longman.

Ditton, James. 1977. *Part-Time Crime: An Ethnography of Fiddling and Pilferage*. London: Macmillan.

Dotter, Daniel, and Julian Roebuck. 1988. "The Labeling Approach Re-examined: Interactionism and the Components of Deviance." *Deviant Behavior* 9: 19–32.

Douglas, Jack. 1967. *The Social Meanings of Suicide*. Princeton: Princeton University Press.

————. 1970. "Deviance and Respectability: The Social Construction of Moral Meanings," in *Deviance and Respectability*, ed. Jack Douglas. New York: Basic.

————. 1976. *Investigative Social Research*. Beverly Hills, CA: Sage.

Downes, David, and Paul Rock. 1998. *Understanding Deviance: A Guide to The Sociology of Crime and Rule-Breaking*. 3rd ed. New York: Oxford University Press.

Durkheim, Emile. 1895. *The Rules of the Sociological Method*, trans. S.A. Solvay and E.G. Catlin. New York: Free Press (1958).

————. 1897. *Suicide*, trans. J.A. Spaulding and G. Simpson. New York: Free Press.

Ebaugh, Helen Rose. 1988. *Becoming an EX: The Process of Role Exit*. Chicago: University of Chicago Press.

Edgerton, Robert. 1967. *The Cloak of Competence: Stigma in the Lives of the Mentally Retarded*. Berkeley, CA: University of California Press.

Ekins, Richard. 1997. *Male Femaling: A Grounded Theory Approach to Cross-dressing and Sex-changing*. New York: Routledge.

Emerson, Joan. 1970. "Behavior in Private Places: Sustaining Definitions of Reality in Gynecological Examinations," *Recent Sociology*, ed. Hand Peter Dreitzel, vol. 2. New York: Macmillan

Emerson, Robert M. 1969. *Judging Delinquents*. Chicago: Aldine.

————. 1981. "On Last Resorts." *American Journal of Sociology* 87: 1–22.

————. 1983a. *Contemporary Field Research: A Collection of Readings*. Boston: Little, Brown.

————. 1983b. "Holistic Effects in Social Control Decision-Making." *Law and Society Review* 17: 425–455.

————. 1988. *Contemporary Field Research: A Collection of Readings*. Prospect Heights, IL: Waveland.

————. 1994. "Doing Discipline: The Junior High School Scene," in *Doing Everyday Life: Ethnography as Human Lived Experience*, ed. Mary Lorenz Dietz, Robert Prus, and William Shaffir. Toronto, ON: Copp Clark Longman.

————. 2001. *Contemporary Field Research: Perspectives and Formulations*. Prospect Heights, IL: Waveland.

Emerson, Robert, E. Burke Rochford, Jr., and Linda Shaw. 1983. "The Micro-politics of Trouble in a Psychiatric Board and Care Facility." *Urban Life* 12: 349–367.

Emerson, Robert M., and Sheldon L. Messinger. 1977. "The Micro-Politics of Trouble." *Social Problems* 25: 121–134.

Ennis, Philip H. 1967. *Criminal Victimization in the United States: A Report of a National Survey*. Field Surveys II, President's Commission on Law Enforcement and Administration of Justice. Washington, DC: U.S. Government Printing Office.

Ericson, Richard V. 1981. *Making Crime: A Study of Detective Work*. Toronto, ON: Butterworths.

Erikson, Kai T. 1962. "Notes on the Sociology of Deviance." *Social Problems* 9: 307–314.

———. 1966. *Wayward Puritans*. New York: Wiley.

Ermarth, Michael. 1978. Wilhelm Dilthey: *The Critique of Historical Reason*. Chicago: University of Chicago Press.

Estes, Carol, and Beverly Edmunds. 1981. "Symbolic Interaction and Social Policy Analysis." *Symbolic Interaction* 4: 75–86.

Evans, A. Donald. 1987. "Institutionally Developed Identities: An Ethnographic Account of Reality Construction in a Residential School for the Deaf," in *Sociological Studies of Child Development*. Greenwich, CT: JAI.

———. 1988. "Strange Bedfellows: Deafness, Language and the Sociology of Knowledge." *Symbolic Interaction* 11: 235–255.

———. 1994. "Socialization into Deafness," in *Doing Everyday Life: Ethnography as Human Lived Experience*, ed. Mary Lorenz Dietz, Robert Prus, and William Shaffir. Toronto: Copp Clark Longman.

Evans, Donald, and W.W. Falk. 1986. *Learning to be Deaf*. Berlin: Mouton.

Farrell, Ronald A., and Victoria Lynn Swigert. 1988. *Social Deviance*. 3rd ed. Belmont, CA: Wadsworth.

Faulkner, Robert R. 1971. *Hollywood Studio Musicians: Their Work and Careers in the Recording Industry*. Chicago: Aldine.

Faupel, Charles E. 1991. *Shooting Dope: Career Patterns of Hard-Core Heroin Users*. Gainesville, FL: University of Florida Press.

Festinger, Leon, Henry Riecken, and Stanley Schacter. 1956. *When Prophecy Fails*. New York: Harper & Row.

Fine, Gary Alan. 1983. *Shared Fantasy: Role Playing Games as Social Worlds*. Chicago: University of Chicago Press.

———. 1987. *With the Boys: Little League Baseball and Preadolescent Culture*. Chicago: University of Chicago Press.

———. 1996. *Kitchens: The Culture of Restaurant Work*. Berkeley, CA: University of California Press.

———. 2001. *Gifted Tongues: High School Debate and Adolescent Culture*. Princeton, NJ: Princeton University Press.

Fishman, Laura T. 1990. *Women at the Wall: A Study of Prisoners' Wives Doing Time on the Outside*. Albany, NY: State University of New York Press.

Freidson, Eliot. 1966. "Disability as Social Deviance," in *Sociology and Rehabilitation*, ed. M.B. Sussman. New York: American Sociological Association.

Garfinkel, Harold. 1956. "Conditions of Successful Degradation Ceremonies." *American Journal of Sociology* 61:420–424.

———. 1967. *Studies in Ethnomethodology*. Englewood Cliffs, NJ: Prentice-Hall.

Geertz, Clifford. 1973. *Interpretations of Culture*. New York: Basic Books.

Glaser, Barney, and Anselm Strauss. 1967. *The Discovery of Grounded Theory*. Chicago: Aldine.

Goffman, Erving. 1959. *Presentation of Self in Everyday Life*. New York: Anchor.
———. 1961. *Asylums*. New York: Anchor.
———. 1963. *Stigma: Notes on the Management of Spoiled Identity*. Englewood Cliffs, NJ: Prentice-Hall.
———. 1967. *Interaction Ritual*. New York: Anchor.
———. 1971. *Relations in Public*. New York: Basic.
Goode, Erich. 1978. *Deviant Behavior: An Interactionist Approach*. Englewood Cliffs, NJ: Prentice-Hall.
Grills, Scott. 1989. Designating Deviance. Ph.D. diss., McMaster University, Hamilton, ON.
———. 1994. "Recruitment Practices of the Christian Heritage Party," in *Doing Everyday Life: Ethnography as Human Lived Experience*, ed. Mary Lorenz Dietz, Robert Prus, and William Shaffir. Toronto: Copp Clark Longman.
———. 1998. *Doing Ethnographic Research: Fieldwork Settings*. Thousand Oaks, CA: Sage.
Grupp, Stanley, and Raymond Schmidt. 1980. "The Assessment of Stigma: Implications for Theory and Prevention." *International Journal of the Addictions* 15: 1253–1263.
Gubrium, Jaber F. 1975. *Living and Dying at Murray Manor*. New York: St. Martin's.
Gusfield, Joseph R. 1955. "Social Structure and Moral Reform: A Study of the Women's Christian Temperance Union." *American Journal of Sociology* 61: 221–232.
———. 1963. *Symbolic Crusade: Status Politics and the American Temperance Movement*. Urbana, IL: University of Illinois Press.
———. 1981. *The Culture of Public Problems*. Chicago: University of Chicago Press.
———. 1984. "On the Side: Practical Action and the Social Constructionism in Social Problems Theory," in *Studies in the Sociology of Social Problems*, ed. Joseph W. Schneider and John I. Kitsuse. Norwood, NJ: Albex.
———. 1989. "Constructing the Ownership of Social Problems; Fun and Profit in the Welfare State." *Social Problems* 26: 431–441.
———. 1996. *Contested Meanings: The Social Construction of Alcohol Problems*. Madison, WI: University of Wisconsin Press.
Haas, Jack. 1972. "Binging: Educational Control among High Steel Ironworkers." *American Behavioral Scientist* 16: 27–34.
———. 1977. "Learning Real Feelings: A Study of High Steel Ironworkers' Reactions to Fear and Danger." *Sociology of Work and Occupations* 4: 147–170.
Haas, Jack, and William Shaffir. 1987. *Becoming Doctors: The Adoption of a Cloak of Competence*. Greenwich, CT: JAI.
Hall, Ian. 1983. Playing For Keeps: The Careers of Front-Line Workers for Developmentally Handicapped Persons. Master's thesis, University of Waterloo.
Hammersley, Martyn. 1989. *The Dilemma of Qualitative Method*. London: Routledge.
Hargreaves, David, Stephen Hester, and Frank Melor. 1975. *Deviance in Classrooms*. London: Routledge & Kegan Paul.
Harrington, C. Lee, and Denise D. Bielby. 1995. *Soap Fans: Pursuing Pleasure and Making Meaning in Everyday Life*. Philadelphia: Temple University Press.
Harrison, Deborah, and Lucy Laliberte. 1994. *No Life Like It: Military Wives in Canada*. Toronto, ON: Lorimer.
Hawkins, Richard, and Gary Tiedman. 1975. *The Creation of Deviance: Interpersonal and Organizational Determinants*. Columbus, OH: Merrill.

Hayano, David M. 1982. *Poker Faces: The Life and Work of Professional Card Players.* Berkeley, CA: University of California Press.

Henslin, James. 1970. "Guilt and Guilt Neutralization: Responses and Adjustment to Suicide," in *Deviance and Respectability*, ed. Jack Douglas. New York: Basic.

———. 1972. "Studying Deviance in Four Settings: Researcher Experiences with Cabbies, Suicidees, Drug Users, and Abortionees," in *Research on Deviance*, ed. Jack Douglas. New York: Random House.

Herman, Nancy J. 1994. "Former Crazies in the Community," in *Doing Everyday Life: Ethnography as Human Lived Experience*, ed. Mary Lorenz Dietz, Robert Prus, and William Shaffir. Toronto, ON: Copp Clark Longman.

———. 1995. *Deviance.* Dix Hills, NY: General Hall.

Herodotus [484–425 B.C.E.] *The Histories*, trans. Aubrey de Selincourt. New York: Penguin (1996).

Hewitt, John P., and Randall Stokes. 1975. "Disclaimers." *American Sociological Review* 40: 1–11.

Heyl, Barbara Sherman. 1979. *The Madam as Entrepreneur: Career Management in House Prostitution.* New Brunswick, NJ: Transaction.

Higgins, Paul C. 1980. *Outsiders in a Hearing World: A Sociology of Deafness.* Beverly Hills, CA: Sage.

Himmelfarb, Alexander, and John Evans. 1974. "Deviance Disavowal and Stigma Management: A Study in Obesity," in *Decency and Deviance.* ed. Jack Haas and William Shaffir. Toronto, ON: McClelland and Stewart.

Hobbes, Thomas. 1651. *Leviathan* (With selected variants from the Latin Edition of 1668), ed. Curley. Reprint, Indianapolis: Hackett (1994).

Hochstetler, Andy. 2002. "Sprees and Runs: Opportunity Construction and Criminal Episodes." *Deviant Behavior* 3: 45–73.

Holstein, James A., and Gail Miller. 1990. "Rethinking Victimization: An Interactional Approach to Victimology." *Symbolic Interaction* 13: 103–122.

Holyfield, Lori. 1999. "Manufacturing Venture: The Buying and Selling of Emotions." *Journal of Contemporary Ethnography* 28: 3–32.

Horowitz, Ruth. 1995. *Teen Mothers: Citizens or Dependents?* Chicago: University of Chicago Press.

Humphreys, Laud. 1975. *Tearoom Trade: Impersonal Sex in Public Places.* Chicago: Aldine.

Hunt, Jennifer. 1995. "Divers' Accounts of Normal Risk." *Symbolic Interaction* 18: 439–462.

Hunt, Morton. 1966. *The World of the Formerly Married.* New York: McGraw Hill.

Ingraham, Larry H. 1984. *The Boys in the Barracks: Observations on American Military Life.* Philadelphia: Institute for the Study of Human Issues.

Irini, Styllianoss, and Robert Prus. 1982. "Doing Security Work: Keeping Order in the Hotel Setting." *Canadian Journal of Criminology* 24 (1): 61–82.

Irwin, John. 1970. *The Felon.* Englewood Cliffs, NJ: Prentice-Hall.

Jackson, Joan. 1954. "The Adjustment of the Family to the Crises of Alcoholism." *Quarterly Journal of Studies on Alcohol* 15: 564–586.

Jacobs, Bruce A. 1994. "Undercover Social-distancing Techniques." *Symbolic Interaction* 17: 395–410.

———. 1999. *Dealing Crack: The Social World of Street Corner Selling.* Boston: Northeastern University Press.

Jacobs, Jerry. 1967. "A Phenomenological Study of Suicide Notes." *Social Problems* 15: 62–72.

———. 1970. "The Use of Religion in Constructing the Moral Justification of Suicide," in *Deviance and Respectability*, ed. Jack Douglas. New York: Basic.

James, William. 1907. *Pragmatism: A New Name for Some Old Ways of Thinking.* Cambridge, MA: Harvard University Press (1975).

———. 1909. *The Meaning of Truth: A Sequel to 'Pragmatism.'* Reprint, Cambridge, MA: Harvard University Press (1975).

Jankowski, Martín Sánchez. 1991. *Islands in the Street: Gangs and American Urban Culture*. Berkeley, CA: University of California Press.

Jewell, Donald P. 1952. "A Case of a 'Psychotic' Navaho Indian Male." *Human Organization* 11: 32–36.

Joas, Hans. 1985. *G.H. Mead: A Contemporary Reexamination of His Thought*. Cambridge, MA: MIT.

Johnson, John. 1975. *Doing Field Research*. New York: Free Press.

Jonas, Lilian. 1999. "Making and Facing Danger: Constructing Strong Character on the River." *Symbolic Interaction* 22: 247–267.

Jorgensen, Danny. 1989. *Participant Observation*. Newbury Park, CA: Sage.

———. 1992. *The Esoteric Scene, Cultic Milieu, and Occult Tarot*. New York: Garland.

Kando, Thomas. 1973. *Sex Change: The Achievement of Gender Identity among Feminized Transsexuals*. Springfield, IL: Charles C. Thomas.

Karp, David A. 1996. *Speaking of Sadness: Depression, Disconnection and the Meanings of Illness*. New York: Oxford University Press.

Karsh, Bernard, Joel Seidman, and Daisy M. Lilienthal. 1953. "The Union Organizer and His Tactics: A Case Study." *American Journal of Sociology* 59: 113–122.

Katz, Jack. 1988. *Seductions of Crime*. New York: Basic Books.

Keiser, Lincoln R. 1969. *The Vice Lords: Warriors of the Streets*. New York: Holt, Rinehart & Winston.

Kelly, Delos H. 1996. *Deviant Behavior: A Text-Reader in the Sociology of Deviance*. 5th ed. New York: St. Martin's Press.

Kitsuse, John I. 1961. "Societal Reaction to Deviant Behavior." *Social Problems* 9: 247–256.

———. 1975. "The 'New Conception of Deviance' and Its Critics," in *The Labelling of Deviance*, ed. W. Gore. New York: Wiley.

Klapp, Orrin. 1962. *Heroes, Villains, and Fools*. Englewood Cliffs, NJ: Prentice-Hall.

———. 1964. *Symbolic Leaders*. Chicago: Aldine.

———. 1969. *Collective Search for Identity*. New York: Holt, Rinehart and Winston.

———. 1971. *Social Types: Process, Structure and Ethos*. San Diego, CA: Aegis.

Kolakowski, Leszek. 1978. *Main Currents of Marxism*. (3 vols). Oxford: Oxford University Press.

Konvitz, Milton, and Gail Kennedy. 1960. *The American Pragmatists*. Cleveland, OH: Meridian.

Kotarba, Joseph, and Darlene Hurt. 1995. "An Ethnography of an AIDS Hospice: Toward a Theory of Organizational Pistach." *Symbolic Interaction* 18: 413–438.

Kotarba, Joseph, and Paul K. Rasmussen. 1996. "The Bar as a Context of Social Control," in *Contested Meanings: The Social Construction of Alcohol Problems*, ed. Joseph R. Gusfield. Madison, WI: University of Wisconsin Press.

Kuhn, Manford. 1954. "Kinsey's View on Human Behavior." *Social Problems* 1: 119–125.

Kuhn, Thomas S. 1970. *The Structure of Scientific Revolutions*, rev. ed. Chicago: University of Chicago Press.

Lauderdale, Pat. 1976. "Deviance and Moral Boundaries." *American Sociological Review* 41: 660–675.

Lemert, Edwin. 1951. *Social Pathology*. New York: McGraw-Hill.

———. 1953. "An Isolation and Closure Theory of Naive Check Forgery." *The Journal of Criminal Law, Criminology and Police Science* 44: 296–307.

———. 1962. "Paranoia and the Dynamics of Exclusion." *Sociometry* 25: 2–25.

———. 1967. *Human Deviance, Social Problems and Social Control*. Englewood Cliffs, NJ: Prentice-Hall.

———. 1974. "Beyond Mead: The Societal Reaction to Deviance." *Social Problems* 21: 457–468.

Lesieur, Henry R. 1977. *The Chase: The Career of the Professional Gambler*. Garden City, NY: Anchor.

Letkemann, Peter. 1973. *Crime as Work*. Englewood Cliffs, NJ: Prentice-Hall.

Levitan, Teresa. 1975. "Deviants as Active Participants in the Labeling Process: The Visibly Handicapped." *Social Problems* 22: 548–557.

Lindesmith, Alfred R. 1959. "Federal Law and Drug Addiction." *Social Problems* 7: 48–57.

Locke, John. 1693. *An Essay Concerning Human Understanding*. Reprint, Amherst, NY: Prometheus (1995).

Lofland, John. 1966. *The Doomsday Cult: A Study in Conversion, Proselytization and Maintenance of Faith*. Reprint New York: Irvington Publishers (1977).

———. 1969. *Deviance and Identity*. Englewood Cliffs, NJ: Prentice-Hall.

———. 1976 *Doing Social Life*. New York: Wiley.

———. 1995. "Analytic Ethnography: Features, Failings, and Futures." *Journal of Contemporary Ethnography* 24: 30–67.

Lofland, John, and Lyn Lofland. 1984. *Analyzing Social Settings*. Belmont, CA: Wadsworth.

———. 1995. *Analyzing Social Settings*. 3rd ed. Belmont, CA: Wadsworth.

Lofland, John, and Rodney Stark. 1965. "Becoming A World Saver: A Theory of Conversion to a Deviant Perspective." *American Sociological Review* 30: 862–875.

Logan, C. H. 1972. "Evaluation Research in Crime and Delinquency: A Reappraisal." *Journal of Criminal Law, Criminology, and Police Science* 63: 378–387.

Loseke, Donileen R. 1989 "Evaluation Research and the Practice of Social Services: A Case for Qualitative Methodology." *Journal of Contemporary Ethnography* 18: 202–223.

———. 1992. *The Battered Woman and Shelters: The Social Construction of Wife Abuse*. Albany, NY: State University of New York Press.

Lundman, Richard J. 1996. "Extralegal Variables and Arrest." *Journal of Research in Crime and Delinquency* 33: 349–353.

Lundman, Richard J., Richard E. Sykes, and John P. Clark. 1978. "Police Control of Juveniles: A Replication." *Journal of Research in Crime and Delinquency* 15: 74–91.

Lyman, Karen A. 1993. *Day In, Day Out with Alzheimer's: Stress in Caregiving Relationships*. Philadelphia: Temple University Press.

Lyman, Stanford, and Marvin Scott. 1975. *The Drama of Social Reality*. New York: Oxford University Press.

———. 1989. *Sociology of the Absurd*. 2nd ed. Dix Hills, NY: General Hall.

MacLeod, Bruce A. 1993. *Club Date Musicians: Playing the New York Party Circuit*. Urbana, IL: University of Illinois Press.

Maines, David R. 1996. "On Postmodernism, Pragmatism, and Plasterers: Some Inter-actionist Thoughts and Queries." *Symbolic Interaction* 19: 323–340.

Manning, Peter K. 1988. *Symbolic Communication: Signifying Calls and the Police Response*. Cambridge, MA: MIT Press.

March, Karen. 1994. "Needing to Know: Adoptee's Search for Self Completion," in *Doing Everyday Life: Ethnography as Human Lived Experience*, ed. Mary Lorenz Dietz, Robert Prus, and William Shaffir. Toronto, ON: Copp Clark Longman.

Martin, Wilfred. 1975. "Teacher-Pupil Interactions: A Negotiation Perspective." *Canadian Review of Sociology and Anthropology* 12: 529–540.

Martinson, Robert, and Juth Wilks. 1975. *The Effectiveness of Correctional Treatment: A Survey of Treatment Evaluation Studies*. New York: Praeger.

Maurer, David. 1955. *Whiz Mob: A Correlation of the Technical Argot of Pickpockets with their Behavior Pattern*. New Haven, CT: College and University Press.

———. 1964. *The Whiz Mob*. New Haven, CT: College and University Press.

Mauss, Armand. 1975. *Social Problems as Social Movements*. Philadelphia: Lippincott.

McCleary, Richard. 1975. "How Structural Variables Constrain the Parole Officer's Use of Discretionary Powers." *Social Problems* 23: 209–225.

———. 1983. *Dangerous Men: The Sociology of Parole*. Beverly Hills, CA: Sage.

McNamara, Robert P. 1994. *The Times Square Hustler: Male Prostitution in New York City*. Westport, CT: Praeger.

McNulty, Elizabeth. 1994. "Generating Common Sense Knowledge among Police Officers." *Symbolic Interaction* 17: 281–294.

Mead, George H. 1934. *Mind, Self and Society*. Chicago: University of Chicago Press.

Meehan, Albert J. 1986. "Record-Keeping Practices in the Policing of Juveniles." *Urban Life* 15: 70–102.

———. 1992. "I Don't Prevent Crime, I Prevent Calls: Policing as Negotiated Order." *Symbolic Interaction* 15: 455–480.

Meltzer, Bernard, John W. Petras, and Larry T. Reynolds. 1975. *Symbolic Interactionism: Genesis, Varieties and Criticism*. London: Routledge & Kegan Paul.

Merton, Robert. 1957. *Social Theory and Social Structure*. New York: Free Press.

Miller, Gale. 1983. "Holding Clients Responsible: The Micro-Politics of Trouble in a Work Incentive Program." *Social Problems* 31: 139–151.

———. 1991. *Enforcing the Work Ethic: Rhetoric and Everyday Life in a Work Incentive Program*. Albany, NY: State University of New York Press.

Millman, Marcia. 1980. *Such a Pretty Face: Being Fat in America*. New York: Berkeley.

Mills, C. Wright. 1969. *Sociology and Pragmatism*. New York: Oxford University Press.

Mitchell, Richard G., Jr. 1983. *Mountain Experience*. Chicago: University of Chicago Press.

———. 1993. *Secrecy and Fieldwork*. Newbury Park, CA: Sage.

Morris, Charles. 1970. *The Pragmatic Movement in American Philosophy*. New York: Braziller.

Mulcahy, Aogan. 1995. "'Headhunter' or 'Real Cop'?: Identity in the World of Internal Affairs Officers." *Journal of Contemporary Ethnography* 24: 99–130.

Mullins, Nicholas, and Carolyn Mullins. 1967. *Theories and Theory Groups in Contemporary American Society*. New York: Harper & Row.

Nanda, Serena. 1990. *Neither Man Nor Woman: The Hijras of India*. Belmont, CA: Wadsworth.

Newman, Donald J. 1956. "Pleading Guilty for Considerations: A Study of Bargain Justice." *The Journal of Criminal Law, Criminology and Police Science* 46: 780–790.

Newton, Esther. 1979. *Mother Camp: Female Impersonators in America*. Chicago: University of Chicago Press.

Otto, Rudolph. 1970. *The Idea of the Holy*. New York: Oxford University Press.

Ouellet, Lawrence. 1994. *Pedal to the Metal: The Work Lives of Truckers*. Philadelphia: Temple University Press.

Owen, Barbara. 1998. *In the Mix: Struggle and Survival in a Women's Prison*. Albany, NY: State University of New York Press.

Padilla, Felix. 1992. *The Gang as an American Enterprise*. New Brunswick, NJ: Rutgers University Press.

Palmer, Vivian. 1928. *Field Studies in Sociology*. Chicago: University of Chicago Press.

Park, Robert, and Ernest Burgess. 1924. *Introduction to the Science of Sociology*. Chicago: University of Chicago Press.

Parnas, Raymond. 1967. "The Police Response to Domestic Disturbances." *Wisconsin Law Review*: 914–960.

Parsons, Talcott. 1951. *Toward a General Theory of Action*. New York: Harper & Row.

Paterniti, Deborah A. 2000. "The Micropolitics of Identity in Adverse Circumstances: A Study of Identity Making in a Total Institution." *Journal of Contemporary Ethnography* 29: 93–119.

Patton, Michel Quinn. 1981. *Creative Evaluation*. Beverly Hills, CA: Sage.

———. 1982. *Practical Evaluation*. Beverly Hills, CA: Sage.

Peirce, Charles Sanders. 1934. *The Collected Papers of Charles Sanders Peirce*, Vols. 5 and 6. Cambridge, MA: Bellknap Press of Harvard University Press.

Petrunik, Michael. 1974. "The Quest for Fluency: Fluency Variations and the Identity Problems, and Management Strategies of Stutterers," in *Decency and Deviance*, ed. Jack Haas and William Shaffir. Toronto: McClelland and Stewart.

Petrunik, Michael, and Clifford Shearing. 1983. "Fragile Facades: Stuttering and the Strategic Manipulation of Awareness." *Social Problems* 31: 125–138.

Peyrot, Mark. 1985. "Coerced Voluntarism: The Micropolitics of Drug Treatment." *Urban Life* 13: 343–365.

Pfuhl, Erdwin H., Jr. 1980. *The Deviance Process*. New York: D. Van Nostrand.

Pfuhl, Erdwin H., and Stuart Henry. 1993. *The Deviance Process*. 3rd ed. New York: Aldine de Gruyter.

Plato. [c427–347 B.C.E.]. Ion, in *Plato: Complete Works*, ed. John M. Cooper. Indianapolis, IN: Hackett (1997).

———. Laws, in *Plato: Complete Works*, ed. John M. Cooper. Indianapolis, IN: Hackett (1997).

———. Republic, in *Plato: Complete Works*, ed. John M. Cooper. Indianapolis, IN: Hackett (1997).

———. Sophist, in *Plato: Complete Works*, ed. John M. Cooper. Indianapolis, IN: Hackett (1997).

Platt, Anthony. 1969a. *The Child Savers*. Chicago: University of Chicago Press.

————. 1969b. "The Rise of the Child-Saving Movement: A study in Social Policy and Correctional Reform." *The Annals*: 21–38.

Ponse, Barbara. 1978. *Identities in the Lesbian World: The Social Construction of Self.* Westport, CT: Greenwood.

Prus, Robert. 1975a. "Labeling Theory: A Reconceptualization and a Propositional Statement on Typing." *Sociological Focus* 8: 79–96.

————. 1975b. "Resisting Designations: An Extension of Attribution Theory into a Negotiated Context." *Sociological Inquiry* 45: 3–14.

————. 1976. "Religious Recruitment and the Management of Dissonance: A Sociological Perspective." *Sociological Inquiry* 46: 127–134.

————. 1982. "Designating Discretion and Openness: The Problematics of Truthfulness in Everyday Life." *Canadian Journal of Sociology and Anthropology* 19: 70–91.

————. 1983. "Drinking as Activity: An Interactionist Analysis." *Journal of Studies on Alcohol* 44 (3): 460–475.

————. 1987. "Generic Social Processes: Maximizing Conceptual Development in Ethnographic Research." *Journal of Contemporary Ethnography* 16 (3): 250–291.

————. 1989a. *Making Sales: Influence as Interpersonal Accomplishment.* Newbury Park, CA: Sage.

————. 1989b. *Pursuing Customers: An Ethnography of Marketing Activities.* Newbury Park, CA: Sage.

————. 1992a. "Influence Work in Human Service Settings: Lessons from the Marketplace," in *Current Research on Occupations and Professions*, ed. Gale Miller, vol. 7. Greenwich, CT: JAI.

————. 1992b. "Producing Social Science: Knowledge as a Social Problem in Academia," in *Perspectives in Social Problems*, ed. Gale Miller and James Holstein, vol. 3. Greenwich, CT: JAI.

————. 1993. "Shopping With Companions: Images, Influences and Interpersonal Dilemmas." *Qualitative Sociology* 16: 87–109.

————. 1994. "Consumers as Targets: Autonomy, Accountability, and Anticipation of the Influence Process." *Qualitative Sociology* 17: 243–262.

————. 1996a. "Adolescent Life-Worlds and Deviant Involvements: A Research Agenda for Studying Adolescence as Lived Experience," in *Not a Kid Anymore*, ed. Gary O'Berick. Toronto, ON: Nelson Canada.

————. 1996b. *Symbolic Interaction and Ethnographic Research: Intersubjectivity and the Study of Human Lived Experience.* Albany, NY: State University of New York Press.

————. 1997. *Subcultural Mosaics and Intersubjective Realities: An Ethnographic Research Agenda for Pragmatizing the Social Sciences.* Albany, NY: State University of New York Press.

————. 1999. *Beyond the Power Mystique: Power as Intersubjective Accomplishment.* Albany, NY: State University of New York Press.

————. 2003. "Ancient Precursors to Symbolic Interaction: Pragmatist Dimensions of Early Greek Scholarship," in *Handbook of Symbolic Interactionism*, ed. Larry Reynolds and Nancy Herman. Walnut Creek, CA: Altamira.

Prus, Robert, and Lorne Dawson. 1991. "Shop 'til You Drop: Shopping as Recreational and Laborious Activity." *Canadian Journal of Sociology* 16: 145–164.

———. 1996. "Obdurate Reality and the Intersubjective Other: The Problematics of Representation and the Privilege of Presence," in *Symbolic Interaction and Ethnographic Research: Intersubjectivity and the Study of Human Lived Experience* by Robert Prus. Albany, NY: State University of New York Press.

Prus, Robert, and Augie Fleras. 1996. "'Pitching' Images to the Generalized Other: Promotional Strategies of Economic Development Officers," in *Current Research on Occupations and Professions: Societal Influences,* ed. Helena Znaniecki Lopata. vol. 9. Greenwich, CT: JAI.

Prus, Robert, and Wendy Frisby. 1990. "Persuasion as Practical Accomplishment: Tactical Manoeuverings at Home Party Plans," in *Current Research on Occupations and Professions: Societal Influences,* ed. Helena Znaniecki Lopata. vol. 5. Greenwich, CT: JAI.

Prus, Robert, and Styllianoss Irini. 1980. *Hookers, Rounders, and Desk Clerks: The Social Organization of the Hotel Community.* Reprint, Salem, WI: Sheffield (1988).

Prus, Robert, and Lorraine Prus. 2000. "Generating, Intensifying, and Redirecting Emotionality: Aristotle and the Study of Rhetoric." Paper presented at the American Sociological Association meetings, Washington, DC.

Prus, Robert, and C.R.D. Sharper. 1977. *Road Hustler: The Career Contingencies of Professional Card and Dice Hustlers.* Lexington, MA: Lexington Books.

———. 1991. *Road Hustler: Grifters, Magic, and the Thief Subculture.* New York: Kaufman and Greenberg.

Prus, Robert, and John Stratton. 1976. "Parole Revocation Related Decision Making: Private Typings and Official Designations." *Federal Probation* 40: 48–53.

Quinney, Richard. 1974. *Criminal Justice in America.* Boston: Little, Brown.

Quintilian [c35–95 C.E.]. *The Institutio Oratoria of Quintilian.* trans. H.E. Butler. 4 vols. Cambridge, MA: Harvard University Press.

Ray, Marsh B. 1961. "Abstinence Cycles and Heroin Addicts." *Social Problems* 9: 132–140.

Reiss, Albert J., Jr. 1960. "Sex Offenses: The Marginal Status of the Adolescent." *Law and Contemporary Problems* 25: 309–333.

———. 1961. "The Social Integration of Queers and Peers." *Social Problems* 9: 102–120.

Reynolds, Larry T. 1993. *Interactionism: Exposition and Critique.* 3rd ed. New York: General Hall.

Rock, Paul. 1973. *Making People Pay.* London: Routledge & Kegan Paul.

———. 1979. *The Making of Symbolic Interaction.* London: Macmillan.

Roebuck, Julian B., and Wolfgang Frese. 1976. *The Rendezvous: A Case Study of an After-hours Club.* New York: Free Press.

Rogers, J.W., and M.D. Buffalo. 1974. "Fighting Back: Nine Modes of Adaptation to a Deviant Label." *Social Problems* 22: 101–118.

Rosenau, Pauline Marie. 1992. *Post-modernism and the Social Sciences: Insights, Inroads, and Intrusions.* Princeton, NJ: Princeton University Press.

Rosenblatt, Paul C., Terri Karis, and Richard Powell. 1995. *Multiracial Couples: Black-and-White Voices.* Thousand Oaks, CA: Sage.

Rosenhan, David L. 1973. "On Being Sane in Insane Places." *Science* 179: 250–258.

Rosnow, Ralph L., and Gary Allan Fine. 1976. *Rumor and Gossip: The Social Psychology of Hearsay.* New York: Elsevier.

Ross, H. Lawrence. 1970. *Settled Out of Court*. Chicago: Aldine.

Rossi, Peter H., and Howard E. Freeman. 1989. *Evaluation: A Systematic Approach*. 4th ed. Newbury Park, CA: Sage.

Roth, Julius. 1962. "The Treatment of Tuberculosis as a Bargaining Process," in *Human Behavior and Social Process*, ed. A. Rose. Boston: Houghton-Mifflin.

———. 1972. "Some Contingencies of the Moral Evaluation and Control of Clientele: The Case of the Hospital Emergency Service." *American Journal of Sociology* 77: 839–856.

Rubinstein, Jonathon. 1973. *City Police*. New York: Ballantine.

Rubington, Earl. 1968. "Variations in Bottle-Gang Controls," in *Deviance: The Interactionist Perspective*, ed. E. Rubington and M. Weinberg. New York: Macmillan.

Rubington, Earl, and Martin S. Weinberg. 1968. *Deviance: The Interactionist Perspective*. New York: Macmillan.

———. 1995. *The Study Of Social Problems: Seven Perspectives*. 5th ed. New York: Oxford University Press.

———. 2002. *Deviance: The Interactionist Perspective*. 8th ed. Boston: Allyn & Bacon.

Rucker, Darnell. 1969. *The Chicago Pragmatists*. Minneapolis, MN: University of Minnesota Press.

Sanders, Clinton. 1989. *Customizing the Body: The Art and Culture of Tattooing*. Philadelphia: Temple University Press.

———. 1995. "Stranger than Fiction: Insights and Pitfalls in Post-modern Ethnography," in *Studies in Symbolic Interaction*, ed. Norman K Denzin, vol. 17. Greenwich, CT: JAI.

Sanders, William B. 1977. *Detective Work: A Study of Criminal Investigations*. New York: Free Press.

Sandstrom, Kent L. 1990. "Confronting Deadly Disease: The Drama of Identity Construction among Gay Men with AIDS." *Journal of Contemporary Ethnography* 19: 271–294.

Scheff, Thomas J. 1963. "Decision Rules, Types of Error, and Their Consequences in Medical Diagnoses." *Behavioral Science* 8: 97–107.

———. 1964. "The Societal Reaction to Deviance: Ascriptive Elements in the Psychiatric Screening of Mental Patients in a Mid-Western State." *Social Problems* 11: 401–13.

———. 1966. "Typifications in the Diagnostic Practice of Rehabilitation Agencies," in *Sociology and Rehabilitation*, ed. M.B. Sussman. New York: American Sociological Association.

Scheffler, Israel. 1974. *Four Pragmatists: A Critical Introduction to Peirce, James, Mead, and Dewey*. New York: Humanities.

Schervish, Paul G. 1973. "The Labeling Perspective: Its Bias and Potential in the Study of Political Deviance." *American Sociologist* 8: 47–57.

Schmid, Thomas, and Richard S. Jones. 1991. "Suspended Identity: Identity Transformation in a Maximum Security Prison." *Symbolic Interaction* 14: 415–432.

———. 1993. "Ambivalent Actions: Prison Adoption Strategies of First-Time, Short-Term Inmates." *Journal of Contemporary Ethnography* 21: 439–463.

Schneider, Joseph W., and Peter Conrad. 1983. *Having Epilepsy*. Philadelphia: Temple University Press.

Schutz, Alfred. 1962. *Collected Papers I: The Problem of Social Reality*. The Hague: Martinus Nijhoff.

———. 1964. *Collected Papers II: Studies in Social Theory*. The Hague: Martinus Nijhoff.

Scott, Lois. 1981. Being Somebody: The Negotiation of Identities in a Community Context. Master's thesis (Kinesiology). University of Waterloo, Waterloo, ON.

Scott, Marvin. 1968. *The Racing Game*. Chicago: Aldine.

Scott, Marvin B., and Stanford M. Lyman. 1968. "Accounts." *American Sociological Review* 33: 46–62.

Scott, Robert. 1969. *The Making of Blind Men: A Study of Adult Socialization*. New York: Russell Sage.

Shaffir, William. 1974. *Life in a Religious Community: The Lubavitcher Chassidim in Montreal*. Toronto, ON: Holt, Rinehart & Winston.

———. 1993. "Jewish Messianism Lubavitch Style: An Interim Report." *The Jewish Journal of Sociology* 35: 115–128.

———. 1995. "When Prophecy is Not Validated: Explaining the Unexpected in a Messianic Campaign." *The Jewish Journal of Sociology* 37: 119–136.

Shaffir, William, and Robert Stebbins. 1991. *Experiencing Fieldwork: An Inside View of Qualitative Methods*. Newbury Park, CA: Sage.

Shaffir, William, Robert Stebbins, and Alan Turowetz. 1980. *The Social Experience of Fieldwork*. New York: St. Martin's Press.

Shalin, Demetri. 1986. "Pragmatism and Social Interactionism." *American Sociological Review* 51: 9–29.

Shaw, Clifford. 1930. *The Jack-Roller*. Chicago: University of Chicago Press.

———. 1931. *The Natural History of a Delinquent Career*. Chicago: University of Chicago Press.

Shibutani, Tamotsu. 1966. *Improvised News: A Sociological Study of Rumor*. Indianapolis, IN: Bobbs-Merrill.

———. 1961. *Society and Personality: An Interactionist Approach to Social Psychology*. Englewood Cliffs, NJ: Prentice-Hall.

Shover, Neal. 1979. *The Sociology of American Corrections*. Homewood, IL: Dorsey.

———. 1996. *Great Pretenders: Pursuits and Careers of Persistent Thieves*. Boulder, CO: Westview.

Simmel, Georg. 1907. *The Philosophy of Money*, trans. T. Bottomore and D. Frisby. Reprint, London: Routledge & Kegan Paul (1978).

———. 1950. *The Sociology of Georg Simmel*, ed. Kurt Wolff. New York: Free Press.

Simmons, J.L. 1969. *Deviants*. Berkeley, CA: Glendessary Press.

Sinclair, Andrew. 1962. *Prohibition: The Era of Excess*. New York: Little, Brown.

Smith, Charles W. 1989. *Auctions: The Social Construction of Value*. Berkeley, CA: University of California Press.

Smith, Kenneth J., and Linda Liska Belgrave. 1995. "The Reconstruction of Everyday Life: Experiencing Hurricane Andrew." *Journal of Contemporary Ethnography* 24 (3): 244–269.

Snow, David A. and Leon Anderson. 1993. *Down on Their Luck: A Study of Homeless Street People*. Berkeley, CA: University of California Press.

Snyder, Eldon E. 1994. "Getting Involved in the Shuffleboard World," in *Doing Everyday Life: Ethnography as Human Lived Experience*, ed. Mary Lorenz Dietz, Robert Prus, and William Shaffir. Toronto, Ontario: Copp Clark Longman.

Spector, Malcolm, and John I. Kitsuse. 1977. *Constructing Social Problems*. Menlo Park, CA: Cummings.

Spencer, Jack W. 1983. "Accounts, Attitudes, and Solutions: Probation Officer-Defendant Negotiations of Subjective Orientations." *Social Problems* 30: 570–581.

Spradley, James P. 1970. *You Owe Yourself a Drunk: An Ethnography of Urban Nomads*. Boston, MA: Little, Brown.

Sprague, Rosamond Kent. 1972. *The Older Sophists: A Complete Translation by Several Hands of the Fragments in Die Fragmente der Vorsokratiker*, ed. Diels-Kranz. Columbia, SC: University of South Carolina Press.

Stachnik, Thomas, and Roger Ulrich. 1965. "Psychiatric Diagnoses: Some Cracks in the Crystal Ball." *Psychological Reports* 17: 989–990.

Stanley, Liz, and Sue Wise. 1993. *Breaking Out Again: Feminist Ontology and Epistemology*. New York: Routledge.

Stanton, Ester. 1970. *Clients Come Last*. Beverley Hills, CA: Sage.

Stebbins, Robert. 1990. *The Laugh Makers: Stand-up Comedy as Art, Business, and Life-Style*. Kingston, ON: McGill-Queen's University Press.

Steffensmeier, Darrell J. 1986. *The Fence: In the Shadow of Two Worlds*. Totowa, NJ: Rowman and Littlefield.

Stoll, Clarice S. 1968. "Images of Man and Social Control." *Social Forces* 47: 119–127.

Strauss, Anselm. 1993. *Continual Permutations of Action*. Hawthorne, NY: Aldine de Gruyter.

Suchar, Charles S. 1978. *Social Deviance: Perspectives and Prospects*. New York: Holt, Rinehart and Winston.

Sudnow, David. 1965. "Normal Crimes: Sociological Features of the Penal Code in a Public Defender Office." *Social Problems* 12: 255–276.

———. 1970. "Dead on Arrival." Pp. 111–130 in Anselm Strauss (ed.), *Where Medicine Fails*. Chicago: Aldine.

Sutherland, Edwin. 1937. *The Professional Thief*. Chicago: University of Chicago Press.

———. 1939. *Principles of Criminology*. 4th ed. Philadelphia: Lippincott.

———. 1950. "The Diffusion of Sexual Psychopath Laws." *American Journal of Sociology* 56: 142–148.

———. 1955. *Principles of Criminology*. 5th ed. Philadelphia: Lippincott.

Sykes, Gresham, and David Matza. 1957. "Techniques of Neutralization: A Theory of Delinquency." *American Journal of Sociology* 22: 664–670.

Szasz, Thomas S. 1970. *The Manufacture of Madness*. New York: Delta.

Tannenbaum, Frank. 1938. *Crime and the Community*. New York: Columbia University Press.

Taylor, Ian, Paul Walton, and Jock Young. 1973. *The New Criminology*. London: Routledge & Kegan Paul.

Theberge, Nancy. 2000. *Higher Goals: Women's Ice Hockey and the Politics of Gender*. Albany, NY: State University of New York Press.

Thomas, William I. 1928. *The Child In America*. New York: Knopf.

Thomas, William I. and Florian Znaniecki. 1918–1920. *The Polish Peasant in Europe and America*. Vols. I–V. Boston: Richard Badger.

Thorsell, Bernard, and Lloyd Klemke. 1972. "The Labeling Process: Reinforcement or Deterrent?" *Law and Society Review* 6: 393–403.

Thrasher, Frederick M. 1927. *The Gang: A Study of 1,313 Gangs in Chicago*. Chicago: University of Chicago Press. Reprinted and abridged (James F. Short, ed.), University of Chicago Press (1963).

Thucydides [c460–400B.C.E.]. *History of the Peloponnesian War*, trans. Rex Warner. New York: Penguin Putnam (1972).

Traub, Stuart H., and Craig B. Little. 1999. *Theories of Deviance*. 5th ed. Itasca, IL: F.E. Peacock Publishers.

Trice, Harrison M. 1993. *Occupational Subcultures in the Workplace*. Ithaca, NY: IRL Press.

Trice, Harrison M., and Janice M. Beyer. 1993. *The Cultures of Work Organizations*. Englewood Cliffs, NJ: Prentice-Hall.

Vail, Angus. 1999. "Tattoos are Like Potato Chips . . .You Can't Have Just One: The Process of Becoming and Being a Collector." *Deviant Behavior* 20: 253–273.

Van Zandt, David E. 1991. *Living in the Children of God*. Princeton, NJ: Princeton University Press.

Vaughan, Diane. 1986. *Uncoupling: Turning Points in Intimate Relationships*. New York: Oxford.

Waddington, P.A.J. 1999. "Police (Canteen) Sub-Culture: An Appreciation." *British Journal of Sociology* 39: 287–309.

Walker, Samuel. 1989. *Sense and Nonsense about Crime: A Policy Guide*. Pacific Grove, CA: Brooks/Cole.

Waller, Willard. 1930. *The Old Love and the New*. Reprint, Carbondale, IL: Southern Illinois University Press (1967).

Warren, Carol A.B. 1974. *Identity and Community in the Gay World*. New York: Wiley.

———. 1983. "The Politics of Trouble in an Adolescent Psychiatric Hospital." *Urban Life* 12: 327–348.

Wax, Rosalie. 1971. *Doing Fieldwork*. Chicago: University of Chicago Press.

Weinberg, Martin. 1970. "The Nudist Management of Respectability: Strategy for, and the Consequences of, the Construction of a Situated Morality," in *Deviance and Respectability*, ed. J.D. Douglas. New York: Basic Books.

Wharton, Carol S. 1989. "Splintered Visions: Staff/Client Disjunctions and Their Consequences for Human Service Organizations." *Journal of Contemporary Ethnography* 18: 50–71.

———. 1991. "Why Can't We Be Friends?: Expectations Versus Experiences in the Volunteer Role." *Journal of Contemporary Ethnography* 20: 79–106.

Whyte, Willliam F. 1934. *Street Corner Society*. Chicago: University of Chicago Press.

Wiseman, Jacqueline. 1970. *Stations of the Lost: The Treatment of Skid Row Alcoholics*. Englewood Cliffs, NJ: Prentice-Hall.

———. 1979. "Towards a Theory of Policy Intervention in Social Problems." *Social Problems* 27: 3–18.

———. 1991. *The Other Half: Wives of Alcoholics and Their Social-Psychological Situation*. New York: Aldine de Gruyter.

Wolf, Charlotte. 1994. "Conversion into Feminism," in *Doing Everyday Life: Ethnography as Human Lived Experience*, ed. Mary Lorenz Dietz, Robert Prus, and William Shaffir. Toronto: Copp Clark Longman.

Wolf, Daniel. 1991. *The Rebels: A Brotherhood of Outlaw Bikers*. Toronto, ON: University of Toronto Press.

Yarrow, M.R., C.G. Schwartz, H.S. Murphy, and L.C. Deasy. 1955. "The Psychological Meaning of Mental Illness in the Family." *Journal of Social Issues* 11: 12–24.

Young Jock. 1986. "The Failure of Criminology: The Need for Radical Realism," in *Confronting Crime*, ed. by R. Matthews and J. Young. London: Sage.

Xenophon [c430–340B.C.E.] *The Persian Expedition [Anabasis],* trans Rex Warner. New York: Penguin Putnam (1972).

———. "Hellenica" in *Xenophon Vol I–II.* trans. Carleton L. Brownson. Cambridge, MA: Harvard University Press (1918).

Zurcher, Louis, Jr., R. George Kirkpatrick, Robert G. Cushing, and Charles K. Bowman. 1971. "The Anti-Pornography Campaign: A Symbolic Crusade." *Social Problems* 19: 217–238.

Index of Names

Index of Terms

About the Authors

ROBERT PRUS is Professor of Sociology at the University of Waterloo. His published books include *Symbolic Interaction and Ethnographic Research, Subcultural Mosaics and Intersubjective Realities,* and *Beyond the Power of Mystique,* among others.

SCOTT GRILLS is Dean of Arts and Associate Professor of Sociology at Brandon University in Manitoba. He is the editor of *Doing Ethnographic Research: Fieldwork Settings* and has served on the editorial board of the *Canadian Review of Sociology and Anthropology* and the interdisciplinary journal *Dianoia*.